THE REINVENTION OF BRITAIN
1960–2016

The Reinvention of Britain 1960–2016 explores the transformation of contemporary Britain, tracing its evolution from the welfare state of the post-1945 era to social democracy in the 1960s and 1970s and the liberal market society of 1979 onwards. Focusing primarily on political and economic change, it aims to identify which elements of State policy led to the crucial strategy changes that shaped British history over the past six decades.

This book argues that since 1960 there have been two reinventions of the political economy of the United Kingdom: a social-democratic shift initiated by the Conservative government of Harold Macmillan and developed by Labour under Harold Wilson, and a subsequent change of direction towards a free market model attempted by the Conservatives under Margaret Thatcher. Structured around these two key policy reinventions of the late twentieth century, chapters are organized chronologically, from the development of social democracy in the early 1960s to the coalition government of the early 2010s, the Conservative election win that followed and the 'Brexit' referendum of 2016.

Providing a comprehensive yet accessible introduction to the political and economic history of this period, *The Reinvention of Britain 1960–2016* is essential reading for all students of contemporary British history.

Scott Newton is Emeritus Professor of Modern British and International History at Cardiff University, having taught there for 33 years before retiring in 2016. He has written on British economic history and policy and the interaction between socio-economic change and international relations, and his work has appeared in journals such as *Diplomacy and Statecraft*, *The Economic History Review* and the *English Historical Review*. His best-known books are *Modernization Frustrated* (1988, with Dilwyn Porter), *Profits of Peace: The Political Economy of Anglo-German Appeasement* (1996) and *The Global Economy, 1944–2000: The Limits of Ideology* (2004).

THE REINVENTION OF BRITAIN 1960–2016

A Political and Economic History

Scott Newton

LONDON AND NEW YORK

First published 2018
by Routledge
2 Park Square, Milton Park, Abingdon, Oxon OX14 4RN

and by Routledge
711 Third Avenue, New York, NY 10017

Routledge is an imprint of the Taylor & Francis Group, an informa business

© 2018 Scott Newton

The right of Scott Newton to be identified as author of this work has been asserted by him in accordance with sections 77 and 78 of the Copyright, Designs and Patents Act 1988.

All rights reserved. No part of this book may be reprinted or reproduced or utilised in any form or by any electronic, mechanical, or other means, now known or hereafter invented, including photocopying and recording, or in any information storage or retrieval system, without permission in writing from the publishers.

Trademark notice: Product or corporate names may be trademarks or registered trademarks, and are used only for identification and explanation without intent to infringe.

British Library Cataloguing in Publication Data
A catalogue record for this book is available from the British Library

Library of Congress Cataloging in Publication Data
Names: Newton, Scott, 1956- author.
Title: The reinvention of Britain 1960-2016 : a political and economic history / Scott Newton.
Description: Abingdon, Oxon ; New York, NY : Routledge, 2017. | Includes bibliographical references and index.
Identifiers: LCCN 2017008627 | ISBN 9781138800038 (hardback : alk. paper) | ISBN 9781138800045 (pbk. : alk. paper) | ISBN 9781315161853 (ebook)
Subjects: LCSH: Great Britain--Politics and government--1945- | Great Britain--Economic conditions--20th century. | Great Britain--Economic conditions--21st century.
Classification: LCC DA589.7 .N487 2017 | DDC 941.085--dc23
LC record available at https://lccn.loc.gov/2017008627

ISBN: 978-1-138-80003-8 (hbk)
ISBN: 978-1-138-80004-5 (pbk)
ISBN: 978-1-315-16185-3 (ebk)

Typeset in Bembo
by Taylor & Francis Books

To the memory of my parents,
Charles Henry Newton (1920–2015)
and
Margaret Joan Newton (1919–2006)

CONTENTS

List of illustrations	*viii*
Acknowledgements	*ix*
Introduction: Why a political and economic history?	1

PART I
The rise and fall of social-democratic Britain — 11

1	Conservative social democracy, 1961–64	13
2	Labour's New Britain, 1964–70: National plan	43
3	Quiet revolution, 1970–74	75
4	The crisis of the post-war settlement, 1974–79	97

PART II
Neo-liberal Britain — 141

5	Thatcher's revolution, 1979–90	143
6	Major interlude, 1990–97	185
7	New Labour in power, 1997–2010	201
8	Envoi	242

Bibliography	*250*
Index	*257*

ILLUSTRATIONS

Figures

2.1 Estimated size of the Eurodollar market ($bn)	52
2.2 Growth per quarter, 1964–70	56
2.3 Exports and imports of goods and services, 1960–66	60

Tables

1.1 United Kingdom trade, 1952–62	21
2.1 Public investment in certain sectors, 1964–70: forecast and outturn	64

ACKNOWLEDGEMENTS

Many people, colleagues, friends and family, living and dead, have contributed to this book. Neither they nor I realised that congenial encounters in private homes, meetings, pubs, restaurants, cricket and football matches, railway trips and car journeys, all going back over decades, as well as telephone conversations, letters and emails, were providing the ideas and arguments which would help to shape a work of history. But these exchanges turned out to be as important as academic seminars, archival visits and secondary texts in providing the insights and raw material which has been processed into *The Reinvention of Britain*. So I would like to acknowledge my debt in particular to Dan Anthony, Peter Cain, Ralph Cummins, John Davies, John Drakakis, the late Lionel Guest, Gerry Harris, the late Terry Hawkes, Merion Hughes, Paddy Kitson, the late Ronnie Kowalski, Steve Latham, the late Rhodri Morgan, the late John Lawrence, the late Alan Milward, my late parents Charles and Margaret Newton, Dil Porter, Gwynn Pritchard, Robin Ramsay (whose experienced editorial eye has proved invaluable), John Smith, Rob and Helen Stradling, Doris and the late Tony Trott, all good companions over many years. On a more formal note, I must thank the School of History, Archaeology and Religion at Cardiff University for the sabbatical period which allowed me to start writing the book in 2013 and the ESRC for the opportunity to take paid leave to research the 1964–70 Labour governments and the international economy. My long-suffering editor at Routledge, Amy Welmers, has been patient and understanding throughout. I cannot close without mentioning my wife, whose love and support continues to be a wonderful source of strength.

INTRODUCTION
Why a political and economic history?

Histories of contemporary British life have not been in short supply over recent decades. Many of these have tended to focus on how, in the decades since 1945, aspects of British society have altered and become more open and tolerant in attitudes to sexuality, marriage, cultural production (in broadcasting, the theatre and cinema especially) and ethnic differences. Important contributions have been made in the overviews by Grace Davie (1994), Peter Leese (2006), Jane Lewis (1992), and Andrew Rosen (2003). Andrew Marr (2009) effectively caught something of the shifting attitudes. Dominic Sandbrook (2005 and 2006) captured the rapid changes of the 'long 1960s', while Andy Beckett (2009) provided an evocative popular history of the 1970s which punctured some of the more lurid myths about that decade. Paul Addison and Harriet Jones (2005), and Addison's *No Turning Back* (2010)[1] both provide a broader survey, covering not only society and culture but the making of the post-war state, Britain's changing international role, and the economy.

The economic dimension has perhaps been the most controversial. For many years much of the debate has raged around the concept of 'decline', as Peter Clarke noted at the start of *Hope and Glory: Britain 1900–1990* (1997).[2] The thesis that post-war Britain had lurched from one economic failure to another was first popularized in the late 1950s by left-leaning writers such as Andrew Schonfield (*British Economic Policy since the War*, 1958).[3] It became commonplace to argue that the experience of the next quarter century did not suggest that governments knew how to break free from this process. Sidney Pollard lamented in *The Wasting of the British Economy* (1982)[4] that what required explanation was why post-war Britain had not enjoyed the kind of post-war 'economic miracle' enjoyed by all its west European competitors. Martin Wiener (*English Culture and the Decline of the Industrial Spirit*, 1981)[5] pointed to the continuing hegemony within the UK of a gentlemanly elite which had always despised 'trade'. Corelli Barnett (*The Audit of War*, 1986, and *Lost Victory*, 1995)[6] identified a fundamental misallocation of resources after 1945 in the construction of a socialist or social democratic version of the New Jerusalem rather than in industrial reconstruction, education and training and the reform of labour practices. The accounts of both Wiener and Barnett became very influential in media and political circles.[7]

In more recent years there has been something of a reaction against this 'declinism', for example in the work of David Edgerton (1991), Peter Clarke (1997), Kenneth Morgan (1992) and George Bernstein (2004).[8] Edgerton has argued that post-war Britain remained a significant industrial and military power. Morgan, Clarke and Bernstein all point to the fact the British people enjoyed unprecedented levels of rising affluence for over a generation after 1945 – even if the social and economic achievements of the countries which had been defeated in World War Two remained more striking than those of unconquered Britain. Middleton (2001) took this argument further, pointing not only to the UK's record of sustained economic growth for most of the post-war era but also to its retention of a position as one of the world's leading economic powers into the twenty-first century.[9] Newton and Porter (1988)[10] took issue with Barnett's line in *The Audit of War*, while Jim Tomlinson, in a 1997 article[11] questioned the methodology of *Lost Victory*. Historians now tend to accept that, like its European competitors, Britain did in fact enjoy a 'Golden Age' after 1945: but that increasing prosperity was not accompanied by increasing equality and failed to bring to a large proportion of the electorate the happiness and contentment that politicians had assured them it would.[12]

Yet even if declinism is more of a problem than decline, there can be little argument that the British economy has *changed* quite dramatically since the middle of the century. This development has been characterized by a shift from specialization in a number of labour-intensive manufacturing and heavy industrial concerns (for example, shipbuilding, textiles, steel manufacturing, coal mining and automotive production), to a more diverse economy. Manufacturing has not disappeared (Britain remains one of the world's leading producers in the chemical and aerospace sectors), but now occupies just over 10 per cent of the GDP compared with almost 30 per cent in 1979. The financial sector has grown along with enterprise in small and medium sized concerns in the service sector and the 'knowledge economy' (centred on IT and design). The worlds of fashion, sport, leisure and culture have become big business.

Running alongside this development has been a shift in the dominant form of political economy in modern Britain. For the best part of thirty years after 1945 this was dominated by the '1944 settlement' in which the political parties, the economic core of the State – in the form of the Treasury and the Bank of England – and what Middlemas (1979)[13] has called the 'peak institutions', namely the Confederation of British Industry (CBI – representing corporate industry), the City and the trade unions, accepted that post-war Britain should become a society in which there was full employment, free secondary education, and a welfare state. J. M. Keynes had shown, notably in his *General Theory of Employment, Interest and Money* (1936)[14] that governments could sustain this new welfare state through taxation and spending policies which ensured that the level of demand within the economy for goods and services remained high enough to absorb the available resources of capital and labour; the mass joblessness of the inter-war years seemed to have been banished for ever. After 1979 this consensus was eroded by a liberal economic philosophy, whose vigorous promotion of the free market would not have been unfamiliar to the Manchester School in the mid-nineteenth century. Its members, as Marx once wrote, viewed 'every institution of old England … in the light of a piece of machinery as costly as it is useless'.[15]

This metamorphosis of contemporary Britain is not really explained by the existing historiography. *The Reinvention of Britain* attempts to fill this gap. While acknowledging that some economic change is autonomous (the growth of the service sector and the relative decline of manufacturing is common to all advanced industrial societies) it argues that alterations in the priorities of State policy have been fundamental to Britain's transition from the welfare state of the post-1945 era to social democracy in the 1960s and 1970s and the liberal market society of the post-1979 era. This contention does of course need to be demonstrated, and the book seeks to identify the key agents of shifting views within the State and peak institutions about what should be the most appropriate politico-economic strategy for Britain. *The Reinvention of Britain* is therefore, of necessity, a work of political and economic history which views the transformation of Britain through the prism of the reinventions of its political economy.

Prelude: reinventions of Britain

Post-war Britain was a self-confident nation which saw itself as a prosperous welfare state and a great power with global responsibilities. This society was itself a reinvention of the British State which had greeted the start of the twentieth century with the coronation of the Queen's great-grandfather, Edward VII. Yet the Edwardian order itself had been built upon reinvention. With the passing of Roman 'Britannia' in the fifth century, 'Britain', like 'Germany' and 'Italy' had become little more than a geographical expression (though the forceful English medieval King Edward I did attempt a recreation in the thirteenth century). The Britain of modern history did not exist until the 1707[16] Act of Union, and it was formed in order to promote the external commercial interests of the landowning and mercantile elite whose plantations in the Americas and trading connections with India had led to the creation of the 'first British Empire'. Britain had from the start been an Imperial state.[17] In its first manifestation it was a mercantilist power. It protected the home market through the taxation of imports and used force (above all the Royal Navy) to keep its hold over overseas trading concessions and colonial possessions. The strategy led to conflict with other imperial states, notably Spain and France, in a series of wars financed by the City of London.

Britain showed great resourcefulness in defeating its rivals as well as in adapting to the most profitable forms of enterprise and developing the domestic politico-economic order required to support this activity. In a first reinvention it abandoned mercantilism for free trade during the decades after the final victory over Napoleon in 1815 had destroyed the French challenge to British global hegemony. The old agrarian ruling elite was replaced by an alliance, sealed with the repeal of the Corn Laws in 1846, between financiers based in the City of London and manufacturers whose wealth was founded on exploitation of the new techniques developed in the industrial revolution. The new dominant coalition of bankers and the producers of the textiles, iron, coal, steel and ships which formed the core of the nineteenth-century industrial economy, relied on overseas connections just as much as its predecessors. The external orientation of the British Imperial state was sustained in order to secure export markets for goods and capital as well as sources of imports, notably of cheap food and of raw materials. Many of these markets were outside the formal Empire: by 1913 almost two-thirds of all British trade was extra-imperial while one quarter of all British overseas investment was in Latin America. The opening of Britain to free trade encouraged the reciprocal tariff reductions which expanded the markets available to British manufactures and investment. On occasion diplomacy was not enough to promote British commerce. The British invasion of Egypt in 1882 and expansion into West Africa during the 1890s are examples of occasions when, despite much liberal and internationalist rhetoric, successive governments were not afraid to sanction the use of force.[18]

By 1913 the British Empire had embraced one-quarter of the world's surface[19] and one fifth of its population – 412 million people, 330 million of them living in Asia.[20] Britain was the dominant economic power, with 30 per cent of world exports. London was not only the political hub of this vast Empire, but the world's financial centre: the pound sterling was the world's main international currency, used throughout the British Empire and beyond for trading and to support national reserves. British banks in the City of London provided short-term credits for international trade, 60 per cent of which was carried in ships made in the United Kingdom and insured in London. British capital, channelled through the City, accounted for 43 per cent of the world's foreign investment.[21] A significant proportion of this investment financed the construction of ports, harbours and transportation systems throughout the Americas, Africa, the Near East, India and Australasia. These in turn created a global market which generated income for British finance and industry. Indeed, by the first decade of the twentieth century Britain's earnings from 'invisible trade' based on finance and the service sector were growing more rapidly than from its 'visible trade' centred on sales of manufactured goods. This nexus of wealth and power was policed by the Royal Navy, ensuring that the trade routes which sustained profits, wealth and living standards throughout the Empire (and especially in the metropole) remained open.

The fractured state

Imperial Britain was not a united country. Industrialization had called into existence a new social class, composed of landless labourers and impoverished artisans who abandoned agriculture and small scale production for work in the new factories.

This was the working class, or proletariat, which at various times in the period from the end of the Napoleonic wars until the late 1840s showed itself capable of organizing in favour of revolutionary political change based on universal (male) suffrage. After 1850 the advent of free trade, facilitating imports of cheap food along with a period of steadily increasing prosperity which lasted for a generation, reduced the pressure for radical change. Working class willingness to work for the improvement of the existing system rather than replace it was strengthened by limited social reforms and gradual extensions of the franchise. By the early years of the twentieth century the majority of working-class voters were supporting either the Liberal or the new Labour Party, both advocating leglislation which would give the State a responsibility for establishing a 'National Minimum'. This was to be characterized by improvements to working-class housing, along with social welfare and wage bargaining arrangements designed to provide a basic standard of living for all, funded by taxes on the wealthy. Key parts of the programme (such as old age pensions and the introduction of National Insurance, as well as the tax increases on high incomes in Chancellor David Lloyd George's 1909 People's Budget) were enacted by the Liberal governments of Henry Campbell-Bannerman and H. H. Asquith after 1906.

The political arguments surrounding the introduction of the Liberal reforms were intense and revealed Britain to be a profoundly divided country. The year 1910 saw two closely fought General Elections. After the first one the liberal-socialist economist and sociologist J. A. Hobson published 'The General Election: A Sociological Interpretation',[22] identifying the fracture which ran through the British state and society. This was between 'Producer's England' and 'Consumer's England'. The first of these was centred on manufacturing industry and to be found in northern England, parts of the Midlands, south Wales and southern Scotland. It tended to be nonconformist (or Roman Catholic) in religious observation. The predominant social classes were composed of provincial industrialists (mostly Liberals) and the organized working class. The dominant political parties in 'Producer's England' tended to be Liberal or Labour and committed to programmes of domestic social reform. Consumer's England, by contrast, based its wealth on the financial sector centred on the City of London. It was composed of 'large numbers of well-to-do and leisured families'[23] whose incomes derived from overseas or domestic investments managed by City firms. These were people who had a material interest in the free movement of capital, the global role of the City and the international status of sterling as the world's leading reserve currency. They tended to be Anglican, vote Conservative, send their children to the public schools and Oxbridge and generally live in the London suburbs and the Home Counties.[24]

The City institutions which handled their money were often more interested in foreign than home economic developments. As *The Economist* commented in 1911 'London is often more concerned with the course of events in Mexico than what happens in the Midlands and is more upset by a strike on the Canadian Pacific than by one in the Cambrian Collieries'.[25] In 1905–1906 only

12 per cent of all the securities quoted on the London Stock Exchange were 'home industrials'.[26]

The existence of this split in British society has been confirmed by research which has shown that the south-east was the fastest growing region in Britain on the eve of World War One. The 1911 census revealed that 25 per cent of the country's population lived there, earning the income which generated a thriving consumer society along with suburbs and seaside holiday resorts such as Southend and Margate. The region had become 'the focal point of an affluent society enjoying conspicuous consumption and giving employment to a wide-range of domestic services'.[27] Prominent among these were both the well-paid professional services provided by the legal, medical and (private) educational professions and the much less generously remunerated domestic services which were essential to the daily maintenance of middle-class homes as well as aristocratic establishments. The prosperity of the area, many of whose inhabitants were financially dependent on the income from 'rentier home and foreign stocks'[28] fed demand for consumer and light industry such as fashion and luxury clothing, furniture manufacturing, printing and publishing as well as for retailing, distribution and transport.

Between 1914 and 1945 this fractured Imperial Britain faced its most serious challenges, now from Germany and (from the mid-1930s) Japan, since the French Revolutionary wars against Napoleon. Full use of all the country's productive resources became essential to the creation of a military machine powerful enough to resist and, in conjunction with Soviet and American allies, defeat these rival powers. In order to retain public support and build the national solidarity central to the success of this mobilization, both in 1914–18 and in 1939–45 wartime governments embraced the political agenda of 'Producer's England'. David Lloyd George's 'land fit for heroes to live in' may not have been constructed after 1918, but World War One and its aftermath did see significant social reforms, a process which was of course carried much further during and after World War Two.

It cannot be argued that Hobson's 'two Englands' had ceased to exist by 1950. The Conservative Party and its allies retained both their connections to the City and their commitment to its economic internationalism. Its core voters were still linked to finance, the service sector and light industry. They continued to live mainly in Home Counties England and sent their children to the public schools. Labour still represented 'Producer's England'. Yet whereas in Hobson's time it seemed as if the financial and service sectors of the economy were more dynamic than industry, in post-1945 Britain the position was more balanced. Britain's share of world trade in manufactured goods rose from 17.5 per cent in 1938 to 20.5 per cent in 1950. The share of national income taken by wage earners grew from 37.8 per cent in 1938 to 41.9 per cent in 1950, a greater increase than apparent at first blush since over the same period wage-earners fell as a proportion of the labour force from 71.4 per cent to 66.2 per cent.[29] There was full employment, the National Health Service (NHS), full-time state education for all to the age of 15, and the extremes of poverty and wealth characteristic of Edwardian Britain no longer existed. The Imperial state was now a welfare state.

Post-war Britain: change and continuity

Not surprisingly, by the mid-1950s Britain was a confident society. It had emerged on the winning side from the two world wars. During the second of these it had (in 1940) come close to defeat. Its people had, however, shown great courage and determination in the face of military reverses and sustained bombing while its government had shown more skill, inventiveness and abililty in mobilizing the nation's resources for war than any other belligerent nation. These formidable qualities alone prevented defeat: in conjunction with the special relationship with the USA and the extraordinary sacrifices of the USSR in the 'Great Patriotic War' they guaranteed victory. The mood of solidarity had lasted into the post-war era. It had sustained the population through the years of rationing and deferred personal consumption which allowed the Labour government run by Prime Minister Clement Attlee to devote scarce resources to the export drive and the construction of the welfare state. However, middle-class disaffection with high taxation and austerity began to grow at the start of the 1950s, and delivered a narrow General Election victory to the Conservative Party late in 1951. The new Churchill administration did not attempt to return the nation to 1939. It embraced the essentials of the 1944 settlement in its domestic policy.[30] Rationing was gradually dismantled, though the process was not completed until 1954.[31]

By 1955 British citizens were starting to enjoy the fruits of austerity. The economy had been growing at an annual average rate of 2.9 per cent since 1951. Unemployment was less than 2 per cent of the workforce. Rationing had ended. There is no doubt that pockets of deprivation existed yet the advent of job security, the NHS and social security from the cradle to the grave for all meant that the country was becoming one where 'freedom from want' was gradually being abolished. The government had embarked on an ambitious housing programme, presided over by Harold Macmillan, which aimed (successfully) at the construction of 300,000 new units each year. Government expenditure on education, health and social security rose from £1537 million in 1951 to £3171 million in 1959.[32] The combination of full employment with high government spending generated expanding consumer demand, which was now being met as high street showrooms filled with goods designed to provide greater ease of life for individuals and families. Working-class families were increasingly able to purchase their own car, television set, washing machine and refrigerator. Shops were selling a far greater range of foodstuffs, clothes and household goods than had been available prior to the early 1950s.

The Conservative accommodation with the post-war order proved popular with the electorate: in the May 1955 General Election, the party, now led by Anthony Eden, was returned to power with a comfortable majority. The mood of satisfaction with Britain's internal configuration was paralleled with pride in its position on the world stage. Its international prestige had received a major boost with the first known successful ascent of Everest, in an expedition led by a British subject, John Hunt (though the last stages of the climb were conducted by the Nepalese Tenzing Norgay and the New Zealander, Edmund Hillary) in 1953. Britain had been the first country to build a commercial jet airliner, the De Havilland Comet, which entered service in 1952. It had successfully exploded its own atomic warhead in October of the same year, joining the USA and the USSR as members of the exclusive nuclear club. The days of the British Empire were clearly numbered, as had been demonstrated in 1947 when the Attlee government had presided over the transfer of power in the Indian subcontinent. But the change did not seem to involve a diminution of global influence. The new nation-states of India, Pakistan and Ceylon now joined Australia, New Zealand, Canada and South Africa in the British Commonwealth, an association of independent countries which were not only staunch allies but large markets for British overseas investment and exports of goods (indeed, at the start of the decade exports to and imports from the Commonwealth accounted for almost one half of all British trade). Britain's military forces were deployed in bases scattered through Europe, the Middle East and South East Asia. The country's obvious wealth and power gave it significant diplomatic authority, exercised most recently in 1954 when Eden, then Foreign Secretary, had played a central role in organizing the Geneva Accords which had brought an end to the war in Indochina between the French and the Viet Minh nationalists. Post-war Britain seemed to have successfully embraced the mid twentieth century in its economy and society while retaining a global presence which harked back to the days of the Pax Britannia – a blend of the modern and the traditional embodied in the televised 1953 Coronation of the young Queen Elizabeth II. This British 'era of good feelings'[33] was, however, to prove very short-lived. It was brought to a peremptory conclusion by a combination of national crisis, economic difficulties and internal divisions which drove successive governments to seek the reinvention of the post-war British nation-state.

Notes

1 Grace Davie, *Religion in Britain since 1945* (Oxford: Blackwell, 1994); Peter Leese, *Britain since 1945: Aspects of Identity* (Basingstoke: Palgrave Macmillan, 2006); Jane Lewis, *Women in Britain Since 1945* (Oxford: Blackwell, 1992); Andrew Rosen, *The Transformation of British Life 1950–2000: A Social History* (Manchester: Manchester University Press, 2003); Dominic Sandbrook, *Never Had It So Good: A History of Britain from Suez to the Beatles* (London: Abacus, 2005) and *White Heat: A History of Britain in the Swinging Sixties* (London: Abacus, 2006); Andy Beckett, *When the Lights Went Out: Britain in the Seventies* (London: Faber and Faber, 2009); Paul Addison and Harriet Jones (eds), *Companion to Contemporary Britain* (Oxford: Blackwell, 2005); Paul Addison *No Turning Back* (Oxford: Oxford University Press, 2010).
2 Peter Clarke, *Hope and Glory: Britain 1900–1990* (London: Penguin, 1997).
3 Andrew Schonfield, *British Economic Policy since the War* (London: Penguin, 1958).
4 Sidney Pollard, *The Wasting of the British Economy* (London: Croom Helm, 1982).
5 Martin Wiener, *English Culture and the Decline of the Industrial Spirit* (Cambridge: Cambridge University Press, 2004).
6 Corelli Barnett, *The Audit of War* (London: Macmillan, 1986), and *Lost Victory* (London: Macmillan, 1995).
7 See also Perry Anderson, 'Origins of the Present Crisis', *New Left Review*, 161 (1963), pp. 20–77; Andrew Gamble, *Britain in Decline: Economic Policy, Political Strategy and the British State* (London: Palgrave Macmillan, 1994).

8 David Edgerton, *England and the Aeroplane: An Essay on a Militant and Technological Nation* (Basingstoke, Palgrave Macmillan, 1991); Clarke, *Hope and Glory: Britain 1900–1990*; Kenneth O. Morgan, *The People's Peace: British History 1945–1990* (Oxford: Oxford University Press, 1992); George Bernstein, *The Myth of Decline* (London: Pimlico, 2004).
9 Roger Middleton, *The British Economy since 1945* (Basingstoke: Macmillan, 2001), pp. xv, 137.
10 Scott Newton and Dilwyn Porter, *Modernization Frustrated: The Politics of Industrial Decline in Britain since 1900* (London, Unwin Hyman 1988), pp. 107–108.
11 Jim Tomlinson, 'Correlli Barnett's History: The Case of Marshall Aid', *Twentieth Century British History*, vol. 8, no. 2 (1997), pp. 222–238.
12 Jim Tomlinson, 'After Decline?' *Contemporary British History*, vol. 23, no. 3 (2009), pp. 395–406.
13 Keith Middlemas, *Politics in Industrial Society* (London: Andre Deutsch, 1979).
14 J. M. Keynes, *General Theory of Employment, Interest and Money* (London: Macmillan, 1936).
15 Karl Marx, *Surveys from Exile*, edited by David Fernbach (London: Penguin, 1973), p. 262. The quote is from an essay on the Chartists written on 10 August, 1852.
16 An argument developed in two pioneering studies: Hugh Kearney's *The British Isles: The Four Nations* (Cambridge: Cambridge University Press 1989 and 2006) and in Norman Davies's *The Isles* (Basingstoke: Macmillan, 1999).
17 This argument is central to another seminal work, Tom Nairn's *The Break-up of Britain* (London: Verso, 1977 and 1981).
18 See the discussion in P. J. Cain and A. G. Hopkins, *British Imperialism 1688–2000* (London: Pearson Education, 2002), chs. 11–13.
19 Niall Fergusson, *Empire: How Britain made the Modern World* (London: Penguin, 2004), p. 15.
20 Angus Maddison, *The World Economy: A Millennial Perspective* (Paris: OECD, 2006), p. 99.
21 Paul Kennedy, *The Rise and Fall of the Great Powers: Economic Change and Military Conflict from 1500 to 2000* (London: Unwin Hyman 1988), p. 296.
22 J. A. Hobson, 'The General Election: A Sociological Interpretation', *Sociological Review*, 3 (1910), pp. 112–115.
23 Ibid., p. 115.
24 These questions have been intensively explored by W. D. Rubinstein. See for example 'The Victorian Middle Classes: Wealth, Occupation, Geography', *Economic History Review*, 2nd ser., XXX (1977), pp. 602–623.
25 Newton and Porter, *Modernization Frustrated*, p. 8.
26 Scott Newton, 'Joseph Chamberlain and Tariff Reform: British Radicalism, Modernization and Nationalism', in Robert Stradling, Scott Newton and David Bates (eds), *Conflict and Coexistence: Democracy and Nationalism in Modern Europe* (Cardiff: University of Wales Press, 1997), p. 88.
27 See C. H. Lee, 'Regional Growth and Structural Change in Victorian Britain', *Economic History Review*, 2nd ser., XXXIV (1981), pp. 438–452.
28 P. J. Cain, 'J. A. Hobson, Financial Capitalism and Imperialism in Late Victorian and Edwardian Britain', in A. N. Porter and R. F. Holland (eds), *Money, Finance and Empire 1790–1969* (London: Frank Cass, 1985), p. 15.
29 Sidney Pollard, *The Development of the British Economy 1914–1990* (London: Edward Arnold, 1992), p. 220.
30 See for example, Morgan, *The People's Peace*, ch. 4; Paul Addison *Churchill on the Home Front* (London: Cape, 1992), ch. 12.
31 See Peter Hennessy's study of this period, *Having it So Good: Britain in the Fifties* (London: Allen Lane, 2007), chs. 1 and 2.
32 Kevin Jeffreys, *Retreat from New Jerusalem* (Basingstoke: Macmillan, 1997), p. 131.
33 'The era of good feelings' was an expression used to describe the period in US history following the conclusion of the Napoleonic wars. It was marked by bipartisanship, an extension of the powers of the Federal Government and by political optimism.

PART I
The rise and fall of social-democratic Britain

1

CONSERVATIVE SOCIAL DEMOCRACY, 1961–64

The fall

The first major event to shatter the self-satisfaction of the mid 1950s was the 1956 Suez crisis. The story of this affair is well known and there is no need to go into detail here. Suffice it to say that the Anglo-French bid to use force to occupy the Suez Canal and overthrow Egypt's President Nasser, in response to his decision to nationalize the waterway, was a fiasco. The expedition was halted short of its objectives not by military defeat but by diplomatic outcry. From the British perspective the most alarming aspect of this was the attitude of the USA and of Commonwealth nations.

British external strategy had been rooted in the 'three circles' doctrine, set out by Churchill in a speech to the Conservative Party conference in 1948. He had argued that Britain could best promote its welfare in the world by remaining at the point where three circles of influence intersected. The first of these was the British Commonwealth and Empire. The second was 'the English-speaking world', which included Canada, the British Dominions and (most important of all thanks to its wealth and military power) the United States of America. The third was 'United Europe'. It was not accidental that Churchill had mentioned Europe last: European upheaval could certainly threaten Britain but the experience of the two world wars had shown that the nation's security and prosperity depended in the last resort upon its military, political, trading and financial connections with the first two circles. At the time of the Suez crisis, however, the only members of the British Commonwealth to support Britain were Australia and New Zealand. India and Canada meanwhile condemned the operation. In Washington, where the incumbent President Eisenhower was fighting a campaign for his re-election, there was outrage. Neither Eisenhower nor John Foster Dulles, the Secretary of State, had been forewarned of the expedition. Dulles spoke out against the British. The pound came under pressure on the foreign exchanges, a development Harold Macmillan (now Chancellor of the Exchequer) attributed to US influence. Both Dulles and the President considered the action a betrayal of the Anglo-American relationship and a diplomatic blunder of the first order, a throwback to the crudest form of imperialist aggression which could only strengthen the determination of newly independent countries in the developing world to follow a neutral rather than pro-Western path in the Cold War. But the damage did not stop there: at the very moment the British and French forces were fighting their way towards Suez the Soviet Union had invaded Hungary in order to suppress an anti-Communist revolution. The USA led attempts to generate international condemnation of the Soviet move but given the actions of its closest ally these reeked of hypocrisy.

The episode distanced Britain from the two most important of the three circles. As John Young has commented, it revealed that Commonwealth countries could no longer be relied on to follow a British lead. It also showed that now, even in conjunction with France and despite the great network of bases and the appearance of military power, the country no longer possessed the resources to undertake large-scale military operations overseas in the absence of support from the USA.[1] Domestic opinion was split down the middle and there were powerful demonstrations against the expedition. At the same time many who had supported it were shocked by the experience of failure and by the country's apparent weakness in the face of international pressure. Macmillan, who replaced Eden as Prime Minister in the wake of the crisis, liked to say that Britain was and would remain 'a great power', but he knew that the rebuilding of global influence required a repairing of the special relationship with the USA and accommodation with nationalist movements as a prelude to decolonization in Britain's African and West Indian colonies.

The next blow to British pride came in defence policy. Like the Suez expedition, this was predicated for much of the 1950s on the assumption that Britain was a great power and had the weapons systems, in the form of nuclear weapons, to back up its pretensions. The delivery system for the British bomb was the 'V' force of Vulcan, Victor and Valiant long-range strategic bombers. However, the development of the ballistic missile by the USSR and the USA damaged the credibility of the British deterrent. In order to retrieve this position the government determined that the country should now have its own, and embarked on the construction of a British medium-range ballistic missile, known as Blue Streak, capable of carrying a nuclear warhead. Unfortunately the project ran into difficulties, the most serious of which was steadily escalating costs, going from estimates of £65 million in 1955 to £600 million in 1960. It became clear that the country lacked the financial resources needed to complete Blue Streak – unless the government was prepared to raise taxes or sacrifice budgets elsewhere. This was not deemed good politics, and cancellation followed in 1960. The government opted to buy the ready-made American Skybolt instead, designed for aerial launching. In the end even this deal collapsed, when the US government decided that Skybolt was unreliable. A somewhat desperate Prime Minister was, however, able to salvage Britain's deterrent at Nassau in the Bahamas at the end of 1962, when President Kennedy agreed to provide the UK with the American submarine-launched Polaris ballistic missile programme (with the warheads to the British version being made in the UK, which amounted to a gesture in the direction of independence). This off-the-shelf choice was certainly cheaper than Blue Streak, but it was another blow to national perceptions of enduring British strength in the post-war world.

A further blow to British perceptions of the country's ability to exert significant influence in its own right on the world stage came with the disastrous Paris summit of May 1960. Macmillan was eager to mediate between the USA and the USSR, just as Churchill and Eden had done, with some success, in the 1951–55 period. The Prime Minister had played a central role in the organizing of a Four Power meeting between the heads of the US, Soviet, British and French governments. He hoped the result would be a reduction in the international tensions resulting from disagreement between the USSR and the West about Berlin, from an escalation in the arms race (seen in the development of ballistic missiles and the testing of nuclear weapons on both sides in the Cold War), and from US anxieties about the implications of the recent revolution in Cuba. Progress towards a resolution of these issues would have the beneficial result of making the world a safer place. Beyond this, however, in demonstrating that Britain retained the power to achieve such a change in the climate it would reassure a domestic electorate anxious about the country's declining capacity for unilateral action on the world stage and show the growing numbers supporting the Campaign for Nuclear Disarmament that the government cared about peace as much as they did.

As is well known, the summit collapsed without reaching agreement on any of the issues it had been convened to discuss, following the revelation that an American spy plane had just been shot down over Soviet territory. Instead of progress towards a more harmonious world there had been a major international incident – and Britain had been powerless to do anything about it. The setback was a big shock and upset to Macmillan, who now became preoccupied with how to develop a national strategy which would enable Britain to continue playing a major role in world affairs. According to his Private Secretary, Philip de Zulueta, the Prime Minister's thoughts turned increasingly to the question of Britain's relationship with the newly formed European Economic Community (EEC, also known as 'the Common Market') in Western Europe and the feasibility of joining the organization.[2]

Suez, Blue Streak and the Paris Summit all gave a strategic dimension to a growing conviction of economic vulnerability, shared by the major political parties, both sides of industry and sections of the press. There was increasing evidence that Britain's economy was underperforming. In 1950 Britain's real GDP was 158 per cent of its closest continental rival, France.[3] Yet by the late 1950s it was clear that the advanced industrial states of Western Europe, apparently in ruins not much more than a decade earlier, were experiencing rapid annual growth. Britain however was not sharing in this progress, averaging annual GDP growth of 2.5 per cent between 1955 and 1960 against 5.3 per cent on the part of the nations making up the European Economic Community (Belgium, France, West Germany, Italy, Luxembourg and the Netherlands) over the same period.[4] Although the record was certainly respectable by comparison with the country's past, the statistics show a relative decline from economic leadership in Western Europe to a position of apparent mediocrity by the end of the decade.

In recent years historians have expressed doubts about whether Britain was ever in a position to match the achievements of the continental economies in the 1950s and 1960s. These were able to take advantage of the movement of workers from the countryside to the cities. They were exchanging work on what were often small and uneconomic farms, generally characterized by low productivity (low output per head), for labour in industry.[5] Although this tended to pay better than agriculture, rates initially were low compared with wages in the USA and the UK. In consequence costs were held down, allowing for an expansion of investment in plant, equipment and machinery. Productivity in industry therefore rose sharply, without which the growth 'miracles' would not have occurred. This was not a development that the British economy could easily reproduce (although as we shall see the Labour government of 1964–70 made an ingenious attempt to do just this), given that here the migration of labour from agriculture to industry had peaked in the decades prior to 1914. It is arguable, therefore, that the continental states were merely 'catching up' with Britain and once they had reached comparable levels of income their growth would drop back towards the British level.[6]

These subtleties were not employed by economists any more than they were by politicians in the late 1950s. The figures were taken as evidence of Britain's slide downhill from its position in the first half of the decade. Prime Minister Macmillan's comment in the summer of 1957 that 'most of our people have never had it so good' was not a complacent comment but intended as the prelude to a warning that the new status quo was threatened by inflation – in other words, persistently rising prices. Were full employment and price stability compatible? The Chancellor, Peter Thorneycroft, agreed with Macmillan and expressed anxiety about the nation's tendency to 'live beyond its means', with increases in incomes outstripping those in output by a factor of three over the previous eight years.[7] Thorneycroft's anxieties about the economy were reinforced in the autumn of 1957, when fears of a sterling devaluation from the current rate of £1 = \$2.80 (fixed in 1949) flared after holders began a wave of panic selling, many of them deserting the currency for the German deutschmark.

This run on sterling was especially disturbing to opinion within the City and the Bank of England. During and after the war the convertibility of the pound for current and capital transactions had been suspended. This meant that official permission had been necessary before pounds could be exchanged for other currencies and that balances of sterling could not freely be transferred outside the 'sterling area', namely the association of states (most within the Commonwealth and Empire) which continued to use sterling as a trading and reserve currency. This had been inescapable given the heavy import requirements of the war and reconstruction eras. The need to divert production to the military effort meant that offsetting earnings from exports became exiguous. In 1944 export values were 33 per cent of their 1938 level. It followed that there was real danger of Britain's reserves suffering rapid depletion in the absence of restrictions on the use of sterling. This would have left the nation unable to buy the volume of food, raw materials, capital goods and machine tools needed to fight the war and rebuild afterwards without falls in living standards which were already austere.

By the early 1950s opinion in the Treasury, the Bank of England and the City was turning against the regulations. Within all these organizations there was a desire to see sterling resume its pre-1939 role as an international currency whose attractiveness derived from its reliability as an asset and the lack of restrictions governing its use. Fearful that the decontrol of sterling would expose the domestic economy to serious risk, Labour had not been in a hurry to promote this agenda, which reflected the priorities of 'Consumer's England'. The Conservatives, given their historic links to the City, unsurprisingly took the opposite view. At the same time, however, they were aware that the political balance of forces in post-war Britain did not favour rapid liberalization and followed a cautious approach, which led them to abandon the 'Robot' plan for a dash to sterling convertibility in 1951–52.[8] Thereafter they had encouraged a slow and at times erratic dismantling of controls on sterling. The panic selling of September 1957 was therefore especially unwelcome since it threatened sterling's return to its pre-war glory. The Bank and the City viewed the shift of market sentiment in favour of the deutschmark both as another national embarrassment, following hard on the heels of Suez, and as a clear indication that Britain needed to control inflationary pressures as effectively as West Germany.

Thorneycroft's response to the crisis was to raise the Bank Rate by two percentage points to 7 per cent and introduce a credit squeeze along with reductions to public spending programmes. The rationale for these measures was a view, shared between Thorneycroft and his junior Ministers Nigel Birch and Enoch Powell, that inflation was the economy's most serious problem and that the only way to eliminate it was by curtailing demand, even if this meant a rise in unemployment and a temporary check to the expansion of output. The package did seem to reassure the markets, and speculation against the pound had ceased to be a problem by early October. Thorneycroft, however, now took the view that in order for Britain's competitive position to be restored and all danger to sterling removed, it would be necessary to go a good deal further than he had in September. He proposed that public spending projections for 1958–59 be held at 1957–58 levels. Since Ministers were proposing an overall increase of £153 million this would represent a dramatic cut in expenditure. By December the Chancellor was calling for 'an agonising reappraisal' of public spending commitments, including even those needed to improve the welfare state.[9] There was a revolt in the Cabinet. Macmillan refused to back his Chancellor. Thorneycroft, Birch and Powell all resigned together in January 1958.

Macmillan famously dismissed this event as 'a little local difficulty', but the resignation of a government's Treasury team is a dramatic event at any time. The Prime Minister was prepared to face down his own Chancellor (whom he regarded as 'stupid, rigid')[10] because he did not share the same set of politico-economic priorities. For Macmillan, as for senior Conservatives such as R. A. Butler, the continuing accommodation of their Party with the post-war order was essential. This was not simply out of tactical concern about Conservative prospects at the General Election which was expected at some point in 1959. Although the Prime Minister recognised that all was not well with the British economy the Chancellor's remedy offended his social conscience. As a young man in the 1920s Macmillan had been appalled by the suffering inflicted by unemployment on his constituents in Stockton.[11] This had led him to embrace Keynesian economics and on occasion advocate the adoption by governments of 'socialistic methods and principles'.[12] Attlee had called him 'a real left-wing radical in his social, human and economic thinking'.[13] Macmillan was therefore completely committed to the 1944 settlement and sought solutions to Britain's relative decline compatible with its continuation. Thorneycroft's agenda was not, and this was the reason for its rejection.

In the aftermath of Thorneycroft's departure Macmillan and his new Chancellor, Derick Heathcoat Amory, gradually switched to an expansionary macroeconomic policy. Unlike Thorneycroft, Birch and Powell, Macmillan saw nothing wrong with a small touch of inflation if it meant higher growth. He therefore continually pressed for new public investment and in early 1959 gained Treasury agreement to both increases in capital spending and a giveaway budget characterized by cuts in direct and indirect taxation.[14] Economic activity accelerated and a boom developed which was to last until the following year. Unsurprisingly the Conservatives won the 1959 General Election, being returned to power with a very comfortable 100-seat majority, but the clear skies darkened during the first half of 1961. Heathcote Amory's replacement at the Treasury, Selwyn Lloyd, became as concerned about the country paying itself more than it was earning as Thorneycroft had been five years before. He noted that average income had risen over the past year by 8 per cent but output per head had increased by just 3 per cent.[15] The high level of demand was attracting an excessive level of imports: a current account balance of £234 million in 1960 swung to a deficit of £171 million the following year.[16] As in 1957 there was a wave of speculation against sterling and in favour of the deutschmark. To protect the pound the Conservatives once again pushed up the Bank Rate (all the way back to 7 per cent in 1961) and introduced a credit squeeze. They committed themselves to public spending cuts and, without consulting trade union leaders, announced a 'Pay Pause' to check wage and salary rises.

These sudden lurches in macroeconomic policy became known as 'Stop-Go' and appeared to contrast very sharply with the continuing high and smooth levels of growth evident in the economies of EEC members. They were frustrating for the Prime Minister, unpopular on both sides of industry, and delivered further shocks to public confidence in the state of post-war Britain. Macmillan did not abandon his pro-expansionist views but came to the conviction that reflation alone was not going to restore British economic leadership to Western Europe and restore the economic foundations essential to lasting global influence. Along with many in the major political parties as well as management, unions and the press he concluded that Britain should adopt the strategies which had underpinned success on the continent. The most successful of these appeared to be economic planning and membership of the EEC. Macmillan had been an advocate of the first of these as far back as the 1930s and had come round to supporting the latter by late in 1960, but these enthusiasms were at first not widely shared in the Conservative Party. In 1961–62, however, Britain's changing fortunes led to a reappraisal throughout the government, which ultimately embraced both of these causes. The long struggle to reinvent Britain as a West European social democracy was beginning.

Turn to Europe

Harold Macmillan's successful revival of Conservative fortunes after the Suez fiasco and the Thorneycroft embarrassment, with the switch to economic expansion following the squeeze imposed in late 1957, guaranteed his domination of the domestic political scene. At the same time he acquired a reputation for successful international statesmanship. The Prime Minister was able to repair the special relationship with the USA and sought to encourage a thaw in Cold War tensions, flying to Moscow to meet the leaders of the USSR early in 1959 on a mission to facilitate closer cultural links and discuss nuclear disarmament. By the start of 1960 the unlikely status of comic book hero, reflected in the figure of 'Supermac' and intended as a joke by the left-leaning political cartoonist Vicky, had stuck to the Prime Minister and lent him an aura of political invincibility. Over the next three years, however, this masterful image was replaced by a far less flattering one: as the economy stagnated while competitor nations prospered and international influence appeared to shrink, Supermac disappeared from the scene. He was replaced by a doddering pensioner approaching his seventieth birthday, an aristocratic relic from the Edwardian era unable to come to terms with the pace of change not only in science and innovation but also in social and sexual relations. By the spring of 1963, with the Profumo affair transforming the Conservative Party into a vehicle for sleazy political soap opera, Macmillan seemed an out of touch and bewildered figure.

Macmillan did have aristocratic connections; to the Devonshire family whose seat was Chatsworth House in Derbyshire. He enjoyed some of the traditional pursuits of the English gentleman, notably grouse shooting. These links and tastes, along with a manner characterized at times by studied vagueness or even slightly fey disposition, gave him the appearance of an old-fashioned Tory squire straight from central casting. It all made him increasingly vulnerable to the satire boom of the time, and the Prime Minister became a familiar figure of fun (and sometimes contempt) in the pages of *Private Eye* and the sketches of the stage show *Beyond the Fringe* and the weekly television broadcasts of *That Was The Week That Was*. The impression was very misleading. Macmillan was no traditional Conservative. His link to the Devonshires was through marriage: his wife Dorothy was daughter of the ninth Duke. Macmillan's own background was that of the professional upper middle class: his father was a publisher and his mother an American artist and socialite. The two Parliamentary constituencies he represented in his career as an M.P. were Stockton-on-Tees and Bromley in Kent, neither of which was known for its grouse moors and stately homes.[17]

As Attlee had noted, Macmillan was an uncomfortable Tory: between the wars he had opposed the Party leadership on the appeasement of Germany and on economic policy. Surveying the wreckage of traditional British industries, Macmillan had urged politicians, industrialists and investors to abandon their commitment to liberal economics and pursue not self-interest but a 'national economic policy', their actions guided by a State planning structure capable of taking a synoptic view.[18] Much influenced by the work of J. M. Keynes, he had been a consistent advocate of cheap money and had argued for public investment schemes designed to improve the infrastructure and reduce unemployment. His 1938 publication, *The Middle Way*, called for the reorganization of industry through the creation of government-backed trade associations grouped into separate councils organized along the lines of industrial sectors. These in turn would come under the guidance of a National Industrial Council responsible for the development and, if necessary, compulsory implementation of reconstruction and rationalization plans. Overall co-ordination of the plans would be executed by a central National Economic Council composed of members of the sectoral councils, government representatives and independent experts.[19]

Concern about Britain's economic and strategic vulnerability and the incumbent National Government's apparent torpor in the face of the strategic and economic challenges of the 1930s had led Macmillan to resign the Tory whip in June 1936. By 1961, given the course of events since 1956, Macmillan's anxieties about Britain's international position and domestic economic performance had once more become acute, and had led him to work on a strategy for national modernization which he now sought to make central to government policy. A closer relationship with the EEC seemed a good place to start. The 'Common Market' was composed of six fast growing economies committed to the removal over time of all barriers to the movement of goods, people and capital between them, and surrounded by its own common tariff. Its existence was a problem for the British: their trade with Western Europe had been increasing throughout the 1950s (see Table 1.1) and they did not wish to be excluded from the emerging economic unit. At the same time they were aware that membership would not be compatible with the system of trade preferences which linked the UK to markets in the Commonwealth. Commonwealth markets no longer enjoyed the near 50 per cent share of all British imports and exports they had taken in 1950, but ten years on they remained the UK's best customers and most significant suppliers. Britain's initial reaction to the creation of the EEC had therefore been to call for its transformation into a free trade area in which commitment to the elimination of trade restrictions remained but members were allowed to retain an independent tariff policy towards nations outside the group. This attempt to make the common tariff redundant was unacceptable to the Six: no West European Free Trade Area came into being.

In order to counter economic isolation the British led a rival group, the European Free Trade Area (EFTA), known sometimes as the 'Outer Seven' and composed of the UK and the six smaller West European economies (Norway,

TABLE 1.1 United Kingdom trade, 1952–62

Percentage of total UK exports

	1952	1956	1960	1961	1962
Commonwealth	48.4	45.5	37.8	35.5	32.7
EEC	11.3	13.6	14.6	16.7	18.9
EFTA	10.2	11.9	10.7	11.7	13.6
Other (OEEC) Europe	4.4	2.3	5.1	6.0	3.2
Total W. Europe	25.9	27.9	30.4	34.3	35.8

Percentage of total UK imports

	1952	1956	1960	1961	1962
Commonwealth	45.8	44.4	36.3	35.5	34.7
EEC	12.3	12.7	14.6	15.4	15.3
EFTA	9.2	11.6	10.1	10.4	12.0
Other (OEEC) Europe	3.6	2.3	4.7	5.5	2.3
Total W. Europe	25.1	26.6	29.5	31.5	29.6

Source: *Annual Abstract of Statistics* (various issues)

Denmark, Sweden, Portugal, Austria and Ireland). For London, however, EFTA was no permanent home. Rather, it was seen as the key to a process of tariff bargaining with the EEC which would, through mutually agreed reductions, lead to the wider free trade area the British had wanted since the EEC had started. It soon became clear that occupation of this half-way house was not tenable. The disparity in size of the markets represented by the EEC (200 million) and EFTA (80 million) resulted in an asymmetry of bargaining power: the Six had less incentive to offer tariff reductions than the Seven. This was not encouraging for Britain given that by late 1960 its trade with Western Europe was growing a good deal more rapidly than with the Commonwealth markets. The situation reinforced a growing conviction within Downing Street and the Treasury, under its new Joint Permanent Secretary, Sir Frank Lee[20] that the economy would gain from joining the EEC. Lee argued that the shock of competition with successful European firms would force British companies to modernize through rationalization and investment in new plant and machinery, while the extension of the domestic market to much of Western Europe would facilitate economies of scale and longer production runs.

The view from Whitehall was gaining purchase in the Federation of British Industries (FBI),[21] which tended to represent the larger corporations, and the Association of British Chambers of Commerce. Companies such as Courtaulds,

Imperial Chemical Industries (ICI) and General Electric Company (GEC) were keen to expand their business in European markets but had become frustrated at the disruptive impact on production of 'Stop-Go'.[22] The Director General of the FBI, Sir William McFadzean, was an enthusiastic advocate of closer links with the EEC, all the way to membership if possible. Government recognition of his key position at the interface between corporate capital, foreign trade and the State led to his appointment as the first Chairman of the Export Council for Europe, established in 1960 to promote more commerce with the continental economies and composed of civil servants, trade associations and industrialists. The growing interest in the possibilities of increased prosperity was shared by the Trades Union Congress (TUC), where the rapid rise of the continental worker's living standards in the form of higher pay, better pensions and improved conditions of service had made a strong impression.[23] By late July 1961 this developing identity of opinion between Government and the peak institutions was powerful enough to ensure a favourable domestic climate for the news that the Cabinet had resolved to make a 'conditional application' for membership of the EEC, with TUC members voting in favour of the Government's recent application for membership at their September conference[24] even though some powerful organizations such as the Transport and General Workers Union (TGWU) tended to be suspicious of the implications of membership for job security and a future Labour Government's ability to plan the economy.[25]

The generally warm reception given to the announcement of the British application did not extend to some circles of the Conservative Party. Those who were committed by sentiment and commercial interest to the maintenance of ties to Commonwealth and Empire, as well as farmers anxious about the implications of EEC membership for agricultural price support, expressed their unease.[26] The Prime Minister overrode these objections out of a conviction that membership of the Common Market on good terms would stimulate faster economic growth and from a tactical awareness that the European issue signalled a fundamental change of direction for the Party. It was intended to show that modern Conservatism did not seek to restore Britain's imperial glory; there were to be no more episodes like Suez. Britain's future was to be part of a democratic association of progressive nation states co-operating to promote mutual trade, rising living standards and full employment.[27]

In taking this line Macmillan and the younger, pro-European Cabinet Ministers he promoted in 1961, such as Edward Heath and Christopher Soames (both to posts which would be crucial to the negotiations with the Six, Heath at the Foreign Office and Soames at Agriculture) were not only acting from conviction but from the awareness of professional politicians that the electorate was changing. Over the previous decade the share of the workforce taken by white collar workers (mainly administrative, technical and scientific) had grown from 30.9 per cent to 35.9 per cent.[28] From the mid-1950s onwards more young people had been staying on at school beyond the leaving age of 15 in order to gain qualifications which would permit them to find not just white collar jobs in the commercial and service sectors but also in industry where scientific and technical posts were expanding.[29] The number leaving school with two or more A Levels each year grew from 25,000 (1955) to 64,000 (1964). The trend led to intensified competition for university places, and in acknowledgement the number of available places within the system was raised from 90,000 students in 1956 to a target of 175,000, set in 1959 for the late 1960s and early 1970s. In 1961 the government approved the creation of seven new universities.[30] The turn to Europe was only one element of the government's response to the changing nature of British society but it was indicative of Macmillan's determination to modernize Conservatism so that it became an appropriate vehicle for the transformation of Britain. The Party was now to be identified with a set of policies attractive to an increasingly well-educated and skilled working population. The political loyalties of this group were known to be volatile and determined not by commitment to the old causes of class solidarity (on the Left) and Empire (on the Right) but by perceptions of personal well-being determined especially by income, job security, career prospects and low mortgage costs.[31] On foreign policy issues many were attracted by the internationalism of the Liberal Party, which had condemned Suez, supported mediation between the Superpowers and advocated British membership of the EEC. 'Europe' as a political issue therefore encapsulated idealism, peace, modernity and the promise of greater prosperity. It represented a new departure for Nation and Party and was designed to appeal to a constituency whose numbers were to rise over the coming decade.

Interest in the potential economic benefits of joining the EEC and conviction that membership would help to refurbish the image of the Conservatives in the eyes of the electorate were not the only reasons for the application. The bid also emerged from the Prime Minister's concern about the country's declining influence, seen so graphically at the Paris Summit. It was designed to lead to a strengthening of the country's world position by placing it at the heart of an international environment likely to guarantee its security and prosperity. There is, then, no doubt that membership of the Common Market was a central part of Macmillan's new strategy for Britain. Yet economic modernization could if necessary proceed for a time outside the EEC, whereas continuing influence as an independent global power would be unsustainable in the absence of the Anglo-American alliance – as the fate of the British nuclear deterrent demonstrated. This reality became evident when the French President, Charles de Gaulle, seized on what he saw as the contradictory implications of Britain joining the EEC while retaining its close Atlantic and Commonwealth connections. In January 1963, citing the UK's links with the USA (recently reaffirmed by the agreement on the Polaris missile system) and the Commonwealth as likely to mean that British membership of the Common Market would turn the organization into a giant Atlantic free trade area, de Gaulle vetoed the British application. In the short term at least the EEC would not be a springboard for the renewal of Britain's international influence nor an external stimulus to economic growth. The drive had to be from within: Britain's regeneration and Conservative fortunes rested on the programme of domestic led economic reform and expansion.

Planning modernization

Of course, even if Britain had joined the Common Market the anticipated beneficial economic effects would not necessarily have been felt very quickly. In the meantime it was clear that the country needed an economic strategy capable of delivering faster growth. The implications of the disappointing annual average rate of British economic growth were underlined by what was happening to the country's international economic position. The share of world exports taken by British goods (including both manufactures and services) had been falling steadily throughout the 1950s, slipping from 25.5 per cent in 1950 to 16.5 per cent ten years later.[32] Of course this trend should not have been surprising, given that neither Germany nor Japan had been competitors in global markets in 1950, but it was taken as evidence that the economy needed reform if it was to remain competitive enough to support full employment, the welfare state and a world-wide military presence.

'Declinism' now developed as commentators and politicians sought to identify the causes of the national malaise and propose measures likely to cure it.[33] The texts most commonly cited in this connection are Hugh Thomas's collection of essays on *The Establishment* (1959), Michael Shanks's *The Stagnant Society* (1961), Anthony Crosland's *The Conservative Enemy* (1962), Anthony Sampson's *The Anatomy of Britain* (1962) and *Suicide of a Nation?* (1963), edited by Arthur Koestler.[34] Together they produced an agenda for change which influenced both the main political parties for the best part of a decade. There was general support for entry to the EEC. The case for professional training of civil servants so that they possessed the specialist knowledge to offer informed advice on, for example, economic policy issues to Government was widely accepted. Following from the work of Shanks it became conventional wisdom that a new approach to industrial relations was necessary, in order to reduce division between management and unions and create a climate conducive to the acceptance of pay restraint and innovation in the workplace. Shanks also argued for the State to enlarge its role in the management of the economy. He called for economic planning, the government co-operating with both sides of industry to promote industrial modernization, and for the State purchase of shares in profitable private companies.[35] Finally it was common ground that the Conservative governments of the 1950s had neglected the national infrastructure and that a significant expansion of public investment was now overdue.

The list of deserving causes was long. Education was an obvious candidate: it was taken as axiomatic that high quality secondary and tertiary education was needed in order to produce a more skilled and qualified working population. Yet spending had been held back for much of the 1950s, with predictable results. A government report issued in 1963 found two-thirds of all schools overcrowded, with 45 per cent lacking a dining room and only a minority possessing adequate library or science facilities.[36] Despite the recent decision to increase the number of universities there remained a shortage of places and courses, especially in science and technology. Other areas most often singled out were the transport system, where Britain had only made a start on the construction of a motorway network in 1958, and the National Health Service (not one new hospital had been constructed in the ten years after 1948).[37] Housing, a success story in the mid-1950s, was an increasing problem by the start of the 1960s: 3 million were living in slums and homelessness was rising in many cities, including London. The shortage of accommodation, together with a permissive attitude to private landlords, led to a combination of overcrowding and high rents. Transport, health and housing were not luxuries; improvements in the first reduced costs and delivery times both in the internal market and for goods being exported; money spent on the NHS would lead to a fitter and healthier work force; an increased and refurbished housing stock would assist labour mobility.

The case for investment in the nation's social infrastructure was not only technocratic. It went to the heart of the argument about what kind of society Britain was becoming. When J. K. Galbraith had written about 'private affluence and public squalor' in *The Affluent Society* (1958)[38] he had, of course, been concerned with the USA. Yet his words were often used to describe what had gone wrong with Britain in the 1950s. The historian David Thomson commented in his widely used *England in the Twentieth Century* (1965) that if the significant innovations of affluent society Britain were commercial television, betting shops and Bingo

> Even more significant...was what was not done. The equipment neededand expected by the Welfare State was not provided: 'it could not be afforded'. The public sector did not keep pace with the private, and the neglected classes of the old-age pensioners and the sick were left behind in the race for affluence and status.[39]

Running in parallel with the neglect of the Welfare State was a divergence between the prosperous new towns around London, in old Consumer's Britain,[40] and the traditional working-class communities still to be found in Producer's Britain, clustered around the coal, steel and shipbuilding industries of south Wales, northern England and southern Scotland. Here could be found many of the new poor identified by the work of Brian Abel-Smith and Peter Townsend, working people whose income was too low to pay for basic needs.[41] This deprivation was reinforced by the appearance of heavy regional unemployment, concentrated especially in the north-east and in Scotland; by early 1963 the national figure stood at 3 per cent of the work force but in the old centres of heavy industry it was up to 5 per cent, a post-war high. Yet growing inequality was becoming apparent even in south east England, much of it connected to housing. Social support through National Assistance and unemployment benefit left much to be desired and the idealistic commitment to eradicate poverty which had been intrinsic to early post-war Britain seemed to have faded. Cultural critics such as Richard Hoggart and Raymond Williams reflected a concern, growing across society, that the new era set a premium on individualistic materialism and ignored older qualities more conducive to social solidarity, such as work, duty and community.[42] The nation's values as well as its fabric seemed in need of repair.

Macmillan's government worked hard to develop an agenda for national renewal. This embraced membership of the EEC, the construction of new State structures to promote modernization, a growth-oriented macroeconomic policy, supply-side reforms to encourage competition and a significant expansion of public investment focused on education, health, housing, transport and regional development. It was an ambitious project, reflecting Macmillan's determination that 'In or out of Europe, Britain needs to be brought up to date in every sphere of life'.[43] It did not appear in finished form in 1961. At this point it was characterized by two items. One of these was Britain's relationship with the EEC; the other involved the promotion of measures to encourage greater competition. A Treasury report delivered to Ministers (with tactically acute timing) during the sterling crisis of July 1961 recommended the introduction of stronger Monopolies and Merger legislation, tariff reductions and the abolition of Resale Price Maintenance[44] (which gave manufacturers legal authority to fix a price for goods leaving their outlets, in agreement with the distributors). The rest of the agenda developed, rapidly but piecemeal, over the next two years. Key elements reflected the Prime Minister's own definition of what constituted a 'national economic policy' and sought to build on the philosophical and structural innovations of the wartime and post-war years designed to foster co-operation between industry and labour. Yet it became apparent that these had become somewhat etiolated: in consequence, 'In or out of Europe', Britain needed to look across the English Channel and adopt the economic strategies and institutional arrangements which had seemed to underpin the recent achievements of its continental neighbours.

The programme of national development to which the government became committed during 1962–63 did not need to be justified by reference to what had been done within the Six. All the same it was undeniable that throughout the Common Market the post-war decades had seen substantial levels of public spending on transport, energy, agriculture, education and health by governments keen to break with the post-1929 legacy of lost production, unemployment and social division, culminating in war, defeat and occupation. Alan Milward characterized the modernization which had followed from this investment as 'the European rescue of the nation-state'.[45] The verdict of 1945 had appeared to make so dramatic a departure unnecessary in Britain but the failures and setbacks which had been evident since 1956 indicated that, after all, it was now appropriate to follow a path which promised to lead to the country's reinvention as a social democracy, given that empirical observation suggested this to be the template for prosperity.

The two years closing the long era of Conservatism which had started in 1951 saw a burst of constructive and reforming government, much of it focused on infrastructural renewal. In 1962, the government agreed to raise the annual housing target from 300,000 to 325,000, most of the expansion to occur as a result of support for more local authority housebuilding. At the end of the year the figure was raised to 350,000 and in 1963, following the recommendations of a Housing

White Paper it was expanded again to 400,000.[46] In the autumn of 1962 Minister of Health Enoch Powell announced a ten-year programme worth £500 million, devoted to hospital refurbishment and construction (ninety new ones were scheduled); in 1963 the budget for this project was increased to £800 million. In 1963 the Ministry of Transport unveiled plans to modernize the road network, including the building of a motorway system across the country, amounting to £1,000 million over the next six years.[47] In the same year, following the recommendation of the Prime Minister's Committee on Higher Education, chaired by Lord Robbins, that higher education should be available to all 18–21 year olds who were able and willing to take advantage of it, the Department of Education secured Cabinet agreement for the expenditure of £3.5 billion over ten years (the total annual government budget at the time was £11 billion) on the expansion of tertiary education. Most of this was to be devoted to augmenting the number of available university places so that the system would be able to accommodate an extra 50 per cent by 1967, rising to 250 per cent by 1980.[48] At the same time the government responded to growing concern about the state of the nation's schools, devoting more funds to primary and secondary education so that the overall budget on education was set to rise by 10 per cent in 1963–64, becoming 'the most rapidly developing feature of the whole public outlay'.[49]

The magnitude of the shift in public expenditure policy following from these commitments was dramatic: it grew by 10 per cent in 1963–64 and the estimates for 1964–65 showed a further increase of 9.75 per cent to be in the pipeline for 1964–65.[50] It all indicated government acceptance of the idea, common to the reconstruction strategies pursued by the six Common Market nations, that the State was an agent of modernization. This view, described by Middlemas as 'Conservative Social Democracy', did not command universal support in the Conservative Party. There were suspicions among grass-roots supporters that they were being dragged towards 'socialism'.[51] Indeed, it was perhaps not unreasonable for a traditional Conservative, sceptical of grand designs and committed to the small state and lower taxes, to entertain such feelings. At the time however such opinions and those who held them were in a minority within the Party. They were outnumbered by colleagues and outgunned by powerful corporate interests who argued that only the new approach was compatible with the imperative of national regeneration.

Between 1960 and 1962 an increasing number of key figures and organizations representing opinion throughout large-scale industry came to share the Prime Minister's interest in planning. A 'great reappraisal' of economic strategy was under way[52] within the government and the FBI. The frustration with 'Stop-Go' which had led to the FBI's backing for British membership of the Common Market also converted it to planning. Firms had been buffeted by the oscillations resulting from government policy shifts without being able to moderate them or influence the thinking behind them. The fluctuating output of the economy was making long-term decisions on investment hazardous. This, in turn, was likely to damage the competitive position of British goods in home and overseas markets. Noting the conjunction on the continent of planning machinery involving the State and both sides of industry with smooth and high levels of economic growth, senior FBI figures argued in favour of co-operation with government in a 'conscious attempt to assess plans and demands in particular industries for five or even ten years ahead'.[53]

Following the conference, commitment to planning became FBI policy. The problem was, of course, what sort of planning. Many in the West had been impressed by the apparent successes of planning in the Soviet Union during the 1950s. Here, a strategy of State-led development involving import substitution along with high investment in heavy industry and social overhead capital (especially education) had generated an annual average growth rate of 5.7 per cent during the decade.[54] Given its aversion even to Labour's rather improvised version of planning after 1945 this model was not likely to attract the FBI, and in 1960–61 representatives of the organization began to travel to west European countries in order to see which examples of planning there could be applied at home. The most popular destination was France, largely on account of its transformation from 'sick man of Europe'. The post-war French recovery had been characterized by successful infrastructural modernization, especially in the transport and energy sectors, and striking advances in industrial output (by 1960 this was 60 per cent above its 1938 level), notably in automobile production. These achievements had run in parallel with significant progress in social policy, with death rates (especially the infant death rate) falling from a disturbingly high 112 per thousand in 1945 to 22 per thousand in 1962.[55]

Observers attributed these impressive achievements to the planning process which the French had established to guide national development immediately after the war. During the period since liberation the country had suffered from considerable political turbulence but its economic strategy had demonstrated continuity. The *Commissariat du Plan*, independent of government, had been established in 1946. It had been given the task of supervising the modernization of France, a task it undertook through the establishment of small commissions whose membership was composed of civil servants, industrialists and trade unions. Each commission took responsibility either for specific sectors of the economy (such as transport, energy, agricultural machinery, fuel and fertilizer) or for issues of common concern (over the period since the start of the Plan these had come to include research, marketing, productivity and training). The Commissariat set goals for growth, both global and by sector, and for the balance of payments. Over the period since 1946 there had been four plans, each one prioritizing what the Commissariat judged the most critical problems confronting the economy as these had developed over time. The First (1946–53) had been addressed to the modernization and re-equipment of basic industry. The Second (1954–57) saw extension of the process to cover all the economy and a commitment to macroeconomic expansion. The Third (1958–61) continued the emphasis on growth (the goal was an annual rate of 5 per cent) and set targets for higher output (33 per cent for manufacturing) and increased exports (70 per cent) over the period. The Fourth, which had started in 1962 and was to last until 1965, raised the growth target to 5.5 per cent and turned attention to social and economic reform (notably social benefits, urban renewal, housing provision and education).[56]

Doubt has been expressed about the extent to which the Plan was responsible for the French post-war boom.[57] Economic historians have pointed to specific factors such as the tendency of economies passing through a phase of 'catch up' with more prosperous neighbours to demonstrate brisk growth. The French economy had lagged behind both Britain and Germany for much of the twentieth century; in 1951 output per head in France was 20 per cent lower than the level in the UK and did not reach parity with it until 1968. Special factors operating after 1945 drove a process of economic convergence within Western Europe and between the West European economies and the world's leading economy, the USA. These included the high levels of demand resulting from heavy expenditure on investment during the period of reconstruction, the availability of relatively cheap labour for industry, and the rapid development of international trade in consumer goods.[58]

There may be scope for debate about the extent of the Plan's contribution to the French post-war achievement but claims that it was irrelevant are not supported by the evidence. The Plan, in making economic growth the main objective of macroeconomic policy, raised the expectations of business and civil servants whose experience throughout the interwar years had been characterized by stagnation. Governments now stuck by the commitment to expansion in circumstances which would have led them to abandon it in the 1920s and throughout most of the 1930s. Budgetary policy was countercyclical. After 1948 the franc was devalued five times,[59] a sharp contrast with practice between the wars when successive administrations had prioritized the strong franc and low inflation, notwithstanding the consequent low output and high unemployment. At the same time the Plan facilitated the allocation of cheap funds for investment projects. Its forecasts of growth were generally accurate. This in turn generated a confidence which was conducive to spending by the private sector on research and development, innovation and new plant and equipment at a rate consistent with the predictions of the Plan for sectoral and national expansion. All participants knew what was expected of them; as one French observer commented at the time, 'the Plan…carries itself out'.[60]

When it came to planning, British visitors and observers came to the conclusion that for the most part it was the French who provided the example of best practice which the UK should adopt. The coincidence of the Plan with France's record on growth impressed British civil servants and business groups. The government's retiring Chief Economic Adviser, Robert Hall, and the senior Treasury official R. W. B. Clarke were converted from sceptics to supporters following discussions with members of the Commissariat. Their views were shared by representatives of the trade unions and business who visited the Commissariat in 1961, as well as by senior FBI figures such as Sir Hugh Beaver.[61] Indeed backing for a British turn to planning was cross party and embraced all the peak institutions. Labour and trade union circles might have been expected to endorse the French model but the interest shown by a growing number of Conservatives (including the Chancellor, Selwyn Lloyd) as well as by industrialists such as Beaver was notable. They were converted by the 'indicative' nature of the Plan, in other words by its reliance not on State direction but on the role of targets agreed between government, industry and the unions and on the maximization of information, including the availability of forecasts concerning national growth and the balance of payments, for all participants. In fact this was a little misleading, since the French State's controls over nationalized industry and ownership of much of the financial system ensured that it possessed an ability to direct the economy not available to its British counterpart. All the same compulsion was rarely obvious; more relevant was the willingness to use market mechanisms which had become evident during the 1950s, as France embraced de-control of prices and production, and the tariff reduction programme made necessary by its membership of the EEC. As O'Hara has noted, a liberal approach to planning appeared to have been found, in which the State built a framework for expansion through infrastructural spending, targets and forecasts while industrialists concentrated on the encouragement of growth within their own sectors.[62]

There was, however, another dimension to Britain's 'great reappraisal' of economic strategy. This related to wage bargaining. Concern about wage rates had been a constant in discussions about economic policy since the second half of the 1950s, and the evidence suggested that it was not misplaced. Between 1954 and 1959 total labour costs per unit of output in British manufacturing rose by 25 per cent, about twice the rate experienced in other advanced industrial countries. The implications for competitiveness were grim, as indicated not just by the nation's falling share of world exports but also by its shrinking portion of global trade in manufactured goods, the latter dropping from just over 20 per cent in 1950 to 12.7 per cent in 1961.[63] There was a school of thought at the time, promoted by the economist F. W. Paish, which argued that the problem could be resolved by management of the economy at a more significant margin of unused capacity than had been customary since 1945.[64] Paish himself suggested this could be achieved if the average rate of unemployment was allowed to rise from the post-war norm of between 1.5 and 2 per cent to a figure somewhere between 2 and 2.5 per cent (the 3 per cent level which it reached in 1962 was regarded as undesirably high even by Paish and his supporters).[65] His argument was that the existence of more idle resources in the economy would be translated into lower inflation (following from a reduction in the pressure exerted by rising costs on the price level) and a healthy balance of payments (a function of falling import demand in the home market combined with more competitive pricing of exports). This theory had some support in the Treasury but the Prime Minister was hostile. He argued that there was an extra ingredient which made it possible to reconcile full employment with price stability, growth and an external surplus; and this was an incomes policy.

Government concern about the implications of rising incomes for the rest of the economy had led it to proclaim the 'Pay Pause', a move which caused it considerable unpopularity among both traditional trade unionists and middle-class professionals working in the public sector (especially teachers). Indeed the electoral fallout became increasingly threatening as safe Conservative seats suddenly became vulnerable to opposition candidates (notably the Liberals, who achieved spectacular successes at the Orpington Parliamentary by-election as well as in Council contests). Within Downing Street and the Treasury it followed that there was a growing conviction that the incomes policy, without which a strategy for growth would be likely to break down, could only be reached by consent: there had to be agreement between government, the employers and the unions on a figure for pay increases which was compatible with sustainable economic expansion.

The era of the 'great reappraisal' therefore saw representatives of government, business and the unions looking for inspiration to France, with its system of planning based on *concertation* between employers, unions and the State. Both government and employers favoured the French approach, which provided the closest guide to what the government wanted. There were parallels with practice across the Channel in the package which Chancellor Selwyn Lloyd announced to the House of Commons in July 1961. The initiative was launched at the same time as the Pay Pause in an attempt to demonstrate that the government was not simply returning to 'Stop-Go' but embarking on a path intended to lead to long-term growth. It was now establishing a new institution within the State but like the *Commissariat du Plan* independent of all other public agencies and departments, in order to promote its objective of stable and high long-term growth. The new body was to be called the National Economic Development Council (NEDC). The NEDC was to act as the vehicle for a British version of indicative planning. It would be a forum in which representatives of government, industry and the trade unions could develop a consensual approach to the nation's economic development, featuring agreement not only regarding levels of pay but on targets for investment, exports and growth, on innovation in the workplace and on measures to encourage research and development. Its recommendations would be set out in reports based on forecasts and information about the economy, at macro and sectoral level, prepared by a National Economic Development Office staffed by professional civil servants. The reports would be submitted to the government, which would have the final say about how far they should be progressed.[66] The NEDC, along with the commitment to expand public investment, showed that a new relationship between the State and the economy was developing in the UK. The next objective, without which the modernization strategy could not succeed, was growth.

Dash for growth

The creation of NEDC was a significant step in Britain's reinvention as a social democracy, but in its early days its impact was largely symbolic. Although the FBI was enthusiastic about the new organization, the TUC was not. The TUC remained well disposed to the idea of planning, and in fact shared the FBI's enthusiasm for a more expansionary economic strategy than the government had hitherto been following, but suspected that the NEDC was in reality the latest in a series of attempts to impose wage restraint on the unions.[67] There seemed to be good grounds for this view when Lloyd announced a successor to the Pay Pause in February 1962. This was his 'guiding light', intended to keep money wages from rising at an annual rate of more than 2.5 per cent over the next twelve months.[68] The 'guiding light' was not a formal incomes policy, but it was seen by the TUC as a rather crude attempt to set a national pay norm. The TUC did not give ground, and argued that trade union participation in the NEDC could not occur unless its agenda included the question of price and dividend controls. These objections delayed the first meeting of the NEDC, even after Macmillan insisted that the Pay Pause was temporary.[69] It was only after the Chancellor made it clear that the government's intention was to link pay to productivity (thereby moving away from the simple percentage limit on incomes which characterized the Pay Pause) and conceding that the government would act to limit excessive price and dividend increases, that the TUC's resistance to participation in the NEDC came to an end.[70] Its first meeting was held in March 1962.

TUC reluctance to discuss wage restraint within the NEDC did not prevent both it and the FBI co-operating within the new organization to influence the government in the direction of policies designed to generate faster growth. In its first meetings the NEDC fell back on the work of an industrial inquiry commissioned by the FBI the previous year, when it had asked the larger firms how they would respond to an annual growth rate of 4 per cent and on the Treasury report of July 1961 which had stressed the importance of steps to increase competition. The result was two documents, *The Growth of the UK Economy to 1966,* and *Conditions Favourable to Growth*, both appearing in the first months of 1963. O'Hara questions their value: they did not cover small or medium sized enterprises, so leaving open the question about how these firms would adjust to 4 per cent growth. Furthermore they assumed British membership of the EEC, incomes rising in line with productivity and a macroeconomic climate characterized by steady expansion. On the other hand it can be argued that there was merit in the work. For a start, it covered seventeen industries, which accounted for 40 per cent of national employment and of visible exports as well as almost 50 per cent of total fixed investment.[71] Given the short time the NEDC had been in existence it would have been difficult to have produced anything more wide-ranging. As it was the impact of so large a fraction of the national economy on overall output was bound to have been of major significance. Secondly, the NEDC documents stressed the importance of increasing investment in scientific research and education, reinforcing the government's own sense of urgency about the need to address these issues. Thirdly, the national and international context in which the 4 per cent target was developed suggested that it was realistic. The public investment projects being unveiled by the British government, the strong expansion of the European economies and the Kennedy administration's economic stimulus in the USA, designed to deliver 50 per cent growth between 1961 and 1971 (indeed annual output rose by over 5 per cent per annum from between 1961 and 1966),[72] could not fail to inject higher demand into the economy over the planning period.

The Chancellor had invested much time and effort on the establishment of the NEDC. Now, to the annoyance of the FBI and the TUC, and, it soon became clear, the Prime Minister, he stopped short of embracing the cause of expansion even though steps to encourage it appeared overdue. The world's leading industrial nations were enjoying accelerating growth yet the British economy was stagnant. In April 1962 the United Nations' Economic Commission for Europe issued a report showing that UK output was virtually unchanged from its level a year earlier.[73] Yet Lloyd's 1962 Budget was a disappointment; it contained very little likely to encourage investment or provide relief for exporters. It lacked changes to personal or indirect taxation likely to assist consumer spending. Indeed, in a bizarre and counterproductive move by the Chancellor, the Budget's most famous innovation, a tax on confectionery and ice cream, seemed likely to have the opposite effect. The government's unpopularity grew. In July a frustrated and, some thought, panicking Prime Minister, sacked Selwyn Lloyd. The new Chancellor was Reginald Maudling, an expansionist. Urged on by Macmillan, Maudling began work on a programme designed to deliver the macroeconomic stimulus which would provide the country with the 4 per cent annual rate of growth the NEDC had endorsed. Its central features were to be unveiled in the 1963 Budget and it was to last until October 1964.

Lloyd's caution had derived from two sources. First of all there was a strong feeling in the Treasury that demand in the economy was already sufficient to deliver faster growth over the next year. Secondly, there was concern about the failure of the trade unions to sign up to any scheme of wage restraint.[74] A further stimulus (it was feared) would push the balance of payments into the red, with damaging consequences for sterling.[75] Macmillan, of course, believed that it was possible to reconcile expansion with full employment, a healthy external balance and stable prices if an agreement was reached between the State, employers and the trade unions regarding pay settlements. He therefore introduced his own version of a grand bargain intended to win trade union backing for the institutionalization of incomes policy when, side-stepping the NEDC, he established the National Income Commission (NIC).

The agenda for the NIC was first set out in comments to the Cabinet late in May 1962. Macmillan called this his 'new approach', based on not a Conservative but a 'national policy', designed to replace the Pay Pause with an 'acceptable incomes policy' which would become 'a permanent piece of machinery', with a standing tribunal to cover special cases. The NIC would, however, cover more than wage determination. Macmillan recognised that in order to secure the commitment of the TUC to this 'new approach' the government needed to show willingness to act on other issues of major concern to trade union members. These included day and hourly contracts (both of which the Prime Minister wished to abolish), redundancy pay and re-training in the event of unemployment, improved health and welfare arrangements at the workplace and more generous sick pay.[76] From the perspective of contemporary West European societies what Macmillan was offering resembled the common post-1945 practice of embedding ongoing dialogue between the government and the 'social partners' within the machinery of the State. In the British context, however, it was a radical programme, the first in a series of similar initiatives launched by governments of both major parties over the next decade and a half. A rassemblement was occurring around the priorities and values of Producer's Britain.

Macmillan never achieved the grand bargain with the unions. The reluctance to discuss wage restraint which had been shown after the Pay Pause did not fade. Some leading trade unionists such as Frank Cousins, General Secretary of the TGWU, spoke of a readiness to consider 'planned growth of wages', in return for growth, price and dividend restraint and more generous social security benefits. A sympathetic Prime Minister expressed willingness to establish a price investigation authority if employers were using periods of wage restraint to inflate prices and profits.[77] With strong opposition coming from the Board of Trade, however, the best the government could offer was referral of profiteering allegations to the NIC, which having investigated them would 'report' on guilty parties. It was not enough to appease the unions, whose leadership preferred to await the coming General Election (it could not be held any later than October 1964) which Labour was looking increasingly likely to win.

By early 1963 Labour was well ahead in the opinion polls. The chaotic political climate of 1963, characterized by the Profumo affair, Macmillan's surprise autumn resignation on health grounds and an unseemly struggle for the leadership of the Conservative Party and Prime Ministership[78] did little to shake the trade unions' confidence in a Labour election victory. Macmillan's successor, to general incredulity, was the Fourteenth Earl of Home (Foreign Secretary in Macmillan's Cabinet), who agreed to disclaim his peerage and sit in the House of Commons as Sir Alec Douglas-Home. His name had emerged not as a result of an election on the part of Conservative MPs but after a mysterious process of consultation among Tory grandees. The high society scandal and exclusive process of leadership selection seemed to confirm that the Conservatives had not changed after all; their roots still seemed to lie in privileged and aristocratic circles. They appeared out of touch with the increasingly meritocratic country they governed. It was an impression which played to Labour's advantage, especially when Harold Wilson, its leader after February 1963, sought with increasing success to identify the Party as one at home with scientific innovation, computers, the techniques of economic planning and the aspirations of all workers, including the growing new cadre of those in skilled and white collar occupations, for a better life.

The reluctance of the unions to enter into discussions about an incomes policy did not fade, notwithstanding a threat to call off the programme of expansion by Maudling himself in February 1964. This spat developed after the Chancellor's proposal for a 'Declaration of Intent', relating to pay, prices and productivity, to be jointly signed by the TUC and the FBI as well as the government, had failed to win union endorsement. The initiative developed out of growing concern that pay settlements were exceeding the 'guiding light', even though this had been raised in the previous year to 3.5 per cent. The unions knew they were on safe ground when they rejected the deal; it was most unlikely that the government would exchange the current 'Go' for a 'Stop' so soon before a General Election.

Political calculation played its part in the government's determination to persist with Maudling's stimulus. But the Conservatives would in all likelihood have pressed on even if no General Election had been looming. By the spring of 1963 what became known as 'the dash for growth' had become the centrepiece of the government's modernization strategy. Maudling's first Budget introduced the most generous system of incentives for capital investment in Western Europe, loans to support the shipbuilding industry and tax relief for middle and lower income families equivalent to a wage increase of 2 per cent for many workers.[79] The critical role now being assumed by macroeconomic expansion followed from reverses on two other fronts of the modernization campaign. First of all there was the ongoing failure to agree a bargain with the unions on a British version of the institutionalized incomes policies operating on the continent. Secondly, the bid to enter the EEC had failed, with the exercise of de Gaulle's veto in January 1963. Subsequently, Macmillan had minuted Maudling that the coming Budget 'and all that goes with (it) will be the key to the success or failure of the Government, the Party and in my view of the Country's efforts over the next period'.[80]

The modernization programme continued throughout the Premiership of Sir Alec Douglas-Home. The Board of Trade, under Edward Heath after October 1963, assumed growing responsibility for the development of an interventionist approach to industrial policy 'in which kicks and kindness took equal part'.[81] Its new role was indicated by an extension of Heath's title, which also designated him Secretary of State for Industry, Trade and Regional Development. Heath worked hard to fulfil all the aspects of the ambitious brief. He shared the widely held view that greater competition would stimulate efficiency throughout the economy (having seen membership of the EEC as a means to that end). He now persuaded a reluctant Cabinet to abolish Resale Price Maintenance, much to the discomfiture of many traditional Conservative supporters, notably small shopkeepers and businesses. But Heath's drive to install more competitive practices to the economy also extended to larger firms; following a White Paper of March 1964 on *Monopolies, Mergers and Restrictive Practices* the government committed itself to the strengthening of the Monopolies Commission (originally established by the Attlee government in 1948), giving it powers to investigate mergers.[82] Legislation followed – but was introduced by the subsequent, Labour administration in 1965.

The move towards competition was accompanied by a significant increase in State intervention, through regional policy and government-led supply side reform. The new approach to regional policy followed a limited number of initiatives on the part of the Board of Trade to persuade firms to locate themselves in areas of relatively high unemployment during the decade after 1950. These had generally taken the form of support for factory construction, such as the 1959 Triumph Standard plant at Speke. But the overall spend had been low, and it was not until 1963 that a more ambitious approach to the question of regional development had followed, with the creation of Development Districts. Areas so designated now gained government backing for major projects such as the Rootes factory at Linwood in south-west Scotland, the Vauxhall plant at Ellesmere port in north-west England, and investment in the modernization of the docks in Teeside, north-east England. Funding rose from an annual average of £4 million on such schemes from 1950–59, to £14 million in 1960–63, and to £91 million from 1964–67:[83] it was the Labour government which inherited this innovatory approach. Supply-side reform featured the Industrial Training Act of 1964. Following on from Macmillan's 'new approach' of 1962, its aim was to improve the level of technical education available to the workforce, especially at the level of apprenticeships. The Act gave the Minister of Labour the power to establish Industrial Training Boards (ITBs), on which sat representatives of both sides of industry. These would be funded by a government grant and from the exercise of a levy on employers, while rebates would be provided to those running training schemes which met an approved standard. Only four ITBs had been established by the time the government left office (in wool, jute and flax; engineering; iron and steel; and construction). As with the legislation to intensify supervision of monopolies and the enhancement of regional policy, the fruits did not mature until the next government had come to power.[84]

By early 1964 there were encouraging signs for the government's modernization project. Unemployment had fallen rapidly in response to the government's determined attempt to stimulate demand, from over 3 per cent of the work force at the start of 1963 to just 1.4 per cent by February 1964. Growth accelerated to over 5 per cent by the first quarter of 1964 as manufacturers' order books began to fill. The partners in the NEDC had agreed to the Chancellor's suggestion that a series of 'little Neddies', otherwise known as Economic Development Committees (EDCs), be established. Each one was to cover a different industry and develop plans for improving its performance, with membership composed of representatives from unions, management and the relevant government department. Given that only eight little Neddies had started work by the time the government left office some historians have questioned the significance of this innovation[85] yet it was clear evidence that Britain was indeed starting to adopt the approach to co-operation between the social partners on sectoral modernization which was common on the continent. Finally, even the government's loss of support in the opinion polls seemed to have stalled.

There were, however, darker omens. It seemed clear by the spring of 1964 at the latest that exports were not responding to the government's strategy as fast as imports. In fact their growth in value slightly exceeded 5 per cent both in 1963 and 1964; the problem was that the level of imports was rising more rapidly (indeed the rate of increase in 1963–64 was 11 per cent).[86] A significant fraction of the import bill could be accounted for by orders for machine tools, chemicals and capital equipment necessary for industrial re-equipment; but there was also evidence of buoyant consumer demand for foreign household goods.[87] With the cost of living rising at 4 per cent and the average level of wage settlements at 8 per cent the likelihood of pressure on the external balance was starting to grow. By May the Treasury was forecasting a current account deficit of £300 million for the year.[88]

Anxiety that the impact of wage costs on prices could weaken export prospects while stimulating imports was the main reason why Maudling had proposed his grand bargain. The failure of this initiative led to the abandonment of the attempt to construct an incomes policy. The unions saw no incentive to talk to the government; Ministers on the other hand, unable to gain consent to wage restraint, had no desire to risk a re-run of the obloquy they had incurred with the Pay Pause. In consequence they tended to passivity in the face of pay claims and increases, especially in the public sector, in excess of the 3.5 per cent 'guiding light'.[89]

Neither Maudling's inability to negotiate the grand bargain nor indications that the external balance was likely to deteriorate led him to consider that the economy needed a shot of deflation. Rejecting Treasury advice to raise up to £225 million via tax increases (slightly over 0.7 per cent of GDP) he settled for an extra £100 million through higher duties on drink and tobacco. The Governor of the Bank of England, Lord Cromer, who was beginning to develop doubts about Maudling's judgement and character,[90] argued that spending cuts and increases in Bank Rate were becoming necessary, in order to assure holders of sterling that the government was serious about bridging the gap in the balance of payments at the current exchange rate.[91] He worried that in the absence of any remedial action, sterling holders would start to sell their assets in favour of other currencies, leading to a crisis of confidence in the ability of the pound to continue with its role as an international trading and reserve currency.[92] Maudling, however, was unmoved. Early in 1963 he had discussed with Macmillan the possibility that the 'dash for growth' would lead to pressure on the external balance and both had agreed that the policy should be supported by borrowing from abroad in order to support the reserves, followed if necessary by an import surcharge.[93] Cromer was overruled but he was to revisit the argument after Labour's arrival in office, in a series of bitter clashes with the new Prime Minister which were to show how uncomfortable sections of the old financial establishment were with the implications of social democratic modernization.

Maudling's rationale was clear: a rise in imports during the early stages of expansion was predictable, but this was expected to be a 'one-off', a function of the rising level of stocks being held at each stage of the production process, including imported raw materials and semi- and finished manufactures.[94] As Maudling himself admitted, short-term damage to the balance of payments was predictable in the time-lag before exports responded to re-equipment.[95] What occurred in 1964, however, was that the pick-up in exports came later than expected and the pressure on the external balance was correspondingly more intense than anticipated. By October 1964 the Treasury was forecasting an £800 million deficit for the year as a whole. The headline figure, a function of heavy capital outflows as well as of rising imports, was misleading.[96] In the event the current account deficit for 1964 amounted to a rather less dramatic £376 million, about 1 per cent of GDP. The complexities were however lost during and after the General Election campaign, when the Labour Party had seized on the deteriorating external balance as indicative of the Conservative Party's inability to run the economy with competence. Given that the boom conditions of 1963–64 had been accompanied by a narrowing of the gap between the two main parties in the opinion polls, it is arguable that Labour's manipulation of the current account issue made the difference in what became a very tight General Election.

The balance of payments deficit, together with the Election defeat, has led most commentators to view the 'dash for growth' as a failure. This is unfair. First of all, TUC General Secretary George Woodcock had always suspected that Maudling's gamble could have worked if the Chancellor had had more time.[97] Had the Election been held a year later the result may have been different: the long-awaited revival in exports did occur in 1965 and 1966, when they grew, respectively, at rates of 6.7 per cent and just under 10 per cent.[98] Secondly, concentration on the current account leads the historian to ignore the fact that the expansion was one part, albeit an essential one, of a wider programme which left an enduring mark on British politics, economic policy and society. Not all the measures pursued by Macmillan after 1960 came to fruition (the bid to join the EEC and the search for agreement with the unions on incomes policy being notable examples). Overall, however, the public spending projects, the promotion of industrial modernization via indicative planning and the attempt to break out of the 'Stop-Go' straitjacket set the British politico-economic agenda up to the end of the 1970s. Both main political parties would now prioritize investment in the welfare state, housing, secondary and tertiary education, public transport and communications and regional policy. Both became committed to indicative planning. They would compete to deliver sustained and buoyant growth. Both would search for detente between government, industry and the unions on pay, prices and productivity while establishing mechanisms for tripartite co-operation on training, innovation and research and development. These issues became central to the discourse of British politics, which for the best part of two decades now came to revolve around the social democratic aspirations and values shared by leading political actors on the continent since 1950.

Macmillan had taken the Conservative Party and the country to the Left. Seizing the crisis moment which had resulted from Suez, Blue Streak and the revelation of relative economic failure he had led his party in a direction quite alien to most of its supporters. The government had constructed the foundations of a social democratic state at home. The Commonwealth was being deserted for Europe and in what was left of the Empire there had been a rapid process of decolonization.[99] It all led this new version of Conservatism being regarded with suspicion by an articulate minority of traditional supporters. Many of their misgivings were rehearsed in a series of articles by 'a Conservative' and published in *The Times* in April 1964.[100] These attacked the way the Party had allowed itself to enter into a competition with Labour about 'planning' and the best way to manage the welfare state. They argued that Conservatives should re-examine their commitment to the post-war settlement. In common with other Tory grandees Macmillan regarded such opinions as '*Poujadisme*',[101] reflecting the fact that they tended to come from the lower middle class, especially small business and property owners committed to the politics of low taxation, the small state and anti-union legislation.[102] The Prime Minister's views showed a thinly veiled contempt for a group whose political philosophy he did not share and whom he saw as out of step with the trend of history. Yet twenty years later a political clique led by a politician whose robust views were characterized by more than a touch of '*Poujadisme*' would be Party leader and Prime Minister, and it would be Macmillan's turn to mount a despairing critique from the margins.

Notes

1 John Young, *Britain and the World in the Twentieth Century* (London: Arnold, 1997), pp. 166–167.
2 See Michael Charlton, *The Price of Victory* (London: BBC Books, 1983), pp. 238–238; Wolfram Kaiser, *Using Europe, Abusing the Europeans: Britain and European Integration 1945–63* (Basingstoke: Palgrave, 1996), pp. 119–120.
3 Figures derived from Roger Middleton, *The British Economy since 1945* (Basingstoke: Palgrave Macmillan, 2000), Table 1.1, p. 4.
4 See D. T. Jones, 'Output, Employment and Labour Productivity in Europe since 1955', *National Institute Economic Review*, no. 77 (August 1976), p. 80.
5 Glen O'Hara, *From Dreams to Disillusionment: Economic and Social Planning in the 1960s* (Basingstoke: Macmillan, 2007), pp. 21–22.
6 Jim Tomlinson, *The Labour Governments 1964–1970, Volume 3: Economic Policy*. (Manchester: Manchester University Press, 2004), pp. 226–227.
7 Jefferys, *Retreat from New Jerusalem* (London: Palgrave Macmillan, 1997), p. 65.
8 See Scott Newton, 'Keynesianism, Sterling Convertibility and British Reconstruction 1940–52', in Ranald Michie and Philip Williamson (eds) *The British Government and the City of London in the Twentieth Century* (Cambridge: Cambridge University Press, 2004), pp. 257–275.
9 See Dominic Sandbrook, *Never Had It So Good: A History of Britain from Suez to the Beatles* (London: Abacus, 2006), p. 87.
10 Jefferys, *Retreat from New Jerusalem*, p. 75.
11 Peter Hennessy, *Distilling the Frenzy: Writing the History of One's Own Times* (London: Biteback, 2012), pp. 39–40.
12 Sandbrook, *Never Had It So Good*, p. 68.
13 Ibid., p. 69.
14 Jeffreys, *Retreat from New Jerusalem*, p. 78.
15 Ibid., p. 93.
16 Middleton, *The British Economy since 1945*, table II.3, pp. 150–151.
17 D. R. Thorpe, *Supermac: The Life of Harold Macmillan* (London: Chatto and Windus 2010), pp. 583f.
18 Scott Newton and Dilwyn Porter, *Modernization Frustrated: The Politics of Industrial Decline in Britain since 1900* (London, Unwin Hyman 1988), p. 79.
19 See E. H. H. Green, *Ideologies of Conservatism: Conservative Political Ideas in the Twentieth Century* (Oxford: Oxford University Press, 2002), ch. 6.
20 Samuel Brittan, *The Treasury under the Tories 1951–64* (London: Penguin, 1964), p. 213. The other Joint Permanent Secretary was Sir Norman Brook.
21 The FBI predated the CBI and ceased to exist when the latter was created.
22 Keith Middlemas, *Power, Competition and the State*, vol. 2: *Threats to the Post-war Settlement 1961–74* (Basingstoke: Macmillan, 1990), pp. 7–8.
23 Kaiser, *Using Europe, Abusing the Europeans*, pp. 171–172; Middlemas, *Power, Competition and the State*, vol. 2, p. 16.
24 Kaiser, *Using Europe, Abusing the Europeans*, p. 172.

25 Middlemas, *Power, Competition and the State*, p. 65.
26 Andrew Gamble, *The Conservative Nation* (London: Routledge & Kegan Paul, 1974), pp. 198–201.
27 Kaiser, *Using Europe, Abusing the Europeans*, p. 146.
28 Sidney Pollard, *The Development of the British Economy, 1914–1990* (London: Edward Arnold, 1992), p. 292.
29 David Edgerton, *Warfare State: Britain 1920–1979* (Cambridge: Cambridge University Press, 2005), pp. 174ff.
30 Nicholas Timmins, *The Five Giants: A Biography of the Welfare State* (London: Harper Collins, 2001), pp. 199–200.
31 Jefferys, *Retreat from New Jerusalem*, p. 173.
32 Ibid., p. 111.
33 Jim Tomlinson, 'Inventing "Decline": the Falling Behind of the British Economy in the Post-War Years', *Economic History Review*, 49 (1996), pp. 731–757.
34 Hugh Thomas (ed.), *The Establishment* (London: Ace Books, 1959); Michael Shanks, *The Stagnant Society* (London: Penguin, 1961); Anthony Crosland, *The Conservative Enemy* (London: Cape, 1962); Anthony Sampson, *The Anatomy of Britain* (London: Hodder and Stoughton, 1962); Arthur Koestler (ed.), *Suicide of a Nation?* (London: Hutchinson, 1963).
35 Newton and Porter, *Modernization Frustrated*, p. 137.
36 Jefferys, *Retreat from New Jerusalem*, p. 149.
37 Timmins, *The Five Giants*, p. 209.
38 J. K. Galbraith, *The Affluent Society* (Boston: Houghton Mifflin, 1958).
39 David Thomson, *England in the Twentieth Century* (London: Penguin, 1965), pp. 260–261.
40 From this point the terms Producer's Britain and Consumer's Britain will be used in preference to the now somewhat dated language of Producer's England and Consumer's England employed by Hobson, even though the meaning of the terminology remains the same in this text as it was when first deployed by him.
41 Jefferys, *Retreat from New Jerusalem*, pp. 137–138.
42 Ibid., pp. 192–193.
43 TNA CAB 129/111, C (62) 201, 3 December 1962, memorandum by the Prime Minister, 'Modernisation of Britain'.
44 O'Hara, *From Dreams to Disillusionment*, p. 46.
45 See Alan S. Milward, *The European Rescue of the Nation-State* (2nd edition, London: Routledge, 2000).
46 TNA CAB 129, C (63) 80, 'White Paper on Housing Policy', 10 May 1963.
47 Thomson, *England in the Twentieth Century*, pp. 265–266.
48 Timmins, *The Five Giants*, p. 202.
49 *The Times*, 9 April 1963, p. 9 col. A.
50 TNA CAB 128/37, C. C. (63) 28th Conclusions, 3 May 1963; TNA CAB 128/37, C. C. (63) 47th Conclusions, 18 July 1963.
51 Middlemas, *Power, Competition and the State*, pp. 55–56.
52 Brittan, *The Treasury under the Tories*, ch. 7.
53 Ibid., p. 218.
54 Scott Newton, *The Global Economy 1944–2000* (London: Arnold, 2004), p. 163.
55 David Thomson, *Democracy in France since 1870* (Oxford: Oxford University Press, 1969), p. 249.
56 Charles Kindleberger, *French Planning* (Harvard: National Bureau of Economic and Social Research, 1965), pp. 280–281.
57 See for example Andrew Knapp and Vincent Wright, *Government and Politics in France* (5th edition, London, 2006), pp. 18–24.
58 Newton, *The Global Economy*, pp. 56–60; O'Hara, *From Dreams to Disillusionment*, pp. 21–22.
59 O'Hara, *From Dreams to Disillusionment*, p. 22.

60 Ibid., p. 21, quoting Pierre Massé.
61 Brittan, *The Treasury under the Tories*, pp. 219–220.
62 O'Hara, *From Dreams to Disillusionment*, pp. 20–22.
63 Newton and Porter, *Modernization Frustrated*, p. 120.
64 Brittan, *The Treasury under the Tories*, pp. 295–300.
65 Samuel Brittan, 'A Backward Glance: The Reappraisal of the 1960s', lecture to the Institute of Contemporary British History, April 1997.
66 O'Hara, *From Dreams to Disillusionment*, p. 46.
67 Newton and Porter, *Modernization Frustrated*, p. 141.
68 Brittan, *The Treasury under the Tories*, pp. 238–240.
69 O'Hara, *From Dreams to Disillusionment*, p. 48.
70 Newton and Porter, *Modernization Frustrated*, p. 141.
71 O'Hara, *From Dreams to Disillusionment*, p. 49.
72 Richard Parker, *John Kenneth Galbraith* (New York: Farrar, Strauss, Giroux, 2005), p. 342.
73 Sandbrook, *Never Had It So Good*, p. 540.
74 Brittan, *The Treasury under the Tories*, pp. 242–244
75 Newton and Porter, *Modernization Frustrated*, pp. 141–142.
76 TNA PREM 11/3390, transcript of the Prime Minister's remarks to the Cabinet, 28 May 1962.
77 Newton and Porter, *Modernization Frustrated*, p. 147; O'Hara, *From Dreams to Disillusionment*, p. 51.
78 There is a good description of this in Jefferys, *Retreat from Jerusalem*, pp. 176–186.
79 Brittan, *The Treasury under the Tories*, p. 259; Newton and Porter, *Modernization Frustrated*, p. 143.
80 TNA PREM 11/4202, Prime Minister to Chancellor, 20 February 1963.
81 Middlemas, *Power, Competition and the State*, vol. 2, p. 74.
82 Jim Tomlinson, 'Conservative Modernization, 1960–64: Too Little, Too Late?' *Contemporary British History*, vol. 11 (1997), p. 31.
83 Barry Moore and John Rhodes, 'Evaluating the Effects of British Regional Economic Policy', *Economic Journal*, vol. 84 (1973), p. 89.
84 Barrie Petman, 'The Industrial Training Act; Progress and Attitudes', *Management Decision*, vol. 4, no. 4 (1970), p. 9.
85 O'Hara, *From Dreams to Disillusionment*, p. 52.
86 Figures derived from Middleton, *The British Economy since 1945*, Table II.3, pp. 150–151.
87 Newton and Porter, *Modernization Frustrated*, p. 144.
88 Scott Newton, 'The Two Sterling Crises of 1964', *The Economic History Review*, vol. 62 (2009), p. 75.
89 Middlemas, *Power, Competition and the State*, vol. 2, p. 85.
90 Esme Cromer, *From this Day Forward* (Stoke Abbot: Thomas Harmsworth, 1991), p. 126.
91 TNA T171/755/1 (xxxi), meeting of the Chancellor, Sir W. Armstrong, Mr Governor, and others, 28 August 1964.
92 Newton, 'The Two Sterling Crises', p. 76.
93 TNA PREM 11/4202, 'Note for the Record', 21 February 1963; Newton, 'The Two Sterling Crises', p. 75.
94 John Cooper, *A Suitable Case for Treatment: What To Do About The Balance of Payments* (London: Penguin, 1968), pp. 173f.
95 Ibid., p. 181.
96 Newton, 'The Two Sterling Crises', p. 76.
97 Middlemas, *Power, Competition and the State*, vol. 2, p. 85.
98 Figures derived from Middleton, *The British Economy since 1945*, Table II.3, pp. 150–151.
99 See for example, Bernard Porter, *The Lion's Share: A History of British Imperialism from 1850 to the Present*, 5th edition (London: Routledge, 2012), pp. 70–75.
100 Middlemas, *Power, Competition and the State*, vol. 2, p. 86; Jonathan Rutherford, *Forever England* (London, 1997), pp. 112 and 124. The articles appeared on 1, 2 and 3 April

1964. Rutherford attributes them to Enoch Powell (ironically one of the architects of the modernization of the National Health Service in the 1960s).
101 Pierre Poujade (1920–2003), a bookshop owner turned politician, led a populist movement, supported strongly by small business people, against high taxation in the French Fourth Republic during the 1950s.
102 Middlemas, *Power, Competition and the State*, vol. 2, p. 55; E. H. H. Green, 'Thatcherism: an Historical Perspective', *Transactions of the Royal Historical Society*, vol. 9 (1999), pp. 26–27. Alan Clark, in *The Tories: Conservatives and the Nation State 1922–1997* (London: Phoenix, 1998), p. 380, writes of Macmillan's 'apparent disregard, perhaps even contempt, for the interests and values of the British middle class'.

2

LABOUR'S NEW BRITAIN, 1964–70

National plan

The result of the October 1964 General Election was much closer than had seemed likely a year earlier. Labour won, but with an overall majority of just five seats (soon reduced to three following an early by-election defeat). Maudling's expansionist strategy had led to rapid growth, rising living standards and to the disappearance of the disturbingly high levels of unemployment evident in 1962–63. The Conservatives, even under the unlikely leadership of Alec Douglas-Home, were able to recruit sizeable support from the skilled workers and educated professionals Macmillan had sought to attract. Their ability to stimulate economic expansion and combine this with a generous programme of public investment almost eclipsed the association with privilege, selfish materialism and incompetence which had led to their earlier unpopularity. In the end, however, they were unable to convince enough voters that modern Conservatism was capable of delivering the prosperous and meritocratic Britain which both major political parties aspired to build. Macmillan's version of social democracy notwithstanding, the Conservative Party and its allies retained both their connections to the City and their commitment to its economic internationalism. Its core voters were still linked to finance, the service sector and light industry. They continued to live mainly in Home Counties England and sent their children to the public schools. Set against this was the Labour coalition which brought Harold Wilson to power, rooted in manufacturing industry, the unions and in the growing middle-class salariat educated in the grammar schools. The longstanding identification of these groups with Producer's Britain and a political economy which privileged growth, social justice, industrial efficiency and innovation led voters to give Labour the benefit of the doubt.

There can be little doubt that Labour's victory was assisted by the personality and politics of its leader, whose character was a winning combination of the ordinary and the extraordinary. Wilson himself was a Nonconformist Northern meritocrat, whose background, unlike that of his two most recent predecessors, was shared by many British voters. He struck up a good rapport with the public. He appeared at home in working men's clubs and public houses. Yet he was no average figure. He had a sharp and ready wit. He had been educated at grammar school, had pursued an outstanding academic career at Oxford followed by five years as a highly successful and respected wartime civil servant. Elected to Parliament as a Labour MP in 1945 he was rapidly promoted to Ministerial roles, first junior and then, aged just thirty-one, Cabinet (President of the Board of Trade). During most of Labour's long spell in opposition after 1951 he had been an influential front-bench spokesman for the Party, holding at various times the portfolios of Shadow Chancellor and Foreign Secretary before succeeding Hugh Gaitskell as leader in 1963.

Although briefly identified with the Labour Left in the early 1950s, Wilson was no doctrinaire socialist. His politico-economic views combined the radical liberalism of David Lloyd George with a Fabian enthusiasm for planning, conducted by humane technocrats. Perhaps his strongest conviction was a hatred of unemployment, which he came to see as 'not only a severe fault of government, but…in some way evil, and an affront to the country it afflicted'.[1] This stemmed from bitter personal experience. During his Yorkshire boyhood Wilson had seen the cruel effects of joblessness on families and communities at first hand: his father had been out of work along with many others in the Colne Valley area of west Yorkshire where the Wilson family had lived. Since the early 1950s he had consistently argued that the State, working in conjunction with private industry, should use its resources to promote reconstruction and economic growth while protecting the consumer from exploitation at the hands of public and private monopolies.[2] Wilson was therefore precisely located, both politically and sociologically, to reflect the impatience of the emerging class of experts, technicians and planners with a system which still seemed biased towards corporate complacency and the rewarding of social privilege above professional achievement. Throughout the period between his assumption of the Party leadership in February 1963 and the General Election twenty months later he stressed Labour's commitment to the modernization of Britain, developing the talents of the nation's scientists, engineers, skilled workers and managers in order to build an economy comparable with those now flourishing in Europe.

Labour proposed to pursue the task of modernization through a set of policies which economic historians have called 'Keynesian plus'.[3] This involved an acknowledgement that the management of the economy at high levels of demand in order to generate full employment and growth, unless supplemented by more fundamental change, was likely to result in a return to the old 'Stop-Go' cycle. Wilson was convinced that sustainable long-term expansion could not be achieved in the absence of structural and supply-side reforms designed to improve competitiveness and so generate a volume of exports large enough to break through the external constraint hitherto presented by the tendency of the current account to go into the red after short bursts of economic expansion. He argued that this challenge could not be met in the absence of a National Plan developed by a 'Ministry of

Economic Planning' and 'covering industrial policy, financial policy and the application of science to industry'.[4] The NEDC had already started this work, but it lacked the power and authority to drive home its reforms which a new Ministry would possess.

Commitment to planning was a constant theme in Labour's pre-election publicity as well as its election manifesto, *Let's Go with Labour for the New Britain*. Wilson's conviction that planning was likely to prove essential was set out in what was perhaps his most famous speech as leader of the Opposition, given at the Labour Party's Scarborough Conference of 1963. Here he drew attention to the coming of rapid and dramatic industrial change, based on automation, computing and electronics.[5] A new Britain was being forged in 'the white heat of this technological revolution'.[6] Labour's mission was to harness this technological change through planning so that it could be 'directed to national ends'. These featured four priorities. First, there should be a large expansion of places for the study of science in higher education. Secondly, the transition to an economy based on high technology would be managed by a Ministry of Science, established to manage the deployment of resources to stimulate innovation, especially in the commercial, non-military sector of the economy.[7] Thirdly, the State would stimulate both economic growth and the development of a more competitive industrial sector by increasing support for research and development (R and D) and establishing public enterprises based on government-funded innovation, to be located in regions experiencing relatively high unemployment. Finally, a Labour government would invest in scientists through measures which enhanced their status and improved the facilities in which they worked, encouraged mature ones to stay in Britain rather than join the 'brain drain' to the USA and attracted more young people into scientific careers.[8] The Scarborough speech made a powerful impression. It tapped into what was at the time a widespread faith in the capacity of scientific innovation to provide humanity with the means not just to overcome poverty but also to develop all the sophisticated technological and electronic equipment conducive to the good life. In doing so it showed Labour both to be more aware than the Conservatives about what the increasing technological complexity of this new era meant for Britain and more capable of developing a political agenda for managing it to the nation's advantage.

By the time the 1964 General Election arrived Labour had developed a well-prepared programme, much of which followed from Wilson's Scarborough speech the previous year. Its first year in office saw a series of institutional reforms to the structure of the State, designed to enhance its ability to promote modernization and growth. Two of the most notable innovations were the Department of Economic Affairs (DEA) and the Ministry of Technology. The first of these was the 'Ministry of Economic Planning' Wilson and his colleagues had called for in the approach to the General Election. The second was in due course to evolve into something close to the 'Ministry of Science' discussed by Wilson at Scarborough but at this stage it was quite small. Under its first Minister, Frank Cousins (persuaded to join the government by Wilson), it took important steps to support high technology and new industries (especially computing), but its main responsibility was the Atomic Energy Authority (AEA). The DEA, by contrast, was at the heart of the government's effort to modernize and plan the economy. Its establishment marked the first time the priorities of growth and industrial expansion had become the explicit mission of a Cabinet level government department. Its head, known as Secretary of State for Economic Affairs, was Labour's Deputy Leader George Brown. The priority accorded to the DEA was so great that it was accorded equal status with the Treasury. Under a concordat between the two departments Brown and the new Chancellor, James Callaghan, agreed that the DEA take responsibility for long-term measures to improve industrial performance while the Treasury concentrated on short-term financial policy and the balance of payments.

The DEA's objective was the raising of the British economy's long-term growth rate, a task to be achieved via the structural reforms Wilson had envisaged. These involved, first, sector by sector attempts to improve industrial efficiency and competitiveness, undertaken, just as they had been since the establishment of the NEDC, through tripartite co-operation within the little Neddies. Now, however, with Brown taking over the Chair at the NEDC, these bodies would be subordinate to the DEA. Secondly, it would encourage mergers in order to promote rationalization and more efficient use of plant. Thirdly, it aimed for a shift in the pattern of investment with a view to reducing the share taken by declining sectors such as the coal industry. Fourthly, it encouraged an alteration in the balance and direction of public spending: this was set to rise as a proportion of GDP but a larger share of the global target was to be devoted to education, health, housing, transport and R and D, with less being taken by defence and associated prestige military projects such as the TSR-2 fighter-bomber. Finally, Labour was determined to expand upon the previous government's regional planning initiatives. This ambition was set out in the National Plan, but even before the document had been published the new government had established regional planning Boards and Councils. These were intended to operate under the DEA on schemes bringing work to regions where unemployment exceeded the national average. This would (it was hoped) ensure that the benefits of growth were spread equitably across the nation and in so doing offset the inflationary pressures resulting from the concentration of activity in areas which were already prosperous.

The political climate was favourable to the DEA's mission and Labour's commitment to deliver planned growth. Wilson's willingness to challenge what he had called in his Scarborough speech 'restrictive practices' and 'outdated methods on either side of industry' brought the new government the goodwill of many industrialists. Many were prepared to work with Labour, and there was a large influx of senior businessmen into Whitehall.[9] Most went into the DEA's Industrial Policy Division or the Ministry of Technology. Their enthusiasm was matched by trade union leaders, who had already made it clear that they would accept 'planned growth of wages' in exchange for price and dividend restraint as well as increases in social security benefits. With employers' associations explicitly committing themselves to price restraint, and increases in spending on the welfare state a central feature of Labour's programme, the conditions had been created for a rassemblement between the social partners, in the form of the grand bargain between government, industry and the unions which had eluded Macmillan, Maudling and the Conservatives.

Labour wasted no time in implementing the government's side of this bargain. Its first weeks in power saw an increase in old age pensions, the abolition of prescription charges and the announcement of proposals to introduce corporation tax (designed to encourage companies to retain profits for the purposes of investment rather than distribute them to shareholders via generous dividends) in 1965. These measures had the desired effect of securing TUC backing for the *Joint Statement of Intent on Productivity, Prices and Incomes*, signed jointly with the government and employers' associations in December 1964.[10] In approving this document the TUC was committing the trade union movement to the restraint of demands for pay and salary increases which exceeded the growth of real national output. The way was now prepared for an institutionalized incomes policy, which duly emerged in September 1965 with the establishment of the National Board for Prices and Incomes (NBPI). Both sides of industry declared their support for the NBPI, whose role was to advise whether pay and price increases referred to it by the government were 'in the national interest'. As far as incomes were concerned this meant the Board would decide if grounds (stemming from improvements in productivity, for example) existed for increases beyond an annual rate of 3.5 per cent, the 'norm' identified by the government as compatible with the growth of the economy. The NBPI did not initially possess any statutory powers, but if it found against a pay claim unions were expected to accept the decision and settle in accord with the norm. The same principle applied to price increases in excess of the norm, which would only be regarded as acceptable if they had followed from unavoidable rises in costs. The *Joint Statement* and the NBPI could plausibly be seen as the foundations of an economic constitution designed to facilitate low-inflationary growth.

Work on the National Plan proceeded in step with the creation of the machinery for an incomes policy. The Plan, launched in September 1965, envisaged growth of 25 per cent up to 1970, a task which would require an annual rate of 3.8 per cent. Commentators at the time and since have argued that the term 'Plan' was rather misleading.[11] This is somewhat harsh. The Plan was in fact three things. The first was a set of responses from industrialists in the private and public sectors explaining how they would adapt to 3.8 per cent per annum growth between 1965 and 1970. The second involved an attempt to establish a synoptic overview of government strategy so that all key departments were working in the same direction – to promote growth through industrial restructuring, public investment and a rebalancing of priorities in government spending. This was what Wilson liked to call 'purposive planning' or what the Labour Party called 'planning with teeth', in contrast to the Conservative experiment of 1962–64 in which tripartite co-operation and macroeconomic strategy were not reinforced by efforts to reorganize industry and switch funds away from prestige and military projects. The third was the rebalancing of public spending priorities, including an increase in the volume of resources for industry via funding for R and D and innovation (especially related to the machine tool and computing industries) and for management training.[12] Labour's attempt to reorganize the government machine was a genuinely new peacetime departure, an attempt 'at recasting the needs of government to meet the needs of the twentieth century ... the opening campaign of a major social revolution', as Brown later argued,[13] and perhaps not as unsuccessful on this front as he (and others) came to think.

Businesses responded with plans showing their needs for labour, capital goods, raw materials and imports, along with likely export levels, given the growth target and the government's public spending forecasts up to 1970. Their forecasts were encouraging. With the incomes policy holding down private consumption to yearly expansion of 3.2 per cent there would be resources available for investment and exports. The forecasts pointed to annual rises in productivity of just over 3 per cent and of 5.5 per cent in fixed investment, along with an increase in volume of 5.25 per cent in exports (twice the rate of recent years) against one of 4 per cent in imports.[14] This was extremely promising, suggesting that striking improvements in Britain's economic performance were feasible over the next five years. The problem was that such an achievement depended on fulfillment of the growth target, and the Plan did not explain how this was to be sustained.

This lacuna in the Plan did not prevent it from receiving a favourable reception. The CBI (formed in January 1965 through a merger between the FBI and other employers' associations) and the TUC both greeted it warmly. But goodwill would not be enough: in the end the economy grew at an annual average rate of 2.6 per cent up to 1970 (just over 14 per cent overall). Indeed, few of the National Plan's projections relating to investment and output had been met by 1970. Gross fixed capital formation was up by 20 per cent instead of the expected 38 per cent. Industrial production rose by 15.7 per cent between 1965 and 1970 whereas over the same period it increased, respectively, by 38.9 per cent and 41.6 per cent in France and West Germany.[15] Meanwhile personal consumption rose by 13 per cent instead of the predicted 21 per cent.[16]

Critics argued that Labour failed to commit itself to a sufficient degree of economic expansion. It had come to power facing the significant balance of payments deficit which was the legacy of Maudling's 'dash for growth'.[17] The government's response generated considerable disappointment. Far from breaking out of the 'Stop-Go' cycle, Labour embarked on one set of deflationary policies after another throughout most of its time in office. This harsh verdict can be found in a series of highly critical analyses of its years in office, of which works by Paul Foot, David Mackie and Chris Cook and Clive Ponting are characteristic examples.[18] Despite the appearance of revisionist literature,[19] these texts have continued to exercise considerable influence: their arguments have been used in more recent accounts of this period, for example by Andrew Marr and Dominic Sandbrook.[20] By 1970 few of the projections set out in the National Plan had been achieved, since (it has been argued) the tough economic regime discouraged rather than stimulated private investment.[21]

Forever unmentionable

Critics of the Wilson governments' economic record have fastened onto its reaction to the external financial difficulties greeting it on arrival in power. An emergency package, much of which had been prepared under Maudling, was introduced late in October. It centred on a 15 per cent tariff on all imports of manufactured goods, tax incentives for exports and a review of government spending. This failed to calm the markets for more than a few weeks. Renewed speculation broke out in mid-November and was not quelled by a sharp rise in the Bank Rate, from 5 per cent to 7 per cent. Soon it became clear that the large external deficit and weak confidence in the sterling parity on the part of the financial markets were going to force Labour to choose between three options. The first was devaluation. The second was to borrow from overseas financial institutions and foreign governments in order to sustain the sterling rate. The third involved deflation so that imports fell in response to weak demand. Lord Cromer made it clear that the third option was the one most compatible with the restoration of confidence in sterling to the financial markets. Wilson however considered such action, which would mean the immediate dumping of Labour's manifesto commitments, a travesty of the democratic process. He refused to take this course and threatened to call another General Election on the theme of who ran Britain – the international financial community or the elected government – followed (if Labour were to win) either by devaluation or the floating of sterling.[22] Worried by the implications of Wilson's threat, Cromer organized a $3 billion credit for sterling late in November. In December this was supplemented by $1 billion from the International Monetary Fund (IMF).

The critics have argued that in reality Wilson's radical threats to Cromer in November 1964 were bluff.[23] He had had no intention of devaluing or floating sterling and ruled that cabinet Ministers and civil servants regard the entire subject of sterling's rate as 'forever unmentionable'. This did not of course prevent discussions of the subject between the Prime Minister and senior Ministers,[24] while the Treasury prepared contingency plans for devaluation, the series of files covering the question being called 'FU' in response to the Prime Ministerial injunction.[25] The Prime Minister had been heard to argue that since Labour had devalued sterling in 1931 and 1949, to do so again would leave it labelled by the press and public as the 'Party of devaluation', with dire consequences for its future electoral prospects. This political distaste was reinforced by Wilson's limited faith in the price mechanism: he believed that altering the value of the currency would not lead to an efficient allocation of resources in the economy so that they shifted into the production of goods for the export market. This was a process which required planning and intervention in industry.[26]

The credits did not silence the doubters in the markets. Sterling came under attack both in 1965 and 1966, forcing the government into more borrowing.

Labour gradually lost control over the British economy as the defence of the parity became the government's major preoccupation. Its bold plans for the modernization of Britain were either abandoned or postponed in a series of forlorn efforts to satisfy foreign creditors. Economic policy came to revolve around crisis management.[27] Each year saw a round of spending cuts, restrictions on pay increases, tax rises and dear money. A package of such measures in July 1966 put paid to the growth aspirations of the National Plan. It seemed that Labour had become more orthodox in its macroeconomic policy than the Conservatives after 1962. Yet despite all the government's efforts, devaluation of just over 14 per cent occurred in November 1967. After this, policy came to focus not on steps to increase growth but on the creation of a balance of payments surplus of £500 million, large enough to remove all doubts about the new sterling rate (£1 = $2.40) and ensure repayment of the debts incurred during the course of the attempt to defend the indefensible. By 1969–70 the government had achieved its target. Indeed exports, rising by 42 per cent in volume between 1965 and 1970, were one of the few areas where a forecast made in the Plan (36 per cent) had been exceeded.[28] But the cost to growth and living standards brought bitter disappointment. This was expressed in the alienation of many Labour voters and defeat at the polls in the June 1970 General Election.

This narrative presents a seriously distorted interpretation of Labour's record. Much of it is rooted in the political and economic debates of the late 1960s and early 1970s. Many of the arguments reflect a frustration that Wilson had not brought socialism in our time (on the part of the Left)[29] or a growing distaste for planning and intervention (on the Right).[30] The smoke of ideological battle has obscured the historical realities within which Labour had to operate. If we can let this clear it becomes possible to see that the government's commitment to £1 = $2.80 did not derive from political vanity. It is true that Labour's rather precarious position in Parliament meant there was a political constraint, at least until the March 1966 General Election which saw the Party returned to power with an emphatic 97 seat majority. But Wilson's misgivings about a change in the value of sterling were well-founded. First, he was concerned that devaluation would panic the holders of the £4 billion held as sterling balances in London. They would start to withdraw their funds, diversifying into other currencies such as the dollar or the deutschmark, so provoking a massive capital outflow that could only be contained by the imposition of wartime style controls. Secondly he worried that other nations would retaliate with alterations in their own exchange rate parities, which would nullify any price advantage gained by Britain. Thirdly, Wilson feared that devaluation would retard modernization even more than sticking to the old parity. Given the existence of full employment it would be unlikely to have the desired result of facilitating a transfer of resources into production for exports unless accompanied by a reduction of demand in the home market, damaging the government's expansionist aspirations in the process.

It followed that the decision to defend sterling was in fact central to the pursuit of Labour's original strategy, which was not abandoned but modified in July 1966.

The strategy followed what one of Wilson's economic advisers, Thomas Balogh, called 'the third way' – not devaluation or deflation but the organization of international financial support for sterling to buy time while the domestic economy was reformed in accordance with the National Plan, leading to a transformation of Britain's competitive position in world markets. As late as June 1967 the evidence suggested this approach was working and that there was no reason to assume that devaluation was bound to happen. The fact that it did does not mean that the struggle against it was foredoomed to failure. It does however indicate that social democracy was becoming vulnerable to external shocks.

Footloose funds

These shocks were functions of the growing instability of the Bretton Woods international monetary system established shortly after World War Two. This was based on stable (but adjustable) exchange rates and the convertibility of the world's leading reserve currency, the dollar, into gold at the fixed price of $35 to one ounce. Sterling, as the second most widely used international trading and reserve currency after the dollar, played a critical part in the Bretton Woods system: as late as the mid-1960s it accounted for a third of all foreign exchange reserves.[31] Now, however, global monetary arrangements were being threatened by two separate, but inter-related developments. First of all both major international reserve currencies were under pressure. They had accumulated considerable liabilities by 1964. Since the late 1940s there had been a steady outflow of dollars from the USA, caused initially by foreign aid programmes such as the Marshall Plan but then sustained by military spending overseas (including the commitment to supporting South Vietnam), imports, and foreign investment mainly on the part of multinational corporations. The latter had from the late 1950s been building factories or buying up firms overseas, especially in Western Europe. The result was an accumulation of dollars in the world economy, some of which were held by the central banks of countries such as West Germany or France, while others were deposited in private banks, many of them in London. They became known as 'Eurodollars' (Figure 2.1) and for a time were attractive to hold because of the dollar's convertibility into gold at the fixed price of $35 to 1 ounce. By the early 1960s, however, anxieties were growing on the part of the Americans and their creditors that US liabilities far exceeded the reserves available to honour such obligations.

As far as the UK was concerned, the use of London's banking facilities for deposits held by foreign governments, banks, corporations and individuals had been encouraged by successive British administrations during the 1950s, so that sterling could resume its pre-war role as a worldwide trading and reserve currency.[32] Gross liabilities to the Sterling Area reached £4,572 million, five times the size of the published gold and foreign exchange reserves (£907 million).[33] As a result, the British economy was left with an exposed external financial position, which was not improved by the significant expenditure incurred as a result of the country's

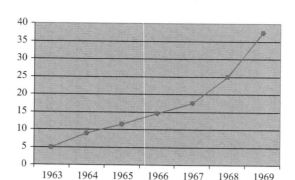

FIGURE 2.1 Estimated size of the Eurodollar market ($bn)
Source: BIS *Annual Reports*, 1965–70

overseas military commitments in Europe, the Middle East and in South East Asia, where political instability was at this very time involving British and Commonwealth forces in armed conflict.[34] This all contributed to a febrile mood on the part of the foreign exchange markets, leading sterling holders to switch away from the currency when the current account went into the red, even by a small amount, out of anxiety that the government would seek to correct the external position via devaluation.

The existence both of the dollar surplus and of sterling's vulnerability threatened the stability of the post-war world economy. What would happen if and when US policy began to focus on correcting the currency imbalance? If supplies of dollars and of gold in the world economy became inadequate some countries would seek to build up their own reserves, essential for the financing of external deficits, through protectionist or deflationary steps whose effects would reduce the reserves of other countries, which would then have to respond in kind. The upshot would be a downward spiral of world trade, production and employment. Anxiety about this prospect on the part of governments, the IMF and central banks led to a series of papers and discussions about the creation of extra reserve assets. In the UK, by 1963 both the Conservative Chancellor Maudling and the Labour leader Wilson were proposing that the IMF 'create international credit *parri passu* with the development of world trade'.[35]

This commitment to an international economic order supportive of domestic growth inspired British enthusiasm for international monetary reform. The UK hoped for extra liquidity, both so that it could avoid being forced into deflation to safeguard its external position at the current exchange rate, and because it believed that it might be possible for sterling holders to exchange their balances for a new international reserve asset to be held by the Fund, hence reducing the susceptibility of the British reserves to runs on the pound caused by 'confidence' rather than trade factors.[36] But the talks lasted for the best part of six years,[37] meanwhile global trade and finance depended on two reserve currencies whose value was not universally trusted. Moreover, with no rapid external solution to the sterling problem

London became reliant on IMF support, short term central bank loans and currency swap agreements largely with the Federal Reserve Bank of New York (FRBNY) to protect the parity and the reserves.

The absence of agreement on international monetary reform therefore left the reserve currencies vulnerable to speculation. The growth of these speculative flows of funds into and out of national currencies was the second reason for questioning the future prospects of the post-war global monetary system. It arose from the progressive liberalization of trade and payments after the mid-1950s, promoted by the national governments of the leading capitalist states and international organizations such as the IMF as a means to the achievement of high and smooth economic growth.[38] A key date in this history is December 1958, when non-resident sterling convertibility for current transactions was restored. This enabled bank branches and large firms to switch surplus cash in and out of local European currencies in search of the best short-term return. As a result 'a highly efficient international market in short-term money'[39] developed, with London the most important centre. Continental banks and companies contributed to this new market, but the most significant input came from the USA.

London was the favourite destination for these Eurodollar funds because there were, for a start, a large and growing number of US subsidiaries in the UK compared to the rest of Europe at this time. Indeed, over the decade from 1959 US direct investments in the UK grew by 188 per cent to reach a figure of $7.2 billion (25 per cent of all US long-term private investment in Europe).[40] There was also the unrivalled range of banking services available in London arising from its historic specialization in insurance, shipping, and acceptances. As early as 1953 there were ten US banks with branches in London. This number grew after 1960, and by the end of 1965 there were twenty-one overseas branches, including prestigious names such as the Bank of America, Chase Manhattan, First National City Bank, and Morgan Guaranty.[41] By the end of 1965, 46.8 per cent of total Eurodollar deposits worth $9,102 million were banked in London.[42] There was a large short-term money market there which was highly attractive to the US banks, and these in turn could deploy their dollars in a variety of ways. They could offer them on the European inter-bank market or convert them into sterling loans (usually of three months) to UK local authorities and hire purchase companies, where rates were generally between 0.5 and 1 per cent higher than those offered by Treasury Bills.[43]

This increasing interdependence of capital markets in leading industrial states during the 1960s, arguably a key stage in the development of economic globalization, generated an international financial community with its own priorities. The most significant of these was 'confidence', which when applied to Britain meant assurance that the government was genuinely committed to an economic strategy capable of delivering a balance of payments surplus at the prevailing exchange rate within the short to medium term. Between early 1963 and the summer of 1964, the new freedom of movement for international payments, the pound's status as a reserve currency, London's history as an international financial centre, and the favourable short-term rates available there, had all worked together to draw in the substantial volume of official and private sterling balances. But given the structural weaknesses in the international financial system and the increasing exposure of sterling, all these factors could operate as effectively to promote an exodus of funds from London as they could to attract them.

Sterling crisis

The fragility of sterling's position was demonstrated in the November 1964 crisis: the catalyst was indeed a lack of confidence in the currency's future as an international reserve currency, which provoked a run on the pound. Given the absence of any institutional mechanism to provide extra long-term international liquidity, Labour had had little choice but to go for external credits. But its programme, notably its commitments in health and social welfare, did not sit comfortably with the prevailing sentiments on the part of Britain's creditors, the City of London and the Bank of England. There was real doubt in these circles about Labour's willingness to take appropriate steps to correct the balance of payments deficit.[44] Even though the government successfully negotiated a $1.4 billion credit from the IMF in April 1965, most of which ($1.1 billion) was needed to repay the November credits, there was some concern within the Fund about whether the UK would reach external balance by the end of 1966.[45] These doubts were echoed by Lord Cromer, who argued that confidence could only be restored via implementation of the public spending cuts and wage restraint the bankers themselves believed indispensable to the correction of external imbalances. Wilson made it clear on several occasions that he was not prepared to allow central bankers to dictate policy to a democratically elected government,[46] but the final shape of the 1965 budget indicated that both he and Callaghan were aware that anxiety about sterling could not be ignored.[47] It saw steps to reduce demand by £250 million, mainly via higher indirect taxes, and the scrapping of the TSR-2.

Although the budget was well received on the foreign exchange markets, confidence remained weak. The pound remained vulnerable to speculation provoked by a poor set of trade figures, shifts in international interest rates, perceptions on the part of foreign central bankers and overseas holders of sterling that British costs were not under control, or strike action at home. Over the next two years all of these influences, sometimes working separately and sometimes in combination, operated on sterling, provoking a crisis in the summer of 1965 and again twelve months later. The first followed measures by President Johnson to encourage a repatriation of dollars. These transformed a net outflow of $2 billion in 1964 into a net inflow of $850 million in 1965. The demand for dollars was accompanied by a shift of market sentiment against sterling, exacerbated by a cut in the Bank Rate and disappointing trade figures for May and June. In fact it is now understood that the current account deficit was eliminated in 1965, being turned into a surplus of £33 million,[48] with exports over the year growing at a rate of 6.7 per cent, some way above the 5.25 target for annual increases set out in the National Plan. But the statistics *seemed* to confirm all the doubts which had been expressed about the government's willingness to reduce domestic demand and wage costs. The existence of weak confidence and relatively low lending rates in London led to significant selling of sterling, with the sterling balances falling by £136 million between June and December.

The government responded with an emergency package, designed to reduce demand by £200 million. This included the deferment of social spending commitments (a minimum income guarantee and abolition of remaining health charges), a six month delay to the start of public spending projects (apart from industrial building, schools, hospitals and housing) and cuts in defence spending. The measures were followed at the start of September by an agreement between the government, unions and employers that the incomes policy be given statutory backing: in the event of the voluntary approach failing, the Secretary of State would be able to enforce NBPI decisions by Ministerial Order and defer any wage or price increase while the Board's enquiries were ongoing. It was also accepted that the Board should receive 'early warning' of price increases and wage claims.[49] The agreement to strengthen pay restraint and so reduce the pressure of rising wages on costs (between July 1964 and June 1965 prices had risen by 5 per cent but average wage settlements had been running at almost 6 per cent, leaving the incomes policy 'in great danger')[50] was the trigger for another international rescue operation. It was worth $925 million, the most significant contributions coming from the USA ($400m) and West Germany ($120m).

The emergency measures, along with external support and good trade figures from July onwards, allowed the government to launch the National Plan in a crisis-free atmosphere. This lasted well into 1966, enabling Wilson to call a General Election for March, when Labour's conclusive victory reflected the ringing endorsement of its modernization plans that it had not quite achieved in 1964. Yet there were critics at the time and among subsequent commentators. Crossman[51] reports the dismay of Labour backbenchers; Stewart, who was an economic adviser in 10 Downing Street at the time, lamented 'the preservation of the existing exchange rate over other objectives, particularly growth'.[52] Ponting and Middlemas repeated these criticisms, adding that US support was conditional on deflationary measures, a toughening of the incomes policy and on commitment to maintaining an expensive British military presence in the Far East.[53]

There is no doubt that the measures were welcome as far as Britain's creditors were concerned but the criticisms are misplaced. To begin with, the July package was far less dramatic than the headlines had suggested. It amounted to less than 0.6 per cent of the GDP – and may have been even gentler than that. Unemployment, having increased briefly in the third quarter, resumed a downward path thereafter.[54] Quarterly growth figures indicate that, if anything, growth was faster in the last half of the year than in the first (see Figure 2.2). Secondly, the government had become increasingly anxious about wage settlements during the spring and had determined to strengthen the pay policy before the crisis supervened. Given these worries it was not unreasonable for Wilson to welcome statutory backing for the pay policy as a 'positive development of the Government's policy for planned and controlled increases in incomes' and a reinforcement of the tripartite alliance whose existence was crucial to the success of Labour's project. Finally, Wilson was not blackmailed by Washington into prolonging an expensive British military presence in the Far East. Johnson and his senior advisers certainly wanted the Labour government both to retain Britain's strategic role in the region and to send forces to Vietnam, but Wilson repeatedly refused to make such commitments.[55] US pressure notwithstanding, the government was clear that the costs of Britain's stay east of Suez were high enough to be detrimental to sterling, and following the end of the Confrontation with Indonesia in 1966 a process of withdrawal began.[56]

The calmer external environment allowed the government to begin implementing the Plan. Infrastructural spending was increased in accordance with the Plan, with ambitious programmes for housing, hospitals and education. The number of council houses built each year rose from 119,000 in 1964 to 142,000 in 1966.[57] The annual average level of housing completions moved steadily towards 400,000 (its target of 500,000 was never met), a long way beyond the 310,000 per year achieved by the Conservatives in the Macmillan and Douglas-Home years. Education Secretary Anthony Crosland swung the government behind a series of seminal reforms, especially in secondary and tertiary education. All local authorities were requested to produce plans for the replacement of the grammar and secondary modern school (their intake determined by the results of the Eleven Plus examination) by non-selective comprehensive schools. The number of teachers in training increased by over a third between 1964 and 1967 and the percentage of pupils remaining in education over the age of sixteen rose by a similar level.[58] In higher education Labour accepted the Conservative target of 390,000 places by 1973–74 and aimed at reaching 700,000 by 1980. To meet this expansion it created ten new universities, increased investment in staff and capital development at existing institutions and established thirty polytechnics and three new Business

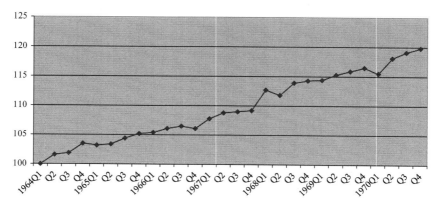

FIGURE 2.2 Growth per quarter, 1964–70
Source: Office of National Statistics

Schools (London, Manchester and Cranfield School of Management)[59] in order to develop applied, vocational and managerial skills.[60]

At the same time determined efforts were made to promote industrial modernization. The Ministry of Technology supported the application of scientific innovation to industry through grants, funding for R and D and investment in high technology industries. It also encouraged fusion between military and civil research projects, aiming to steer advances away from concentration in the defence sector. There was backing for restructuring.[61] This was pursued by an expansion in the numbers of the 'little Neddies', or EDCs, established by the Conservatives. Now, each one contained officials from the DEA as well as representatives from both sides of industry. The EDCs were tasked with the development of agreements on import-saving, productivity improvements and rationalization. By July 1966 there were twenty of them (an advance on the eight left by the Conservatives), covering 66 per cent of private industry. One of the government's most significant innovations was unveiled in the May 1966 Budget; this was the Selective Employment Tax (SET), which imposed a payroll levy discriminating against employers in the service sector. SET's objective was to facilitate the release of labour from services into manufacturing, based on the theory that the virtuous circle of high productivity, rapidly increasing exports, and high levels of economic growth had by-passed Britain because the share of its labour resources occupied in the service sector, inherently less productive than manufacturing, had been too high. Throughout much of post-war Europe, fast growth had been sustained by the migration of under-employed agricultural labourers into industry. SET represented an attempt to replicate this in the somewhat different conditions of 1960s Britain.[62] It was highly controversial and much disliked by employers in the service sector, but there is evidence (admittedly not conclusive) that it did assist an improvement in productivity in both the service and manufacturing sectors after the mid-1960s.[63]

At the very moment when Labour seemed most secure a new crisis overtook the currency. Structural changes to the international economy once again interacted with weakening confidence. As in July 1965, a policy shift in the USA was a key influence. At the end of 1965 there was a tightening of US monetary policy, with the discount rate going up from 4 to 4.5 per cent.[64] The impact was felt first in the Eurodollar market, as US banks with branches in Europe withdrew funds for redeployment at home. There was a switching out of European currencies into dollars. This process was especially marked in the UK, where an outflow of sterling developed, leading to pressure on the reserves.

The effect of interest rates was magnified by a crisis of confidence. This was provoked initially by disappointment in the post-election Budget. Foreign observers argued that it left demand too high and should have done more to hold back public spending and private consumption.[65] This difficult climate was worsened by a seamen's strike, starting in mid-May. It immobilized ships being loaded with exports.[66] The effect on the trade figures was serious: a modest May deficit doubled to one of £55 million in June.[67] Expectation that Britain would end the year in surplus disappeared at home and abroad. As a result, a run on the pound started in June and accelerated in July. The introduction of a State of Emergency, intended to demonstrate the government's determination not to allow the seamen to breach the incomes policy, actually generated more nervousness about sterling's prospects. The situation failed to improve in July even though the seamen's strike had been called off at the end of June. The Bank Rate went up from 6 per cent to 7 per cent but sterling struggled for most of July. The sterling balances were run down by £180 million[68] between June and August. By mid-July losses to the reserves were exceeding those experienced in the preceding crises of 1964 and 1965.

The Cabinet debated the merits of devaluation but in the end its response to the crisis was another set of July measures to reduce internal demand. On July 20 a new emergency package was announced. There was to be a six month freeze on all prices, wages and salaries, followed by a six month period of 'severe restraint'. This would be accompanied by increases in indirect taxes worth 10 per cent, rises in postal and telephone charges, reductions in domestic public spending programmes and in overseas spending, and an intensification of building controls designed to ensure a cutback of £180 million in new projects. At the same time hire purchase controls were tightened and an allowance of £50 per head was introduced for foreign travel outside the sterling area. Wilson and Callaghan both argued that the measures would take 'about £500 million a year from the pressure of demand'.[69] A Treasury analysis of the July measures supported this contention, calculating 'that the level of GDP in the second half of 1967 will have been brought down by 1.72 per cent compared with our previous forecast'.[70]

The government's clear determination to transform the external position by squeezing internal demand went down well abroad,[71] especially in Bonn and Washington. Sterling started to recover.[72] But the measures were not welcomed by many of the government's own supporters. The TUC was hostile, although the General Council did agree to 'acquiesce' in the policy, and the annual TUC Congress endorsed it following a strong plea from the Prime Minister.[73] There was great unease in the Parliamentary Party. An angry Frank Cousins left the government and returned to his post as General Secretary of the TGWU. George Brown considered resignation.[74] Supported by a group of leading Ministers, he argued that the cuts only made sense if they were accompanied by devaluation or a downward float of sterling, which would insulate the reserves from speculative attacks while stimulating exports.[75] The issues were discussed in Cabinet on 19 July, but the Prime Minister and Chancellor had a clear majority.[76] Contemporary observers concluded that the result was fatal for the National Plan: given the introduction of the cuts, its growth target was clearly unachievable. Brown left the DEA in September, swapping places with Foreign Secretary Michael Stewart. His departure seemed to confirm the view that the July measures 'made nonsense of everything Labour had been saying for the past few years'.[77]

This negative view of the July measures has become the orthodoxy in the historical literature.[78] Yet, as Wilson had argued, there is no reason to assume that depreciation would have implied less deflation than the July measures. Calculations by Wynne Godley and Fred Atkinson, from the Treasury Economic Section, showed that for a devaluation (estimated to be in the region of 14 or 15 per cent) to be successful, an external surplus running at an annual rate of at least £400 million by the end of 1968 would be required. To reach this figure there would have to be a shift of resources into the balance of payments amounting to at least £740 million (this being the sum of the adverse shift in the terms of trade caused by devaluation plus the target of £400 million), requiring the reduction of demand by 2 per cent (or slightly more) of GDP.[79] The July measures were less severe than this. They allowed the government to develop a modified economic programme for the period to 1970, on the basis of annual surpluses worth at least £100 million. Tax increases of £300 million, with cuts of £200 million in defence spending and of £100 million in other government commitments, were judged adequate for its modified strategy. The framework was compatible with annual growth of 3 per cent, with unemployment between 2 and 2.5 per cent. Devaluation would have struck harder at growth without necessarily having a beneficial impact on exports, which had in any case performed respectably since 1964 (Figure 2.3).

The decision not to devalue in July 1966 represented not the abandonment of but a major adjustment to the strategy the government had followed since October 1964. It had consistently avoided devaluation and sharp deflation as correctives for the inherited balance of payments deficit and the July 1966 measures were consistent with this 'third way'. By the spring of 1967 there seemed good grounds for thinking that its approach was working. The trade figures had stayed in the black for six months in a row. There had been a significant reduction of external debt and the IMF signalled its confidence by encouraging countries borrowing from it to draw sterling.[80] By May–June 1967 the government's attention was concentrated on action to reduce unemployment, which had almost doubled over the previous twelve months, from 280,000 (1.2 per cent) to 540,000 (2.3 per cent). This was slightly above the target rate; with the improved external position it now seemed appropriate to consider selective reflation. A Bank Rate cut from 6 per cent to 5.5 per cent in May was generally welcomed: *The Times*, noting the favourable external position and the 'depressed' state of industrial activity, argued that 'a further mild shot in the arm is not out of place'.[81] The government established 'special development areas', to encourage new enterprise in parts of the country affected by the contraction of old industries, especially coalmining (where employment fell by 208,000 between 1964 and 1969).[82] This initiative was reinforced by Regional Employment Premium (REP), whose objectives were in accordance with the government's aim of encouraging output without stimulating cost inflation. To this end it provided employers in the development and special development areas with a subsidy worth about 7 per cent of labour costs and reduced unemployment in these areas by 15–20 per cent.[83]

By summer 1967 it appeared that the prospects for sustained expansion might soon be enhanced by membership of the EEC. In 1966 Wilson and Brown had come to the conclusion that membership would be in Britain's interests. This would not only allow Britain to avoid strategic dependence on the USA but provide it with the framework which would allow for the pursuit of smooth and high growth in the long-term.[84] It was clear that western Europe, and especially the EEC, was absorbing a steadily increasing share of British trade at the expense of Commonwealth markets. At the end of April the Cabinet agreed that the government should once again apply to join the Common Market.[85] The application was well received by five of the EEC six, but doubts remained about the French government given President de Gaulle's well-known suspicions that British participation in the EEC would transform it into an Atlantic free trade area. Wilson, however, remained optimistic that he might be able to persuade the President. He looked ahead to the possibility that with Britain in the EEC there was the potential for co-operation between member governments and corporations in the modernization and restructuring of European industry; the drive to harness the white heat of the technological revolution could be relocated to the Common Market, strengthening efforts to resist the expansion of US multinationals.

The hopeful start to Britain's second bid to join the EEC increased the optimism felt by the government at the start of June 1967, as it appeared that sterling's problems were in the past. In July the Organisation for Economic Co-operation and Development (OECD, bringing together the most developed countries in the world) predicted that Britain was heading for 'calmer waters'. Exports in 1967 would rise more rapidly than imports, 'and the balance of payments should continue to improve'.[86] At this point progress was disrupted by a series of events outside the control of the government. First of all there was a slowdown in the growth of world trade. This had much to do with deflation in the USA (from late 1965) and West Germany (where there was anxiety about inflation).[87] The German performance affected growth throughout continental Western Europe, where it slipped from 3.7 per cent in 1966 to 2.9 per cent in 1967.[88] British exports were hit; France and Italy recorded deficits in 1967.[89] Secondly, there was the Arab-Israeli Six Day War, which provoked an oil embargo and the closure of the Suez Canal. The embargo forced the UK to replace Middle Eastern oil with more expensive supplies (largely because of freight costs) while the Canal closure was estimated to have cost the balance of payments £20 million a month.[90] In September, before

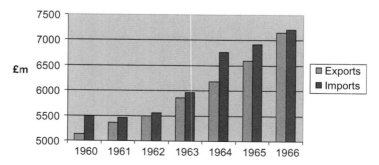

FIGURE 2.3 Exports and imports of goods and services, 1960–66
Source: Middleton 2001, Table II.I, pp. 146–147

the economy had a chance to recover from these shocks, unofficial dock strikes started in Liverpool and London, with damaging results: the fall in income from exports amounted to nearly £140 million between October and January,[91] and the disputes were largely responsible for some freakishly bad October trade figures. The reappearance of pressure on the balance of payments eroded confidence in sterling on the foreign exchange markets. By the start of November the losses across the exchanges were so great that either another rescue package or devaluation was unavoidable. At the IMF the consensus was that a successful support operation would require $3 billion. But it became clear that the conditions of such a package would involve the surrender of autonomy over monetary, credit and budgetary policy[92] and replacement of the government's chosen economic strategy with a more deflationary approach. In consequence, devaluation, of 14.2 per cent, was chosen.[93]

There had been arguments for devaluation in 1965 and 1966, but they were not overwhelmingly powerful ones; in reality the choice between sticking to the parity and devaluation to promote faster growth was illusory. The defence of sterling involved difficult and uncongenial measures, but the modified economic strategy adopted in 1966–67 indicated that it was consistent with modest expansion in the medium term. This ceased to apply in the autumn of 1967. The argument for devaluation then became a compelling one for Wilson. Until that point the long campaign to protect the parity appeared both to have been more consistent with the government's long-term objectives than devaluation, and to be succeeding.

These subtleties were not, however, apparent to the many who had been critical of Labour's strategy over the previous three years. For them the sterling devaluation was predictable – and overdue. The National Plan was now widely regarded as a failure. The DEA had been sidelined by the Treasury. The latter's preoccupation with the balance of payments and the need to hold down public spending had been allowed to eclipse the expansionist aims of the former, to no good result. The Prime Minister's reputation took a hard knock as he was portrayed as a Canute-like figure who had committed his government, the repository of so many hopes, to a futile effort at avoiding economic reality. The demoralising impact of the devaluation was compounded by another French veto of the British EEC application, partly on familiar grounds concerning the special relationship with the USA – but de Gaulle also argued that Britain's economy was not strong enough for it to join. It was a bad moment for Labour; notwithstanding the realities behind economic strategy after October 1964, public confidence in the government was seriously damaged. March 1966 seemed a long time ago.

Hard slog

The temptation to write off the National Plan and Labour's modernization campaign was strengthened by the aftermath of devaluation. Deflation followed as external crises buffeted sterling in 1968. The Bank Rate went up to 8 per cent and with Roy Jenkins succeeding James Callaghan as Chancellor financial policy became austere: 1968 and 1969 were years of tight credit restrictions.[94] Jenkins warned the electorate that the country faced 'two years of hard slog'. Living standards were squeezed by continuing pay restraint (until late in 1969) and sharp increases in taxation (mostly indirect). Taxes (personal and indirect) and social contributions rose to 37.2 per cent of GDP in 1970 and household consumption went up by just 0.5 per cent in 1969 (its lowest rise for over a decade). Two later commentators concluded that

> the second half of the 1960s is striking as the most (or, perhaps, the only) significant and sustained increase in the tax burden seen over the twentieth century that did not reflect war or pre-war military build-up: between 1964 and 1970, general government revenue increased from 33.6 per cent of GDP to 42.1 per cent, an increase of 8.5 percentage points.[95]

The Government's abandonment of its growth agenda seemed clear.[96] Senior Cabinet Ministers such as Barbara Castle lamented that 'whatever the economic situation…the only course of action was to deflate'.[97] Disillusionment spread throughout the electorate. By spring 1968 Labour was 20 per cent behind the Conservatives in the opinion polls.

It is fair to argue that there have been times in modern British history when governments have given way to Bank and Treasury advice that external financial probity took priority over the welfare of industry and the level of employment. Sterling's 1925 return to the gold standard at its pre-1914 parity is often cited as a prime example.[98] In the circumstances of the late 1960s, however, it is misguided to argue that there was a polar opposition between growth and the achievement of exchange rate stability and external surplus. Lord Kahn, who led a contemporary enquiry into the factors behind the sterling crises of 1964 and 1965, concluded that

> if economic policy is to be developed on its merits, and not under pressure of international monetary disturbances, then it is essential that the development and maintenance of a really substantial balance of payments surplus, taking one year with another, shall be accepted as an important element of economic policy, to be pursued with vigour in good times and bad.[99]

As Jenkins told his colleagues in December 1968, there was in fact 'no choice between balance of payments and growth'; Britain's debts now stood at £3 billion and a substantial external surplus, worth £500 million a year, was essential.[100]

Given the very volatile international financial environment, the £500 million figure (equivalent to 1 per cent of GDP, a level not seen since 1958–59) was regarded as essential to quashing doubts in the markets about sterling's ability to stay at the new rate. If these were allowed to persist there would be ongoing pressure on the pound and more losses to the reserves. These would have to be made good by further borrowing, the extent of which would be determined by Britain's creditors. If they ran out of confidence, the government would be facing either another devaluation or a downward float of the currency. Either would be disastrous. Within the Treasury a sterling collapse to £1 = $1.50, 37.5 per cent below the $2.40 level and 46 per cent below the pre-devaluation rate of $2.80, was feared. This would prompt a withdrawal of as much as £2 billion from the sterling balances,[101] leading to bank failures in London and a drastic contraction of credit in the UK.[102] It would also intensify strains on the current account, provoke price increases and jeopardize trade union consent to pay restraint. On the external front there was every chance that many other countries would let their currencies float,[103] leading to a return to the trade wars of the 1930s – just at the moment when Britain was seeking to expand exports.[104] Clearly, neither further devaluation nor a float was compatible with the conditions required for the success of Labour's post-devaluation strategy. An annual £500 million surplus would, however, reassure Britain's creditors and allow the government to expand the economy without having to borrow more. It would be freed from anxiety that external constraints would yet again frustrate the attempt to achieve west European levels of growth. The curse of 'Stop-Go' would finally be lifted. Wilson and Jenkins were now very clear that fulfilment of Labour's social democratic mission required a large, sustained external surplus.

Tax rises and spending reductions were therefore central to what the government called a 'Switch of Resources Strategy', designed to rebalance the economy by reducing demand in the home market in order to promote export-led expansion. A White Paper giving details of public spending cuts was released in January 1968. Labour backbenchers on the whole did not object to cuts in the defence budget, which heralded the acceleration of Britain's retreat from its historic military commitments in the Far East. But they found the reintroduction of prescription charges, the postponement of raising the school leaving age to 16 and the announcement of reductions worth almost £700 million in civil expenditure programmes up to 1970 deeply unpalatable. The White Paper was followed in March 1968 by a budget described by Wilson himself as 'the most punishing' in British peacetime history. It raised taxes (mainly indirect) by £923 million, equivalent to 2.1 per cent of the GDP, even more than Britain's financial creditors thought necessary.[105]

Both domestic press and international reaction to the Budget was favourable,[106] although the pound continued to be buffeted by foreign exchange turbulence resulting from the unstable international monetary environment, even after agreement in July 1968 between the Bank of England and the Bank for International Settlements (BIS) in Basle on a $2 billion loan to insulate the British reserves from diversification out of sterling by balance holders.[107] The government did not, however, deviate from its strategy, which began to show dividends. The trade figures for the last part of 1968 showed real improvement. In December the OECD accepted that 'there was now a good chance of the United Kingdom reaching its goal'.[108] By mid-October 1969 sterling was exceeding $2.39, where it remained (occasionally reaching parity) for the rest of Labour's time in power.

Sterling's freedom from turbulence followed from evidence that the switch of resources to production for exports was succeeding as well as from international co-operation designed to remove some of the factors behind currency volatility, seen (for example) in the Basle arrangements. In consequence, Labour was to complete its post devaluation strategy successfully. By March 1970 the combination of large external surpluses (£554 million in 1969, with an even more sizeable one forecast for the current year)[109] and expectations of sustained growth running at 3 per cent had led the OECD to declare that Britain was 'no longer a problem country'.[110] The problem for Labour was that success had come at a high price: the squeeze on living standards was widely blamed for its defeat in the 1970 general election.[111] The turnout was 72 per cent, the lowest figure since 1935, and the Labour vote dropped by 900,000 (7 per cent) over its level in 1966. In addition it seems that a significant group of skilled manual labourers, normally Labour supporters, switched allegiance.[112] The Conservative Party therefore inherited the opportunity for sustained expansion. For Labour, the outcome of the Switch of Resources Strategy was a case of virtue being its only reward.

Wilson's Britain

Labour did not abandon its mission in the face of successive sterling crises. Wilson was throughout his career frequently accused of putting tactics before strategy, but the record of his 1964–70 governments is one of persistent, dogged commitment to its modernizing project. The Switch of Resources strategy built on the projections of the National Plan and the work of the DEA prior to devaluation. This continuity was characterized by a focus on two particular areas. One was public investment. Despite the July 1966 measures Labour sustained the expansion which had started when Macmillan was Prime Minister. Between 1965 and 1970 investment in health (which included a major programme of hospital building) as well as in housing, schools, higher education and management education and training, was protected. Other sectors (notably coal and defence) were run down – indeed defence more rapidly than foreseen in the Plan. The picture emerges clearly from a comparison of the Plan's forecasts for certain categories of public spending with the outturn for the same group over the lifetime of the governments (Table 2.1). This

TABLE 2.1 Public investment in certain sectors, 1964–70: forecast and outturn

	Annual percentage growth forecast 1964–70	Annual percentage growth achieved 1964–70
Roads	8.3	6.1
Public housing	6.6	4.6
Education	6.4	5.5
Defence	0.0	-0.8
Health and welfare	4.7	5.1

Derived from: *The National Plan*, Cmnd. 2764, pp. 177–179 and Table 18.1, p. 178; Tomlinson, *The Labour Governments 1964–70*, Table 9.1, p. 202.

shows a reasonably successful effort to safeguard programmes which were seen as 'beneficial to the national economy'. Although the Plan's growth targets were not attainable, many of its aspirations remained alive, even if the strategy required a greater squeeze on the consumer than had been expected.

The second area was support for technological change through structural intervention in the economy. Here, the key agents were the Industrial Reorganisation Corporation (IRC), established in 1966, and the Ministry of Technology – frequently known at the time as Mintech. The IRC was an independent agency financed from public funds but run by private businessmen. It was created as a result of concern that sectors of the economy, manufacturing products for which there was growing international demand, such as the motor industry, electrics, electronics and computing, were not competing as effectively as they might because of the relatively small size of many firms. Economies of scale were needed to facilitate longer production runs and lower costs. The IRC was therefore encouraged to back mergers where it considered these to be in the national interest, usually (and in keeping with the Switch of Resources Strategy) defined in terms of the need to develop import substitution and increase exports, and it used its budget of £150 million to encourage rationalization and undertake selective investment.

The IRC was only responsible for 2 per cent of all mergers between 1967 and 1970, but this small figure included some of the most significant, which were often strategically located in the high-technology sectors Labour was keen to encourage. A process of concentration was encouraged in the electricity, electronics and aerospace industries, with the General Electric Company (GEC) being transformed into a major international corporation following its takeover of Associated Electrical Industries in 1967 and English Electric and Marconi in 1968. It continued to grow throughout the 1970s and by 1983 was the economy's largest private employer, with a workforce of 250,000. The car industry, characterized by wasteful competition and producing too many models for a limited market, was rationalized with the creation of British Leyland from a merger between the British Motor Corporation and Leyland (though the outcome was to provide successive governments with headaches for years to come). The IRC also took the initiative in electronics and was directly involved in the creation of International Computers Limited (ICL), the largest manufacturer of computers outside the USA.[113]

The IRC had started out under the wing of the DEA. In 1969, however, Mintech took over the DEA's functions concerning regional development, industrial modernization and the IRC. Mintech, under Tony Benn (Minister since 1966), now became the government's principal instrument for economic planning. It had been supporting investment and innovation in the nuclear, computing and machine tool industries since 1964 and owned large government research establishments such as the Atomic Weapons Research Establishment (AWRE) and the Royal Radar Establishment (RRE). By 1970 Mintech's responsibilities embraced most of British manufacturing.[114] The 1968 Industrial Expansion Act gave Mintech the power to lend money to or take a direct stake in firms manufacturing products at the cutting edge of technological development, but whose immediate commercial prospects were limited by the cost of innovation. Examples were funding for new aluminium smelters and for production of the supersonic Concorde airliner.[115] In 1968 it provided financial support to Rolls Royce for the RB 211 aero-engine after orders which had been anticipated failed to materialize. This high-capacity engine was needed for a new generation of wide-bodied aircraft, including the Lockheed Tri-Star – which was to prove a highly successful and long-lived civil and military airliner and indeed remains in service with the RAF at the time of writing. Without Mintech's intervention the project would have collapsed, taking Rolls Royce right out of the aero-engine business and leaving the market dominated by two US corporations, General Electric and Pratt and Whitney.[116] As it was, the commitment saved Rolls Royce (though further aid was to be needed three years later) and kept Britain in the forefront of the international aerospace industry.

In 1988 Newton and Porter claimed that Mintech's work was interesting but that its budget was too small for it to make the most of its potential.[117] This comment now appears unfair. In addition to its work with different industrial sectors Mintech presided over the first attempt in modern British history to convert defence-related research into civilian use,[118] examples being the work of the AWRE on the improvement of artificial limbs using servo motors built for guided missiles or the Royal Radar Establishment's involvement in the development of computer languages, CAD (computer assisted design), air traffic control systems and thermal imaging.[119] By 1969 government spending on non-military R and D was indeed above resources committed under the same heading to defence. The shift of emphasis followed the revelation that British R and D spending had not been lower than in comparable states such as France and West Germany: there was, after all, no automatic correlation between growth and investment in R and D.[120] It became clear that what mattered was the *application* of R and D; in Britain it had become closely identified, especially after 1939, with the defence sector. Benn and Wilson favoured not an indiscriminate expansion of R and D funding but a reallocation of the scientific effort to projects with potential for commercial exploitation. The civilian sector therefore took priority; and Mintech achieved some success in redirecting national scientific and technological efforts. Given more time it could have made more progress in transforming for the better the international prospects of the high value-added manufacturing industries whose success was central to Wilson's vision of a new Britain.[121]

The government's interventionism had been clearly signalled in Labour's 1964 and 1966 manifestos but it started to provoke a reaction which weakened Wilson's attempts to create a lasting grand bargain between the state and both sides of industry. First, the CBI started to complain about government interference, even accusing it (absurdly) of threatening the existence of private enterprise. Some of this noise came from doctrinaire liberals such as Arthur Shenfield (previously Executive Director of the CBI) and the representatives of firms in finance, distribution and services. But some emanated from senior figures such as Director-

General John Davies, who spoke for many senior executives when he accused Mintech of using the Industrial Expansion Act to implement back-door nationalization, criticized the levels of personal and company taxation, attacked restrictions on dividends and called for firm measures to curtail unofficial strikes. Government relations with the CBI became somewhat strained at times and in 1970 the organization came out in support of Conservative proposals to row back from Labour's interventionism.[122]

At the same time, the work of the IRC and Mintech notwithstanding, Labour came under pressure from its own supporters. The long period of pay restraint, with the NBPI, backed by statutory power, policing a 3.5 per cent pay limit along with the restrictions on price and dividend increases, generated resentment in the unions and on the left of the Labour Party as well as in private industry.[123] TUC efforts to ensure compliance on the factory floor were undermined by a growing number of unofficial strikes. Between 2 and 3 million days had been lost in strikes between 1963 and 1967; in 1968 the number rose to 4.7 million. The government became increasingly concerned about the trend to shop steward power, inter-union disputes and local pay deals; in 1965 it had appointed a Royal Commission on Industrial Relations chaired by Lord Donovan to investigate these issues. Donovan reported in 1968, having concluded that British industrial relations were characterized by two parallel systems, one of which was the 'system embodied in the official institutions', while the other was the 'informal system' arising from the 'actual behaviour of trade unions, employer associations, shop stewards and workers'.[124] He recommended that the government avoid legislative attempts to impose greater order on industrial relations and the pay bargaining process and instead opt for reform on the basis of self-regulation supervised by the TUC. Neither Wilson nor Barbara Castle at the new Department of Employment and Productivity (DEP: replacing the Ministry of Labour) were satisfied with this conclusion and in 1969 the government introduced its own proposals, entitled *In Place of Strife*, which included pre-strike ballots, a 28-day 'Cooling Off' period prior to strikes and legal sanctions against unofficial strikes provoked by inter-union disputes. In return, conciliation procedures would be strengthened and workers would receive a statutory right to join a trade union (this had never existed in the UK). Both Castle and Wilson saw *In Place of Strife* not just as an attempt to tackle the troublesome issue of unofficial strikes but the charter for a social democratic constitutional settlement. It was a step up from Brown's *Joint Statement* and would help the government to plan the economy given that long-term stability in relations between it and both sides of industry was central to the construction of an effective incomes policy and, therefore, the maintenance of full employment at stable prices.

As is well known, *In Place of Strife* was never turned into legislation. The underlying climate of frustration with the statutory pay policy (abandoned later in the year), along with Parliamentary Labour Party and TUC anxieties about the implications of government intervention in collective bargaining arrangements, ensured that Wilson and Castle's attempt to build a legal framework for industrial relations met with defeat. This was a setback for efforts at the institutionalization of tripartite co-operation; Wilson and Castle withdrew their own proposals in favour of a 'Solemn and Binding Agreement' with the TUC, in which the latter made a commitment to use its own authority to intervene in inter-union disputes and prevent unofficial strikes. The deal was derisively dubbed 'Solomon Binding' in the press[125] and was widely regarded as another blow to the Prime Minister's authority, coming as it did less than two years after devaluation.

In point of fact significant reforms did result. TUC General Secretary Vic Feather was responsible for the resolution of several disputes which looked likely to lead to unofficial strikes. Talks between government and the TUC concerning how the Commission on Industrial Relations, established in the wake of the Donovan Report, could become a forum for what Middlemas called 'voluntarily bargained corporatism' led to rule changes concerning procedure agreements, the regularization of institutional bargaining at plant level and the promotion of industry-wide agreements. The 1970 TUC *Economic Review* endorsed key aspects of government policy such as the urgency and importance of pay restraint (albeit voluntary), the need for greater union contributions to productivity improvement and acceptance that the £500 million external surplus was an essential precondition of reflation. Against all the odds, given the embarrassment of *In Place of Strife*, the government and the unions were moving together towards the kind of collaboration envisaged back in 1964, even though 'planned growth of wages' remained an elusive goal.[126]

There is no doubt that Labour had endured a bumpy ride over the period since 1964. Annual average growth of 3.8 per cent had eluded it. The sequence of July measures, wage restraint, tax rises and 'two years' hard slog' disappointed Labour supporters and provoked hostility on the part of Labour's enemies, especially those in the financial establishment. Indeed this bitterness was to culminate in the bizarre attempt of Cecil King (a director of the Bank of England and Chairman of the International Publishing Corporation, then the largest publishing group on the planet and owner of the *Daily Mirror* amongst many other newspapers) to contemplate the organization of a military coup in 1968 and the replacement of Labour by a National government led by Earl Mountbatten of Burma, the Queen's cousin.[127] Yet much had been achieved. This is to leave on one side the remarkable liberalization of British cultural and personal life resulting from the reforms relating to the laws governing censorship, homosexuality, race relations, abortion and divorce and the reorientation of British external strategy away from the global commitments of its old imperial days. Combined with the cuts in defence spending (and redirection of R and D spending) these measures drew a line under Britain's past and marked the start of a new era in which, EEC member or no, it aspired to be a progressive, prosperous modern European state. On the economic front Labour had removed the external constraint on macroeconomic expansion which had dogged successive governments since the 1950s. Productivity, possibly held back by the measures to suppress domestic demand, did not reach the 3 per cent annual target in the Plan but the application of new technology, the shedding of labour in traditional industries such as coal mining and the railways and the effects of SET helped it to rise to 2.9 per cent by 1970.[128] Annual increases in national output between 1964 and 1970 remained close to the average level throughout the period from 1951 but given the large surpluses of 1969 and 1970 (and the March 1970 OECD assessment) it is reasonable to argue that Labour achieved one of its key objectives – a rise, albeit unspectacular, in the sustainable long term growth rate of the UK.

By 1970, therefore, it seemed reasonable to suppose that an opportunity existed for the British economy to approach the west European levels of annual growth Labour had been aiming for when it developed the National Plan. The government's infrastructural spending (especially on roads) and investment in communications, health, housing and education (including the establishment of the Open University) had left an enduring mark on the country. By 1968–69 Labour had developed (in the words of Middlemas) 'a machine for a powerful and generally coherent policy for industrial change'[129] based on rationalization and investment in innovation, education and training led by Mintech and the DEP. This was underpinned by the work of the NEDC and the EDCs, which conducted ongoing reviews of how industrial sectors were adapting to the demands of modernization and export expansion. External indebtedness was paid off and in 1969 *The Task Ahead*, a new planning document, appeared.

The Task Ahead was a successor to the old National Plan. Covering 1969–72, this was called a 'planning document' rather than a plan and aimed for a 'dialogue with industry'. It projected a range of growth scenarios ranging from slightly under 3 per cent to a maximum of 4 per cent, dependent on the state of the external balance, and accepted that a continuing shift of resources into exports would be necessary throughout the period. *The Task Ahead*, and a further document in 1970, *Economic Prospects to 1972: A Revised Assessment*, were both more modest in their aspirations than the National Plan, the caution deriving from the impact of the external constraint on Labour's original ambitions. By the time the government left office it was widely argued that it had fallen short of some key objectives, notably its aspirations for annual growth. Labour had become a victim of the expectations it had generated in the exciting days of 1963–64 but in fact it had delivered a large part of the modernization agenda Wilson had set before the electorate. The government had been true to its roots in Producer's Britain: Cecil King notwithstanding, the normative discourse in British politics and economic policy was now social democratic, as the experience of the new Conservative administration was about to demonstrate.

Notes

1 Harold Wilson, *Memoirs: the Making of a Prime Minister 1916–1964* (London: Weidenfeld and Nicholson, 1986), p. 49.
2 See Martin Chick, *Industrial Policy in Britain 1945–1951: Economic Planning, Nationalisation and the Labour Governments* (Cambridge: Cambridge University Press, 2002), pp. 100–102; Ilaria Favoretto, 'Wilsonism' Reconsidered: Labour Party Revisionism

1952–64, *Contemporary British History*, vol. 14 (2000), pp. 54–80; Noel Thompson, 'The Fabian Political Economy of Harold Wilson', in Peter Dorey (ed.), *The 1964–70 Labour Governments* (London: Routledge, 2006), pp. 53–72.
3   Roger Middleton (ed.) *Inside the Department of Economic Affairs: Samuel Brittan, the Diary of an 'Irregular', 1964–66* (Oxford: Oxford University Press, 2012), p. 5.
4   Middleton, quoting Wilson, *Inside the Department of Economic Affairs*, p. 17.
5   See Stephen Fielding, '"White Heat" and White Collars: The Evolution of Wilsonism', in Richard Coopey, Steven Fielding and Nick Tiratsoo (eds), *The Wilson Governments 1964–1970* (London: Pinter, 1993), pp. 39–41; David Horner, 'The Road to Scarborough: Wilson, Labour and the Scientific Revolution', in Coopey, Fielding and Tiratsoo, *The Labour Governments 1964–1970*, pp. 65–66.
6   Historians and commentators too numerous to mention by name have made a habit of stating that Wilson committed Labour to the forging of a new Britain in 'the white heat' of technological revolution. This is misleading. Wilson was drawing attention to a development which was already under way: the question was how should Britain respond to, and take advantage of, a process which threatened to disrupt society unless it was managed in the national interest.
7   David Edgerton, *Warfare State: Britain 1920–1979* (Cambridge: Cambridge University Press, 2005), p. 240.
8   Horner, 'The Road to Scarborough', p. 66.
9   Stephen Blank, 'Britain: The Politics of Economic Policy, the Domestic Economy and the Problem of Pluralistic Stagnation', *International Organization*, 31(1977), pp. 674–721; Newton and Porter, *Modernization Frustrated*, p. 148.
10 See James Callaghan, *Time and Chance* (London: Collins, 1987), p. 169.
11 See Sidney Pollard, *The Wasting of the British Economy* (Beckenham: Croom Helm, 1984), p. 47; Brittan diary entries for 12 and 18–20 September 1965, in Middleton, *Inside the Department of Economic Affairs*, pp. 114, 118–120.
12 See *The National Plan* (Cmnd 2764, London: HMSO, 1965), pp. 6–9, 176–181.
13 George Brown, *In My Way* (London: Gollancz, 1971), p. 95.
14 Jacques Leruez, *Economic Planning and Politics in Britain* (London: Martin Robertson, 1975), p. 173.
15 Newton and Porter, *Modernization Frustrated*, p. 155.
16 Ibid., Table 6.1, p. 152.
17 Middleton, *British Economy since 1945*, Table II.3, pp. 150–151; Scott Newton, 'The Two Sterling Crises of 1964', *The Economic History Review*, vol. 62 (2009), p. 76.
18 Paul Foot, *The Politics of Harold Wilson* (London: Penguin, 1968); David Mackie and Chris Cook, *Decade of Disillusion: British Politics in the Sixties* (London: St Martin's Press, 1972); Newton and Porter, *Modernization Frustrated*, pp. 147–159; Clive Ponting, *Breach of Promise: Labour in Power 1964–70* (London: Penguin, 1990).
19 Tim Bale, 'Dynamics of a Non-Decision: The "Failure" to Devalue the Pound, 1964–7', *Twentieth Century British History*, 10 (1999), pp. 192–217; Glen O'Hara, '"Dynamic, Exciting, Thrilling Change": The Wilson Government's Economic Policies, 1964–70', *Contemporary British History*, 20 (2006), pp. 383–402; Jim Tomlinson, *The Labour Governments 1964–70: Economic Policy* (Manchester: Manchester University Press, 2004), p. 14 and ch. 10.
20 Andrew Marr, *A History of Modern Britain* (London: Pan Books, 2007), pp. 225ff; Dominic Sandbrook, *White Heat: A History of Britain in the Swinging Sixties* (London: Abacus, 2009).
21 See also Roger Opie, 'Economic Planning and Growth', in W. Beckerman (ed.), *The Labour Government's Economic Record, 1964–70* (London: Duckworth, 1972).
22 Newton, 'The Two Sterling Crises', pp. 87–88.
23 See Ponting, *Breach of Promise*, p. 71.
24 Apart from the well-known Cabinet discussion of the matter in July 1966 it was raised by Wilson himself with representatives of the US government in the late summer of 1965, and discussed by him with Michael Stewart (Secretary of State for Economic

Affairs) early in 1967 and with Barbara Castle (then Minister of Transport) in July 1967; Wilson told her that 'devaluation must be a political issue when it comes: we devalue to preserve our independence'. See Scott Newton, 'The Sterling Devaluation of 1967, the International Economy and Post-war Social Democracy', *The English Historical Review*, vol. CXXV (2010), p. 935.

25   There is no reason to believe that Wilson, who was after all both a former Cabinet Minister with experience of helping to manage a sterling devaluation (in 1949) as well as an ex-civil servant, was unaware of the FU exercise.

26   Michael Stewart, *The Jekyll and Hyde Years: Politics and Economic Policy since 1964* (London: Dent, 1977), pp. 27–29.

27   Alec Cairncross and Barry Eichengreen, *Sterling in Decline: the Devaluations of Sterling 1931, 1949 and 1967* (Oxford: Blackwell, 1983), pp. 164–166. Brittan's diaries, revealed in Middleton, *Inside the Department of Economic Affairs*, provide a vivid illustration of one insider's disillusionment with the progress of the Plan.

28   Newton and Porter, *Modernization Frustrated*, Table 6.1, p. 152.

29   See for example, Stuart Hall, Edward Thompson and Raymond Williams, *New Left: May Day Manifesto* (London: Goodwin Press, 1967). This was republished as a Penguin Special in 1968, edited solely by Raymond Williams, with the amended title of *May Day Manifesto 1968*.

30   Richard Cockett, *Thinking the Unthinkable: Think-Tanks and the Economic Counter-Revolution, 1931–1983* (London: Harper Collins, 1995), ch. 5 and especially pp. 167–181.

31   Catherine Schenk, *The Decline of Sterling: Managing the Retreat of an International Currency 1945–1992* (Cambridge: Cambridge University Press, 2010), figure 7.1, p. 242.

32   Alan S. Milward, *The European Rescue of the Nation-State* (London: Routledge, 2000), p. 389.

33   TNA: PREM 13/866, Lord Kahn's enquiry into the position of sterling, 1964–65, p. 11; statistical table A.

34   This was the Indonesian Confrontation of 1962–66, which involved a successful British-led operation to prevent the destabilization of the new Commonwealth state of Malaysia by the radical nationalist Indonesian government of President Sukarno.

35   Harold Wilson, *Purpose in Politics* (London: Weidenfeld and Nicolson, 1964), p. 209.

36   TNA T267/35, Treasury Historical Memorandum 25, 'International liquidity: an account of the negotiations leading up to the creation of special drawing rights in the International Monetary Fund 1962–1968', pp. 59–60.

37   See Scott Newton, *The Global Economy, 1944–2000. The Limits of Ideology* (London: Hodder Arnold, 2004), pp. 94–95.

38   Ibid., pp. 62–63 and 74–76.

39   TNA PREM13/866, Lord Kahn's Enquiry, p. 5.

40   Frank Tipton and Robert Aldrich, *An Economic and Social History of Europe from 1939 to the Present* (Basingstoke: Macmillan, 1987), p. 145.

41   *The Banker*, 116 (November 1966), pp. 782–785.

42   TNA PREM 13/866, Lord Kahn's Enquiry, p. 9.

43   Ibid., p. 7; Newton, 'The Two Sterling Crises', p. 90.

44   Gianni Toniolo (with the assistance of Piet Clement), *Central Bank Cooperation at the Bank for International Settlements, 1930–1973* (Cambridge: Cambridge University Press, 2005), pp. 391–392.

45   TNA PREM 13/3151, Washington telegrams from Dean to FO, 30 April and 12 May, 1965. In February 1965 the EEC's Committee of Governors began making contingency plans in the event of a sterling devaluation. See Toniolo, *Central Bank Co-operation at the Bank for International Settlements*, p. 392).

46   See for example TNA PREM 13/261, note of a meeting at 10 Downing Street at 10.30 p.m., 24 November 1964.

47   Barbara Castle, *The Castle Diaries 1964–76* (Basingstoke: Macmillan, 1990), pp. 4–5, entry for 28 Jan.1965; Alec Cairncross, *The Wilson Years: A Treasury Diary 1964–69*, (London, 1997), pp. 45–46, entries for 22 March and 5 April 1965.

48 Middleton, *The British Economy since 1945*, table II.3, p. 151.
49 Tomlinson *The Labour Governments, 1964–1970*, 135; Harold Wilson, *The Labour Governments, 1964–1970: a Personal Record* (London: Weidenfeld and Nicolson, 1971), p. 133.
50 TNA CAB 128/39, CC 33(65), 15 July 1965.
51 Richard Crossman, *The Diaries of a Cabinet Minister*, vol. 1: *Minister of Housing 1964–1966* (London: Jonathan Cape, 1975), p. 293, entry for 28 July 1965.
52 Stewart, *The Jekyll and Hyde Years*, p. 54.
53 Ponting, *Breach of Promise*, pp. 83–84; Middlemas, *Power, Competition and the State*, vol. 2: Threats to the Post-war Settlement 1961–74 (Basingstoke: Macmillan, 1990), pp. 117, 137–138.
54 Cairncross and Eichengreen, *Sterling in Decline*, p. 178.
55 *Foreign Relations of the United States (hereafter FRUS) 1964–68*, XII, doc. 250, report from Ball, 10 September 1965, http://history.state.gov/historicaldocuments/frus1964-68v12/d250 (accessed 2 April 2017).
56 Saki Dockrill, *Britain's Retreat from East of Suez: The Choice between Europe and the World* (Basingstoke: Macmillan, 2002), pp. 216–217; O'Hara, 'Dynamic, Exciting, Thrilling Change', pp. 275–276.
57 Sandbrook, *White Heat*, p. 628.
58 Henry Pelling, *A Short History of the Labour Party*, 5th edition (Basingstoke: Macmillan, 1976), p. 146.
59 See Nick Tiratsoo, 'Management Education in Post-war Britain', in L. Engwall and V. Zamagni, *Management Education in Historical Perspective* (Manchester: Manchester University Press, 1998).
60 Peter Dorey, 'Education, Education, Education', in Dorey, *The Labour Governments 1964–1970*, p. 278.
61 TNA PREM 13/851 'An Economic Strategy for Britain', summary and comment by Balogh, 28 January 1966.
62 R. Price, 'Budgetary Policy', in Frank Blackaby (editor), *British Economic Policy, 1960–74* (Cambridge: Cambridge University Press, 1978), p. 152; and TNA PREM 13/852, 'The Causes of the Low Rate of Manufacturing Growth in Britain' (undated and unsigned, but probably by Kaldor, March 1966).
63 Tomlinson, *The Labour Governments, 1964–1970*, pp. 132–133 and 225–226.
64 The Bank for International Settlements (BIS), *37th Annual Report* (1967), p. 49.
65 TNA T318/137, Cromer to Callaghan, 15 June 1966.
66 Wilson, *The Labour Governments, 1964–1970*, p. 229.
67 *The Times*, 14 July 1966, 1, col. A, 'Bank Rate May Rise Today'.
68 TNA T295/904, Kahn, 'Enquiry', pp. 21–22.
69 Callaghan addressing a meeting of the Ministers and Governors of the Group of Ten, 25 July 1966, and PM to Cabinet, 20 July 1966: TNA T318/103 and TNA CAB 128/41, CM (66) 38, respectively.
70 TNA T318/103, 'Note by the Treasury: Revised Forecasts to the End of 1967', 25 July 1966.
71 *The Times*, 21 July 1966, 'Europe Welcomes New Measures', 18, col. F.
72 *The Times*, 23 July 1966, 'Better Day for the Pound', 17, col. C.
73 Middlemas, *Power, Competition and the State*, vol. 2, p. 145.
74 George Brown, *In my Way* (London: Gollancz, 1971), pp. 115–116.
75 Tony Benn, *Out of the Wilderness: Diaries 1963–67* (London: Arrow, 1988), p. 457, entry for 19 July; Crossman, *Diaries of a Cabinet Minister*, vol. 1, pp. 571–573, entries for 17 and 18 July.
76 Castle, *The Castle Diaries*, p. 76, entry for 19 July.
77 Cecil King, *The Cecil King Diaries 1965–70* (London: Jonathan Cape, 1972), p. 79, entry for 16 July 1966; Stewart, *The Jekyll and Hyde Years*, p. 74.
78 Middleton *The British Economy since 1945*, p. 89; Newton and Porter, *Modernization Frustrated*, p. 154; Tomlinson *The Labour Governments, 1964–1970*, p. 54.

79 TNA T312/1635, 'Accompanying Measures', draft by Godley and Atkinson, 22 August 1966.
80 *The Times*, 'IMF Aid for Sterling', 15 May 1967, 21, col. B.
81 *The Times*, 'Good Reasons for Bank Rate Cut', 5 May 1967, 23, col. A.
82 Tomlinson, *The Labour Governments, 1964–1970*, Table 10.3, p. 221.
83 Middlemas, *Power, Competition and the State*, vol. 2, p. 165.
84 Helen Parr, *Britain's Policy towards the European Community: Harold Wilson and Britain's World Role, 1964–1967* (Abingdon: Routledge, 2005), p. 86.
85 Helen Parr and Melissa Pine, 'Policy towards the European Economic Community', in Dorey, *The Labour Governments 1964–1970*, pp. 112, 114.
86 *The Times*, 'Calmer Waters for Britain, Says OECD', by Frances Cairncross, 24 July 1967, 8, col. A.
87 BIS, *38th Annual Report* (Basle 1968), p. 45.
88 Ibid., p. 47.
89 Ibid., pp. 5–6 and p. 91.
90 Wilson, *The Labour Governments, 1964–1970*, p. 400; A. P. Thirlwall, *Balance of Payments Theory and the United Kingdom Experience* (Basingstoke: Macmillan, 1986), p. 186.
91 Cairncross and Eichengreen, *Sterling in Decline*, p. 193.
92 Wilson, *The Labour Governments, 1964–1970*, p. 453.
93 See Scott Newton, 'The Sterling Devaluation of 1967, the International Economy and Post-War Social Democracy', *The English Historical Review*, vol. CXXV, no. 515 (2010), pp. 912–945.
94 Peter Jay, 'OECD Urges Jenkins to Make Sharp Increases in Tax Rates', *The Times*, 8 March 1968, p. 17, col. B.
95 Tom Clark and Andrew Dilnot, 'Long-Term Trends in British Taxation and Spending', *The Institute for Fiscal Studies*, Briefing Note No. 25 (London, 2002), p. 4. General government revenue is composed of all sources of taxation. It therefore includes corporate as well as personal taxation, revenue from import charges and the proceeds of social security contributions.
96 Newton and Porter, *Modernization Frustrated*, pp. 155–156.
97 Barbara Castle, *Fighting all the Way* (London: Macmillan, 1993), p. 397.
98 Geoffrey Ingham, *Capitalism Divided: The City and Industry in British Social Development* (London: Macmillan, 1984), pp. 175–181.
99 TNA PREM 13/866, Lord Kahn's Enquiry. It would have been difficult to have found anyone less impressed by old-fashioned Treasury orthodoxy than Lord (Richard) Kahn. He had been a longstanding friend and colleague of J. M Keynes and in 1931 had developed the concept of the multiplier, which was to play a crucial role in the argument made in Keynes's *The General Theory of Employment, Interest, and Money* (1936).
100 Tony Benn, *Office without Power: Diaries 1968–72* (London: Arrow, 1989), p. 136, entry for 15 December 1968.
101 TNA PREM 13/2051, 'Blocking', 17 March 1968. The £2 billion figure was a Bank of England estimate.
102 TNA T312/2549, paper by McMahon on 'The Question of Planning for Floating', 20 December 1967.
103 TNA PREM 13/2051, 'The Consequences of Floating', 16 March 1968.
104 TNA T267/21, 'The Gold Crisis March 1968', p. 19.
105 Scott Newton, 'Sterling, Bretton Woods and Social Democracy, 1968–70', *Diplomacy & Statecraft*, vol. 24 (2013), pp. 427–455.
106 Peter Jay, 'Jenkins to the Rescue', *The Times* 20 March 1968, p. 25, col. C.
107 *The Economist*, 'A Year at $2.40', 16 November 1968.
108 TNA T277/2052, minutes of OECD Working Party 3 meeting held in Paris on 19 December 1968.
109 Middleton, *The British Economy since 1945*, Table II.3, pp. 150–151.
110 Peter Jay, 'UK "No Longer a Problem Country"', *The Times*, 6 March 1970.
111 Newton and Porter, *Modernization Frustrated*, p. 159.

112 Stewart, *The Jekyll and Hyde Years*, p. 117.
113 The argument here follows Newton and Porter, *Modernization Frustrated*, p. 156.
114 Richard Coopey, 'Industrial Policy in the White Heat of the Scientific Revolution', in Richard Coopey, Steven Fielding and Nick Tiratsoo, *The Wilson Governments 1964–1970* (London: Pinter, 1993), p. 113.
115 Edgerton, *Warfare State*, p. 261. It has to be said that Labour had initially wanted to cancel Concorde, but found that the Anglo-French Treaty governing the project was legally impossible to break. See Roy Jenkins, *A Life at the Centre* (London: Macmillan, 1991), pp. 160–166.
116 Benn, *Office without Power*, pp. 51–54, entry for 27 March 1968.
117 Newton and Porter, *Modernization Frustrated*, p. 157.
118 Edgerton, *Warfare State*, pp. 264–265.
119 Coopey, 'Industrial Policy in the White Heat of the Scientific Revolution', p. 114
120 Edgerton, *Warfare State*, pp. 250–251.
121 Coopey, 'Industrial Policy in the White Heat of the Scientific Revolution', p. 120; O'Hara, 'Dynamic, Exciting, Thrilling Change', pp. 383ff.
122 Newton and Porter, *Modernization Frustrated*, pp. 157–158.
123 Dorey, 'Policy for Incomes to Incomes Policies', in Dorey, *The Labour Governments 1964–1970*, pp. 82–89.
124 Dorey, 'Industrial Relations Imbroglio', in Dorey, *The Labour Governments 1964–1970*, p. 94.
125 Peter Jenkins, *The Battle of Downing Street* (London: Charles Knight, 1970), esp. ch. 8; Middlemas, *Power, Competition and the State*, vol. 2, p. 243.
126 Middlemas, *Power, Competition and the State*, vol. 2, p. 253.
127 See Scott Newton, 'Harold Wilson, the Bank of England and the Cecil King "coup" of May 1968', *Lobster*, 56 (2008), pp. 3–8.
128 Tomlinson, *The Labour Governments, 1964–1970*, p. 225.
129 Middlemas, *Power, Competition and the State*, vol. 2, p. 216.

3
QUIET REVOLUTION, 1970–74

Disengagement

Britain in 1970 was commonly regarded as one of the world's leading capitalist economies. Yet it is arguable that the Conservative government which came to power in the summer of 1970 was not taking over a capitalist State. Indeed as early as 1956 Labour's leading theoretician of social democracy, Anthony Crosland, had claimed that major shifts in the political economy of Britain since the mid-1930s had transformed the country to such an extent that it could scarcely be considered 'capitalist' any longer. He had suggested designating the new formulation 'Statism' or 'mixed economy'. To support his case he had pointed to the expansion in the size and functions of the State (concerning its role in managing the economy and its ownership of key industries); the existence of the welfare state and full employment; the much higher rates of income tax paid by the wealthy; the trend towards more equal distribution of income away from property owners; the falling share of wealth accruing to the owners of industrial capital (just 3% of all incomes after tax in 1954); the transfer of power in industry from the owners to professional managers; and controls on bank lending and on the movement of capital. These material changes, which had driven down the rewards to the capitalist class to historically low levels, seemed by the middle of the 1950s to have been accepted (to varying degrees) by both main political parties and therefore to have become permanent. They had led to the withering away of the 'explicit, assertive' ideology of capitalism, based as it had been on the 'veneration of individualism and competition'.[1] By the start of the new decade 'social democracy' seemed as apt a label for Britain as 'mixed economy'.

Despite appearances, Labour's defeat did not herald a fundamental shift away from social democracy. Nor did it mean any weakening in the commitment to modernize Britain embraced by Macmillan eight years earlier.[2] It is, however, reasonable to argue that Edward Heath, the new Conservative Prime Minister, initially employed a different strategy from his predecessor in pursuit of this objective. Heath, supported by CBI leaders and the managerial salariat, argued that the incentives for wealth creation had been crushed by high personal and corporate taxes. Excessive State intervention had entangled firms in red tape. The use of public subventions from bodies such as MinTech and the IRC had diverted resources away from profitable enterprises. A shift to more market-oriented policies than had been customary under Labour was seen to have become necessary. Despite the sudden death of Chancellor of the Exchequer Iain Macleod after a few weeks in office, the Conservatives' first year was characterized by a reforming zeal which recalled Labour's energy in 1964 and 1965. They introduced what Heath, addressing the Tory Conference in October 1970, called a 'quiet revolution'.[3] This amounted to a set of well-prepared policies designed to promote higher growth and industrial modernization. The theme which ran through this process was to be 'disengagement', by which the State would retreat from a number of the functions it had acquired during the 1960s. To this end Macleod's replacement Tony Barber's first Budgets (in October 1970 and March 1971) reduced income and corporation tax and announced the replacement of investment grants by allowances, the termination of SET, the abolition of the NBPI, the scrapping of the IRC and the winding up of MinTech. Labour's public spending plans were scaled down, by £330 million in 1971–72 and rising to £900 million in 1974–75, in a drive to reduce its annual average growth from 3.5 per cent to 2.8 per cent.[4]

The macroeconomic policy changes were accompanied by reforms to the machinery of government. Heath and his colleagues believed that there was scope for slimming down the Whitehall bureaucracy so that government became less expensive and more efficient. To this end, the Department of Trade and Industry (DTI) was established, taking on the functions of MinTech and the Board of Trade; the Ministry of Overseas Trade lost its autonomy and became part of the Foreign Office. The Ministries of Housing and Local Government, Public Buildings and Works and Transport were all subsumed in a new super-Ministry, the Department of the Environment, designed to develop a synoptic approach to housing, town and country planning and transport.[5] These changes were accompanied by the creation of the Central Policy Review Staff (CPRS) within the Cabinet office, reporting to the Prime Minister, and the introduction of Programme Analysis Reviews (PAR), to be managed by a new inter-Ministerial committee.[6] The first of these two new initiatives was to be responsible for long-term strategy and co-ordination of policy across government departments; the second was designed to assess the cost and efficiency of public spending programmes with a view to recommending whether they were value for money.

The last two key reforms in Heath's modernization campaign were entry to the EEC and legislation to reduce trade union power. The former had of course been attempted by Macmillan and Wilson. They had both considered strategic factors, relating to Britain's ability to project its influence in the world, to be as significant as the economic benefits of joining the Common Market. For Heath the emphasis was different. The new Prime Minister had witnessed the rise of Nazism in pre-war Europe and had seen active service on the continent during the 1939–45 conflict. These experiences had led him to the conclusion that Britain could not avoid being engulfed by European crisis and to the belief that his generation of politicians had a duty to ensure that the continent would never again be scarred by the trauma of Fascism and war. He was personally and deeply committed to the view that the new Europe marked a profoundly hopeful development for humanity: a continent where millions had been killed only a few decades earlier was now building the institutions which would guarantee lasting peace and co-operation. Heath was convinced that Britain should join in this process[7] and believed, in addition, that the stimulus of participation within the large European market would be good for industry and growth.

Heath's mission to take Britain into the EEC at last was strongly backed by the corporate interests who supported the new Prime Minister. The combination of Heath's evident commitment to the European project with a new President in France (de Gaulle had resigned late in 1969 and was replaced by the more pro-British Georges Pompidou) led to a successful outcome for Britain's third attempt to enter the Common Market. With formal accession set for the start of 1973, the CBI and both large-scale and medium-sized corporations were strongly attracted by the rewards they believed likely to follow from competing on equal terms with continental firms in a market of 250 million consumers.[8]

The legislation to curb the power of the unions was embodied in the 1971 Industrial Relations Act. This provided the government with the authority to order compulsory ballots before strikes if the proposed industrial action threatened the 'national interest'; established a National Industrial Relations Court (NIRC) with the authority to grant injunctions to prevent damaging strikes and settle disputes; granted unions legal immunities and exemption from potentially crippling fines imposed by the NIRC if they signed up to a Register of recognised trade unions; and declared the closed shop unlawful.[9] On the surface the Act seems far removed from 'disengagement', but Heath saw it as central to the shift of macroeconomic policy away from the interventionism of Labour. Its aim was to shift the balance of power on the factory floor back towards management after the labour unrest of the later 1960s. Two results were expected to follow. First, more industrial discipline would mean fewer strikes and therefore more investment. Secondly, the Act would lead to responsible trade union behaviour, facilitating in turn co-operation with government and the employers on productivity improvement, organization and pay.[10] Incomes policies would become unnecessary: the State could step away from interference with the collective bargaining process and leave the unions and management to undertake it within the new legal framework.

The 'disengagement' project had been worked out during the period since the 1966 election, but it became associated with a special moment: a meeting of leading Conservatives, including much of the Shadow Cabinet, at the Selsdon Park Hotel in London one weekend in January 1970. Much of the discussion centred on the questions of tax cuts, pensions, welfare spending, immigration controls, and law and order. The conclusions were not intended to set out a bold new departure in Conservative thinking; rather, they reflected policy developments over the previous four years. All the same, the conference was the subject of an unexpectedly large amount of press attention and in a hurried statement afterwards the Conservatives laid some emphasis on their willingness to take tough steps to deal with crime[11] along with the setting of a 'framework for an economy regulated by the market'.[12] This led Harold Wilson to claim that the Conservatives had veered sharply to the Right and abandoned their commitment to the post-war state. He invented the term 'Selsdon Man' to describe the modern Conservatives, echoing the sobriquet of the prehistoric 'Piltdown Man'. It proved to be rather a successful attempt to depict the Conservatives as having turned their backs on twentieth-century social democracy in favour of 'a system of society for the ruthless and the pushing, the uncaring…(the) message to the rest is: you're out on your own'.

Many commentators have argued that Edward Heath's brand of Conservatism did indeed seek to roll back the years to a time when capitalists enjoyed higher rewards than in the post-1945 era. They were joined by many Conservatives, who wore Wilson's insult as a badge of honour. The free market think tank, the Institute for Economic Affairs (IEA), which had a number of supporters on the Tory Right, genuinely believed that the new administration would break with the postwar consensus and promote the politics and philosophy of economic liberalism.[13] And certainly, in 1970–71, the government's rhetoric and conduct did nothing to dispel the impression that its 'quiet revolution' involved the replacement of the postwar settlement with a radical free market agenda. John Davies, former Director-General of the CBI and now Secretary of State at the DTI, explained in November 1970 that the new government intended 'to gear its policies to the great majority of people, who are not "lame ducks", who do not need a hand, who are quite capable of looking after their own interests'. The implication was clear: the Conservatives would not use public funds to support failing concerns and rejected universal benefits.

The government showed its willingness to allow market forces a greater role in industrial policy than Labour when Davies refused to follow Labour's example of supporting ailing shipbuilding concern Upper Clyde Shipbuilders (UCS). Davies did not consider that UCS was receiving enough business to be viable. Though thousands of jobs on Clydeside were at stake, he refused to extend credits to ship owners intending to place orders for the construction of ships by UCS.[14] The Cabinet stood firm, with some success, against pay claims in the public sector even when (as in the case of a dispute with the postmen) there was widespread public support for the action. Meanwhile admission charges were introduced for museums and art galleries. Charges for school meals, prescriptions and glasses as well as fees for dental treatment were raised. Free school milk was abolished for the over sevens, resulting in Education Secretary Margaret Thatcher being dubbed 'milk snatcher' by angry parents and teachers. It all seemed to amount to a significant break with the recent past; Crosland, writing in early 1971, argued that the 'new

Conservative government is showing itself the most ideological and reactionary right-wing government that Europe has seen in two decades'.[15]

In fact, both the government's more ideological supporters and its opponents on the Left were wrong to assume that Heath was leading Britain away from social democracy. The new Prime Minister was a committed supporter of the post-war settlement. His intention was not to sweep it away but to modernize it through an injection of more 'enterprise and efficiency into the economy'[16] so that it delivered the economic growth which would permit rising living standards and full employment to continue along with generous public funding for education, housing, health, and the social services.[17] Heath did not favour a move to the free market in industrial policy any more than he wished to undermine the unions and restore managerial authority to pre-1939 levels. The government remained committed to the NEDC and to indicative planning. Heath saw the trade unions as 'an estate of the realm with which co-operation was both desirable and necessary'.[18] He believed that the unions would come to see the Industrial Relations Act as a benevolent reform which strengthened the authority of the paid trade union official and gave workers the legal right to join a union and take strike action.[19] It was in fact intended to entrench consensus between both sides of industry not undermine it. Heath's willingness (and that of colleagues such as Davies) to use abrasive rhetoric and at times act in a confrontational manner (as in the case of the postal workers), along with his readiness to accept the 'Selsdon' label, was a serious tactical error, as he later recognised.[20] By the time the limitations of the disengagement strategy became apparent during 1971–72 an entirely misleading image of the Prime Minister had gained currency not just on the Left but in the Centre of British politics. In doing so it had alienated the very people and institutions, notably the TUC leadership and the trade unions, whose co-operation were to prove essential to the government's success.

U-turn

The year 1971 was one of crisis for the disengagement strategy. It did not survive. It was undermined by a combination of disappointing industrial output and rising joblessness. The impact of Barber's October 1970 Budget had been broadly neutral, with the reductions to public spending projections being offset by the tax cuts.[21] Aiming to hit a growth rate of 3 per cent, a level in line with Labour's projections for sustainable growth in *The Task Ahead*, the Chancellor did not deviate far from this path in his March 1971 Budget. Further tax changes did little to stimulate demand but tended to favour the top 5 per cent of income earners.[22] The government was initially relaxed about the jobless figures, despite the fact that they had grown from 2.6 per cent of the workforce (600,000) at the end of 1970 and to 2.9 per cent by March.[23] Its attitude shifted, however, as the rising trend continued. By July the figure was 3.5 per cent (800,000), a post-war high. Concern about unemployment was reinforced by evidence that output in the first half of 1971 was 1 per cent lower than the Treasury had estimated; by the end of the year it had risen only 2 per cent over its level in December 1970. The growth of slack in the economy came as a surprise; in retrospect it seems initially to have been a function of Labour's squeeze on consumption to make room for investment in production for exports. The problem was that these stalled during 1971 (an experience shared by several other advanced industrial States at the time) therefore generating only very modest expansion.[24]

The government showed its true colours in its response to the faltering growth. Despite the Selsdon rhetoric it was committed to Keynesian political economy and Conservative social democracy. Heath had been arguing for action since the spring of 1971. By early summer Barber, initially sanguine about the prospects for the economy, had concluded that the combination of spare capacity with the large external surplus inherited from Labour left scope for a stimulus. Over the next eighteen months a series of measures were introduced to promote expansion, embracing credit, taxation, public spending, and external economic policy. The Bank Rate was lowered from 7 per cent to 5 per cent between April and September (this meant that the real rate was negative given that the Retail Price Index (RPI) providing a measure of inflation was running at an annual rate of 9 per cent by late 1971) and all hire purchase controls were abolished in July.[25] That month a mini-Budget saw the government exchange its objective of 3 per cent growth for one of 4.5 per cent. To this end purchase tax was cut by 20 per cent, investment allowances increased and extra funding promised for regions where unemployment was especially high. Further reductions in income and purchase tax followed in the 1972 Budget, and the growth target was revised, this time up to 5 per cent. The looser fiscal stance was accompanied by new public spending projections. A White Paper of November 1971 revealed these were to be £500 million above those announced in January but they were increased further in 1972 by £1.2 billion (which meant a 4 per cent rise above the total figure set out in the November 1971 spending programme).[26]

The government's change of course led to some anxieties on the foreign exchange markets and in June 1972 these intensified: a large capital outflow developed as a result of poor trade figures and nagging concern about the UK's relatively high rate of inflation. Heath and Barber's response was to float sterling, an initiative facilitated by the floating of the dollar in response to speculative attacks and the deepening of the US deficit in 1970–71. It was clear that the government was not going to follow Labour's example and downgrade its growth target for the sake of the balance of payments and exchange rate stability: it allowed sterling to float down against a basket of other currencies by 15 per cent over the subsequent eighteen months.[27] The commitment to expansion seemed absolute.

Although Heath and Barber had (for now) removed the external constraint on expansion they shared the anxieties about inflation which had become evident in the markets.[28] Wage rates rose by 12 per cent in 1971 and in 1972 this figure approached 15 per cent.[29] These and other costs were likely to escalate as spare capacity in the economy shrank, a trend which the falling pound would certainly intensify given its implications for the price of imported goods. The logic of Selsdon

Man, in so far as he had ever existed, dictated bearing down on inflation by reducing demand: cuts in public spending and tighter credit. This was evidently out of the question. It left one option: a return to a prices and incomes policy. The fate of the NBPI notwithstanding, Heath now attempted to put back together the producers' alliance or 'grand bargain' between employers, unions and government which had, for a time, marked Labour's period in office.

Heath was confident he would be able to gain the agreement of both sides of industry to a voluntary policy but the Industrial Relations Act proved to be an insuperable stumbling block. The problem was that the government was distrusted by organized labour, which saw the Act, along with the abrasive rhetoric which had marked Heath's first year in office, as indicative of a desire to destroy the power of the trade union movement. There were massive demonstrations against the Bill. Once it became law many unions embarked on a strategy of non-co-operation by refusing to sign up to the Register of recognised trade unions. This was not at all an encouraging background to Heath's efforts to restore tripartite co-operation but the Prime Minister made a genuine effort to establish partnership with the TUC. A bitter dispute between the National Union of Mineworkers (NUM) and the National Coal Board (NCB) in the winter of 1971–72, reaching a climax when flying pickets prevented deliveries from entering the Saltley coke depot, led some in the Cabinet to fear class war and social breakdown.[30] The episode however reinforced Heath's determination to find a consensual way of resolving pay issues. He was impressed by the results, in terms of industrial harmony, economic growth and inflation, of the regular round-table consultations with the unions held by West German Social Democratic Chancellor Willy Brandt. He embarked on a search to establish a similar practice in the UK, one which would leave the British unions with 'an acknowledged role in the running of the economy'.[31]

By the autumn of 1972 Heath was offering 5 per cent growth, measures to help the low paid and pensioners, price controls and subsidies for nationalized industries in exchange for agreement to a £2 per week pay increase across the board. The TUC leadership were impressed by Heath's commitment to reaching common ground with the unions; he gained personal respect from them and in return found them more sympathetic and congenial personal and political company than many of the employers. TGWU General Secretary Jack Jones later commented (writing in 1986) that no Prime Minister before or since had tried harder 'to establish camaraderie with trade union leaders and to offer an attractive package which might satisfy large numbers of work-people'.[32] Yet the grand bargain remained elusive, partly because the government would not repeal the Industrial Relations Act (though it offered concessions) and because the experience of 1964–70 had resulted in disillusionment with any form of institutionalized pay policy, a development the Labour opposition now turned to its advantage. At the same time that Heath was holding out the prospect of partnership the Shadow Cabinet was offering the unions a 'Social Contract', whereby Labour promised joint consultation on economic policy, food subsidies, a freeze on rent increases and, most important, the repeal of the Industrial Relations

Act. In return the TUC would agree to persuade its members to accept voluntary wage restraint.[33] This was more attractive than anything Heath could offer unless he proposed concessions so sweeping that he would forfeit the support of the CBI (and much of the Cabinet).

Thwarted in his bid for trade union consent, Heath introduced a statutory prices and incomes policy on 6 November. Policed by a Pay Board and Price Commission (the NBPI by other means), this was to remain in place until the government left office. Though there had been no overt deal between the government and the TUC, there was certainly informal co-operation. The pay policy actually worked reasonably smoothly up to late 1973, when it was challenged by the NUM and the train drivers' union ASLEF.[34] The unions' willingness to pursue informal co-operation with the government was enhanced by a dramatic shift in its industrial strategy. Here, just as in macroeconomic policy, 'disengagement' was abandoned. It was replaced by a highly interventionist approach, set out in the 1972 Industry Act. This change of course had been in the making for some time. The first signs had been evident early in 1971, when it became apparent that Rolls Royce was in serious difficulty. The costs of developing the RB 211 engine, notwithstanding the assistance already provided by Labour, had far exceeded the price agreed with Lockheed in the contract, with the result that the company was facing bankruptcy. Given that Rolls Royce was a major employer at the cutting edge of technological innovation and produced advanced engines for civil and military airlines (and shipping) throughout the world, it was decided not to let market forces do their worst. Rather than accept the consequences of closure for British jobs and export markets, not to mention the smaller industrial concerns dependent on Rolls Royce, the government opted to nationalize it, with the DTI providing funds to meet the losses on development and production of the RB211 series. It was the first new act of public ownership since the time of the Attlee Government.[35]

A similar set of circumstances surrounded UCS, which entered receivership in July 1971. A work-in, led by the shop stewards, followed. Aware that the provision of finance for UCS would be 'contrary to the Government's general industrial policy', the Cabinet nevertheless agreed to work with management and the unions to reconstruct (and rationalize) the company. This was another repudiation of the 'no lame ducks' policy, driven on this occasion by concern about the scale of unemployment likely to result from closure. The Cabinet drew back from risking the consequences, in terms both of personal hardship to the workers and their families and of the possibility that social unrest (driven, it was feared, by trade union militancy) might engulf the area.[36] UCS was split into two new concerns, Govan Shipbuilders and Scotstoun Marine, both being launched in February 1972. They were backed by substantial public investment, amounting to £20 million by the time the government left office.[37]

By late 1971, the crises at Rolls Royce and at UCS, along with mounting unemployment (which peaked at 1 million early in the New Year) and sluggish industrial output in comparison with the annual rate of 4 per cent achieved by Britain's neighbours on the continent, had all convinced Heath and senior colleagues that disengagement was not working. With not much more than a year to go before the UK joined the EEC it seemed evident that British firms were not in good enough shape to perform well in competition with their rivals in the Six. Heath started to be critical of employers and managers, claiming that the government had delivered what they had been requesting when the Conservatives had been in opposition.[38] It was now their turn to create a competitive climate in British industry. They were failing to do this: in consequence the government needed to intervene directly. In November 1971 Heath established a policy review led by Sir William Armstrong (Head of the Civil Service) to outline the steps 'and executive machinery required to bring about the necessary changes in the country's regional and national economic structures, modernise British industry...and also re-establish full employment and put the economy on a path to sustained growth'.[39] The recommendations led to the passage of the Industry Act in May 1972. The Act marked a return to the more dirigiste approach of Labour. The DTI was given the power and funding to act as a rival to the Treasury, becoming a Ministry for the promotion of industrial modernization, just as the DEA and MinTech had been. An Industrial Development Executive was established. The Secretary of State was given the power to provide selective financial assistance to any industry or firm if such action was considered to be in the national economic interest. The Act provided tax incentives for investment and regional development grants for depressed areas. There was to be an infrastructural investment programme embracing road building, large-scale construction projects such as a third airport for London (abandoned in 1974 in the wake of the oil crisis), a Thames Barrier (completed in 1982) and the upgrading of ports.[40] It was estimated that these wide-ranging measures would cost £1.9 billion.[41]

Heath liked to claim that his policies were simply 'a sensible, pragmatic and practical response to a disappointing state of affairs'[42] but they were seen at the time as a dramatic U-turn and indicative (along with the incomes policy and Heath's efforts to establish a partnership with the unions) of an increasingly close rapprochement between modern Conservatism and social democracy. Unsurprisingly, therefore, the Act was greeted with dismay by the Right of the Conservative Party, which had never lived comfortably with the post-war settlement, as a Conservative's April 1964 articles in *The Times* had shown. This constituency saw the Act as a betrayal and established a 'Selsdon Group', embracing backbenchers, peers and Party activists beyond Westminster. As its name suggests, the Group was dedicated to what it believed to be the government's original mission and policies and campaigned within the Party for its conversion to the political economy of free enterprise. Initially, notwithstanding some sympathetic publicity, the Group had little impact, but it became increasingly attractive to those who saw the Heath government's journey as characteristic of a process by which each Tory government moved 'twice as far towards the Socialist millennium as its Labour predecessor'.[43]

Whirlpool

The results of Heath and Barber's new strategy were on the face of it very encouraging, perhaps one reason why Right wing dissent from the government's policies failed to gain backing from the rest of the Conservative Party. In 1973 the economy grew at an annual rate of almost 6 per cent while industrial production rose by 9 per cent. Unemployment fell steadily, back down to 500,000. The rate of expansion exceeded what both the preceding Conservative and Labour administrations thought sustainable. This led *The Times* (among others) to express some anxiety about output exceeding capacity, with serious consequences for inflation and the external balance.[44] The CBI and leading economists however commended the government: Professors James Ball (London Business School) and Robin Matthews (Oxford University) celebrated that 'we now have a major opportunity to run the economy over the next five years at full employment, exploiting the real underlying growth of potential output of which we are capable'.[45] Yet there were mounting problems beneath the surface. In late 1973 and early 1974 these combined with an unforeseen external shock and derailed the government's bid for high and smooth growth. In doing so they posed a major challenge to British social democracy.

A clue to the underlying problems of the economy could be found in the relative levels of net investment both within and outside industry. Between 1970 and 1973 this dropped from an annual rate of 6.2 per cent to 3.6 per cent within industry but outside (including investment by the public authorities) rose from 19.4 per cent to 24.8 per cent.[46] The figures were certainly evidence of expansion but not indicative of the industrial modernization Heath's government was trying to deliver. To some extent they were a function of the Bank rate reductions and abolition of hire purchase controls which had occurred in 1971. But they reflected in large part a property boom which had developed following a major change to the financial system, the Competition and Credit Control (CCC) measures, introduced in 1971. Heath had hoped that the reform would encourage competition between banks, stimulating an expansion of credit for industry and the development of the closer relationship between bank capital and industrial enterprise which was evident in the highly successful West German economy.[47] In reality, however, the CCC changes favoured the interests of the financial system and did nothing to promote industrial modernization.

The reforms stemmed from the frustration of British clearing banks with official regulation of their activities. Since the war the Treasury had maintained ceilings on the size of loans available to private borrowers. The banks had become increasingly restive about this on the grounds that they were prevented from maximizing the profits which could be made through the advancing of credit. These had not been the only restrictions on their independence and indeed they had become informal regulators of the financial system, responsible for much of the administrative machinery behind exchange controls as well as the periodic credit freezes introduced by successive governments to damp down economic activity.[48] Their case for more freedom was pressed on the government by the Bank of England, where the proposals leading to the CCC reforms originated.[49] The key points involved substituting market forces for the ceilings: credit would now be rationed solely by interest rates, in other words on the basis of cost. It would no longer be administratively controlled but would flow freely to the companies and individuals able to pay the highest rate for it. At the same time there was a reduction, from 28 per cent to 12.5 per cent, in the minimum ratio of assets to liabilities banks were required to retain. The Bank of England would replace the Treasury as the key State agency in the credit market, regulating demand for money through manipulation of the Bank Rate, to be known as the Minimum Lending Rate (MLR) from October 1972.[50]

The banks were enthusiastic about the reform. The restriction of their activities under the old system had facilitated the development of an alternative financial market, much of it outside the regulatory authority of the Treasury and the Bank of England, composed of pension funds, building societies,[51] offshore banks (mainly US, dealing in Eurodollars), and fringe, or secondary banks. The secondary banks had grown rapidly in both size and complexity during the 1960s. They tended to be subsidiaries and affiliates of British merchant (and clearing) banks, as well as finance companies whose roots could be located in hire purchase, stock market activity and moneylending, and who were now able to engage in banking following a 1966 legal judgement.[52] They were 'closely related' to City firms, in two ways. First, a large share of their resources was provided by credit from major City banks; and secondly, 'as much as a quarter of the equity of some leading secondary banks' was owned by some of the nation's largest banks and insurance companies such as Barclays, the Crown Agents, Hambros, and the Prudential.[53] CCC's abolition of credit ceilings now liberated the clearing banks to compete freely with the secondary banks in the money markets, and to this end they reorganized, reintegrating subsidiaries they had spun out into the secondary banking system and taking advantage of the opportunity to raise sterling deposits from the wholesale markets[54] without restriction (by 1973 the wholesale markets were accounting for 45 per cent of the London clearing banks' sterling deposits).[55] CCC allowed the banks to commence a transformation from their traditional role as retail bankers lending to individuals and small businesses into 'multinational financial institutions marketing a wide variety of financial instruments'[56] to corporate, domestic and international customers. They did not hesitate to take advantage of the new freedom.

The impact of CCC on the financial system and the economy in general was explosive. Low and negative real interest rates (the MLR hovered between 7.25 and 8 per cent for most of the period between October 1972 and late July 1973, while the RPI was rising towards an annual rate of 10 per cent) combined with liberalization of credit ceilings and competition between banks to cause a dramatic surge in lending. Between the start of CCC in September 1971 and December 1973 sterling bank advances in the UK grew by a factor of 2.5, the greater part of these going as lending to property companies and to financial concerns, many of them in the secondary market.[57] The lending fed a 70 per cent rise in house prices in the two years following the CCC reforms. Property was an attractive hedge against inflation and a source of large and rapid speculative profit; it is perhaps not surprising that between 1970 and 1973 investment in property and in new plant and equipment grew by 83 per cent and 25 per cent respectively.[58] The figures reflected heavy borrowing by the secondary banks to fund investment in the property market so that they could take advantage of asset price rises sufficiently large and rapid to both facilitate payment of debt and a good return.

Clearly, the fastest growing sector in the economy at this time was the financial one. This was not a temporary development. The relatively generous rewards being earned by property development and financial speculation were indicative of more profound politico-economic shifts. For a start, the rate of profit in British industry had generally been less than in other advanced industrial societies throughout the 1960s. By the early 1970s it was lower than at any time since 1945[59] and therefore CCC's freeing up of the financial system was unlikely to deliver a flow of capital favouring manufacturing. Secondly, CCC reflected the resurgence of the City after a long period during which its activities had been subordinated to the macroeconomic priorities of successive governments. Pressure for change from within the Square Mile had been reinforced by the increasing freedom of international trade and finance since the later 1950s, a process especially notable in the foreign currency and capital markets.

These markets had of course experienced the dramatic expansion of the trade in Eurodollars (see chapter 2), a development which had swollen the volume of available funds in the City. As this offshore dollar liquidity grew it helped to finance the US deficit; after March 1973, when the Bretton Woods system of fixed exchange rates was replaced by generalized floating, it was used by a growing number of countries to finance external deficits, a trend which 'opened enormous markets for bank capital'.[60] Even industrial firms now turned to the financial markets to protect their reserves from fluctuating currency values and invest in assets with a high rate of return (particularly property). The Eurodollar market in London took the lead in these activities, much of it conducted by international consortia (whose numbers grew from 10 in 1969 to 117 by 1974).[61] The growth of the financial sector was most obvious in the UK but similar, if less spectacular, developments could be seen in Western Europe and the USA. Income derived from financial and property transactions began to account for a rising share of all profits; the post-war trend to 'the euthanasia of the rentier', a development seen as desirable by Keynes,[62] had started to go into reverse. The shifting nature of international capitalism in turn both reinforced the pressure for liberalization from within the City, traditionally closely geared to the global economy, and gave extra fuel to the revival of liberal political economy already evident in Conservative Party circles linked not just to banking but small business and property ownership.[63]

The property boom was evidence that the simultaneous expansion of private consumption, public spending and investment was producing unsustainable growth, the optimism of Ball and Matthews notwithstanding. By the summer of

1973 the annual rate of inflation was exceeding 10 per cent. The growing domestic market sucked in imports, increasing in volume by 27 per cent between 1971 and 1973. The result was a marked deterioration in the balance of payments, which swung from a surplus of £1 billion in 1971 to an annualized deficit of £750 million in mid-1973. This worsened further during the course of 1973 as the prices of imported food and raw materials rose in response to high global demand. The experience of Maudling's dash for growth was being repeated. This time the impact on inflation and the current account was to be vastly more dramatic; during the first quarter of 1974 the RPI rose over 13 per cent while the external deficit reached an annual rate of £3.3 billion (over 4 per cent of GDP), its plunge into the red being intensified by the quadrupling of the oil price as a result of the October 1973 Arab-Israeli war. By the spring of 1974 it was running at an annual rate of £3.6 billion.[64]

Responding to the economic indicators, Sir Leslie O'Brien, an increasingly anxious Governor of the Bank of England, argued in the summer of 1973 that MLR should rise in order to restrain the demand for credit in accordance with the rules of the game according to CCC. Heath, determined to press on with his modernization strategy, initially resisted. He reiterated the commitment to 5 per cent growth and expressed a determination to 'swim through the whirlpool'.[65] Finally, however, the government agreed to a series of increases which took the MLR up to 11.5 per cent at the end of July and 13 per cent in November. By December it was retreating from its previous expansionism in an attempt to cut demand (and therefore the climbing external deficit): a mini-Budget announced a £1.2 billion cut in the public spending projections for 1974–75, the reintroduction of hire purchase controls, increases in taxation (including surtax) and a new levy on development gains from the sale of land and buildings.[66]

The government hoped these measures, targeted on speculation and escalating property prices, would rebalance activity in the direction of investment in industry and production for the export market. The problem was that by now many fringe banks in particular had allowed themselves to become so heavily indebted in order to take advantage of the property boom that only modest rises in the cost of borrowing were likely to provoke liquidity problems. The warning signals were the suspension of share dealings in the London and County Securities Group and then Cedar Holdings in November and December 1973 respectively. A scramble for cash began as creditors sought to recover their money. Activity stalled and asset prices began to tumble, leading to further liquidity problems for financial institutions which now saw the prospect of windfall gains evaporating. It became clear that a significant number were facing embarrassment. The Bank of England was forced to launch its 'lifeboat', a rescue effort co-ordinated with the clearing banks. At the time the magnitude of this operation was downplayed but subsequently it became clear that by March 1975 the funds advanced under this initiative amounted to £3 billion.[67] The process was accompanied by significant changes of ownership in the rescued concerns, many being taken over by the clearing banks at very low prices.[68]

Liberalization of the banking system, fiscal expansion and cheap money had combined with the increasing volume and instability of the financial markets to produce London's most serious crash since 1914. This outcome was indicative of a shift in the economic terrain away from the post-war variant of capitalism. The certainties of the post-war mixed economy were starting to be eroded by developments which threatened the ability of the modern nation-State to subordinate the activities of the financial and credit markets to the overriding commitment to growth, full employment and price stability. 'Selsdon Man' had quickly been replaced by the social democratic manager and planner but this had not prevented the eruption of a destabilizing speculative boom. Moreover, though the bust of 1973–74 was highly unwelcome to the government and its supporters in industry and commerce, the conditions which led to it did not generate such opprobrium. Within both the Conservative Party and the private sector of the economy both CCC and the deeper shifts from which it sprang had revealed deep-rooted support inside what appeared to be the most dynamic and unstable sector of the economy for a return to the *laissez-faire* values Crosland had thought to be defunct. Capital had begun its transition – its return – to a version more close to the one identified and examined by Marx a century before, one dominated by the search for profit.[69]

Breakdown

By late 1973 the economy was under pressure from inflation, the deteriorating current account and a looming financial crisis. Some commentators began to query the continuing viability of the post-war settlement.[70] These doubts were amplified within the Conservative Party and the financial system on the part of the Selsdon Group, the IEA and among Enoch Powell and his supporters. Here, scepticism about the feasibility of a macroeconomic strategy based on two interconnected trade-offs,[71] one between full employment and price stability and the other between growth and external equilibrium, had been longstanding. The first of these trade-offs had been based on the 'Phillips curve', namely the apparent inverse relationship between inflation and unemployment identified by the New Zealand economist William Phillips in the late 1950s. Successive governments had fine-tuned demand to buy more jobs at the expense of higher prices, deploying prices and incomes policies to keep these from contributing to an escalating cost of living. The second had caused governments to rein in expansionary policies designed to stimulate national output if this had risen beyond a figure consistent with capacity, on the grounds that failure to do so led to a surge in imports. Critics of this orthodoxy had long doubted the lasting validity of the Phillips curve, arguing that the maintenance of full employment appeared sustainable only at the price of increasingly high rates of inflation (see chapter 1). Now they were also able to claim that, given the evidence provided by the current account figures for 1972–73, it appeared that a drive for growth above what were regarded at the time (in both major Parties) as the relatively modest levels achieved by Labour led to a sharp and severe deterioration in the external balance.[72]

The Powellites argued for an alternative strategy, more compatible (they said) with true Conservatism, based on a return to *laissez-faire* capitalism and focused on the control of inflation. The proponents of this thinking now derived support from the work of the Chicago-based academic economist Milton Friedman, who argued that the manipulation of demand to sustain high levels of employment merely led employers and workers to anticipate rising prices. The result was wage agreements which, in being concluded at or slightly over the cost of living, did indeed cause full or high levels of employment to occur only at increasing annual rates of inflation. To overcome this problem it was necessary for governments to adopt a new approach to the management of the economy. Instead of seeking to preserve full employment governments should aspire to control the rate of inflation, a problem they could attack at its root by an approach known as 'monetarism'. This involved regulation of the money supply so that it never exceeded the real growth potential of the economy.[73] Friedman claimed there was a correlation between expansion of the money supply beyond this limit and an accelerating rate of inflation. Governments had it in their power to remedy this situation, since it stemmed from their commitment to sustaining full employment levels of demand. This is what had led them to the profligate printing of money to fund their own excessive borrowing, over-generous wage settlements and companies which would otherwise go bankrupt.

The appeal of monetarism lay in its simplicity and in its political implications: the money supply appeared to be one variable which governments could control. Targeting inflation in this manner would make deals with the unions unnecessary. The interventionism of the post-1945 era was no longer required or feasible (if it ever had been); only the free market could now salvage stable prices and its corollary of social and political stability. Friedman and the economic liberals on the Right now called for a cut to the State's range of activities, leading to a reduction in its share of GDP, on the grounds this was now a strategy of necessity as much as one of choice. Lower public spending, falling taxation, and greater incentives for industry (so it was argued) would be translated into higher investment in products wanted by the market, leading to sustainable growth.[74] The new thinking drew sympathy from beyond the circle of think tanks, economists and ideologues where it had been incubating. It attracted sections of the CBI and the Chambers of Commerce, not only among small businesses, where State interventionism had never been popular,[75] but even from some larger firms such as GEC and Guest, Keen and Nettlefolds (GKN). Here, frustration with what was seen as government *dirigisme* was growing, along with concern that, the Industrial Relations Act notwithstanding, the willingness of Heath and his colleagues to accommodate the TUC was driving the balance of power in industry further and further towards the trade unions.[76]

At this stage neither the majority of mainstream economists nor Heath nor most of the Cabinet were impressed. Most of the former doubted whether there was a clear chain of causality between money supply and the general price level.[77] These misgivings were shared by the Prime Minister, who remained committed to Conservative social democracy. He viewed arguments for embracing a more radical version of disengagement as siren calls whose pursuit would lead to confrontation with the unions, mass unemployment and class war, outcomes he found distasteful on pragmatic and philosophical grounds. Even by the autumn of 1973 he had not abandoned his 5 per cent growth target and aimed to reconcile this with the restraint of inflation and full employment through his incomes policy.

The result of Heath's commitment to a corporatist solution to the economic crisis was Stage Three of the incomes policy. Heath again tried to win trade union support for a voluntary approach. The TUC, notwithstanding the 'social contract', genuinely attempted to find common ground with the government but the Industrial Relations Act continued to be the main obstacle to agreement.[78] The government would not resile from it, even though senior members of the CBI such as Director-General Campbell Adamson had come to regard the Act as counterproductive. In consequence the government imposed Stage Three in October 1973 and hoped that its provisions would lead to union acquiescence. It allowed for an average increase of 8 per cent in pay, the pill being sweetened for the TUC by price controls, a 5 per cent limit on dividends and the introduction of threshold increases. The latter were designed to damp down the impact of inflationary expectations on pay claims by providing for wages to increase automatically in line with prices if the latter rose by more than 7 per cent.[79] By December 1973 over four million workers had settled within Stage Three, fuelling Heath's optimism that his pursuit of consensus was working.[80]

Despite these encouraging results, neither the government's determination to stick by the Industrial Relations Act (in the expectation this would keep the CBI onside) nor its very extensive conciliation to the unions succeeded in creating the enduring alliance between government and the peak institutions for which Heath was looking. The government's willingness to impose Stage Three, along with the price and dividend controls, stoked the feelings of alienation developing within the CBI. At the same time it became clear that the pay policy did not command consent across the trade union movement. With food prices rising at an annual rate of 20 per cent and petrol prices escalating fast thanks to the oil price increases, while pay settlements were averaging 13 per cent, there was increasing union anxiety about falling living standards.[81] Some of the more radical union officials claimed that Stage Three, coming after the Industrial Relations Act and the rise of unemployment to 1 million in 1971–72, was yet another example of the government's determination to undermine the power exercised by the working class through its own institutions. In mid-November the NUM started an overtime ban in pursuit of claims in excess of what was allowed under Stage Three.

Within Whitehall anxieties began to develop about whether the nation's coal stocks would last the winter. These intensified when the miners' example was followed by ASLEF. This came as a serious blow to the government since it made impossible the planned movement of coal around the country in response to local shortages.[82] On 13 December Heath announced that a three day week would commence on 1 January, in order to preserve coal stocks. Television broadcasts were to cease at 10.30 p.m. The Festive Season was approaching, but an atmosphere of foreboding and crisis began to spread through industry and the government. Tony Benn noted in his diary, 'Dinner with Wilfred Brown, head of Glacier Metals, who believes we are headed for a slump and food riots'.[83] John Davies, now Chancellor of the Duchy of Lancaster, told his family that 'we should have a nice time, because I deeply believed that it was the last Christmas of its kind we would enjoy'.[84]

Within the Cabinet and the Conservative Party a conviction grew that the unions were being manipulated by Communists intent on bringing down the elected government and replacing it with a compliant Labour regime nominally led by Wilson but in reality controlled by the radical Left and committed to a large-scale extension of public ownership and union-friendly legislation. The scenario was sheer phantasmagoria: neither the NUM General Secretary Joe Gormley – who in fact regularly informed Special Branch about trade union tactics and internal politics[85] – nor the TUC wanted the government to fall. Indeed the TUC, supported by the General Secretaries of affiliated unions, offered Heath a way out of the dispute: arguing that the miners' claim amounted to a special case, it undertook that no other union would take advantage of a settlement between the NUM and the Coal Board which exceeded Stage Three.[86] The Cabinet turned down the proposal on the grounds that it was a propaganda exercise and any deal beyond the terms of Stage Three would show the public that no government could 'withstand the monopoly powers of the unions', render impossible any attempt to construct a 'rational economic policy' and 'strike at the heart of democratic government'.[87] It was a response which led Amalgamated Engineering Workers Union (AEU) President Hugh Scanlon to ask the Prime Minister, rather desperately, 'Is there anything we can do to convince you this is a genuine offer?'[88]

The government's response to the TUC initiative revealed a growing willingness to turn the industrial crisis into a trial of strength for the administration, and by implication for Parliamentary democracy. Colleagues urged Heath to hold a General Election on the theme of 'Who governs Britain?' confident that such a question would elicit a renewed mandate and lead to the ending of the disputes with the NUM and ASLEF within the parameters of Stage Three. Initially reluctant, Heath bowed to the pressure following a vote by the NUM in favour of a national strike, calling an election for 28 February. From the start there was an undertone of mild hysteria about much of the government propaganda, which focused on a 'Communist threat' to the nation and claimed this was located within the trade unions.[89] Some of this rhetoric was doubtless crude electioneering but there is no doubt that in the heat of the crisis some senior Ministers and civil servants lost their balance. At the start of January Heathrow was surrounded by troops and armed police, apparently after information suggested the possibility of a terrorist missile attack on incoming planes, although Tony Benn suspected the real object of the exercise was to accustom the public to the presence of 'tanks and armed patrols on the streets of London'.[90] A denial of the terrorist story by Home Secretary Robert Carr in a private meeting with James Callaghan (Shadow Foreign Secretary) shortly afterwards strengthened Benn's suspicions.[91] MI5 placed Harold Wilson under surveillance.

Cabinet Secretary Sir William Armstrong became obsessed with 'communist infiltrators' and finally experienced complete mental and physical breakdown.[92]

Heath was not averse to using robust rhetoric himself but never intended the 'Who governs Britain' theme to be a stick with which to beat organized labour. His aim was to rally public support for a continuation of his moderate, tripartite approach to government. He grew concerned about the possibility that a conclusive victory for the Conservative Party would encourage its anti-trade union and pro-free market elements to embark on a campaign to roll back the post-war State. In consequence he retreated from the attempt to use the election to create an anti-Communist rassemblement and moved to conciliate the miners. He referred their claim to the Pay Board and gave it the authority to offer them more money, committing the government to acceptance of its decision in the process. At the same time the Prime Minister announced a modest relaxation to the three day week (coal stocks had not run down as far as expected, partly due to a mild winter) and the 10.30 p.m. television curfew was lifted.[93]

These tactics backfired. Many loyal Conservatives were bewildered by the Prime Minister's moves to defuse the crisis. They wondered why the election had been called in the first place. These views were shared by uncommitted voters, especially given the lifeline Heath had been thrown by the TUC. Confusion about the government's intentions was compounded by growing doubts about its competence after information leaked from the Pay Board suggesting that it had overestimated the level of miners' pay from the start of the negotiations. It suffered a further blow when off the record comments by CBI Director-General Campbell Adamson were broadcast on television in the week before polling day, criticizing the Industrial Relations Act as motivated by 'hatred' and calling for its repeal. Then, on 25 February, the January trade figures were released, showing the largest monthly visible trade deficit in British history (£383 million).[94] It all meant that by the time polling day had arrived Labour had turned the question 'Who governs?' against Heath, pointing to rising inflation, financial crisis, the deteriorating external position and pointless confrontation with the unions. Key objectives of the 'quiet revolution', namely industrial modernization, low inflation and a new climate in industrial relations, now seemed further away than they had been in 1970. Between 1970 and 1973 10 million working days had been lost to strikes, more than at any time since the aftermath of the 1914–18 war.[95] In these circumstances it was not surprising that the electorate failed to return the Conservatives to power. There was a hung Parliament with Labour very narrowly the largest party. Harold Wilson formed a minority administration. He was back in office largely thanks to an election strategy which had focused on Labour's highly experienced Ministerial team along with a commitment to settle the miners' strike, end the three day week and return the country to normal through co-operation with the trade unions.

Heath's experiment had been a failure. The combination of financial liberalization with industrial dirigisme had been contradictory; the tendency of the former to fuel inflation and set off a speculative boom and bust had not enhanced the ability of the latter to promote growth on the scale enjoyed by Britain's new partners in the

EEC. Yet the government's problems had not stemmed purely from faulty judgement or bad management. Its trajectory had reflected tensions between its liberal and social democratic tendencies which had been brewing in the Conservative Party since Macmillan's time as Prime Minister. These tendencies in turn stemmed from the historic fracture between Consumer's and Producer's Britain. Given that the first of these two fractions was demonstrating an increasing dynamism and that the Party's roots were located here, it was unlikely that Heath or any subsequent leader would find it straightforward to resolve these tensions on terms congenial to Conservative social democracy. It is not surprising that the election defeat weakened the appeal of his brand of One Nation Toryism within the Party and strengthened the hand of the economic liberals committed to lower taxes, tamed unions and a small State.[96]

The growing interest in economic liberalism on the Right was fuelled by the apparent breakdown of the compromise between capital and labour which had marked the 1944 settlement. This now seemed to have soured into conflict between the contending parties over the distribution of rewards from the surplus. The attractiveness of the *laissez-faire* solution to some on the Right stemmed from a belief that it would be likely to remove the obstacles to greater profitability created by powerful trade unions and high levels of personal and corporate taxation. Its implications for industrial relations, the welfare state and full employment ensured its attractions would stay limited to a section of the Conservative Party, for the present at least. In the meantime the electorate were prepared to support Labour's attempt to resolve the British crisis within the framework of social democracy.

Notes

1 C. A. R. (Anthony) Crosland, *The Future of Socialism* (London: Cape, 1956), p. 31.
2 Newton and Porter, *Modernization Frustrated*, pp. 159–160.
3 Robert Taylor, 'The Heath Government, Industrial Policy and the "New Capitalism"', in Stuart Ball and Anthony Seldon, *The Heath Government 1970–74* (London: Longman, 1996), p. 139.
4 Stewart, *The Jekyll and Hyde Years*, pp. 312–313.
5 Kevin Theakston, 'The Heath Government, Whitehall and the Civil Service', in Ball and Seldon, *The Heath Government 1970–74*, p. 91.
6 Leo Pliatzky, *Getting and Spending: Public Expenditure, Employment and Inflation* (Oxford: Blackwell, 1982), p. 98.
7 Philip Ziegler, *Edward Heath: The Authorised Biography* (London: Harper Press, 2011), p. 70.
8 See John Cockcroft, *Why Britain Sleeps* (London: Arlington Books, 1971), pp. 190–198.
9 Robert Taylor, 'The Heath Government and Industrial Relations: Myth and Reality', in Ball and Seldon, *The Heath Government 1970-74*, p. 170
10 Taylor, 'The Heath Government and Industrial Relations', p. 163.
11 Sandbrook *White Heat*, pp. 760–761.
12 Shirley Robin Letwin, *The Anatomy of Thatcherism* (New York: HarperCollins, 1992), p. 73.
13 Cockett, *Thinking the Unthinkable*, pp. 202–203.
14 James Mitchell, *The Scottish Question* (Oxford: Oxford University Press, 2014), p. 147.
15 Anthony Crosland, *Socialism Now* (London: Cape, 1974), p. 93.
16 John Campbell, *Edward Heath: A Biography* (London: Pimlico, 1994), p. xviii.
17 Ibid.

18 Andy Beckett, *When the Lights Went Out: Britain in the Seventies* (London: Faber and Faber, 2009), p. 57.
19 Campbell, *Edward Heath*, pp. 365–367.
20 Edward Heath, *The Course of my Life: My Autobiography* (London: Hodder and Stoughton, 1998), p. 330.
21 Donald MacDougall, *Don and Mandarin: Memoirs of an Economist* (London: John Murray, 1987), p. 187.
22 Stewart, *The Jekyll and Hyde Years*, p. 130.
23 MacDougall, *Don and Mandarin*, p. 112.
24 Newton and Porter, *Modernization Frustrated*, p. 162; Alec Cairncross, 'The Heath Government and the British Economy', in Ball and Seldon, *The Heath Government 1970–74*, pp. 114–115.
25 Newton and Porter, *Modernization Frustrated*, pp. 162–163.
26 Stewart, *The Jekyll and Hyde Years*, p. 142.
27 Ibid., p. 173.
28 Newton and Porter, *Modernization Frustrated*, p. 163.
29 See Nicholas Woodward, *The Management of the British Economy, 1945–2001* (Manchester: Manchester University Press, 2004), Figure 5.6, p. 151.
30 Beckett, *When the Lights Went Out*, pp. 69ff., p. 84.
31 Campbell, *Edward Heath*, p. 445.
32 Jack Jones, *Union Man: An Autobiography* (Collins: London, 1986), pp. 259, 262.
33 Middlemas, *Power, Competition and the State*, vol. 2, p. 319.
34 Associated Society of Locomotive Engineers and Firemen.
35 TNA CAB 128/48, CM (71) 6, 2 February 1971; Pliatzky, *Getting and Spending*, pp. 101–102.
36 TNA CAB 128/48, CM (71) 42, 28 July 1971.
37 Stewart, *The Jekyll and Hyde Years*, p. 136.
38 See for example Campbell, *Edward Heath*, p. 452.
39 Richard Wade, *Conservative Economic Policy: from Heath in Opposition to Cameron in Coalition* (London: Palgrave Macmillan, 2013), p. 38.
40 Beckett, *When the Lights Went Out*, pp. 35ff.
41 Wade, *Conservative Economic Policy*, pp. 39–40.
42 Heath, *The Course of My Life*, p. 400.
43 Former Conservative Minister Lord Coleraine (Richard Law) quoted in Cockett, *Thinking the Unthinkable*, p. 211.
44 See for example 'The Boom Speeds Up', *The Times*, 4 May 1973, p. 19 cols. A–C.
45 'Opportunity for Economic Growth', *The Times*, 14 May 1973, p. 13 col. D.
46 Newton and Porter, *Modernization Frustrated*, pp. 165–166; Sidney Pollard, *The Wasting of the British Economy*, 2nd edition (Beckenham: Croom Helm, 1984), p. 46.
47 Robin Ramsay, 'Back to the Future: The British Political Economy of the 1970s Re-examined', *Lobster* 34 (1998), p. 30; and 'The Financial Crisis. Well, How Did we Get Here?' *Lobster* 60 (2010), p. 73.
48 Michael Moran, *The Politics of Banking* (London, Macmillan, 1986), pp. 20–1; 30ff.
49 Ibid., pp. 39–41.
50 Duncan Needham, 'Britain's Money Supply Experiment, 1971–73', CWPESH no. 10, University of Cambridge, 2011, pp. 3–4.
51 The share of all sterling deposits taken by these grew from 18.4 per cent to 28.9 per cent between 1964 and 1970; in the same period the clearing banks' share dropped by 3 percentage points to 32.2 per cent (Moran, *The Politics of Banking*, p. 41).
52 Jerry Coakley and Laurence Harris, *The City of Capital: London's Role as a Financial Centre* (Oxford: Blackwell, 1983), p. 70.
53 Ibid., p. 71.
54 The wholesale financial markets cover the provision of services by banks to other banks and financial institutions such as mortgage brokers, property developers and investment funds, as well as to governments.

55 Moran, *The Politics of Banking*, p. 43.
56 Ibid.
57 Coakley and Harris, *The City of Capital*, p. 71.
58 Newton and Porter, *Modernization Frustrated*, p. 166.
59 Coakley and Harris, *The City of Capital*, p. 76; Andrew Glyn, *The British Economic Disaster* (London: Pluto Press, 1980), pp. 51–54.
60 Kees Van der Pijl, *The Making of an Atlantic Ruling Class* (London: Verso, 1984), p. 263.
61 Van der Pijl, *The Making of an Atlantic Ruling Class*, p. 265.
62 J. M. Keynes, *The General Theory of Employment, Interest and Money* (Cambridge, 1936), ch. 24.
63 Van der Pijl, *The Making of an Atlantic Ruling Class*, pp. 263–264.
64 Bank of England, 'Economic Commentary', *Quarterly Bulletin* 1975, Q4, p. 127.
65 Ramsay, 'Back to the Future: The British Political Economy of the 1970s Re-examined', p. 30.
66 Stewart, *The Jekyll and Hyde Years*, p. 182.
67 Coakley and Harris, *The City of Capital*, p. 73.
68 Ibid.
69 David Harvey, *A Brief History of Neoliberalism* (Oxford, 2005), pp. 55–56.
70 See for example, 'The Good Old Days of Stop-Go Economics', Peter Jay, *The Times*, 5 December 1973, cols A–B; and Samuel Brittan, 'The Economic Contradictions of Democracy', *British Journal of Political Science*, 5 (1975), pp. 129–159. Some of the key arguments are explored in Roger Middleton, 'Brittan on Britain: "The Economic Contradictions of Democracy" Redux', *The Historical Journal*, 54 (2011), pp. 1141–1168.
71 Middleton, *The British Economy since 1945*, pp. 103–104.
72 Ibid., p. 105.
73 See Michael Stewart, *Keynes and After* (London: Penguin, 1975), pp. 229ff.
74 Friedman's views were set out in *Free to Choose* (London: Secker and Warburg, 1980).
75 Middlemas, *Power, Competition and the State*, vol. 2, p. 340.
76 Ibid., p. 360.
77 See Richard Parker, *John Kenneth Galbraith: His Life, His Politics, His Economics* (New York: Farrar, Strauss and Giroux, 2005), p. 542; Stewart, *The Jekyll and Hyde Years*, pp. 160–163.
78 Jones, *Union Man*, pp. 259–261.
79 Max-Stefan Schulze and Nicholas Woodward, 'The Emergence of Rapid Inflation', in Richard Coopey and Nicholas Woodward, *Britain in the 1970s: the Troubled Economy* (London: UCL Press 1996), p. 114.
80 Middlemas, *Power, Competition and the State*, vol. 2, p. 378.
81 Newton and Porter, *Modernization Frustrated*, p. 167.
82 Stewart, *The Jekyll and Hyde Years*, p. 181.
83 Tony Benn, *Against the Tide: Diaries 1973–76* (London: Arrow, 1991), entry for 3 December 1973, p. 76.
84 Stephen Dorril and Robin Ramsay, *Smear! Wilson and the Secret State* (London: 4th Estate, 1991), p. 230.
85 'MI5 Set Agent to Shadow Labour MP: BBC is Told how NUM was Infiltrated to Beat Strike', Richard Norton-Taylor, *The Guardian*, 1 November 2002, p. 5.
86 Taylor, 'The Heath Government and Industrial Relations', p. 185.
87 TNA, CAB 128/51, CM (73) 59th conclusions, 4 December 1973.
88 Taylor, 'The Heath Government and Industrial Relations', p. 186.
89 The author witnessed an example of this when he went to see Chancellor Anthony Barber address an open meeting at Dame Elizabeth Cadbury Hall in Bournville, Birmingham during the election campaign: see also 'TV Broadcast Shows Tories are "Rattled, Afraid and Desperate"', *The Times*, 21 February, p. 5, cols. A and B.
90 Tony Benn, *Against the Tide*, entry for 6 January, p. 86.
91 Ibid., entry for 8 January, p. 89.
92 Dorril and Ramsay, *Smear!*, pp.230–231.

93 Beckett, *When the Lights Went Out*, p. 147.
94 Ibid., p. 150; *The Times*, '£383m Trade Deficit Biggest Monthly Total in British History', p. 1 cols. A–C.
95 Taylor, 'The Heath Government and Industrial Relations', p. 161.
96 Cockett, *Thinking the Unthinkable*, pp. 235–236.

4

THE CRISIS OF THE POST-WAR SETTLEMENT, 1974–79

Sick man

After returning to office in March 1974 Labour was to stay in government for another five years. Histories of this period have not been kind to Labour.[1] They have depicted Britain as the victim of hyperinflation and semi-permanent industrial unrest resulting from irresponsible trade union activity; it was the 'sick man of Europe'.[2] Its economy was characterized by industrial decline, symbolized by the collapse and State-led rescue of its leading motor vehicle manufacturer, the British Leyland Motor Corporation, and by mass unemployment, which hit a post-war high, rising well beyond the 1 million mark during 1975 and never falling beneath it for the rest of Labour's time in office. Presiding over this shambles was a weak government which appeased the unions and indulged in inappropriately high levels of public spending funded in part by penal levels of personal taxation. Only after Labour was forced to borrow $3.9 billion from the IMF in late 1976, following a major foreign exchange crisis caused by the collapse of confidence in its economic policies, did the country's fortunes improve. Yet even this stable interlude concluded unhappily, with a series of bitter and disruptive industrial disputes (mostly within the public sector) in late 1978 and early 1979. Labour's credibility as a governing party was destroyed along with the confidence of employers and many workers in the post-war settlement and social democracy. It seemed time to try a new politico-economic model, and this was duly built by the Conservatives during the course of Margaret Thatcher's long Premiership (1979–90), during which Britain embraced the free market with more enthusiasm than any other major European nation.

There have been dissenters from this viewpoint. These historians have all argued that Labour made a competent job of defending social democracy at a time when the internal and external environment which had sustained it was in crisis.[3] Their efforts have not made much difference to the accepted view, which has indeed been reinforced by the Labour Party itself since the mid-1990s with its willingness to distance itself from 'Old Labour' and the supposed bad old days of the 1970s. As the 40⁻ʰ anniversary of the 'winter of discontent' approaches the Conservative Party still uses folk memory of the late 1970s as a basis for developing policy towards the trade unions and for deterring voters from supporting Labour.[4] The willingness of the political parties and much of the mainstream media, both print and broadcasting, to continue re-cycling the conventional wisdom owes much to the strength of the free market politico-economic paradigm installed since 1979. Yet the historical record supports an alternative reading of the period, one closer to the interpretation of the dissenters.

Hostile world

Post-war social democracy depended on the continuing ability of governments to manage an open economy – in other words one which participated fully within the international trade and financial system – at a level of national income which increased annually while sustaining full employment at stable prices. Keynes had spent the last years of his life attempting to construct the international financial architecture which would sustain this synthesis between liberalism and socialism. His vision was partly realized with the creation of the Bretton Woods institutions, the IMF and the International Bank for Reconstruction and Development (later known as the World Bank). Yet neither of these organizations was operative in the immediate aftermath of World War Two, with dire implications for the Labour Government of Clement Attlee.

Elected by a landslide in the summer of 1945, Labour was pledged to implement an ambitious programme of national and social reconstruction. Its plans were however immediately threatened by Britain's parlous external position. The country had debts to the sterling area worth £3 billion (a vast figure at the time, equivalent to just over one-third of GDP) and a prospective balance of payments deficit between 1945 and 1950 of £1,250 million.[5] How, therefore, were Labour's policies to be financed? In the absence of external assistance it would have had to cut the import bill via either drastic deflation or rigorous protectionism. This would have amounted to deciding whether to abandon its mission or try and salvage it via recourse, for an indefinite period, to a political economy close to the Soviet model based on central planning both of the domestic economy and of the foreign trade sector, with trade and exchange rate arrangements characterized by protectionism and an inconvertible currency. Labour had however been able to reject both of these options thanks to the support from the USA: late in 1945 Keynes negotiated a $3.75 billion loan and after 1948 Britain had been a major beneficiary of the Marshall Aid programme. The willingness of the USA, running a large external surplus, to act as generous creditor to the UK (and to other countries embarking upon their reconstruction programmes) allowed Labour to embark on its project of remaking Britain as a liberal socialist, or social-democratic society.[6]

Labour had remained true to this tradition under the leadership of Hugh Gaitskell and Harold Wilson. The Wilson governments backed international trade liberalization and supported the Kennedy Round of talks in GATT[7] designed to reduce tariff and non-tariff barriers.[8] Labour's National Plan for the modernization of the economy, launched in 1965, explicitly stated the government's commitment to the market economy.[9] During the 1960s both Conservative and Labour governments had drawn on financial support from sources such as the IMF, the central banks of the leading industrialized nations, and the US Federal Reserve Bank of New York to cover balance of payments deficits. Although the 1964–70 Wilson administrations had come under some pressure to rein in its expansionary programme further than it found palatable, it was generally true that external assistance had facilitated the return of the nation's current account to balance without a violent deflationary adjustment.

In other words, 'Stop-Go' notwithstanding, throughout the period since 1945 it had not been necessary to reduce imports via reductions in demand leading to factory closures and unemployment beyond the levels deemed compatible with the norms of the post-war consensus. Public investment had generally been high enough to fund infrastructural renewal (housing, energy, roads, rail and public transport) as well as the expansion of health, education and social services. The existence of a generous creditor (or creditors) in the international economy therefore underpinned full employment and the Welfare State.

The fundamental problem facing Labour in 1974 was that the external environment was changing. One of the foundations of post-war social democracy – the existence of a generous creditor – was crumbling. This new development stemmed from the increasing volatility of international finance. The growth of the US deficit, combined with the rise of the Eurodollar market, had caused Washington to float the dollar in 1971. Subsequent to this both Washington and London had drawn up plans for a new international monetary order in which the dollar would be replaced as the world's main reserve currency by a new unit, the Special Drawing Right (SDR), to be managed by the IMF. Under both plans the IMF would be empowered to lend SDRs to debtors and apply sanctions to persistent creditors who refused to reflate (and in so doing make it difficult for deficit nations to export their way to a current account balance).[10]

Both of these plans reconciled membership of a multilateral trading and financial order with full employment. They failed to make progress for two reasons. First of all surplus nations at the time, especially Japan, West Germany and France, were worried that the proposals contained a built-in inflationary bias. Secondly, the USA itself lost interest in international monetary reform. As the dollar floated down against other currencies, generating the adjustment Washington had long desired between debtor and creditor, demand for imports in the US market was checked yet expansion sustained via export-led growth.

The era of floating rates proved compatible with continuing domestic expansion until this was undermined by spiralling commodity prices in 1973–74. The most dramatic change was of course to the price of oil, quadrupling between October

1973 and January 1974. The result was the arrival of 'stagflation', namely the combination of minimal (or negative) growth and high inflation. Expensive import bills sent countries into external deficit, pushed up the cost of living and at the same time provoked a sharp fall in demand throughout the industrialized world, with the global economy sliding into recession until 1976. The higher cost of raw materials, along with wage demands made by well-organized unions on behalf of hard-pressed members, caused profits to fall throughout the OECD. Private investment was cut and by the autumn of 1975 about 11 per cent of fixed capital in the industrialized world lay idle; unemployment rose from 8 million to 15 million between 1973 and 1975.[11] Most OECD governments sought to narrow their external deficits by reducing public expenditure programmes and increasing interest rates, a course of action which reinforced the deflationary aspects of stagflation. As a result there were falls in output (in 1975 this was lower than it had been in 1973) and in the volume of international trade throughout the capitalist world.

The Labour government therefore came to power at a time when the external environment had become distinctly unfriendly to social democracy. There was no creditor to take on the role played by the USA after World War Two. The IMF did not have the resources to provide liquidity to governments on a scale large enough to prevent the rush to deflation. Yet even as Britain's current account deficit approached £4 billion, Wilson and the new Chancellor of the Exchequer, Denis Healey, eschewed measures to reduce economic activity. They settled the dispute with the miners on terms favourable to the NUM and ended the Three Day Week. Healey's first Budget was intended to be broadly neutral in its impact on domestic output. On the one hand there were tax rises for the better off, the highest rate of income tax increasing from 75 to 83 per cent (it was paid by 750,000 people in 1974), while the top rate on investment income went from 90 to 98 per cent, a post-war high.[12] On the other hand the government took the classical Keynesian path of rejecting cuts in the Public Sector Borrowing Requirement (PSBR: the technical term for how much governments needed to borrow in order to fund their commitments), in the expectation that sustained expansion would after all be embraced by the other OECD nations so that demand for exports would be generated throughout the industrialized world.[13] The external deficit would gradually close and be transformed into a surplus once Britain had built the infrastructure needed to exploit the extensive reserves of oil recently discovered under the North Sea.

Given the absence of a Keynesian creditor, the nation's double-digit inflation rate and the external deficit, this strategy seems to have been ill-advised. Yet it was a rational one, based on the conviction that the international financial system did, after all, possess the resources which would permit debtor countries to avoid economic contraction. This was not wishful thinking. As a result of the quadrupling in the oil price, the producing states, co-operating through their own cartel, the Organisation of the Petroleum Exporting Countries (OPEC) saw their income rise from $33 billion in 1973 to $108 billion in 1974. This was a dramatic transfer of wealth and, since OPEC members were unable to spend it all on importing from the industrialized world, they accumulated large surpluses, reaching $55 billion in 1974.[14] These were offset by the external deficits of western industrial nations and non-oil producing states in the Third World. It therefore made commercial sense for the billions of 'petrodollars' to be re-cycled to the debtor nations through the international financial system. The IMF established an 'oil facility' to assist countries whose current account had been driven deep into the red by the unfavourable shift in the terms of trade while OPEC nations made large deposits in the London Eurocurrency market. These in turn facilitated the extension of credit to western governments and financed an expansion of lending on the part of US banks keen to make a profit from the high demand for dollars experienced by the oil-importing countries. The Labour government was able to take advantage of the plentiful liquidity, covering the external deficit via inward investment ($7.2 billion in 1974) and a $1.2 billion credit from Iran.[15] Oil-exporting countries' sterling balances increased from £719 million to £3,183 million between September 1973 and December 1974,[16] a significant proportion of these belonging to Nigeria and Saudi Arabia.[17]

At first blush, therefore, it would seem that the facilities existed to assist deficit nations like the UK continue to pursue economic strategies which combined domestic expansion with membership of an open trade and financial system. Yet the reality was different. The sudden growth of international credit driven by the oil price rise reinforced the rise of money capital within the world's leading financial markets, London especially, noted in chapter 3. During the 1950s and after, foreign exchange for deficit countries had generally been provided by the IMF and the World Bank or by the central banks of the leading industrialized nations. Now the private sector was becoming more prominent, as European and American banks found there were good profits to be made from financing external imbalances.[18] It followed that, given so much of the finance available within the global economy came from the markets, the creditors would generally wish to see a healthy return on their investments or at the very least would be keen to avoid holding on to monetary assets whose value was decreasing. This meant that they were highly averse to inflation, especially when manifest in falling currency values.

This had serious implications for debtor nations, especially Britain. Here, the combination of a large external deficit with a rising internal price level put sterling under pressure from the markets. During the course of 1974 sterling fell against the dollar by 10 per cent. In the last quarter of the year the pound's effective rate dropped by 4 per cent and inflows from the Gulf Sheikdoms, which had traditionally held their reserves in sterling, dried up. Another indication of the currency's vulnerability came with ARAMCO's decision at the end of the year to start invoicing oil sales in dollars and cease doing so in sterling.[19] Within the Treasury the fall in sterling was greeted with ambivalence. On the one hand it would promote exports. On the other hand there were real worries that continuing decline would lead to large-scale movement out of the currency by those holding it, leading to further falls in its value, in the process draining the gold and foreign currency reserves and putting upward pressure on domestic prices.[20] If such a *dégringolade* were to be averted the government needed the confidence of the markets; but Labour had a serious credibility problem when it came to the question of its counter-inflation strategy.

The struggle to contain inflation centred on Labour's Social Contract with the unions. During the course of 1974–75 this delivered food subsidies and higher social benefits and pensions as well as measures to extend the rights of working people. These included the repeal of the Industrial Relations Act and legislation to strengthen job security (the Employment Protection Act), improve health and safety at work (leading to the establishment of the Health and Safety Executive) and strengthen arbitration arrangements in industrial disputes (the Advisory Conciliation and Arbitration Service). Wilson and Healey, along with Michael Foot at the Department of Employment, relied on the Social Contract to moderate wage claims and therefore bring the wage-price spiral under control. They hoped that trade union leaders and shop stewards would see the reforms as improvements to the worker's wage packet and bargaining position and that in return claims for higher pay would be designed to match but not outstrip the cost of living.

The Social Contract was frequently criticized by Right wing commentators, City bankers and even senior Labour Party figures as a one-sided bargain in which the government could do little apart from exhort the unions to avoid inflationary pay demands.[21] Joel Barnett, Chief Secretary to the Treasury from 1974–79, later said 'the only give and take in the social contract was that the government gave and the unions took'.[22] Indeed, there was little sign that the Social Contract was leading to pay restraint: by the end of 1974 the increase in earnings index had risen to 18.2 per cent (a year earlier it had stood at 13.3 per cent), and it continued to climb through the first half of 1975. Early in the New Year the NUM negotiated a settlement of 35 per cent. Prices continued to escalate: the annual rate of inflation was now approaching 20 per cent. The tendency of wages and prices to chase each other up the scale was exaggerated by the impact of the threshold agreements which had been a feature of Heath's incomes policy. Labour had retained these, which had been designed to head off inflationary pay claims but given the circumstances of 1974 the agreements turned into 'a doomsday machine'.[23] They were activated six times between January and July,[24] with inescapable rises in the price of imports being transmitted into 'spiralling increases in both wage settlements and inflation'.[25]

Criticism of the Social Contract is easy but based on an oversimplified reading of the situation in which the government found itself. Its options were limited. Wilson was frequently urged to follow the path of statutory incomes policy taken after 1966, advice which he firmly rejected.[26] He told Healey that he would support the Chancellor on any measures he deemed necessary to control inflation – barring a statutory incomes policy.[27] Labour had, after all, come to power against a background of political turbulence owing much to union disenchantment with pay policy. Heath's government had foundered on the rocks of its attempt to control wages and Wilson did not wish his administration, in office largely because of its claim that Labour's historic links to the unions meant it could manage relations with them better than the Conservatives, to suffer the same experience. Moreover, the absence of an overall Parliamentary majority in Parliament left the government in a weak position when it came to passing controversial legislation to which many of its own supporters and MPs were likely to be unsympathetic. Even after Labour's victory in the October 1974 General Election had provided it with a majority, the very small size (3) indicated that little was likely to change. It all meant that the political situation not only made the establishment of a statutory incomes policy impossible but also ensured that there were great difficulties facing attempts to make a voluntary one effective.

Labour's apparent inability or unwillingness to tackle the roots of inflation nevertheless damaged its standing at home and overseas. The seemingly relentless upward drift of the cost of living led to alarmist articles in the press. These, often by the same journalists and commentators who had started to question the post-war social-democratic settlement during the winter of 1973–74, suggested that Labour was simply buying short-term political calm by spending resources the country did not possess. This approach, it was argued, only led to higher price levels and ever-larger external deficits. The nation was in danger of tipping into hyperinflation and ungovernability.[28]

The growing sense of impending disaster was reinforced by grim economic statistics: by the end of 1974 the current account deficit amounted to 6 per cent of the GDP at market prices[29] (a peacetime record); GDP was only 0.4 per cent higher in the last quarter than it had been at the same point in 1973; and unemployment had risen by 750,000 over the year.[30] The government's strategy of tunnelling through the crisis, sustaining high demand and promoting exports while borrowing to cover the deficit, had misfired. First of all, Healey's 'neutral' first Budget had provided an unintentional reflationary boost to the economy, given that the changes it made to taxation and spending had been based on an underestimation by the Treasury (by £4 billion) of the Government's borrowing requirement.[31] Secondly, rather than follow Britain most OECD members had stuck to the path of spending cuts and higher interest rates, measures which had narrowed deficits but at the price of lower activity.[32] This would have been enough to ensure that the buoyant external markets Labour needed for its approach to work were not likely to appear, inevitably leading to a widening of Britain's external deficit: as it was, this effect was exaggerated by the consequences of the Treasury's miscalculation.

Social democracy's apparent inability to turn the economy around and deliver lower inflation led a growing number of commentators, Conservative politicians and influential journals to join those who had already abandoned any commitment to the post-war settlement. Disillusionment with it became increasingly common; Keynesian political economy retreated and the appeal of monetarism grew not just on the political Right but in the financial markets. It also became attractive to Britain's creditors in the international financial community. Central banks, the US Treasury, the IMF and the BIS, dealers in money, bonds and foreign exchange, as well as bankers and fund managers, embraced monetarist ideas. They seemed to offer an explanation for persistent external deficits and inflation: these were seen as functions of excessive borrowing, financed by inappropriately large increases in the money supply. As far as the financial institutions were concerned the policy implications were clear: deficit countries like Britain should cut public spending and introduce targets for the growth of the money supply. For the markets the appeal of monetarism was its simplicity: quick decisions to buy or sell could be made on the basis of key indicators such as the latest figures for the money supply (monetary targets) and the PSBR.[33]

Given that monetarism involved the promotion of *laissez-faire*, control of the money supply and a deflationary fiscal policy (to be characterized mainly by lower public spending), it of course implied the abandonment of full employment as an objective of macroeconomic policy and the rollback of the post-1945 State.[34] Support for this revival of economic liberalism (or neo-liberalism as it became known) had long been growing within the Conservative Party. Yet despite its growing popularity after 1970 it had failed to recruit supporters at the highest levels of the Party. The economic crisis acted as a catalyst, however, and facilitated the efforts of Sir Keith Joseph, Secretary of State for Social Services from 1970–74, to promote the new approach. Along with former Education Secretary Margaret Thatcher and shipping magnate Sir Nicholas Cayzer, Chairman of the multinational British and Commonwealth Shipping (BCS) and well known for his strong pro-free enterprise and anti-trade union views, Joseph launched the Centre for Policy Studies (CPS). CPS was committed to repudiation of the post-war consensus and through its efforts monetarism entered the mainstream of British politics.[35]

With the markets and the international financial institutions embracing monetarist ideas, the Conservative Party swinging to the Right, and a domestic press increasingly sceptical about Labour's ability to navigate a way out of crisis, the normative values of British political discourse began to shift away from those of post-war social democracy. From late 1974 confidence in Labour increasingly depended on its ability to cut public sector borrowing and develop a credible target for the money supply. If it failed to meet these criteria for creditworthiness the chances of a run on sterling would become very high, leaving the government with three options, each of which had very bleak implications given the current economic context. The first was to use up its foreign exchange reserves (including the credits and inward flows which had sustained it throughout its first year in power); the second involved allowing the exchange rate to fall; and the third entailed seeking to borrow more from unsympathetic creditors. It was looking more and more likely that participation within the open international trade and financial system was no longer compatible with commitment to the post-war settlement.

Alternative strategy

The tendency to disillusionment with key aspects of Keynesian political economy seen on the Right was shared on the British Left. Here, the major problem was seen to be the difficulty British governments had been experiencing in retaining control of the national economy. For almost 20 years neither the Labour nor the Conservative Parties had found it easy to reconcile constant economic expansion at full employment with a healthy current account and growth at 3 per cent per annum or more. The failure of Heath's government suggested this objective was becoming unattainable. On the radical Left the increasing power of international market forces was identified as the main obstacle to meeting the aspirations of the parties to the post-war settlement. It seemed that the only effective way to reverse this trend was for governments to avail themselves of new economic policy tools and go beyond the indicative planning in vogue since the early 1960s. In its place they needed to embrace the extension of public ownership along with measures to increase State control over capital movements and regulate the level of imports. Whereas sections of the Right were prepared to prioritize the conquest of inflation and the maintenance of Britain's credibility as a leading member of the multilateral trade and financial order above the objective of full employment, many on the Left were persuaded that unemployment (at 4 per cent of the workforce in the first quarter of 1975, with the trend clearly upward),[36] stagflation and external deficits could not be tackled on terms acceptable to Labour and the trade unions unless British governments exchanged multilateralism for protectionism.

The leading advocate of a more radical approach to government was Tony Benn, Secretary of State for Industry from March 1974 and Chair of the Labour National Executive's influential Home Policy Committee from January 1975. Benn's thinking had shifted in the years since he had left MinTech in 1970. At that stage he had been committed to the combination of interventionism and indicative planning which had been a hallmark of Wilson's first two administrations. His views had changed, thanks partly to lessons he personally drew from experience and partly to observation. Benn had become frustrated with the anti-trade union attitudes and what he considered to be the inadequacy of many senior figures in private industry (a sentiment he shared with Heath), and concerned that Britain's economic performance was being set back by the tendency for investment in manufacturing industry to be outstripped by the volume going into finance and services. This combination of poor management and market failure persuaded him that it was necessary for the State to play a much more far-reaching role in the modernization of industry than had been deemed acceptable just a few years before and take leading companies partly or wholly into public ownership. But if the government was going to provide financial support it needed to take strategic control away from owners and managers who had failed to show a capacity to innovate. Instead, it would work with trade unionists: Benn had been impressed by their willingness not just to use solidarity to challenge employers and government over issues relating to pay, conditions at work and job prospects, but to construct what he considered viable futures for the organizations where they worked. The implications of the crisis in Clydeside, and the ability currently being shown by the shop stewards at Lucas Aerospace to develop a corporate plan designed to rescue the company from having to declare mass redundancies, were clear. The regeneration of British industry required an extension of nationalization along with the transfer of power from capital to labour, through the establishment of co-operatives and industrial democracy, in order to unleash the talent available on the factory floor.[37]

Benn's conversion to a radical form of social democracy was given a powerful intellectual rationale by the work of the academic and Labour policy advisor, Stuart Holland. Holland argued, first in *The State as Entrepreneur* (1972) and then in his 1975 text *The Socialist Challenge* that changes in the global economy had undermined the economic sovereignty of the nation-state and in so doing had rendered traditional Keynesian demand management ineffective.[38] According to Holland the critical development in this process had been the rise of the multinational firm, itself a function of the trend to the internationalization of finance and production which had become notable since the late 1950s. He cited the 1968 Industrial Census to argue that multinationals now formed the majority of the top 100 firms in the UK. These were responsible for one-half or more of all output, industrial employment and assets in the economy, and now represented its commanding heights.[39]

Holland maintained that multinationals were able to evade credit controls and the impact of shifts in domestic monetary policy (such as the introduction of credit squeezes) by raising money from within the firm. They could dodge taxation via transfer pricing (the manipulation of charges for goods traded within a multinational in order to reduce profits in regions where company taxation was high) and avoid the price effects of national currency devaluations by forming cartel arrangements with other large firms. They had the power to nullify or at least reduce the influence of regional policy by threatening to relocate their factories. Finally, the multinationals were in part responsible for the revival of a liberal international capital market, tending to place their earnings not within the home country but within local banks where they could be drawn on for reinvestment; alternatively these funds could be shifted from one financial centre to another in search of speculative profit. About 50 per cent of the foreign assets of the multinationals were subject to movements of this kind, which became a significant source of footloose capital and fed the remarkable growth of the 'Eurodollar' market.[40]

Holland concluded from this analysis that Labour administrations needed to challenge the power of the multinational corporations by establishing a State Holding Company. This would be known as the 'National Enterprise Board' (NEB) and its role would be to stimulate investment and innovation in industry. To achieve this it would be necessary to bring into public ownership whole firms, or sections of them, considered by government central to the future of the national economy in terms of output, potential for import substitution and production for the export market, as well as contribution to a successful regional policy. Starting with companies where the government already possessed a substantial share, such as British Petroleum (BP), International Computers Limited (ICL) or Rolls Royce, the NEB would move on to establish a 'controlling interest' in twenty-five leading firms. Central to the NEB's brief was the role of venture capitalist, supporting the development of new products even if this involved establishing its own companies should commercial prospects not encourage the backing of the private sector.[41] Its authority would provide a Labour government with countervailing power to that possessed by the multinationals. Large firms would be unable either to evade governments' fiscal and monetary measures or frustrate exchange rate management and regional policy. National economic sovereignty would be restored, allowing Labour to pursue a 'co-ordinated, planned programme of expansion'.[42]

The work of the NEB would be supported by 'planning agreements' between the government and private firms in which the corporations seeking State support would be required to sign agreements with the government on investment and pricing policies, R and D and plant location over an extended time horizon of up to five years.[43] Companies would be obliged to share information on profits, costs, products and markets with representatives of the relevant trade unions as well as with government officials. Firms unwilling to commit themselves to these arrangements would not receive backing.[44] The model for this new strategy was a continental one: the NEB owed much to the Italian *Istituto per la Ricostruzione Industriale* (IRI) established by Mussolini in 1933 but kept by post-Fascist administrations, while planning agreements drew from the example of programme contracts pioneered by the French after 1966.[45] The entire package was designed to provide Labour with the 'tactical instruments for planning' which had not been available to the DEA, following as it had a largely indicative approach.

Tony Benn and the Labour Left, now in the ascendant on the Party's National Executive Committee (NEC), found Holland's argument persuasive. They concluded that it not only addressed the question of which interests wielded power within the British economy but explained why, even after devaluation, speculative pressures had continued to harass the last Labour government. The NEB and planning agreements followed the interventionist approach adopted by MinTech and the IRC but sought to go beyond this via the connection they made between government investment and structural change at company level. In consequence, Holland's analysis now served as the framework for a strategy which the Left believed would allow Labour to stay true to its historic objectives and its constituency in the electorate while simultaneously promoting industrial modernization.

Indeed Benn and the Left of the Labour Party went beyond Holland. They favoured the idea of 'compulsory planning agreements' with the 'top 100 companies', by which the State, acting through the office of an 'Industrial Commissioner', would be empowered to nationalize firms reluctant to sign them.[46] Holland opposed this, arguing that such an approach was redolent of the 'Gosplan and central command planning' familiar in the USSR. It would reduce planning agreements to a dogmatic weapon against the private sector, with civil servants 'running industry rather than government bargaining outcomes with it'.[47] Moreover the target of one hundred firms was unachievable: in France, the Ministry of Finance and National Economy had managed an average of just twelve planning agreements (or programme contracts) a year – and that with over half of the Ministry's staff of civil servants engaged on them and considerably longer experience of direct bargaining with companies. Given the need to start a British programme from scratch it was unlikely that a Labour government would exceed six or seven a year.[48] Benn, possibly influenced by the frustration he experienced when dealing with private firms at MinTech, ignored Holland's advice and stuck by the figure of one hundred companies.[49]

Aware that this programme was unlikely to be well received either within the City or by the multinationals, its proponents were committed to a strengthening of exchange controls in order to prevent damaging speculation and capital flight.[50] Indeed, Benn and his allies on the Left were now arguing that Labour's efforts to save jobs, address the external deficit and modernize the economy would fail unless there was a fundamental change to Britain's relationship with the international economy. It would be necessary to embrace what Benn called 'Strategy B' but which soon became known as the Alternative Economic Strategy (AES). This was characterized not only by interventionism but the planning of capital movements and import controls

> to encourage the growth of firms concerned with import substitution, to ensure that key industries had the raw materials and components they need, to see that the whole plan is not frustrated by excessive import bills and to maintain full employment.[51]

The implementation of these controls would conflict with Britain's obligations under the Treaty of Rome: it would be necessary for Britain to withdraw from the EEC if Labour were to be able to implement the Left's programme for reversing industrial decline. Pointing to the continental inspiration for the NEB and planning agreements, Holland vainly argued that there was no need to link Labour's new industrial strategy to departure from the EEC.[52] But there was growing conviction within the Labour Party, seen at both trade union and constituency level, that continuing membership of the EEC would undermine national economic planning and weaken Britain's industrial base.

Supporters of British participation in the Common Market had always argued that it would be good for the economy, stimulating the expansion and output of British industry through increased competition within the large trading area of the European Community. Membership had however coincided with a sharp deterioration in Britain's balance of trade in manufactured goods. In 1971 imports of finished manufactures totalled £2,382 million. By 1974 this figure amounted to £3,871 million. £888 million of the overall £1,489 million increase (all at 1970 prices) had occurred just in 1973 (the year Britain had formally become part of the EEC).[53] Most large and medium-sized firms remained optimistic about the results of membership. Within Labour, however, there was growing concern that free trade in the EEC meant factory closures, job losses and the movement of capital out of the UK. By 1973 these convictions were so strong and widespread that Wilson had committed a future Labour government to holding a referendum on the question of whether Britain should stay in the EEC, following a renegotiation of the terms of entry. In April 1975 a special Labour Party conference voted by a majority of 2:1 to campaign for Britain to leave. This was intended to be the first stage of the process by which the Labour government could implement its radical alternative strategy.

Old school

Wilson and the quartet of highly experienced senior Ministers (Chancellor Denis Healey, Foreign Secretary James Callaghan, Home Secretary Roy Jenkins and Environment Secretary Anthony Crosland) who held the leading Cabinet posts, all saw some merit in the idea of a State Holding Company. On the Left there was some hope that Wilson had moved into their camp, especially in the wake of the secondary banking crisis of 1973–74, when he endorsed proposals for a National Investment Bank and called the City of London a 'casino' devoted not to productive investment but to 'exaggerating the sloshing to and fro of the bilgewater of capitalism'. He argued that a public enquiry into the Stock Exchange was necessary, along with State regulation to rein in its speculative activities.[54]

There was, however, growing anger and disillusionment on the Left as it became increasingly clear through 1974–76 that Wilson and the majority of Cabinet members had no intention of endorsing its radical alternative strategy. The Prime Minister was accused, then and later, 'of simply tacking left to appease the activists in his party'.[55] The charge has been supported by some commentators and historians who have suggested that by 1974 Wilson himself had become a tired and cynical operator. Concerned only to stop Labour from fracturing over the question of Europe and economic policy he displayed inertia in the face both of the Left's determination to commit the Party to policies he did not support and of mounting inflation and the widening current account deficit.[56]

These criticisms are inappropriate, for two reasons. First, the tone of Wilson's attacks on the City and its tendency to encourage speculative capitalism was entirely consistent with the radical, productionist position he had taken on assuming the Labour leadership in 1963. At no stage did Wilson desert the liberal socialist political economy which had guided Labour policy since 1945 whether the Party was in or out or power. He supported a limited extension of public ownership (airframe and aero-engine manufacturing, and shipbuilding) but made clear his opposition to proposals from the NEC for the nationalization of over 25 of the leading 100 firms and ensured they never featured as part of Labour's Election campaigns in 1974. Like Jenkins and Crosland he was not persuaded by Holland's view that the power of multinationals now exceed that of nation-states.[57] Sympathetic to the opposition the proposals aroused in private industry, he sought to cajole the Party back to the indicative planning and corporatism which had characterized its period in office between 1964 and 1970.[58] Secondly, Wilson was well aware of the deteriorating economic situation.[59] His apparent inertia reflected a political problem: the question was how to deflect Labour from embracing policies he regarded as 'outlandish'[60] and inopportune, while generating support within the Party and the unions for the measures he believed necessary to transform the nation's prospects for the better. This was especially tricky. For a start, by late 1974 it was clear to Wilson that although the moderating influence of the Social Contract on the wage-price spiral had so far been minimal there was no practical alternative approach to reducing inflation – unless it involved willingness to tolerate mass unemployment.[61]

Wilson had some success with Labour's industrial strategy, winning Cabinet support for the August 1974 White Paper, *The Regeneration of British Industry*, published in July 1974.[62] This rejected both compulsory planning agreements and the compulsory disclosure of information. It set out the case for establishing the NEB as a State Holding Company whose mission was to provide investment capital for industry, but with powers a good deal less extensive than the Left had envisaged. Grants would be made available only to firms with good commercial prospects. The NEB would 'normally' acquire shares in the firms it was supporting but this process would take place only in agreement with the companies involved.[63] Finance from the NEB would supplement but not replace supply from 'existing financial institutions and companies' own resources'. The White Paper generally eschewed the arguments for the NEB set out by Holland, instead drawing a direct connection to the old IRC. In stating that it would follow the latter's example of promoting or assisting the reorganization or development of an industry it explicitly committed the government to Wilson's preferred strategy of selective intervention and indicative planning.[64]

Wilson's success over the powers of the NEB did not, however, mean that the Prime Minister and his supporters in Cabinet had won the struggle over the government's strategy, which now came to centre on British membership of the EEC. It was increasingly clear that the result of the referendum would not only decide whether or not Britain would remain in the Common Market but what shape its future politico-economic development was likely to take. A vote to withdraw would be a great political boost for the Left's case that only the AES could resolve Britain's economic difficulties in a way compatible with Labour's historic mission and values. On the other hand, given this connection, a vote to remain in the EEC was bound to be a major political defeat for the Left and a triumph for Wilson's determination to keep Labour from moving beyond the framework of post-war social democracy. There would be no fundamental shift in the boundary between the public and private sectors, Britain's relationship to the international economy would not change and the government would seek to resolve the crisis via tripartite co-operation.

Decisive action by the government in the face of rising inflation and the external deficit was a matter of timing, as Wilson himself admitted.[65] By June 1975 inflation was running at an annual rate of 26 per cent.[66] Pay settlements were reaching a going rate of 30 per cent. The growing anxieties of Britain's creditors about the economic situation were evident: in May the government of Kuwait warned the Treasury that it was actively considering selling its sterling balances in favour of other currencies.[67] Wilson was clear that a pay policy was both urgent and essential – but two problems stood in the way. The first was the referendum: given the level of support for the AES and the widespread distrust within the Party and the trade unions for any anti-inflation strategy which implied real cuts in workers' living standards, it was necessary to await the outcome of the vote on EEC membership. The second was the annual conference of the NUM, due in early July. Wilson was clear that no incomes policy could work without the agreement of the miners: if they could be persuaded to accept pay restraint, then other unions would follow suit.[68] These two problems were related, since the Prime Minister's authority when approaching the second was contingent on his achieving the result he needed in the first.[69]

The vote on British membership of the EEC was held on 5 June 1975. There was a conclusive victory, by 2:1, for those urging the voters to stay in the Community. A number of factors contributed to this striking result. To begin with, having renegotiated the terms of membership, the government commended them to the electorate as a good deal for Britain. In fact the improvements, concerning regional policy, Britain's contribution to the EEC Budget and imports of dairy produce from New Zealand, were modest, though genuine.[70] Nevertheless the exercise, led by Wilson and Foreign Secretary Callaghan, gave authority to the pro-market argument: it helped persuade the voters that the case for remaining in the EEC was in the national interest, having been derived from a dispassionate analysis of the 'new' terms.[71]

The cause of the anti-marketeers was also damaged by the politics of the campaign. Their organization, simply called 'Get Britain Out' was notable for the political diversity of its supporters. It attracted the backing of neo-Fascists (from the National Front), Right wing Conservatives drawn by Enoch Powell's conviction that participation in the Common Market heralded the end of Parliamentary sovereignty (and subordination to a socialistic Brussels super-State), as well as many on the Left of Labour committed to the AES. The campaign, which was not well funded, was marked by infighting and ideological incoherence. The pro-marketeers of 'Britain in Europe', by contrast, enjoyed generous financial support from private industry. Their political outlook was considerably less fragmented than that of their opponents, tending (in general terms) to reflect the social-democratic perspective of all British governments since the Prime Ministership of Harold Macmillan (who was himself a supporter of the 'Yes' campaign). Their efforts were slick and well organized; the contrast with the amateurish efforts of 'Get Britain Out' impressed many voters.

Wilson told Bernard Donoughue, the Head of his Policy Unit at No. 10, that a referendum victory for those who wanted to leave the EEC would have empowered 'the wrong kind of people in Britain...who were often extreme nationalists, protectionist, xenophobic and backward-looking'.[72] He was therefore able to treat the result as a strengthening of the position of old school social democrats in the Labour movement and a rejection of radical social democracy. His authority enhanced, he moved Benn to the Department of Energy, a demotion from his position at Industry, now taken by Eric Varley (a protégé of the Prime Minister) and then turned with some confidence to the question of pay policy.[73] The need for action on this front was now critical. With retail prices rising every week, the National Union of Railwaymen had just been awarded a pay increase of 30 per cent, having rejected a 27 per cent offer on the grounds that it would have involved a real cut in living standards. The intensifying wage-price spiral alarmed the Treasury, which worried that it would trigger an exodus of funds from sterling, and worked on plans for a statutory policy based on a 10 per cent flat rate increase. The Treasury's fears were realized on Monday 30 June. Large-scale selling of sterling balances by Nigeria and Kuwait led to a fall of 1.3 per cent in the value of sterling against other major currencies in just one trading session, an event without precedent 'in living memory'.[74] The pound ended the day 4 cents down against the dollar, having dropped from $2.22 to $2.18. Saudi Arabia threatened to follow the lead of Nigeria and Kuwait and sell its sterling balances if the rate fell below $2.17. Healey warned Ministerial colleagues that in the absence of a credible counter-inflationary strategy 'the whole of the UK reserves could disappear within 24 hours'.[75]

By this time anxiety about sterling's vulnerability and hyperinflation had started to spread across the political spectrum. TGWU General Secretary Jack Jones and AEU President Hugh Scanlon had become extremely concerned about the impact of rising prices on members' life savings as well as on their living standards; they were clear that the situation was becoming unsustainable.[76] Under their influence the TUC had already started discussions with the government about a pay norm.[77] At the start of July the Cabinet had agreed to the 10 per cent limit on wages, salaries and dividends in the next pay round, enforceable if necessary by legal sanctions on employers.[78] Now, the momentum within the TUC, in conjunction with sterling crisis, helped Wilson make his case for pay restraint to the NUM, where there had been growing support for a 63.9 per cent claim.[79] Asking the miners for 'not a year for the self, but a year for Britain', Wilson's speech echoed Heath's 'Who governs' question from early 1974: what was at stake was whether 'Governments constituted and dedicated to the principles of consent and consensus in our democracy, can lead this nation'.[80]

The NUM backed the appeal and the government was able to launch an incomes policy, based in the end not on the 10 per cent norm but on a TUC proposal (championed most strongly by Jones, on the grounds that it did not disadvantage the low paid) for a flat £6 per week rise for all earning up to £8,500 a year, accompanied by price controls. The result was a hybrid: the policy was voluntary, since it had been agreed between the government and the TUC without any need for State compulsion, but also statutory to the extent that the government equipped itself with reserve powers to act against employers breaking the limit. Known as Phase 1, it was quickly seen not as a one-off emergency measure but the start of a prolonged joint effort on the part of the peak institutions to break the inflationary spiral. Its first year was 'a resounding success', with inflation halved, falling from 26.9 per cent in August to 12.9 per cent by July 1976.[81] The impact on the foreign exchange markets was immediate: sterling stabilized at between $2.17 to $2.20, though it drifted down to $2.02 by the end of 1975 (largely thanks to benign neglect on the part of the Treasury).[82]

The establishment of a successful pay policy was a clear sign that the tripartite alliance had survived the trauma of 1973–74. More evidence that the values and institutions of post-war social democracy were after all still intact, if battered, was provided by Labour's industrial strategy. This was another triumph for Wilson's old school approach. Varley's appointment was followed by a further refinement of the industrial strategy, set out in a White Paper, *An Approach to an Industrial Strategy* (Cmd.6315), jointly produced by the Treasury and the Department of Industry in November 1975. Healey called this 'more a methodology than a strategy'.[83] It was based on tripartite co-operation, operating through sectoral working parties answerable to the NEDC. These were responsible for reviewing industrial performance and identifying, where necessary, what measures were necessary to improve it. The working parties focused especially on improving productivity, rates of investment and the efficiency with which capital was used, as well as the availability of skilled labour.[84] The strategy was supplemented by regional policy, with the establishment of the Scottish and the Welsh Development Agencies in 1975 and 1976 respectively, responsible for promoting business development and investment in the heartlands of Britain's industrial economy, where the old staples such as mining, shipbuilding and even steel manufacturing were now facing contraction. Benn expressed his scepticism, claiming the revamped strategy represented the abandonment of the Manifesto and was a 'weak and watery policy', merely 'a cover for Tory measures'.[85] *An Approach to Industrial Strategy* certainly involved the rejection of *dirigisme* but can only be called 'Tory' in the sense that the document clearly heralded a return to the selective interventionism followed by both Conservative and Labour governments after 1962.

The same pattern became obvious in the application of planning agreements and the work of the NEB. Only two planning agreements were ever signed, one with the ailing car manufacturer Chrysler, the other with the nationalized National Coal Board (NCB). The agreement with the NCB was designed to assist the modernization and expansion of coal mining in order to promote greater self-sufficiency in energy. It was an uncontroversial move, something which could not be said for the agreement with Chrysler in late 1975. The company was granted £55 million in working capital, to assist with the development of new models, as well as a loss subsidy of up to £60 million for the next two years. Chrysler's financial position had become precarious and there was an argument that the bail-out flew in the face of the industrial strategy's concern to promote modernization and operate on the basis of commercial criteria – but the case in favour was also powerful. Chrysler's contribution to exports was estimated to be worth £200 million a year. The decision saved over 16,000 jobs directly and possibly 40,000 indirectly, and rendered the imposition of controls on imports of motor vehicles unnecessary (a move which would have sparked a major row with trading partners and the IMF just when the government was bidding for financial support).[86]

The achievements of the NEB were more striking. Its greatest challenge came with the nationalization and reconstruction of the British Leyland Motor Corporation (BLMC). BLMC, established after IRC intervention to reorganize production in the automotive industry, had not been a success and filed for bankruptcy in 1975. It had failed to establish effective economies of scale. Rationalization of this sprawling conglomerate, with almost 100 companies producing not just vehicles but fridges, road surfacing materials and metal castings, had been limited. Labour relations were poor and management was ineffective. On its formation in 1968 the corporation had no new family saloon models for the 1970s under development barring the Austin Maxi, a situation which led to the rushed production of the Marina. Given the limited range of products and ongoing technical problems it was not surprising that BLMC had lost ground to foreign competitors in home and export markets.[87] As with Chrysler, the rescue of BLMC was open to criticism on commercial grounds but in fact the decision saved the automotive industry. Over the next decade successive governments invested large sums of public money in BLMC (which became known as just BL). The company became the butt of jokes and was used by free marketeers as an object lesson in why governments should leave market forces to work freely. Yet it is arguable that if BL had been allowed to fail, car production in the UK, at the time of writing on course to reach the record 1.92 million figure achieved in 1972,[88] would have collapsed. A strategic industry, with links across the manufacturing sector, would have been lost along with the employment opportunities it provided.

The rescue of BLMC may have been the most high profile of the NEB's projects, but it was by no means the only one. The NEB invested in a range of firms in its role as State holding company (the Treasury allocated it £1 billion for its first four years).[89] In aerospace it took over responsibility for Rolls Royce and supported Fairey and Ferranti. It provided £50 million to the semiconductor company Inmos, then working on production of early microprocessors. Working to the brief established by *An Approach to Industrial Strategy*, it linked new finance to managerial and organizational change, focusing not simply on the level of funding but on non-price factors such as training, managerial skills and the introduction and use of new technology.[90] Along with the sectoral working parties, which numbered forty by 1978–79, covering one-half of all sectors in manufacturing industry, it sought to promote change by consensus and facilitate the spread of best practice.[91]

Middlemas has argued that the CBI's commitment to tripartite co-operation weakened during the 1974–79 period. This was a function of its uneasiness about the Labour Left's advocacy of nationalization and compulsory planning agreements and trade union influence over corporate strategy as well as pay bargaining, anxieties intensified by the implications of the Bullock Report on industrial democracy (1978). In consequence the CBI began to move in a liberal direction, proposing tax cuts and a new attempt to reform industrial relations. This tendency can however be exaggerated: the CBI supported the Industrial Strategy, continuing to advocate co-operation between both sides of industry and government and remaining committed to full employment. Though the Industrial Strategy as reshaped by Wilson, 'a sort of final post-war rassemblement',[92] fell short of the hopes held out for it by Benn, it was probably about as far as State intervention could have been taken given the fraught political and economic climate and the fact that neither of the 1974 General Election results could have been considered endorsements of radical socialism. It was the last time any British government would identify the health of the national economy with the success of manufacturing industry, reflecting the priorities of a time when this still accounted for 30 per cent of all national output.

The incomes policy, along with the industrial strategy and the repudiation of the AES, was supplemented by reductions in public spending targets and by external support from the IMF. These measures, completing the parallel with the macroeconomic strategy followed by Labour in 1964–70 (especially after the November 1967 devaluation), were necessitated by the country's external position. Although the current account had improved during the year, largely due to an 18 per cent rise in income from exports at the same time as the volume of imports had fallen,[93] there was growing concern in the Treasury about the problem of funding the deficit. This anxiety was driven by a sharp decline in the level of gold and foreign exchange reserves, which fell from $7.8 billion in November 1974 to $5.5 billion in October 1975, combined with the absence of any net inflow from the sterling balances. Forecasts suggested a likely financing gap of £500 million over the six months to May 1976.[94] Healey sought to cover this with £1 billion from the IMF's Oil Facility. Meanwhile the transfer of resources into production for exports, in conjunction with a gentle sterling depreciation, would lead to a boost in revenues from trade. Both Healey and Wilson were convinced that domestic consumption would have to be reduced, the burden of this exercise falling on public spending rather than additional tax rises.[95] Given a seemingly remorseless rise in unemployment, which reached a post-war high of 1.1 million in December, there were some difficult Cabinet meetings. Healey, however, backed by Wilson, achieved the agreement of his colleagues to a package of cuts worth £3 billion up to 1978–79. This left the profile of public expenditure after 1975–76 'virtually flat' in constant price terms.[96] The IMF welcomed the package[97] and support was agreed by the Executive Board early in the New Year.

Wilson resigned in the spring of 1976, shortly after reaching his 60th birthday. Interviewed on television he admitted that he wished he could have done the job in happier times. This was an indication that the high hopes he and many others had held in 1964 had not been realized. Yet Wilson had sustained the social-democratic settlement despite the extremely unpromising circumstances of 1974, with ideological divisions in the Labour Party, a tripartite alliance under strain, powerful inflationary pressures, a startling external deficit, and a wafer-thin Parliamentary majority (after October 1974). When Wilson stepped down the supercharged political atmosphere of 1974 had disappeared and he had steered the government into adopting a coherent and viable economic strategy. The Labour Party had remained united; Wilson, who had won four General Elections out of five, seemed to have succeeded in turning it into 'the natural party of government'.[98] Liberal socialism had been sustained, though the cost involved compromises concerning full employment and real wages which were to become increasingly difficult for many core Labour voters (not to mention Party activists within the unions and in the constituency parties) to sustain.[99] It was a formidable achievement and reflected Wilson's ability to operate, as Bernard Donoughue later said, 'on several levels concurrently....He was perhaps the most complex character I have met in my life.'[100]

Pronunciamento

Wilson's success in sustaining the post-war settlement could not disguise a trend to political polarization in Britain. The growing strength of the radical Left within the grass roots of the Labour Party was mirrored on the Right. Here, there developed a worrying tendency to contemplate extra-Parliamentary steps, involving the use of private armies and parts of the military establishment, to overthrow the Labour government. This was a scenario for a coup d'état, or (on the Spanish and Latin American model) a '*Pronunciamento*', characterized by swift action on the part of senior members of the armed forces and security and intelligence services to seize power from the elected government, in the name of the 'National Will'.[101] In this scenario Labour was to be replaced by a 'National Government', led by a distinguished public figure (Mountbatten's name surfaced on several occasions), and composed of Centrist and Right wing politicians, high-ranking servicemen (either still serving or recently retired), non-party technocrats such as Lord Robens (once a Labour MP, then Chairman of the NCB and now head of Vickers), and prominent figures from the City and industry. This administration would be responsible not to Parliament but to the Crown (the official Head of State) and wield emergency powers aimed at curbing union militancy. Public services would be taken over by the military, with dissenters and subversives facing the prospect of detention without trial (already in practice in Northern Ireland, where it had been introduced during the 'Troubles' which had started in 1968); there were plans to remove the Cabinet *en masse* to the QE2 and keep it confined there.[102]

These shadowy forces were not taken seriously by many at the time. Wilson was an exception. When troops re-appeared at Heathrow in June, July and September (on the last two occasions the pretext of a terrorist threat was not invoked) Wilson became worried that they could be 'turned around' and any alert could be used to 'trigger a plan for a coup'.[103] He expressed his concern about the apparent willingness of rogue elements in MI5 to promote this subversive behaviour to two journalists, who published their story, first in the *Daily Mirror* in 1977 and then as a book, *The Pencourt File*.[104] The revelations started a trail followed afterwards by many journalists, seeking to establish the truth of what became known as 'The Wilson Plot'. *Spycatcher,* the memoirs of former MI5 officer Peter Wright, published in 1987, gave more substance to Wilson's allegations.[105] Against this, Christopher Andrew's history of MI5 dismissed the story of a conspiracy against Labour involving members of the Security Service.[106] Yet in fact the evidence supports Wilson. Brian Crozier, a journalist and self-described 'international activist' against the Left who had worked for CIA and SIS (Secret Intelligence Service, also known as MI6) front organizations, revealed in 1991 that there had been interest in the Army in taking action against Labour and the unions, adding that 'I know a great deal of consideration was given to it'.[107] Number 10 Downing Street was indeed bugged, as Wilson had claimed,[108] and elements in the military and the Security Service did try to undermine the government by the covert dissemination of smears and lies in an Operation, code-named Clockwork Orange, designed to wreck its credibility with the public and its reputation abroad.[109]

The idea that it might be possible to call on the armed forces to effect a change of government in Britain had, of course, surfaced in 1968 when Cecil King had urged Mountbatten to lead a National government. At that stage it had been possible for the Director-General of MI5 to dismiss King and his supporters as 'a pretty loony crew'.[110] By 1974, however, backing for emergency action had increased and embraced important sections of the armed forces, the military-industrial sector of the economy, the security and intelligence establishments, multinational corporations, the City and even the press. The complex of groups willing to consider and plan for a 'coup' was no joke but can be seen as an example of the political formation known by the American political scientist Peter Dale Scott as the 'Deep State'. He defined this as 'the wider interface...between the public, the constitutionally established state, and the deep forces behind it of wealth, power, and violence outside the government'.[111] Scott was writing about the USA but his model can be applied to the UK, given that the constellation of interests involved had been identified as the heart of Britain's old imperial ruling class at the start of the twentieth century by J. A. Hobson.[112] Who was involved? One key figure was Sir Val Duncan, Chairman of the multinational mining conglomerate Rio Tinto Zinc (RTZ). Addressing a group of journalists, businessmen, retired generals and intelligence officers at a meeting in May 1975, Duncan claimed that 'the country was on the verge of anarchy and we are going to step in and take over'.[113] Also at this meeting were Cecil King, prime mover in the 1968 plot, and Lord Robens. Shortly after this the *Daily Telegraph* (whose editor, Bill Deedes, had been present) noted that RTZ was 'in a position to furnish a coalition government should one be required', given the presence on the board of leading politicians such as Lord Carrington (Defence Secretary in Heath's government), and Liberal and Labour peers Byers and Shackleton.[114]

Others key figures were Sir Walter Walker, former Commander in Chief of NATO's Allied Forces Europe; George Kennedy Young, Deputy Director of SIS until his retirement to take up a career in the City in 1960; and SAS founder David Stirling. At the end of 1973 Young established a voluntary organization, Unison, composed mainly of former servicemen (and women), to assist the armed forces in the maintenance of public services in times of strike action; in July 1974 Stirling launched GB75, a similar group; and in September Walker formed his own outfit, Civil Assistance. It is easy to dismiss these individuals as mavericks and eccentrics: this would be mistaken since their connections led to the heart of the British establishment. During the first months of 1975 both Walker and Young can be seen at the centre of a financial and political network. This embraced well-established

City institutions such as Consolidated Goldfields, Cater Ryder, Cazenove's and Lazard's, as well as more obscure ones such as the Anglo-Eastern Bank (also an intelligence front),[115] leading figures on the Right of the Conservative Party such as the MPs (and ex-Ministers) Airey Neave and Nicholas Ridley and senior members of the military establishment such as Sir Gerald Templer.[116] In May 1975 Walker received £10,000 from shipping magnate and co-founder of the new Conservative Party think-tank the CPS, Sir Nicholas Cayzer. The previous month Stirling had obtained backing worth over £10,000 from Cazenove's;[117] he also had a long-term connection with Cayzer, having worked for the BCS subsidiary Airwork. This was a defence support company. Mostly used by the RAF it also undertook missions for SIS; a few years earlier it had assisted Stirling and a band of mercenaries in a deniable operation to protect British influence in the Arabian Peninsula from Egyptian attempts to spread the gospel of Arab nationalism.[118]

The expansion of support for a coup among certain circles of British society had been stimulated by a number of developments, but the key concern was what was perceived to be the rising power of the Left. The difficulties experienced by the Heath government in its relations with some unions, notably the NUM (Saltley and then the Three Day Week featuring prominently), had been central to a growing preoccupation within MI5 and the armed forces with the possibility of domestic subversion. It was assumed that the hand of the Soviet Union was behind militancy in the unions and the increasing radicalism of the constituency sections of the Labour Party. This fear of subversion from the Left had contributed to the somewhat overwrought atmosphere of the February 1974 Election and mounted steadily over the following year, driven by domestic and international developments.

At home, the Irish situation was identified as a major cause for concern. In February 1974 the Provisional IRA (PIRA) exploded a bomb it had planted on a coach transporting soldiers to the military camp at Catterick in North Yorkshire. Twelve died, including one civilian and two children. This was its first successful lethal assault on the mainland, and it was followed by a series of others. That year the PIRA was responsible for forty-four deaths, twenty-nine of them being civilian and fourteen military (one was a PIRA bomber killed by his own device). Nineteen of these occurred on the night of 21 November when two pubs in Birmingham were bombed (two more victims died later).The fatalities accounted for 38 per cent of all incurred in terrorist attacks in England between 1973 and 1997.[119] The PIRA was said to be a Marxist organization which aimed to drive the British out of Ulster and then turn a newly united Ireland into a pro-Soviet socialist republic modelled on Cuba. To this end (so it was alleged) it had received guns and ammunition from the USSR. In consequence no political concessions could be made to PIRA; it was essential the British remained in Ireland, both to protect the Protestant community in Ulster and to ensure that the western flank of NATO was not turned, leaving the UK dangerously exposed to Soviet influence.[120]

If the Irish situation was seen to present one strategic threat to the UK, others appeared to develop from events further afield. Parties of the Left were prospering on the European mainland, presenting a challenge to the power of political, business and financial elites: the Swedish Social Democrats (in power since 1932) were promoting the Rehn–Meidner plan, which promoted the acquisition by workers of all the shares owned by employers in their own businesses. At the same time the Italian Communist Party seemed on the verge of taking power through the ballot box; in Spain the Franco regime ended with the death of the old Caudillo in 1975, leaving a political landscape where both Socialists and Communists were strongly represented. A similar situation prevailed in Portugal after a revolution driven through by army officers brought an end to over four decades of authoritarian government.[121] The transformation here had major implications for Western interests in southern Africa, with Portugal's old colonies of Mozambique and Angola becoming independent. The first of these became a Marxist one-party state while the second lurched quickly into a civil war and Cold War trouble spot where the contending sides were backed on the one hand by the USA and its allies in the region (South Africa and Zaire) and on the other by the USSR and Cuba.[122]

Anxiety about the apparent advance of the USSR and the Left was compounded by the conviction that capitalism itself now faced an existential threat. This insecurity was especially acute among the top 0.1 per cent of the population, whose share of the national income had steadily declined since World War One,[123] but it also spread to a new coalition of forces. This embraced four groups in particular. One was senior executives in large corporations who had come to view the nation-state as a threat to the growth and independence of their own organizations. A second was made up from employers and managers convinced that the trade unions were too powerful. Labour's legislative record in office, the high level of trade union membership at the time – 54 per cent of the workforce was unionized, the highest level recorded in the UK experience[124] – and the falling share of profits in GDP were invoked to support these views. In 1975 these fell to a post-war low of just over 20 per cent[125] while the share of wages in GDP rose from a figure at or just below 60 per cent in the 1960s to hit a peak of 65.1 per cent in 1975.[126] The third group was composed of middle-class voters threatened by militant trade unionism and by inflation and high taxes, both of which were eroding their savings and their living standards. With the basic rate (applicable to incomes over £4,500 a year) rising from 33 per cent to 35 per cent in 1975, this resentment of taxation was increasingly shared by affluent workers. They argued that it was funding social security and unemployment benefit for the work-shy while penalising the thrifty and industrious.[127]

Given the growing strength of radical socialist views within the Labour Party, the collapse of economic growth in 1974–75 and the recent high levels of inflation, it seemed that none of the foundations of the free enterprise system – management's right to manage and to hire and fire labour; price stability; the ability to accumulate wealth as individuals or corporations; and the security of private ownership of the means of production – could be regarded as secure and taken for granted. A real conviction developed on the Right that Britain's days as a great power with global influence and possibly even as a liberal-capitalist State and member of the western alliance were numbered, fuelling desperation about the future. Margaret Thatcher told BBC reporter Michael Cockerell during the 1979 election that 'I can't bear Britain in decline, I just can't.' In a 1976 CPS pamphlet, *Stranded in the Middle Ground*, Thatcher's ally Sir Keith Joseph argued that 'Making the rich poorer does not make the poor richer, but it does make the state stronger....The pursuit of income equality will turn this country into a totalitarian slum.'[128] It was a comment which wove together all the different threads making up this tapestry of gloom and despondency about the condition of Britain. The plotters may at times have appeared slightly comical but they were in reality a serious indication of how the Right was becoming increasingly determined to mount a free market counter-revolution against post-war social democracy, in which taxes would be reduced and government spending would fall while industrial relations legislation would be introduced to limit the ability of unions to use the strike weapon.

Of course, no evidence whatever has come to light to suggest that Thatcher and Joseph ever contemplated extra-Parliamentary action to overthrow Labour; but their heartfelt comments articulated the views of those 'apprehensive patriots' (the term was David Stirling's)[129] who were prepared to consider emergency measures. Support for these peaked in 1974–75, tailing off thereafter though not disappearing altogether until Labour lost the May 1979 General Election. The last flickers of the flame can be seen in the early part of that year, when Airey Neave embarked on talks with an ex-SIS agent about the feasibility of 'stopping' Tony Benn and establishing 'an underground army of resistance' if Labour won at the polls.[130] In the end discussion of a coup was overtaken by events, in particular by the shift of the Conservatives to the Right after Margaret Thatcher replaced Edward Heath as leader in February 1975. This triumph, orchestrated by Neave,[131] provided the forces which had contemplated a coup with a populist ally from Consumer's England capable of constructing a political coalition sufficiently broad and deep to take over the State without drama (at least initially).

Margaret Thatcher did not share Heath's social-democratic views: she was a robust supporter of individualism and the free market and suspicious of the trend to detente between the West and the USSR which had characterized the past few years.[132] Sir Walter Walker called her 'the salvation of this country, truly alive' to internal and external threats[133] and although she was careful not to take the Tories on too radical a path as Opposition leader there were straws in the wind from an early stage. One was her association with Airey Neave. Neave combined a visceral distaste for socialism with a commitment to use the power of the State's military arm and covert agencies, if necessary in the most extreme way, against those (usually on the Left or in the Provisional IRA) he considered to be its enemies.[134] Another was the existence of 'Shield', a group of intelligence officers connected to MI5 and SIS. This was established by Brian Crozier to provide regular briefings for Thatcher on 'the deliberate undermining of State and society' by 'the subversive left', which (he claimed) had taken over the Labour Party and the unions and was penetrating other areas, including the schools, the universities, the media and the Churches, with the aim of turning Britain into a 'people's democracy on the East European model'. Thatcher eagerly embraced Crozier's analysis, telling him, 'From now on, Brian, these are *my* ideas.'[135] The third was the creation of the National Association for Freedom (NAFF) in December 1975. Thatcher enthusiastically welcomed this pressure-group, established to promote anti-collectivist, pro-free-market ideas and to give logistical backing to firms facing strike action and provide financial support to employers using the Courts to challenge trade unions.[136] NAFF ran its own newspaper, *The Free Nation*, to which Margaret Thatcher contributed. It recruited members within local Conservative Associations (the fee was £5) and successfully raised a large number of private donations.[137] Most of its funding, however, came via its founder, British United Industrialists, an organization used as a conduit for funds from business into the Conservative Party.

As NAFF grew in strength the private armies withdrew into the shadows, Civil Assistance disbanding in 1976. They became redundant thanks to NAFF's successes in attracting favourable publicity for the fight against socialism. NAFF became the focus for most of the different strands of the radical and discontented Right in the UK, linking them to the grass roots of the Conservative Party and providing Thatcher with a strong following in the constituencies.[138] NAFF 'embodied all the elements – Intelligence, Right-wing Tory, business interests and the City – that would fall in line behind Margaret Thatcher'[139] as Prime Minister after 1979. It had sponsors from the Tory Right (in the persons of MPs such as Rhodes Boyson, Jill Knight, Neave and Nicholas Ridley) and backing from corporate business (seed-money was provided by Aims of Industry, Taylor Woodrow and McAlpine) and key members of the groups and networks involved in consideration of a coup such as Sir Gerald Templer. NAFF Council members included Brian Crozier and the Right wing commentator and publicist Robert Moss, who shared Crozier's connections to the Anglo-American intelligence establishment, Colonel Sir Robert Thompson, a counter-insurgency expert who had served in Malaya under Templer (who was also on the Council) and ex-SIS Deputy Director George Kennedy Young.[140] From now onwards influential forces within British society were able to make common cause with the external advocates of monetarism and neo-liberalism, at this stage most strongly represented within the USA, using the power and influence of this alliance to destabilize social democracy by constitutional means. These efforts to destroy the government, or, failing its collapse, force it to implement an economic strategy designed to reduce taxes and shrink the State, reached a climax with the IMF crisis of late 1976. Labour survived and even prospered for a time; but its victory was not a lasting one.

Last stand

The dire prognostications of Keith Joseph and others on the British Right were shared in the USA. Here they found a sympathetic audience in Wall Street, the US Treasury and in the IMF, all of which were now thoroughly penetrated by monetarist and neo-liberal doctrine. Pessimism about the state of Britain received telling expression in a *Wall Street Journal* editorial, 'Goodbye Great Britain: it was nice knowing you', in April 1975. The piece described a country in which inflation and public spending were out of control, while British industry was collapsing in the face of trade union militancy, high wages, exorbitant taxation and a government 'clearly headed towards a policy of total confiscation'. These were 'the ultimate consequences of the welfare-state-manic-Keynesian syndrome'.[141] In New York and Washington as well as in sections of the British establishment increasing thought was given to the prospects of removing Labour from office or at least forcing it to implement the new free market agenda. The government's opponents at home and in the USA were to have an opportunity to achieve this with the sterling crisis of 1976. The whole affair certainly amounted to a baptism of fire for Wilson's successor, James Callaghan, but he skilfully managed it so that in the end it was resolved in a way which actually sustained Labour and its version of social democracy. Yet just as Labour seemed to have gained the confidence of the electorate, a series of political misjudgements combined with frustration on the part of some trade unions (representing mainly public sector workers) to destroy its credibility.

Callaghan, who became Prime Minister in April 1976, was highly experienced. He was Wilson's choice as successor; the two men had crossed swords over *In Place of Strife* but they had put their differences behind them and established a good working relationship after Labour's return to power in 1974. Callaghan had spent his political life in the Labour movement, starting as a trade union official (at the Inland Revenue) in the 1930s. After distinguished war service in the Royal Naval Volunteer Reserve (where he was commissioned as an officer) he became a Labour MP in 1945 and quickly rose to a Ministerial position. From 1947 onwards he was continuously on the Labour front bench. By the time he succeeded Wilson he had held all the great offices of State – Chancellor (1964–67), Home Secretary (1967–70) and Foreign Secretary (1974–76). Politically, he was on the Right of the Party, a staunch believer in the mixed economy and in Britain's commitment to the Atlantic Alliance.[142] These positions no longer received the largely unqualified backing across most of the movement which they had enjoyed prior to 1974. Callaghan was, however, able to command widespread respect from all sections of Labour as a result of his longstanding connection to the trade union movement. Jack Jones found him 'more approachable' and friendly than Wilson, qualities which boded well for Labour's ability to sustain the Social Contract.[143] Certainly, he possessed an avuncular manner which many found attractive but this could sometimes be used to be blunt and chilling as well as to benevolent effect.[144] It was a quality which together with his bulky figure gave him a commanding personal presence.

Callaghan's objectives on becoming Prime Minister all featured the consolidation of the social-democratic strategy pursued by Wilson. Disturbed by the industrial strife and tensions evident in 1973–75 he aspired to the construction of a 'cohesive society'.[145] To this end he looked to continuing co-operation between both sides of industry and the government and to the modernization of industry through the industrial strategy. He aimed to support this through the promotion of industrial democracy so that workers developed 'a real sense of responsibility' for the steps needed to enhance competitiveness. In the short-term, however, the key problem was inflation. The achievements of Phase 1 of the incomes policy notwithstanding, this was continuing not only to put pressure on savings and living standards but feeding market distrust for sterling. Callaghan had a particular distaste for inflation, stemming from the conviction that it threatened 'the whole fabric of society', with the living standards of working-class voters and the low paid threatened more than any other section of the community.[146] Callaghan aspired to halve the annual rate of inflation by the spring of 1977 and to drive it below 5 per cent by 1980.[147] Meeting these targets would require continuation of the incomes policy which had started the previous summer.

The government's efforts to keep domestic costs under control started well: in May there was an agreement with the TUC on Phase 2 of the pay policy. The talks had been tough, but both parties were satisfied with the final settlement. This turned on TUC consent to a 5 per cent annual limit to wage increases for those earning between £50 and £80 pounds a week, with a maximum rise of £4 per week for those on higher incomes and one of £2.50 for those on less than £50 per week, though the lowest paid would also receive tax cuts. Healey estimated that it amounted to an average pay rise of 4.5 per cent when applied to the nation's wage bill.[148] TUC representatives did have some misgivings about this arrangement, given that inflation was still running at double-digit levels. Jones would have preferred another flat rate deal but in the end settled along with his colleagues in order to avoid 'the risk of a catastrophic run on the pound and a General Election'.[149]

Jones's anxiety that the failure of the talks might have set off a run on the pound was not fanciful. The Phase 2 agreement did stabilize sterling for a time, but the currency remained vulnerable to waves of selling, reflecting persistent lack of confidence in the markets. The trouble had started in March when the Treasury embarked on a strategy designed to improve the external position via a controlled devaluation of just under 10 per cent, from £1=$2.05 to £1=$1.85/90. Given that the government had ruled out Benn's protectionist Alternative Strategy this made sense as a rational attempt to cut imports and increase exports, whose competitiveness would be enhanced by the productivity measures agreed in the NEDC. There was a risk that a fall in the exchange rate might revive the inflationary spiral of prices and wages experienced in 1974–75 but Callaghan and Healey believed this could be managed by the operation of Phase 2.

This was a perfectly coherent policy but it was not received well in the financial markets. These took the government's readiness to see sterling decline as indicative of no confidence in the prospects of keeping sterling anywhere near the £1=$2 level rather than as an effort to set in motion export-led growth. They started to sell the currency.[150] A powerful bear market in sterling developed, stimulated by gloom about its future and concern that the PSBR was too high, crowding out private investment as a result. By the end of May the rate was down to $1.70, with sentiment against the pound so strong that efforts to shore it up by using the foreign exchange reserves to support it simply wasted precious resources. Market pessimism was reinforced by the Treasury figures showing the share of GDP taken by public spending to have reached the very high level of 60 per cent. In fact the figure was based on highly unsound accounting practice, and was revised down to a much more modest 46 per cent not long after.[151] By that time, however, the damage had been done, with the markets as well as Milton Friedman and his supporters in the USA and the UK (including Shadow Ministers) stating this to be unsustainable and further evidence that Britain was heading towards a decrepit form of state socialism.[152]

The government now tried to stop sterling's decline by raising a large short-term credit of $5.3 billion, to be repaid in December, from the BIS and the central banks of the Group of Ten leading industrialized nations. The Cabinet agreed that the UK would turn to the IMF for a stand-by credit should further borrowing be necessary in order to finance the December repayment of the BIS and central bank credit. Healey was keen to avoid this contingency, aware that the IMF considered the UK public sector too large and wanted to see a reduction in the claims it made on resources, as indicated by the PSBR figure. With new forecasts showing a current account deficit of £3 billion for 1977–78 and a PSBR of £10.2 billion for the same year Healey persuaded a reluctant Cabinet to accept a further £1 billion of public spending cuts in July.[153] At the same time he bowed to the fashion for monetarism and introduced a monetary target of 12 per cent for money supply growth, hoping this innovation along with the fiscal tightening would reassure the markets and so bring an end to the pressure on sterling.[154]

The markets were not convinced. August was quiet but pressure on sterling reappeared in September. Large-scale Bank of England intervention failed to stop the speculation and was abandoned to stop the reserves (now worth £2.9 billion) from falling to a level too low to cover the current account deficit and Britain's external liabilities.[155] As a substitute the MLR was raised to 13 per cent, to little effect. By the end of the month confidence seemed to have evaporated following poor August trade figures and a ballot in favour of industrial action by the National Union of Seamen.[156] Sterling was down to £1=$1.68, a record low.[157] Healey told Callaghan that he was being advised by the Bank of England that the pound could fall below $1.50, with no knowing how far it could go.[158] With capital flooding out of the country (it was later estimated that 1976 saw outflows of more than £2.8 billion)[159] and exiguous reserves, it was becoming clear that repayment of the $5.3 billion credit in December was going to be very difficult in the absence of help from the IMF.

The accelerating crisis led to dramatic scenes. Sterling's plunge coincided with the start of the Labour Party's annual conference. Healey and Callaghan agreed that it would after all be necessary to apply to the IMF for a stand-by credit. The Chancellor, about to depart to Manila for the IMF's annual general meeting, turned round at Heathrow and headed instead to Blackpool where the conference was being held, to explain why. He received a stormy reception from delegates concerned about the policy implications and keen to try the Alternative Strategy instead. Callaghan intervened with a remarkable speech in which he told an extremely uncomfortable audience that

We used to think that you could spend your way out of recession, and increase employment by cutting taxes and increasing government spending. I tell you in all candour that that option no longer exists, and in so far as it ever did exist, it only worked on each occasion since the war to inject bigger doses of inflation into the economy, followed by higher levels of unemployment as the next step.[160]

It was now time to return 'to fundamentals', which meant internationally competitive labour costs, improvements in productivity and incomes which did not exceed the value of what the nation was producing.

For Benn the speech appeared to reject the intellectual foundations of Keynesian economics and the welfare consensus and commit Labour to the side of monetarism and the free market.[161] The same sentiments have been expressed from the Right, not as a criticism but as a compliment.[162] They were therefore widely shared, possibly because the section of the speech which drew all the attention had been drafted by Callaghan's son-in-law Peter Jay, then Economics Editor of *The Times* and sympathetic to monetarism. In fact both the accusations and the compliments are misguided. Callaghan took time to defend the Social Contract, the Industrial Strategy and high levels of public expenditure. He did not say that no government should ever increase spending or cut taxation in order to boost employment: rather that in the current circumstances this would not be sustainable and was no substitute for essential changes such as the introduction of monetary discipline in place of the laxity likely to undermine the 'foundations of sustained economic growth'.[163] Neither Callaghan nor Healey saw the IMF credit as the prelude to a new era in political economy. Rather, if successfully negotiated, it would be a source of liquidity and an endorsement of the government's current strategy which, given the Fund's central role in the international financial system, would guarantee market confidence in Labour. The debilitating pressure on sterling and the reserves which was now threatening to destabilize the government would cease.[164]

The Cabinet agreed to an approach to the IMF for a stand-by credit worth $3.9 billion (equivalent to £2.3 billion). Callaghan and Healey argued, in addition, that it would be necessary to negotiate a safety net for the sterling balances, underwritten by leading members of the G10, to prevent sudden, speculative movements in these from precipitating a run on the reserves.[165] The Fund was, however, adamant that agreement on any safety net would only be possible following a successful conclusion to negotiations on the stand-by. Moreover it was clear that there could be no happy outcome to the talks unless the government was prepared to make sweeping policy changes, featuring above all further and drastic cuts.

As far as the Fund was concerned the case for further cuts was now unanswerable, and confirmed by British Treasury figures. A forecast released in October showed the PSBR rising to £12 billion in 1977–78 (over 10 per cent of GDP and £2 billion up on the revised estimate for this year made after the July cuts) and £10 billion for 1978–79.[166] The Treasury corrected the new estimated PSBR for 1977–78 to £10.5 billion but this did not impress the IMF, which was also bothered by

Treasury estimates that the money supply would increase by 14 per cent in 1977–78. Its team arrived in London at the start of November with its own agenda. The leading item here was 'the "adequacy" of existing UK macro-economic policy, in particular the government's budgetary stance in relation to the monetary outlook' and 'the size of the budgetary adjustment...necessary'.[167] In plain English this meant public spending cuts. It demanded £4.5 billion: £3 billion for 1977–78, followed by a further £1.5 billion in 1978–79, reducing the PSBR for that year down to £6.5 billion, some £3.5 billion lower than the figure set out in the 1976 public spending projections.[168] This was too much for Healey and Callaghan. Neither could consent to the Fund's requirement, which amounted to almost 4 per cent of the 1976 GDP.[169]

The scene was set for a serious clash between the Labour Government and the IMF. The fundamental problem in dealing with the Fund was that its Managing Director, Johannes Witteveen, backed by US Treasury Secretary William Simon and his deputy Ed Yeo, were evangelistic economic liberals who supported and indeed helped to promote the economic counter-revolution. Simon wrote that 'There is only one social system that reflects the sovereignty of the individual: the free-market, or capitalist, system'.[170] These views led them to be instinctively suspicious of Britain's Labour government: they shared the outlook of the 'Goodbye, Great Britain' article.

The Fund's support for such arguments was, of course, in part a function of its sympathy for monetarism. This was reinforced by its long-term mission: from the start of its existence the Fund's role had been to uphold a liberal world trading and financial system. Its provision of liquidity to deficit nations while they undertook measures designed to make their exports more competitive was designed to make it unnecessary for them to embrace protectionism. By the mid-1970s, however, Britain being the prime example, it appeared as if embattled post-war social democracies, facing rising living costs, slow growth and large current account deficits, were becoming increasingly attracted by the idea of using trade and exchange controls to reduce imports. Dismay at developments in the Cold War fed anxiety in Washington, New York and in the City that Western governments seeking to protect post-1945 welfare states might stumble into 'socialism'. It had therefore become essential that the Fund act in accordance with its mission, by linking finance for debtor countries to the policy changes which would (it was believed) deliver low inflation and external surpluses, keeping them locked into the liberal capitalist world in the process.

In the British case this meant that the Fund, supported by the US Treasury, sought to use the credit as the catalyst for fundamental change in the UK, whereby the State was to shrink and the economy move onto a more liberal economic path. This approach was encouraged by the Opposition: on 10 November 1976 Treasury spokesman John Nott, acting on behalf of Thatcher and her Shadow Chancellor Sir Geoffrey Howe, met the US Financial Attaché in London, making it clear that 'Conservative Party leaders and financial spokesmen hope the IMF will be very tough in its conditions' and that 'what is needed is sharp cuts in public expenditure'.[171]

At much the same time Callaghan was tipped off that another Conservative front bench politician was briefing against the government in Washington.[172] It followed that the Labour government's discussions with the Fund about the size of the cuts became an ideological battle between post-war social democracy and the new neo-liberalism with powerful supporters on both sides of the Atlantic. Moreover, given Labour's vulnerable position in the House of Commons (its narrow majority was to disappear altogether after a couple of by-election defeats in the New Year) there was a serious possibility of the government's collapse unless the Cabinet and Parliamentary Party could take a united view on whatever package was agreed. If the final shape of this turned out to be as severe as the Fund and its allies wanted, the government's survival was unlikely. It appeared as if Labour was being driven either out of office or to remaining in power at the price of executing a Right wing economic programme: this may not have been a 'Pronunciamento' but it could be called an informal coup d'état.[173]

Healey put the Treasury response to Cabinet on 23 November: satisfying the IMF involved cuts worth £3.5 billion, £1.5 billion of them in 1977–78 followed by £2 billion in 1978–79. The package would lead to slower growth and higher unemployment (an increase of 70,000 above the forecast total of 1.75 million by the end of 1977–78) in the short-term but the current account would be in surplus by the second half of 1977, a year earlier than currently forecast. The implications of the spending cuts were painful. They included economies in the housing, construction and defence programmes, savings on food and rent subsidies and cancellation of the uprating of social security benefits and public sector pensions in 1977.[174]

The Cabinet reacted badly. It failed to agree to Healey's proposals. Ministers argued that the package would cause the collapse of the Social Contract and therefore jeopardize the counter-inflation strategy. Callaghan acknowledged that 'the scale of the public expenditure cuts at present proposed was too great to accept'.[175] The cuts were debated over the next ten days, with the opposition to them being led by three Ministers. Tony Benn argued that it was time to take the route indicated in his Alternative Strategy while Peter Shore (Environment Secretary) proposed temporary import controls to close the external deficit. These arguments did not receive much support – the Alternative Strategy already having been rejected and the measures in Shore's plan criticized as not necessarily adequate to return the current account to surplus. The most formidable counter-argument to the Chancellor came from Anthony Crosland (Foreign Secretary since April), in a series of interventions which were taken very seriously by colleagues. He opposed acceptance of the Treasury package. It was based on a PSBR estimate for 1977–78 which was not credible. In fact, the combination of the counter-inflation strategy, the lower sterling rate and the cuts already agreed would return the country to a current account surplus by 1978. Crosland suggested consideration of import deposits and a very limited fiscal contraction of £1 billion, made up of £0.5 billion raised from asset sales (mainly BP shares) and £0.5 billion from cuts. Failing the Fund's agreement it should be told that the UK would be obliged to embrace protectionism despite the implications of this for the EEC and for world trade generally.[176]

Healey therefore faced a battle on two fronts. One involved winning over colleagues, many of whom were clearly very sceptical about the entire thrust of IMF thinking, to a package which would satisfy the Fund (and therefore the UK's creditors). Success in the other turned on gaining concessions from the Fund important enough to ensure he was able to put a deal to the Cabinet which was politically acceptable. Healey was not unsympathetic to Crosland's position but for him the key issue was confidence – the confidence of the markets – and this was why the Foreign Secretary's proposal was inadequate.

The importance of confidence arose from sterling's vulnerability to the volatile international capital flows now so significant in the global financial system. The events of June 1975 and September 1976 had shown how sensitive these were to changes in market sentiment. Healey pointed out that since 1973 the UK (government, public sector bodies and private institutions) had borrowed £6 billion from OPEC countries. But this credit was now starting to run out. Rightly or wrongly, those who possessed the funds doubted both whether the British government had the public finances under control and whether the current account was likely to go into surplus within the next eighteen months. Without their support it would be impossible to cover the external deficit over the next year 'and probably more' 'at anything like the current exchange rate'. This would have to fall very low; there was a risk of 'continuous and probably accelerating depreciation, leading to South American-style inflation'. Given that the Fund was seen by the markets as 'the bellwether', successful negotiation of the $3.9 billion stand-by would avert this disaster. It would indicate Fund approval for Labour's strategy. The markets would follow suit, sterling would stabilize and the external position would be covered.[177]

By the start of December no deal was in prospect: the Cabinet had no settled position and a gulf remained between the Treasury and 10 Downing Street on one side and the IMF on the other, with the deadline for repayment of the June G10–BIS credit just a week away. At this point, however, the Cabinet shifted. Healey, backed by the Prime Minister, proposed a revised package of £1 billion cuts, supplemented by £0.5 billion asset sales in 1977–78, plus a further contraction of £2.0 billion in 1978–79, £1.5 billion through reductions in spending and £0.5 million via tax increases. This would produce a PSBR of £8.7 billion in 1977–78 and GDP growth of 3.5 per cent by 1978. By 1978 the balance of payments would be running a surplus of between £2.5 and £3 billion. Unemployment would rise by 30,000 in 1977 but this could be offset by micro-economic measures. Healey also argued that if the government could reach agreement with the Fund on this basis, the effect on interest rates would be positive enough to counteract some of the deflationary effects of the measures he was proposing. Dissent crumbled: Healey's opponents were unable to reach a common position and Crosland took the view that the government would be unlikely to survive if the Cabinet rejected the advice of the Chancellor and Prime Minister on such an important issue.[178]

The government now had an agreed position, which was put to the Fund. It was still not good enough for Witteveen, who demanded the full £4.5 billion contraction he had been asking for from the start, made up from £1.5 billion in 1977–78 and another £3 billion the following year. Healey, who had a very distinguished war record and was known to be a tough negotiator with an extensive and colourful vocabulary, was not a man to be intimidated. At this point he simply stated that the Fund's Managing Director should 'take a running jump' and (quite unconstitutionally) threatened the resignation of the government followed by a General Election on the theme of a 'bankers' ramp'. Callaghan supported his Chancellor and the Fund backed down:[179] a compromise position was reached, whereby the additional cuts demanded by Witteveen for 1978–79 would only be implemented if GDP growth that year exceeded the 3.5 per cent Treasury forecast.[180] In return the Fund agreed to the $3.9 billion stand-by, to be released in instalments; this was followed in January by a new Basle Agreement, establishing a $3 billion safety net to manage the run-down of the sterling balances.

The aftermath of the IMF crisis saw a dramatic turnaround in government fortunes. Its policies regained the trust of the markets, as Callaghan and Healey had anticipated: over the next eighteen months sterling rose steadily towards the £1=$2 level. The current account was back in balance as early as mid-1977. Capital inflows during 1977 amounted to £4.8 billion and by December the reserves had increased to £10.7 billion.[181] At the same time the UK's share of the top twelve trading nations' net exports rose while its costs fell. Electrical engineering, clothing, and the distributive trades all enjoyed a period of expansion in sales, profits and investment.[182] Growth between 1976 and 1979 averaged an annual rate of 2.4 per cent. By mid-1978 it was running at 3 per cent;[183] and unemployment, having reached a peak of 6.2 per cent of the workforce in 1977, fell back to 5.7 per cent in 1979. The government and the TUC agreed Phase 3 of the pay policy, whereby the unions agreed to annual pay rises of 10 per cent. With only a few exceptions this limit was observed. At the same time the government kept to its monetary targets, reducing market expectations about inflation in the process. During the course of 1977–78, thanks to Phase 3, the upward path of sterling and the successful monetary policy, the annual rate of inflation dropped below 10 per cent, falling to 7.4 per cent, the lowest level for five years.[184]

No British government since has been able to deliver steady growth and a current account surplus along with falling inflation and unemployment all at the same time. Credit for the successes achieved after 1976 has been given to the IMF by some historians.[185] Yet in fact the aftermath of the agreement with the IMF involved no fundamental change to the macroeconomic strategy which had been developed during Wilson's final year, although there were modifications to government spending plans which both the Prime Minister and the Chancellor reckoned to be necessary in any case. The agreement with the Fund saw the government agreeing to cuts worth not £4.5 billion but £2.5 billion. The transformation of the external balance in 1977 came too rapidly for the Fund package to have had any hand in achieving it. Indeed, only half of the loan was ever borrowed, the last tranche being drawn in August 1977. These credits, along with those negotiated in 1975, were all repaid well before the government left office in 1979, a process made all the easier when the PSBR for 1977–78 turned out to be just £8.5 billion rather than £12 billion as forecast by the Treasury.[186] As Healey pointed out, had the true picture been clear in 1976 there would have been no need to apply for the stand-by.[187] Crosland had been right: the fundamentals concerning public spending and the external balance had been sound. The problem was that the markets had not believed this and had therefore oversold the currency. The correction could not start until the government had received the Fund's stamp of approval.[188]

The strength of the public finances and the external position actually allowed the government to expand the economy without breaching its monetary targets or its commitments to the IMF relating to the PSBR.[189] With growth in 1978–79 just below the forecast level the extra cuts Witteveen had wanted were never implemented. The standard rate of taxation was cut to 33 per cent (with the threshold raised to over £8,000) and Healey embarked on a modest reflationary strategy to boost growth: in May he announced large increases in child benefits, an extension of free school meals and funding for training. In October the government approved a £400 million package for the construction industry: the combination of these measures increased public expenditure by £1 billion in 1977–78 and by £2.5 billion in 1978–79. It all amounted to 'a virtual cancellation' of the cuts agreed in December 1976.[190]

Rotten potatoes

It has been worth telling the story of the negotiations with the Fund at some length, to show not only that they involved an ideological assault on Labour, but that the Callaghan government did not move very far. The cuts, and contraction, that it did agree to were far less extensive than the Fund and its allies had wanted. The government did not abandon its social-democratic programme and started to reap the benefits of the increasingly benign economic climate. By 1977–78 it had not only weathered the political and economic storm but was presiding over a brisk rise in living standards: the pay rises and tax cuts were delivering a 14 per cent rise in incomes even as inflation slipped below 8 per cent.[191] The pay-off was increasing popularity. The autumn of 1978 saw Labour ahead in the opinion polls, its lead over the Conservatives reaching between 5 per cent and 7 per cent.[192] It was widely believed that Callaghan would call an autumn General Election, with a very good chance of winning it, albeit narrowly. There was increasing anxiety in Conservative ranks at the unexpected longevity and now popularity of a government whose collapse had been expected at least two years earlier.[193]

At this point hubris and political misjudgement intervened. Callaghan, who had wanted the unions to accept an annual pay norm of 4–5 per cent in 1977–78, told the Cabinet that he was looking for one of 5 per cent in 1978–79. Healey and other Cabinet colleagues did not think this was feasible but by this time the Prime Minister's dislike of inflation along with his frustration with what he felt was the unions' recurring 'tunnel vision about pay' made him unwilling to accept any compromise. He told Peter Jay, 'they don't deserve 1 per cent. They deserve zero per cent'.[194] Callaghan's hope was that it would be possible to persuade the TUC to accept another year of pay restraint in return for long-term co-operation on the West German model covering pay, prices and productivity as well as social policies and priorities such as pensions and the promotion of job creation schemes.[195] Rejecting the option of an autumn election (he feared it would lead to an inconclusive result and another minority government)[196] Callaghan decided instead to use the breathing space to secure union agreement not simply to Phase 4 of the pay policy but to the creation of an institutional framework for social democracy.

The strategy failed. Although half a million workers had settled within the government's guidelines by the end of 1978, the 5 per cent limit was unacceptable to trade union leaders, who also rejected Callaghan's proposals for the reform of collective bargaining along West German lines.[197] The relationship between the government and the TUC appeared close to collapse: Jones and Scanlon had retired; their replacements, Moss Evans and Terry Duffy, did not possess the same authority or influence. Indeed Evans made it clear that he had no interest in any kind of pay policy: his role was to promote the interests of his members, even if this meant embarrassment for the government.[198]

The changing high politics of trade unionism were paralleled at ground level by a surge in the power of shop stewards, benefiting from reforms to union constitutions made over the past decade. This made for a situation in which full-time regional and national officials sometimes struggled to make their views prevail if they did not coincide with those being expressed at the grass roots.[199] At this level there was frustration with the way real incomes had lagged behind inflation during much of the period covered by the pay policy: between 1975 and 1977 wage restraint, high taxation and economies on the social wage (mainly concerning food and rent subsidies) were together responsible for a fall of 18 per cent in real earnings, net of tax. This represented a fall in living standards for those in work unprecedented since 1931–33.[200] The real increase in average earnings which occurred in 1977–78 was not enough to compensate for the previous two years: in these circumstances asking workers to accept an annual limit of 5 per cent was foolhardy. A more generous limit may not have satisfied Callaghan's determination to crush inflation but it might have avoided many of the ugly scenes witnessed at the start of 1979. At the same time, the behaviour of key trade union leaders such as Alan Fisher of the National Union of Public Employees (NUPE) and Moss Evans betrayed an inability to operate strategically. Rather than accept wage restraint in exchange for co-operation in the construction of a social-democratic constitution, they encouraged their members to pursue short-term gains, even if the price was Labour's defeat at the polls and a Conservative government committed to curtailing the power and influence of the unions, and inclined towards monetarist policies.

The avalanche started late in 1978. Workers at Ford, claiming a 30 per cent pay rise, were in the vanguard. Tanker drivers and workers in the road haulage industry followed with demands of 40 per cent (all three groups were TGWU members); the nurses called for 25 per cent; ambulance drivers, hospital porters and local authority manual workers, most of them covered by NUPE, were looking for up to 20 per cent. Employers in the private sector generally negotiated settlements for the most part well in excess of 5 per cent but the government attempted to hold the line within the public sector. The result was explosive. For a few weeks in January and February the country was hit by a strike wave unprecedented in scale since the 1926 General Strike. On 22 January 1.5 million public sector workers took action. Over the year as a whole 30 million working days were lost, three times as many as in 1978.[201] The result was great inconvenience for many, made worse by freezing weather, as for a brief time some basic services ceased to operate or did so sporadically. Garbage was uncollected and left to rot on the streets. There were allegations of intimidation made against striking lorry drivers. Schools were picketed and closed. In one notorious case the dead went unburied.[202] Calm was restored by the start of March but the impact of these events on the public mind was dramatic: the period of disruption was dubbed 'the winter of discontent', a term still used to describe it even though it lasted for just a few weeks, not for a whole season.

The events of early 1979 damaged the reputation of both unions and the government. The former were seen to act simply for sectional gain, with no concern for the public interest. The latter appeared helpless in the face of militant trade unionism. As the General Election approached one of the more persuasive arguments for voting Labour, used to successful effect in 1974, ceased to apply: experience now suggested that it was not uniquely equipped to govern with the co-operation of the trade unions. Opposition politicians and their supporters in the press lost no time in exploiting the political fallout. A volte-face by the TUC at the end of January regarding Callaghan's initiative for long-term co-operation was 'submerged in the general tide of disillusionment and dislike' engendered by the strikes.[203] The whole affair was a shot in the arm for Margaret Thatcher. In January she suggested during the course of a television interview that legislation was necessary to curtail the ability of trade unions to take industrial action, especially in the public sector. The proposal was well received by both Conservative and uncommitted voters who believed that Labour was incapable of confronting the issue of union power. The opinion polls, which had shown no firm indication of moving in favour of the Conservatives, started to do so. The trend lasted all the way to the General Election, held early in May, which saw Labour defeated: Margaret Thatcher, whose career at the top of the Conservative Party had a few months earlier appeared to be in jeopardy, became Prime Minister with an overall majority of 44.

The events of January and February 1979, which proved so damaging to Labour, occurred against a background which suggested that Britain in the later 1970s was an increasingly fair and prosperous society. In 1977 the Gini coefficient, which measures the level of inequality within advanced economies, reached its lowest recorded level for British households.[204] Given this background and the government's recent record on inflation and unemployment, as well as the level of wage settlements (after 1977), it could be argued that the 'winter of discontent' was a self-destructive spasm on the part of organized labour, acting as a catalyst for a profound shift in public attitudes. Certainly Callaghan appeared to view developments that way. The Prime Minister became demoralized and seemed resigned to defeat at the polls. He sensed a sea-change in opinion, working against the values which had sustained the post-war consensus: solidarity and concern for the less fortunate was being replaced by individualism and growing contempt for 'scroungers'.

There is no doubt that such views were becoming increasingly fashionable, even among working-class voters.[205] All the same, given Labour's lead in the opinion polls during the last months of 1978 it is hard to argue that such sentiments could have provoked a sea-change in the short time left until the General Election of 1979. The evidence suggests that Labour would have stood a good chance of re-election had it not been for the chaotic interlude of January and February 1979. It was not evident that either the CBI or the TUC wished to abandon the post-war consensus. During the campaign Labour made clear its continuing commitment to the values of 1945, modified by the social-democratic reforms pursued since the early 1960s. The election results, which saw Labour's vote hold up but much of the support for the Liberals, the Nationalists Parties and the extreme Right wing National Front migrate to the Conservatives, did not indicate a groundswell of support for neo-liberalism.[206] Wilson, quoting the Duke of Wellington's comment on the connection between starvation in Ireland and fall of Sir Robert Peel's ministry in 1846, claimed 'It was rotten potatoes that did it all'.[207] Yet, whatever the explanation for Labour's defeat, the General Election result heralded the end of one political era and the start of a new one; another reinvention of Britain was about to commence.

Notes

1. See for example Martin Holmes, *The Labour Government 1974–1979: Political Aims and Economic Reality* (London: Palgrave Macmillan, 1985); Andrew Marr, *A History of Modern Britain* (Basingstoke: Macmillan, 2007), ch. 3; Dominic Sandbrook, *Seasons in the Sun: the Battle for Britain, 1974–76* (London: Penguin, 2012).
2. Neil Clark, 'The Seventies Were Great: Don't Believe the Myth of Thatcherism', *The Week*, 1 May 2009.
3. Michael Artis, David Cobham and Mark Wickham-Jones, 'Social Democracy in Hard Times: The Economic Record of the Labour Government, 1974–1979', *Twentieth Century British History*, vol. 3 (1992), pp. 32–58; Beckett, *When The Lights Went Out*; Dorril and Ramsay, *Smear!*; Middlemas, *Power, Competition and the State*, vol. 3, Part 1.
4. See for example Dominic Smith, 'Tories Plan to Raise Threshold for Key Public Sector Industrial Action', *The Guardian*, 10 January 2015.
5. Newton and Porter, *Modernization Frustrated*, pp. 108–109.
6. Newton, 'Sterling, Bretton Woods and Social Democracy 1968–70', pp. 8–9.
7. General Agreement on Tariffs and Trade, established in 1947 to promote international trade liberalization.
8. Parr, *Britain's Policy towards the European Community*, p. 130.
9. *The National Plan* (Cmnd. 2764, London 1965), p. 2, paragraphs 10–12.
10. Newton, *The Global Economy*, pp. 105–106.
11. Newton, *The Global Economy*, p. 108.

12 Clark and Dilnot, *Long-Term Trends in British Taxation and Spending*, p. 8.
13 Denis Healey, *Time of My Life* (London: Michael Joseph, 1989), p. 392.
14 Newton, *The Global Economy*, pp. 108–109.
15 Ibid., Table 5.2, p. 109; Newton and Porter, *Modernization Frustrated*, p. 171.
16 George Zis, 'The International Status of Sterling', in Michael Artis and David Cobham, *Labour's Economic Policies 1974–1979* (Manchester: Manchester University Press, 1971), p. 110.
17 See Douglas Wass, *Decline to Fall: The Making of British Macro-Economic Policy and the 1976 IMF Crisis* (Oxford: Oxford University Press, 2007), p. 103.
18 Coakley and Harris, *The City of Capital*, p. 180.
19 Wass, *Decline to Fall*, pp. 87 and 103.
20 Chris Rogers, 'The Labour Government, the Treasury and the £6 Pay Policy of July 1975', *British Politics* 5 (2010), pp. 224–236.
21 'The Great Priority', *The Times*, 22 June 1974, p. 9.
22 Denis Kavanagh, 'Lord Barnett: Obituary', *The Guardian*, 3 November 2014.
23 Artis, Cobham and Wickham-Jones, 'Social Democracy in Hard Times', p. 41.
24 Healey, *Time of My Life*, p. 392.
25 Artis, Cobham and Wickham-Jones, 'Social Democracy in Hard Times', p. 41.
26 See Stewart, *The Jekyll and Hyde Years*, p. 190.
27 Healey, *Time of My Life*, p. 394.
28 See for example Peter Jay, 'How Inflation Threatens British Democracy with its Last Chance before Extinction', *The Times*, 1 June 1974, p. 14.
29 Middleton, *The British Economy since 1945*, Table II.3, pp. 150–151.
30 Wass, *Decline to Fall*, p. 84.
31 Healey, *Time of My Life*, p. 393.
32 Newton, *The Global Economy 1944–2000*, p. 108.
33 Coakley and Harris, *The City of Capital*, p. 205.
34 Newton, *The Global Economy*, p. 125.
35 Mike Hughes, *Spies at Work* (Bradford: One in Twelve Publications, 1995), p. 213.
36 UK Government, Office of National Statistics, 'Labour Market Statistics – Integrated FR', http://www.ons.gov.uk/ons/datasets-and-tables/data-selector.html?cdid=LF2Q&dataset=lms&table-id=9 (accessed 2 April 2017).
37 Tony Benn, *Arguments for Socialism* (Harmondsworth: Penguin, 1980), ch. 2; Benn, *Against the Tide*, p. 262, entry for 11 November 1974.
38 Stuart Holland, *The State as Entrepreneur* (London: Weidenfeld and Nicolson, 1972); *The Socialist Challenge* (London: Quartet Books, 1975).
39 Noel Thompson, *Political Economy and the Labour Party*, 2nd edition (London: Routledge, 2006), p. 190.
40 Newton, *The Global Economy 1944–2000*, pp. 88–89.
41 James Cronin, *New Labour's Pasts: The Labour Party and its Discontents* (London: Routledge, 2004), p. 135.
42 Thompson, *Political Economy and the Labour Party*, p. 193.
43 Stuart Holland, 'The Industrial Strategy', in Kevin Theakston and Anthony Seldon, *New Labour, Old Labour: the Wilson and Callaghan Governments 1974–79* (London: Routledge, 2004), p. 298.
44 Cronin, *New Labour's Pasts*, p. 137.
45 Ibid.
46 Ibid., p. 137.
47 Holland, 'The Industrial Strategy', p. 298.
48 Ibid.
49 Cronin, *New Labour's Pasts*, p. 138.
50 Newton and Porter, *Modernization Frustrated*, p. 169.
51 Ibid., p. 173; Benn, *Against The Tide*, p. 302, entry for 16 January 1975.
52 Holland, 'The Industrial Strategy', p. 298.

53 Newton and Porter, *Modernization Frustrated*, p. 172. The statistics are drawn from the Cambridge Economic Policy Group, *Economic Policy Review*, no. 1, 1975, ch. 3.
54 Medhurst, *That Option No Longer Exists* (London: Zero books, 2014), p. 48.
55 Ibid.
56 See for example Sandbrook, *Seasons in the Sun*, especially chs. 3 and 4; Beckett, *When The Lights Went Out*, pp. 157–158 and 164–165. Much of this discourse is rooted in Joe Haines, *The Politics of Power* (London: Jonathan Cape, 1977). Haines had been Wilson's Press Secretary from 1969 until 1976. His insider's account of life in No. 10 has valuable insights but is marred by an excessive focus on gossip, personality clashes and feuds with Wilson's Political Secretary Marcia Williams.
57 Thompson, *Political Economy and the Labour Party*, pp. 211ff; Anthony Crosland, *Socialism Now* (London: Jonathan Cape, 1974), p. 34.
58 See Thompson, *Political Economy and the Labour Party*, pp 223–226; Harold Wilson, *Final Term* (London: Weidenfeld and Nicolson and Michael Joseph, 1979), pp. 33–36, 140–143.
59 Ibid., pp. 23–25.
60 Ibid., p. 113.
61 Ibid., pp. 118 and 223.
62 *The Regeneration of British Industry* (Cmnd 5710: HMSO, London, 1974).
63 Newton and Porter, *Modernization Frustrated*, pp. 171–172.
64 *The Regeneration of British Industry*, p. 6.
65 Wilson made this point in *Final Term*, p. 114. This was a retrospective comment but not a disingenuous one. He had said the same in November 1975. See Hugo Young, *The Hugo Young Papers: A Journalist's Notes from the Heart of Politics* (London: Penguin, 2009), p. 58.
66 Stewart, *The Jekyll and Hyde Years*, p. 211.
67 Wass, *Decline to Fall*, p. 110.
68 Wilson, *Final Term*, p. 114.
69 Young, *The Hugo Young Papers*, p. 58.
70 Newman, *Socialism and European Unity*, pp. 237–239.
71 Newton and Porter, *Modernization Frustrated*, p. 174.
72 Bernard Donoughue, *Downing Street Diary: With Harold Wilson in No. 10* (London; Jonathan Cape, 2005), entries for 18 and 19 June 1975, pp. 418–419.
73 William Keegan, 'Cameron Will Pay the EU its Billions; Ukip Will Cost him Much More', *The Observer*, 2 November 2014.
74 Wilson, *Final Term*, p. 115.
75 Wass, *Decline to Fall*, p. 115.
76 Jones, *Union Man*, p. 297.
77 Wass, *Decline to Fall*, p. 114.
78 Healey, *Time of My Life*, p. 385.
79 Wilson, *Final Term*, p. 114.
80 Ibid., p. 118.
81 Healey, *Time of My Life*, p. 397.
82 Rogers, 'The Labour Government, the Treasury and the £6 Pay Policy', p. 233.
83 Healey, *Time of My Life*, p. 407.
84 TNA CAB129/189/6, C (75) 106, 'An Approach to Industrial Strategy', note by the Chancellor of the Exchequer and the Secretary of State for Industry, 14 October 1975.
85 Benn, *Against the Tide*, p. 455, entry for 5 November 1975.
86 Stephen Wilks, *Industrial Policy and the Motor Industry* (Manchester: Manchester University Press, 1983). The decision is also discussed by Bernard Donoughue (Head of Wilson's Downing Street Policy Unity, 1974–76) in his 'The 1975 Chrysler Rescue: A Political View from Number 10', *Contemporary Record*, vol. 8 (1994), pp. 77–83.

87 See Geoffrey Tweedale, 'Industry and de-Industrialisation', in Richard Coopey and Nicholas Woodward, *Britain in the 1970s: the Troubled Economy* (London: UCL Press, 1996), pp. 259–260.
88 Angela Monaghan, 'UK Car Production Will Surpass Record 1970s Level by 2017, Says Trade Body', *The Guardian*, 7 January 2014.
89 Newton and Porter, *Modernization Frustrated*, p. 175.
90 Middlemas, *Power, Competition and the State*, vol. 3, pp. 132–135.
91 Healey, *Time of My Life*, p. 467.
92 Middlemas, *Power, Competition and the State*, vol. 3, p. 134.
93 Wass, *Decline to Fall*, p. 130.
94 Ibid., p. 145.
95 Donoughue, *Downing Street Diary*, p. 566. Donoughue recorded that Wilson thought public spending had been growing too fast and Healey was 'too soft' on the issue.
96 Wass, *Decline to Fall*, p. 125.
97 Ibid., pp. 153–159.
98 Geoffrey Goodman, 'Harold Wilson', *The Guardian*, 25 May 1995.
99 Newton, 'Sterling, Bretton Woods and Social Democracy', p. 450.
100 Beckett, *When the Lights Went Out*, p. 157.
101 Hughes, *Spies at Work*, p. 135.
102 This remarkable proposal was discussed by senior military and intelligence personnel with the Chairman and directors of the Cunard shipping line (owner of the QE2) in July 1975: Dorril and Ramsay, *Smear!*, p. 285.
103 Dorril and Ramsay, *Smear!*, p. 286.
104 Barrie Penrose and Roger Courtiour, *The Pencourt File* (London: Secker and Warburg, 1978). The book became the basis of a BBC documentary, *The Plot against Harold Wilson*, broadcast on 16 March 2006 – the 30th anniversary of Wilson's resignation.
105 Peter Wright, *Spycatcher: The Candid Autobiography of a Senior Intelligence Officer* (New York: Viking, 1987).
106 Christopher Andrew, *Defence of the Realm: The Authorized History of MI5* (London: Allen Lane, 2009), pp. 627–643.
107 Dorril and Ramsay, *Smear!*, p. 286; Brian Crozier, *Free Agent: the Unseen War 1941–1991* (London: Harper Collins, 1993), pp. 121–122.
108 Ironically, this element of the story was backed by Christopher Andrew, who had inserted it into a draft of his book on MI5 but then removed it at the request of 'senior Whitehall officials to protect the public interest'. See Richard Norton-Taylor, 'No 10 Downing Street Bugged by MI5, Claims Historian', *The Guardian*, 19 April 2010.
109 See for example Paul Foot, *Who Framed Colin Wallace?* (London: Macmillan, 1989), David Leigh, *The Wilson Plot* (New York: Pantheon Books, 1988), and Dorril and Ramsay, *Smear!* All these are evidence-based. The last provides the fullest account of the three and demonstrates the strength, longevity and long-term implications of the Right's efforts to topple Wilson.
110 Hughes, *Spies at Work*, pp. 194–195.
111 See Robin Ramsay's review of Peter Dale Scott's 'The American Deep State: Wall Street, Big Oil and the Attack on U.S. Democracy', in *Lobster*, 69 (2015), http://www.lobster-magazine.co.uk/free/lobster69/lob69-american-deep-state.pdf (accessed 2 April 2017). Scott's definition can be found in an April 2011 interview for the Voltaire Network, 'The Deep State behind American Democracy', http://www.voltairenet.org/article169316.html (accessed 2 April 2017).
112 J.A. Hobson, *Imperialism: A Study* (London: Cosimo, 1902), pp. 46–51.
113 Ian Burrell, 'Britain's own Watergate Scandal', *The Independent*, 14 September 2009.
114 Dorril and Ramsay, *Smear!*, p. 284.
115 See Gerald James, *In the Public Interest* (London: Little, Brown, 1995), p. 33.

116 Dorril and Ramsay, *Smear!*, p. 283. Templer was a member of Civil Assistance; he had been High Commissioner in Malaya at the time of the Emergency, Chief of Imperial General Staff from 1955–58 and since 1966 Lord-Lieutenant of London.
117 Dorril and Ramsay, *Smear!*, pp. 283–284.
118 See the television documentary by Adam Curtis, *The Mayfair Set*, episode 1: 'Who Pays Wins', first broadcast on 18 July 1999; Stephen Dorril and Robin Ramsay, 'Wilson, MI5 and the Rise of Thatcher', *Lobster*, 11 (1986), p. 15; Mark Curtis, *Unpeople: Britain's Secret Human Rights Abuses* (London: Random House, 2004), pp. 178, 295–300.
119 Christopher Andrew, *The Defence of the Realm:* The Authorized History of MI5 (London: Allen Lane, 2009), p. 624.
120 See Paul Routledge, *Public Servant, Secret Agent: the Elusive Life and Violent Death of Airey Neave* (London: Fourth Estate, 2003), pp. 289ff.
121 Harvey, *A Brief History of Neo-Liberalism* (Oxford; Oxford University Press, 2005), p. 15.
122 Crozier, *Free Agent*, pp. 182–183.
123 Harvey, *A Brief History of Neo-Liberalism*, p. 17.
124 Beckett, *When the Lights Went Out*, p. 46. Beckett points out that the British level of union density was not especially high in international terms: in Sweden and Denmark, for example, the figure exceeded 70 per cent.
125 Stewart Lansley and Howard Reed, *How to Boost the Wage Share*, TUC: Touchstone Pamphlet no. 13, 2013, p. 15.
126 Stewart Lansley, *Life in the Middle: The Untold Story of Britain's Average Earners*, TUC: Touchstone Pamphlet no. 6, 2009, p. 25.
127 Newton, *The Global Economy*, p. 126.
128 Lansley and Reed, *How to Boost the Wage Share*, p. 15.
129 Sandbrook, *Seasons in the Sun*, p. 137.
130 Duncan Campbell, 'What Did a Tory MP Say in the Cumberland Hotel?', *New Statesman*, 20 February 1981. According to Campbell's informant, a former SIS agent called Lee Tracey, 'stopping' did not exclude the use of violence.
131 See Routledge, *Public Servant, Secret Agent*, ch. 14.
132 See Charles Moore, *Margaret Thatcher: The Authorised Biography*, vol. 1: *Not for Turning* (London: Allen Lane, 2013), pp. 310–311.
133 Dorril and Ramsay, 'Wilson, MI5 and the Rise of Thatcher', p. 17.
134 See Routledge, *Public Servant, Secret Agent*, especially chs. 14–18 inclusive.
135 Crozier, *Free Agent*, pp. 127–129.
136 Its most famous intervention in its early days was in the dispute at Grunwick Film Processing Laboratories in 1977, which turned on the refusal of its owner, George Ward, to permit union recognition on his premises. See Joe Rogaly, *Grunwick* (Harmondsworth: Penguin, 1977).
137 Beckett, *When the Lights Went Out*, p. 378.
138 Ibid., pp. 378–379.
139 James, *In the Public Interest*, P. 50.
140 Dorril and Ramsay, 'Wilson, MI5 and the Rise of Thatcher', p. 22.
141 'Good-bye, Great Britain', *Wall Street Journal*, 29 April 1975.
142 See for example Kenneth O. Morgan, *Callaghan: A Life* (Oxford: Oxford University Press, 1997), p. 413.
143 Jones, *Union Man*, p. 309.
144 The author witnessed one such occasion when he was present as a trade union delegate (for the lecturers' union, then known as the Association of University Teachers), at a meeting with Welsh Labour MPs (of which Callaghan was one) at the House of Commons in 1986.
145 Callaghan, *Time and Chance*, pp. 398.
146 Beckett, *When the Lights Went Out*, p. 329; Callaghan, *Time and Chance*, p. 426.

147 Callaghan, *Time and Chance*, pp. 397–398; Beckett, *When the Lights Went Out*, p. 438, noted Callaghan's distaste for inflation and frustration with (in his opinion) the 'recurring tunnel vision of workers over pay'.
148 Healey, *Time of My Life*, p. 398.
149 Jones, *Union Man*, p. 307.
150 Newton and Porter, *Modernization Frustrated*, p. 177.
151 Leo Pliatzky, *Getting and Spending: Public Expenditure, Employment and Inflation* (Oxford: Blackwell, 1984), pp. 156–161.
152 Pliatzky, *Getting and Spending*, p. 156.
153 Healey, *Time of My Life*, p. 428.
154 Wass, *Decline to Fall*, pp. 210–213.
155 Ibid., p. 223.
156 Beckett, *When the Lights Went Out*, p. 332.
157 Ibid., p. 333.
158 Callaghan, *Time and Chance*, p. 428.
159 Wass, *Decline to Fall*, p. 308.
160 Callaghan, *Time and Chance*, pp. 425–427.
161 See for example Medhurst, *That Option No Longer Exists*, p. 128; Tony Benn, *Fighting Back* (London: Hutchinson, 1988), p. 4.
162 Holmes, *The Labour Government 1974–79*, p. 102. See also Denis Kavanagh, 'Lord Barnett', *The Guardian*, 3 November 2014.
163 Callaghan, *Time and Chance*, pp. 428–430.
164 Ibid. pp. 435–436.
165 Wass, *Decline to Fall*, p. 242. There was a precedent: the 1968 Basle Agreement. The expectation had been that this would facilitate a gentle running down of the balances. Of course, largely as a result of the surge in the price of oil after 1973, the reverse had occurred.
166 Wass, *Decline to Fall*, pp. 238–239.
167 Ibid., p. 257.
168 Ibid., pp. 269 and 277.
169 The GDP figures are from Middleton, *The British Economy*, Table II.1, pp. 146–147.
170 William E. Simon, *A Time for Truth* (New York: McGraw-Hill, 1978), p. 221.
171 https://wikileaks.org/plusd/cables/1976LONDON18141_b.html (accessed 2 April 2017).
172 Callaghan, *Time and Chance*, p. 431.
173 As Bernard Donoughue noted, 'they (the IMF) are saying that a Labour Government must carry out the policies of Mrs Thatcher'. See *Downing Street Diary*, vol. 2: *With James Callaghan in No. 10* (London: Cape, 2008), p. 111, entry for 3 December 1976.
174 TNA CAB129/193, CP (76) 111, 'IMF Negotiations', Memorandum by the Chancellor, 22 November 1976.
175 TNA CAB128/60, CM (76) 33rd conclusions, 23 November 1976.
176 Wass, *Decline to Fall*, pp. 284 and 288.
177 TNA CAB 129/193, CP (76) 193, 'Economic Policy and the IMF Credit', Memorandum by the Chancellor, 30 November 1976.
178 Wass, *Decline to Fall*, pp. 287–289.
179 Callaghan, *Time and Chance*, pp. 440–441.
180 Wass, *Decline to Fall*, p. 294.
181 Middlemas, *Power, Competition and the State*, vol. 3, pp. 140ff. Wass, *Decline to Fall*, p. 308.
182 Middlemas, *Power, Competition and the State*, vol. 3, pp. 136–137.
183 Healey, *Time of My Life*, p. 401.
184 Ibid., p. 462.
185 See Artis, Cobham and Wickham-Jones, *Social Democracy in Hard Times*, p. 49 and footnotes 44–46.
186 Wass, *Decline to Fall*, p. 309.

187 Healey, *Time of My Life*, p. 438.
188 Artis, Cobham and Wickham-Jones, *Social Democracy in Hard Times*, pp. 49–51.
189 Wass, *Decline to Fall*, pp. 309–310.
190 Ibid. p. 311.
191 Beckett, *When the Lights Went Out*, p. 438.
192 Healey, *Time of My Life*, p. 463.
193 Beckett, *When the Lights Went Out*, pp. 414 and 441.
194 Ibid. p. 438.
195 Callaghan, *Time and Chance*, pp. 516–518; p. 521.
196 Ibid., p. 516.
197 Beckett, *When the Lights Went Out*, p. 439; Callaghan, *Time and Chance*, p. 533.
198 Callaghan, *Time and Chance*, pp. 520–521.
199 Healey, *Time of My Life*, p. 467.
200 Middlemas, *Power, Competition and the State*, vol. 3, p.157.
201 Beckett, *When the Lights Went Out*, pp. 464–465.
202 Wilson, *Final Term*, p. 241.
203 Callaghan, *Time and Chance*, p. 540.
204 Beckett, *When the Lights Went Out*, p. 409.
205 Donoughue, *Downing Street Diary*, vol. 2, p. 7; Peter Dorey, 'Should I Stay or Should I Go? James Callaghan's Decision Not to Call an Autumn 1978 General Election', *British Politics* advance online publication 4 May 2015; doi: 10.1057/bp.2015.9, p. 19; Alan Travis, 'The Thatcher Threat – and How Callaghan Saw it Coming', *The Guardian*, 28 December 2007.
206 Beckett, *When the Lights Went Out*, p. 517.
207 Wilson, *Final Term*, p. 241.

PART II
Neo-liberal Britain

5

THATCHER'S REVOLUTION, 1979-90

Waste land

The train from Birmingham to Crewe passes through the old industrial centres of the Black Country, Wolverhampton and then Stoke-on-Trent before heading for its destination through the Staffordshire and Cheshire countryside. From the time the railway was built until the start of the 1980s any traveller on this line would have witnessed widespread and intense industrial activity. The Black Country region, given its name in the mid-nineteenth century because of the smoke which covered large parts of it, was said to turn 'black by day and red by night'. It was the home to an extensive coal mining industry, as well as to metal manufacturing and chain-making, diversifying over time into glass, automotive production, electrical goods, chemicals and paints. Coal mining had finished by 1968 but the area continued to thrive until the later 1970s, after which its fortunes changed for the worse. The transformation was rapid. In the autumn of 1981 this commuter to Crewe,[1] a native of Birmingham, educated at a school whose song celebrated its location in 'the iron heart of England', was struck not by activity but by mounting evidence of dereliction. The view from the train window revealed deserted factories, empty warehouses and vacant car parks. Very few industrial chimneys smoked; silent and decrepit buildings with broken and gaping windows stood where not so long before there had been thousands at work. Some 5,000 jobs were lost between June 1979 and December 1981 just in the small town of Darlaston (whose population was around 25,000), as long-established concerns such as GKN (rationalizing) and Rubery Owen (closing) ceased to operate in the area. Other casualties were the Patent Shaft Steelworks in Wednesbury, whose collapse in 1980 brought an end to 140 years of production in the town, and the famous Round Oak Steelworks in Brierley Hill (opened in 1857), which finished work at the end of 1982 (leaving unemployment there at 25 per cent of those eligible to work, twice the national average at the time) after several years of contraction.

The collapse of these firms, dragging down in turn the suppliers and component manufacturers who depended upon them, turned large parts of the West Midlands, one of the hubs of British industry for a century and a half, into a waste land. Joblessness in the region increased from 4.2 per cent of the working population in 1979 to 12.2 per cent in 1982 (peaking at 12.6 per cent in 1986).[2] Only the fate of BL relieved the gloom: although the company was facing major financial difficulties by 1980 the new Conservative government of Margaret Thatcher reluctantly decided to back it, fearing its collapse would lead to the loss of up to 300,000 jobs in the automotive sector (including component and other supplying industries), with dire political and economic results in the West Midlands in particular. The prospect was too apocalyptic even for an administration keen to strike out on a non-interventionist, pro-free market path when it came to industrial strategy. Through gritted teeth, Thatcher and her Industry Secretary Sir Keith Joseph agreed to a new investment package worth £990 million to support BL's corporate plan and ensure the safety of a link with Honda, which was to lead to the successful relaunch of the Rover.[3]

No other part of the UK experienced so strong and rapid a surge in redundancies as the West Midlands between 1979 and 1982. But over these years the whole economy was convulsed by a vicious recession, and many other regions shared the West Midlands' experience of bankruptcies, factory closures and mass unemployment, albeit in a marginally less spectacular fashion, with rationalization in the steel industry having an especially drastic impact. The works in Consett, county Durham closed on 12 September 1980 with the loss of 3,500 jobs. The town had been built around the steel industry, with a history of continuous production stretching back to 1881. After the closure of the plant unemployment in the town reached 36 per cent of the workforce, leading locals to talk of 'the murder of a town', echoing Ellen Wilkinson's account of nearby Jarrow during the 1930s following the shutdown of the shipyards and ironworks there.[4] Corby in Northamptonshire experienced a similar trauma: its plant had shut in May 1980, with 6,000 jobs lost. These redundancies, and further job losses in allied businesses, sent the unemployment rate in the town to 30 per cent of the workforce.[5] In Deeside, north-east Wales, the closure of the sheet steel plant at Shotton accounted for over 6,000 job losses in March 1980 alone; this shutdown, combined with the others in the local textile industry, left male unemployment in the region at 33 per cent of the workforce. Over the whole of Wales, contraction in the steel and coal mining industries saw unemployment climb from 5.7 per cent in 1979 to 12.4 per cent in 1982 (14.4 per cent in 1986), while in Northern England it doubled from 6.9 per cent to 13.6 per cent (15.5 per cent in 1986).[6] The Linwood car production plant in south-west Scotland closed in February 1981, leading to 6,000 redundancies at the factory and a further 7,000 in indirect job losses.[7] Plant closures in Scotland between August 1979 and August 1981 propelled unemployment there from 6.2 per cent to 10.4 per cent of the total workforce.[8]

Overall, the UK index of industrial production, standing at 113.1 in 1979 (1975 = 100), fell back to 100 in 1982 while manufacturing output declined by 15 per cent.[9] Investment dropped by 28 per cent over the same period. Company liquidations rocketed from 6,890 in 1980 to 13,000 in 1983.[10] Between 1979 and 1982 Britain lost 20 per cent of its manufacturing capacity.[11] It was this sharp fall in economic activity, leading GNP to drop by 5 per cent from 1979–1981,[12] that drove the unemployment total remorselessly upward. The process was at its most dramatic in industrial Britain; those parts of the nation more dependent on finance, services, agriculture and tourism suffered less, and in no part of the Home Counties, East Anglia and South-West England did joblessness rise as high as 10 per cent.[13] Yet the toll, nationally, was a very heavy one: 1 million jobs were lost in the year from April 1980 to April 1981, 700,000 of these being in the manufacturing sector. Unemployment reached levels not seen since the 1930s (in terms of numbers rather than of percentages of those capable of work), passing the 3 million mark by the end of 1982. The total numbers of jobless continued to grow, albeit less rapidly, over the subsequent three years, officially reaching a peak of 12.2 per cent in early 1986 (3.4 million).[14] Membership of trade unions fell steadily, a development which was most pronounced in manual and general unions, dropping from 12.1 million in 1979 to 11.0 million in 1982 (and down to 8.4 million in 1990). At the same time, many of those without work and outside unions tended to drift into a growing underclass composed of unskilled, part-time, casual labourers in and out of employment and sometimes dependent on the 'black' (in other words payment by cash) economy.[15]

The intensity of this recession, in terms of its impact on output, industry and on the workforce, was unprecedented in British post-war history and indeed surpassed the economic impact of the Great Depression between 1929 and 1932. It was also unique in the experience of advanced capitalist countries at the time: unemployment fell rapidly in the USA after 1982, a trend repeated (albeit less dramatically) in Belgium, France, the Netherlands and West Germany.[16] By 1983–84, with large tracts of old Producer's Britain characterized by idle factories, disused plant and equipment and mass unemployment, the share of national production taken by manufacturing had fallen to 21 per cent.[17] The loss of capacity affected Britain's international economic position, with a manufacturing trade deficit approaching 1 per cent of GDP replacing a surplus worth 1.5 per cent in 1979. It was the first time since the start of the industrial revolution that Britain had been in the red on this account, though it was not to be the last, and the deficit grew during the decade.[18] At the time the effect on the current account was disguised by the foreign exchange being generated by very heavy exports of North Sea oil, but this was not to be permanent.

Critics argued that Britain was experiencing deindustrialization. The government responded that what was happening to the economy characterized the transition from dependence on manufacturing to growing specialization in services which was common to all advanced industrial economies, and that Britain was experiencing a 'shakeout' of uncompetitive industries which was particularly violent because the sectors worst hit tended (like steel) to be labour intensive. The first of these observations did contain some truth, although it failed to address the specifics of the British experience, namely that the contribution of manufacturing to the GDP was falling in absolute terms whereas it was still rising, albeit less rapidly, in the UK's competitors.[19] The second was facile: productivity and technical efficiency in the British steel industry were low by comparison with competitors but the industry faced a global crisis, seen in shutdowns throughout Western Europe and the USA. This was a function of substantially higher energy costs which had provoked an international recession.[20] Moreover, many of the factory closures after 1979 involved not simply headline-making shutdowns in the steel, electrical and electronic engineering and automotive industries but the supply chains involved in sustaining these sectors[21] as well as viable businesses whose turnover and profits had suffered when demand collapsed as a result of the dramatic fall in output.[22] Britain's international competitiveness actually *declined* after 1979: the total volume of imports taken by Britain's export markets grew by 12 per cent between 1979 and 1982, yet UK shipments to these markets 'fell by 5 per cent'.[23] Over the same period real value added in British manufacturing fell by 5 per cent per year, a miserable record not approached by any other leading member of the OECD.[24]

In the three years following 1979 the nation experienced an intense economic and social shock, and in 1981 it received a taste of the consequences. In April, as the unemployment total headed to the 2.5 million mark, rioting erupted in the London suburb of Brixton; during the summer this spread further afield, mostly to the inner cities of Birmingham, Leeds, Liverpool, and Manchester. The rioters tended to be young, and (though by no means always) from ethnic minorities. Poor community relations, especially involving frustration with the behaviour of the local police, were invoked to account for much of this;[25] but explanations which dodged or played down the impact of youth unemployment, at 20 per cent, and its concentration in ethnic minorities, were not convincing.[26] These events all tended to undermine the standing of the government, whose popularity plunged as a result of the toxic combination of recession, accelerating mass unemployment and violent disturbances. In July 1981 only 25 per cent of those polled thought that the Prime Minister was doing a good job.[27] For most of the period from August 1981 until February 1982 the government came third in the opinion polls, with many voters being attracted to the new Social Democratic Party (SDP), whose support reached just over 50 per cent in December, by which time Conservative backing had fallen to just 23 per cent. By the end of 1981 even close supporters were coming to the conclusion that the Thatcher administration stood little chance of re-election.[28]

Thatcherism

Few who voted Conservative in 1979 would have expected the economic and social crisis which followed. The Conservative manifesto for the election was a rather vague document and generally non-confrontational, a tone confirmed by

Margaret Thatcher herself as she entered Number 10 Downing Street as Prime Minister for the first time. Stopping to deliver a message to the assembled representatives of the media she famously offered a prayer, mistakenly attributing it to St Francis of Assisi (in fact it was first published in 1912 in a French religious magazine):

> Where there is discord, may we bring harmony. Where there is error, may we bring truth. Where there is doubt, may we bring faith. And where there is despair, may we bring hope.

On the face of it, therefore, there was little indication that the new government would preside over such dramatic and destructive change. Yet there were straws in the wind. Mrs Thatcher's leadership had seen a change of direction within the Party. Although Thatcher's first Cabinet contained many of Heath's leading supporters, corporatist and paternalist Tories committed to the 1945 settlement such as William Whitelaw (Home Secretary), Jim Prior (Employment Secretary), Quintin Hogg (Lord Hailsham: Lord Chancellor), Sir Ian Gilmour (Lord Privy Seal), Peter Walker (Minister of Agriculture) and Lord Carrington (Foreign Secretary), there were clues about the direction in which she intended to travel. Key appointments covering economic policy were reserved for her monetarist allies: Sir Geoffrey Howe was Chancellor of the Exchequer, Sir Keith Joseph Secretary of State for Industry. The manifesto itself opened with a lament that Britain was 'a great country which had lost its way', an echo of Thatcher's comment about Britain in decline. During the election campaign the Conservatives had concentrated on the high levels of unemployment, inflation and industrial conflict Britain had experienced in recent years. The manifesto pointed to the 'dangerously low' level of profits, a situation which was destroying the 'foundations of a free enterprise economy'. They claimed this constellation of problems was at the root of the nation's slide down the international scale, and stemmed from the tendency of successive governments to hand power to the State, which had eroded the ground left for the exercise of individual responsibility, undermined private enterprise and provoked rising interest rates and prices. The process had been accelerated by Labour's willingness to 'heap' the unions with 'privilege without responsibility', thereby fuelling the strikes and disruption which had culminated in the recent winter of discontent.

The Conservatives proposed to restore the nation's fortunes by following a strategy which had seven fundamental features. The first six of these were all intended to raise the rate of profit in the private sector from its average level of 5.5 per cent between 1973–79 (a post-war low: it had been 15 per cent in the early 1950s)[29] and therefore (according to neo-liberal political economy) increase the capacity of the economy to generate wealth. First, they would strike at the causes of inflation by restoring 'proper monetary discipline', 'with publicly stated targets for the rate of growth of the money supply', and by cutting government spending and borrowing. Secondly they would reduce income tax (specifying a cut in the top rate) and reduce the share of national wealth taken by the State. Thirdly, they would abolish all remaining price controls, scale back the activities of the NEB and follow a non-interventionist path in industrial policy, returning the shipbuilding and aerospace industries to private ownership. Fourthly, they would abandon the attempts of successive administrations from 1961 to 1979 to establish a 'grand bargain' with the unions and the employers covering prices, incomes and employment rights, leaving these issues to be covered by 'responsible bargaining' between industry and organized labour. Fifthly, they would introduce legislation to reform the trade unions. A desire not to repeat the mistakes of the Heath years ensured that what was proposed fell short of the old Industrial Relations Act, with initial measures to be aimed at removing the immunities of the trade unions (specifying legislation to outlaw secondary picketing), the modification of the closed shop and the introduction of taxpayer support for postal ballots in union elections. Sixth, they aimed to encourage the spread of home ownership, in large measure by introducing legislation giving council tenants the right to buy their homes. This was intended to promote the establishment of a property-owning democracy, an ambition of Tory Prime Ministers since the mid-1950s and seen by Thatcher to be essential to the construction of a responsible society. Finally, the Conservatives promised to increase defence spending (though no figures were mentioned).[30]

Thatcher was motivated by the idea that 1940, when Britain had stood alone against Nazi Germany under the inspirational leadership of Winston Churchill, represented the zenith of the nation's reputation and influence in the world; its subsequent victory had been assured by partnership with the USA, the other leading representative of the liberal tradition and of the English-speaking peoples.[31] She was a profound admirer of Churchill, whom she often referred to as 'Winston', and invoked 'the instincts and traditions on which (he) founded his appeal to the nation to fight and to survive' during her campaign for the Party leadership in 1975.[32] She was driven by an inner conviction that she had somehow been chosen to revive what she saw as a great nation in decline; in her memoirs she quotes the remarks of William Pitt the elder (Lord Chatham), made after Britain had suffered a series of reverses at the start of the Seven Years' War in 1756: 'I know that I can save this country and that no one else can'.[33]

If 1940 had been a high-water mark, 1956 had been a low-ebb: Thatcher was determined to emulate Churchill's achievement in the different circumstances of the late twentieth century by disposing of the 'Suez syndrome', which had led successive governments to exaggerate British impotence after 1956.[34] The Conservatives' policies appealed to many in management, keen to shift power on the factory floor away from organized labour (though few favoured a complete repudiation of post-war corporatism).[35] They also contained a strong populist component, which appealed to voters favourably inclined to Enoch Powell's *laissez-faire* Little Englandism: non-unionized workers along with small-scale property owners and self-employed voters frustrated with 'red tape' and the demands of the Inland Revenue.[36] Many of these had been alienated from the Conservative Party since the early 1960s, turning instead to the Liberals or to (at best) maverick far Right organizations. They were keen to see smaller government and lower taxes; but the outlook to which they responded so positively in 1979 was rooted in identity as well as in material self-interest. When Thatcher publicly sympathized with those who were 'really rather afraid that this country might be rather swamped by people with a different culture' and held out the possibility that the Conservatives would put 'an end to immigration, except of course for compassionate cases'[37] she was endorsing Powell's vision of a Britain whose traditions and communities were under siege.[38] This rhetorical turn strengthened the Party's identification with a political tradition in both middle-class and working-class culture which was both patriotic and liberal-individualist and drew strength from the experience of two world wars, though it stretched back to the time of Gladstone a century earlier,[39] as did the claim that Britain was 'overtaxed, over-organized and undisciplined'.[40]

The Conservative strategy played well during the election campaign. Voting patterns in May 1979 were testimony to its success. Some 39 per cent of skilled and 33 per cent of unskilled manual workers (social groups C2 and DE respectively) supported the Tories, the highest figures for these groups since the 1950s; in October 1974 the returns had been, respectively, just 26 and 22 per cent. No other group showed such a dramatic swing to the Conservatives from the previous General Election: the white collar vote (C1) rose marginally, from 51 to 52 per cent; professional middle-class support actually fell, from 63 per cent to 61 per cent.[41] Attracted by the emollient manifesto and disturbed by the events of the winter, many working (and lower middle-class) voters believed a Thatcher government would bring back stability to the nation and make it more respected abroad (the Tories and their supporters in the media returned frequently to what they misleadingly called the 'humiliation' of the 1976 sterling crisis and the IMF loan). They supported the proposals to abjure incomes policy and curtail trade union power, encourage home ownership, reduce taxes and reward aspirational workers, take action to reduce inflation, protect savings, strengthen controls on immigration and take a more vigorous line than Labour in the promotion of the nation's influence overseas. In a significant and (for the Tories) promising reversal of post-1945 voters' priorities, opinion polls during the election campaign reflected greater public concern about rising prices than about joblessness. Even though the annual rate of inflation had fallen a long way below the levels it had reached in the middle of the decade the experience had clearly been intense enough to disturb those with savings, a section of the community which had grown during the decade, with the percentage of real disposable income taken by savings increasing from 9.3 per cent (1970–72) to 14.7 per cent (1979). Over the same period personal savings as a proportion of all savings increased from an average level of 27.7 per cent to 53.2 per cent, a development which enhanced the appeal of the Conservative manifesto to existing and would-be property owners.[42]

Overall, the coalition of voters who supported the Conservatives in 1979 did so because they were persuaded that Margaret Thatcher's team had better ideas than Jim Callaghan's about how to improve Britain. They did not wish to destroy the 1944 settlement even if they did believe it should be rebalanced to become less Statist and corporatist and more individualist. Yet the administration they elected had more radical ambitions and a mission to change the course of British history. Mrs Thatcher and her supporters, true to the values which they had come to espouse during the previous decade, were determined to implement a politico-economic project which represented a fracture with the post-war consensus.[43] This was about turning Britain into a neo-liberal society: only a transformation as fundamental as this could (they believed) make democracy secure and provide the political, cultural and economic foundations for renewed prosperity and restored international influence. The agenda becomes clear with a careful reading of the manifesto: the overriding objective was the rolling back of the State and the replacement of the post-war model with a liberal capitalist one. The retreat from planning and corporatism, the transfer of property, in the form of shares and houses, from the collective (namely the State and the local authorities) to the individual, the reduction of taxation and of spending on public sector programmes were all means to this goal. The reaction against social democracy was to be far-reaching.

The project was soon to become known as 'Thatcherism', defined by one of Margaret Thatcher's more radical allies, Nigel Lawson,[44] as 'a mixture of free markets, financial discipline, firm control over public expenditure, tax cuts, nationalism, Victorian values (of the Samuel Smiles self-help variety), privatization and a dash of populism'.[45] For Thatcher the nationalist component included a willingness to mount a robust (some said strident) defence of Britain's global interests, especially (but not exclusively, as the Falklands War and frequent showdowns with Britain's partners in the European Community were to demonstrate) against ideological enemies in the form of the USSR and its allies. But this was not a conflict which could be confined to the world beyond the English Channel. Thatcher's belief that socialism and communism were the enemies of individual freedom and liberal democracy, a view reinforced by the briefings she received from Brian Crozier and his well-placed group of cold warriors, led to the conviction that her government was engaged in a struggle for absolute values at home as well as abroad. In consequence, when it came to national security there was to be no 'small state' but one capable of deploying both military force overseas and heightened domestic surveillance combined, if necessary, with the repression of those Thatcher was to identify as 'the enemy within', a term reserved for those who in her view were promoting the communist cause inside Britain. Willingness to use state power against these organizations in order to remove entrenched opposition within civil society and the wider world to the neo-liberal Britain which the new Prime Minister and her supporters in the Conservative Party were determined to construct led the political scientist Andrew Gamble to characterize Thatcherism as a mixture of 'the free economy and the strong state' while the sociologist Stuart Hall described it as 'authoritarian populism'.[46]

Money

The combination of conviction politics with ruthlessness that characterized the praxis of Thatcherism was soon apparent; from its earliest days the government took a series of steps in economic policy whose radicalism surprised and dismayed both its enemies and many of its supporters. Pragmatic arguments against these measures did not avail (initially at least) even though they precipitated the crisis which engulfed the manufacturing sector, a point acknowledged by some of those responsible for implementing them.[47] On the surface it seems surprising that the government presided over the dramatic downturn of 1979–81, given its intention to improve the economy's performance by facilitating a rise in the rate of return on investment in the private sector. For Chancellor Geoffrey Howe and his team at the Treasury, especially Financial Secretary Nigel Lawson, however, this task could not be fulfilled unless what were identified as crucial obstacles to accumulation were removed. This meant that macroeconomic policy should prioritize the reduction of inflation, changes to the tax system and the deregulation of markets above returning output to a full employment level.[48]

The government's early months in power saw a determined attempt to make progress on all three fronts. Price and dividend controls were abolished. Its first Budget announced cuts in income tax, designed to reward initiative and hard work, reducing the top rate on earned income from 83p to 75p, while the standard rate was reduced from 33p to 30p. The impact on Exchequer revenues was counterbalanced by a rise in VAT from 8 to 15 per cent, in order to prevent an increase in the PSBR. This move had the perverse effect of increasing inflationary pressures, but was compatible with the Thatcherite project in that it would encourage people to save money while commencing a process of rebalancing fiscal policy away from direct taxation. In accordance with its monetarist convictions the government sought to achieve lower inflation through reducing the growth in the money supply, from a range of between 8 and 12 per cent for the current year to one of between 7 and 11 per cent for 1980–81. This was to be accompanied by measures to prune the State, with cuts worth £2.5 billion in planned public spending totals (bearing down hardest on housing).[49] These were designed to shrink the PSBR from 5.25 per cent to 4.75 per cent of GDP, thereby minimizing the danger that (in accordance with monetarist doctrine) government requirements for finance would 'crowd out' private borrowers from the lending markets and provoke increases in interest rates. More reductions, worth £3.5 billion, were announced in November 1979, with £1.5 billion to be raised for the Treasury by sales of public assets including a portion of the North Sea Continental Shelf held by the State-owned British National Oil Corporation (BNOC).[50]

These measures were reinforced by the government's 'Medium Term Financial Strategy' (MTFS), unveiled in March 1980. It sought further reductions in the growth of the money supply to between 6 and 10 per cent in 1981–82 and between 4 and 8 per cent in 1983–84,[51] with a fall in the share of GDP taken by the PSBR to 1.5 per cent by 1984–85 being a key part of the process.[52] This task was complicated by the problem that economists seeking to control the money supply did not agree on what money actually was, leading to considerable discussion within No. 10, the Treasury and the Bank of England. In the end it came down to a choice between two definitions. The first, known as the monetary base, (M0) was the sum held in the form of commercial bank deposits in the central bank reserves plus the total amount of currency circulating in notes and coins in the hands of the public. The second (sterling M3) involved the level of cash in circulation with the public plus all sterling bank deposits.[53] The consensus within the Bank of England and the Treasury (and the City) was against using M0, on the grounds that it would either impede the freedom of the commercial banks by requiring them to retain a fixed level of reserves with the Bank or necessitate constant intervention by the Bank itself to buy or sell securities in order to keep M0 stable.[54] The weight of opinion therefore favoured taking sterling M3 as the operational measure of money supply, on the positive grounds that it seemed to be both sophisticated and easy to manage, through manipulation of the MLR in order to control the demand for money.

The government found control of sterling M3 to be impossible. This was, in part at least, as a result of two significant acts of financial liberalization. The first was the abolition of exchange controls in October 1979. Representing the most radical of the Thatcher administration's early initiatives, this was certainly in accordance with the ideological predilection for deregulation. It was also in the interests of the City, providing the multinational corporations and financial institutions, including banks, unit trusts and pension funds, located there with the freedom to export capital to any part of the world. Between 1979 and 1981 there was no new (net) unit trust investment in the UK; and by late 1981 pension funds were investing 25 per cent of their funds overseas (compared with 'almost nothing' a few years before).[55] At the same time there were substantial inflows of foreign currency into sterling-denominated assets.[56] This reform was followed in mid-1980 by abolition of 'the corset', controls on bank lending introduced by the previous Labour administration. The move led to growth in the availability of credit as banks started to compete with building societies for a slice of the mortgage market, seen as profitable and low-risk at a time when lending to the corporate sector was very risky.[57]

The internationalization of capital flows through the City and the expansion of domestic lending undermined efforts to control monetary aggregates such as sterling M3.[58] The government was far less successful in meeting its monetary targets than Labour had been. Not one of the MTFS targets for sterling M3 (or for the PSBR) was ever hit. Sterling M3 growth for each year in the period from 1980 to 1983 reached, respectively, 74 per cent, 37 per cent and 23 per cent.[59] The Treasury's solution, strongly supported by Howe and Lawson, was to increase the MLR, thereby (it was hoped) rationing demand for credit via the operation of the price mechanism, while pressing ahead with its package of spending reductions in the belief that the resultant fall in the PSBR would eventually moderate the increases in the lending rate. Howe raised the MLR from 14 per cent to 17 per cent in November 1979, the largest interest rate rise on a single day before or since.[60] It remained there until July 1980. Thereafter, a six-month spell at 12 per cent between March and

September 1981 excepted, it did not fall below 14 per cent until early 1982. It remained in double figures for the rest of the decade, apart from the period between March 1987 and late July 1988.

Initially, the spike in the rate of inflation caused by the VAT increase and by the movement of energy (especially oil) prices (the RPI rose by 21 per cent between June 1979 and June 1980)[61] meant that the high nominal MLR did not represent a high real rate of interest. However, the annual rate of inflation subsequently fell to an average of 5.4 per cent in 1982, thereafter hovering between 4 and 5 per cent until 1988. Given the expansion of sterling M3 it is hard to see how this could have been a result of slower money supply growth:[62] it was in fact largely thanks to a combination of domestic recession with sluggish international demand and falling commodity (fuel and non-fuel) prices.[63] The resulting scissors-like movement of MLR on the one hand and the RPI on the other led to high real rates of interest. These provoked upward pressure on an exchange rate which had been climbing since early 1977, thanks to Labour's agreement with the IMF and the impact of North Sea oil revenues on the current account. By late 1980 sterling was over $2.40: the revaluation represented a 50 per cent increase in the real exchange rate which now even surpassed its 1972 value by 30 per cent.[64] The high real MLR and strong pound in turn led banks to accumulate significant cash deposits and attracted inflows of foreign money into the economy, further fuelling the sterling M3 overshoot.[65] This then led the government to maintain the high real MLR, a response which did not remedy but helped to provoke the very circumstances which were causing it to miss its monetary targets in the first place.

The government welcomed the favourable shift in the terms of trade caused by sterling's rise, arguing that falling import costs would reinforce the impact of the MTFS on inflation.[66] Yet whatever the impact of the government's strategy on the RPI it is hard to escape the conclusion that it was largely responsible for the downturn of 1979–81. With little growth in the international economy British exporters were always going to find life difficult at this time. Their problems were however exacerbated by the high interest and exchange rates, the first of these making borrowing expensive while the second forced British manufacturers to compete on disadvantageous terms with foreign producers at home and abroad. The result was tight profit margins, squeezed even further by high energy costs. At the same time the government's determination to meet its PSBR targets meant more turns of the deflationary screw. The mounting toll of joblessness triggered a rise in spending on unemployment benefit and social security payments. This led the Treasury to search for counterbalancing economies. Public investment programmes were cut, causing the State's contribution to gross fixed capital formation to shrink as a proportion of the national product, from 2.1 per cent in 1979 to 1.3 per cent in 1981; in constant money terms this amounted to a fall from £6.85 billion to £4.35 billion.[67] This did not create room for the compensating expansion of the private sector Treasury Ministers had expected: gross fixed capital formation on the part of the private sector (in 1980 prices) slumped from £30.58 billion in 1979 to

£27.57 billion in 1981.[68] The curtailing of State activities simply contributed to the collapse of demand and output.

The scale of the crisis led to protests in Cabinet and from the CBI Director-General, Sir Terence Beckett, who called for 'a bare knuckle fight' with the government over economic policy late in 1980.[69] This never really materialized, largely thanks to the temporary fall in the MLR during the following year. It was, however, not possible to appease colleagues within the government: there was a series of rows in the Cabinet between Thatcher and her allies on the one hand and her opponents, whom she dubbed the 'wets', on the other. These were the Tories who evoked the One Nation tradition and the pragmatic paternalism of leaders such as Baldwin and Macmillan (who himself entered the debate and spoke out against the government's policies)[70] and advocated a Keynesian U-turn. Ian Gilmour accused the government of following 'the economics of the madhouse'; and Defence Secretary Francis Pym complained that Treasury had 'no idea what the implications of the cuts' would be and that Thatcher 'doesn't really understand the problems of real people faced with the present economy: the unemployed, the factory owners'.[71]

The arguments slowed down the Cabinet's progress towards agreement on the 1980 public spending round, causing the Prime Minister a good deal of frustration. Far from changing tack, however, she was determined not to follow the example of the Heath government in 1971–72. Instead she issued a challenge to those arguing for a U-turn: 'You turn if you want to. The lady's not for turning', she told them at the Conservative Party conference in October1980.[72] The March 1981 Budget showed the government's determination to stick to its course: it tightened fiscal policy, aiming for a net increase of £4 billion in taxes (1.6 per cent of GDP).[73] Coming as it did after output had been falling for over a year, this attempt to cut the PSBR flew in the face of conventional Keynesianism as practised by successive governments since the 1940s. It led to protests from 364 economists, who signed a public letter arguing that the measures would deepen the recession. The spring and summer inner city riots added to the falling confidence in the government's macroeconomic strategy, which now began to spread beyond the usual suspects. The year 1981 saw another fraught public spending exercise. On 23 July the Cabinet refused to accept the Chancellor's proposals for yet further cuts. The revolt left him and Thatcher isolated, supported only by Sir Keith Joseph.[74] This amounted to a serious setback; the head of the Prime Minister's Policy Unit, John Hoskyns, suspected it might be 'the beginning of the end'.[75]

Thatcher's response was to strengthen her position in Cabinet with a reshuffle. There was a purge of the 'wets', with Gilmour being the leading victim. Jim Prior was moved to the Northern Ireland Office while Thatcher's allies Nigel Lawson, Norman Tebbit and Cecil Parkinson were all promoted (to Energy, Employment and Conservative Party Chairman, with a seat in Cabinet, respectively). Although Howe's cuts were never restored, from this point the balance of power in the Cabinet did swing conclusively towards the coalition of

Conservatives most strongly behind Thatcher's own blend of neo-liberalism and nationalism: the self-employed, non-unionized labour, existing and aspiring property owners, members of the armed forces (both serving and retired), leading defence contractors and the City of London. Backed by this alliance the Prime Minister was able to implement her free market agenda, transforming Britain in the process.

Battleground

The determination of Thatcher and her supporters not to concede to her opponents testifies to the strength of her commitment to the establishment of a new politico-economic order in Britain. This, reinforced by her own sense of mission, led her into a series of conflicts with those who resisted her vision. The Prime Minister's determination to clear away obstacles on the road to reform, whether in the shape of individuals or interests in civil society, locked the government into a series of battles over the next few years. They tended to be attritional rather than confrontational but on occasion erupted into set-piece spectaculars which divided the nation.

Arguably the most significant of these was with the trade union movement. Firmly rejecting any possibility of co-operation on macroeconomic or industrial policy with the TUC the government consistently sought to weaken the influence of the unions. This process was facilitated by rising joblessness, which fed a decline in union membership and corroded the bargaining power of organized labour. Against this background the government was able to pass legislation between 1980 and 1990 which imposed serious restrictions on trade union activity. This comprised four Employment Acts, the 1984 Trade Union Act and the 1986 Wages Act, along with Codes of Practice on picketing (1980) and on balloting for industrial action (1990). Most of the more far-reaching reforms were introduced after Norman Tebbit succeeded Jim Prior at the Department of Employment. The overall effect was to place logistical obstacles in the way of organizing strikes, criminalize secondary picketing and weaken the finances of trade unions by granting employers the right to obtain injunctions against them and sue them for damages, while providing for the sequestration of union assets in the event of contempt of court being declared.

The legislation contributed to a spectacular fall in the number of days lost to industrial action, from an annual average of around 300 per thousand employees (a total of 7 million) in the mid to late 1970s to one of little over 100 per thousand employees by the late 1980s.[76] Other factors were the growth of unemployment and the expansion of self-employed labour, from 8 per cent of the work-force in 1979 to 12 per cent in 1987.[77] But there can be no doubt that the outcome of the 1984–85 miners' strike also had a significant impact on the new climate of industrial relations. This dispute between the NCB and the NUM, with the government not simply supporting the former but most anxious to ensure the defeat of the latter, was one of the defining conflicts of the Thatcher era. The miners were the first group to be identified by the Prime Minister as 'the enemy within'. She was convinced that NUM President Arthur Scargill, who had replaced Joe Gormley in 1981, 'sought to impose a Marxist system on Britain whatever the means and whatever the cost',[78] and embodied a tendency which she believed to be increasingly evident in the trade union movement, the Labour Party and in local authorities. Scargill, who occupied a special place in the demonology of the Conservative Party, stemming from his role at Saltley in 1972, was certainly on the radical Left: but the dispute was about the future of the mining industry and not an insurgency against the elected government, even though that is how it was frequently portrayed by Thatcher herself and throughout much of the media.[79]

By the autumn of 1983 relations between the NUM and NCB had been poor for several months: it was clear that the NCB Chairman, the Scottish-American businessman Ian MacGregor (who had previously led the rationalization drive at British Steel) intended to shrink the coal industry. He maintained that British coal was uncompetitively priced, being 25 per cent more expensive than the international market price, with the result that there was an operating loss of £3.05 on each tonne:[80] the solution was increased mechanization and fewer pits. The NUM challenged the figures but MacGregor had the complete approval of the government, which was seeking to reduce the dependence of the energy sector on supplies of coal (80 per cent of UK electricity was generated from domestic coal)[81] and cut the cost to the Exchequer of supporting the mining industry. Before MacGregor's arrival in March 1983 the NCB had been closing pits at the rate of about 20 each year, normally with the agreement of the NUM in a case-by-case colliery review procedure, but the new Chairman made it clear to senior ministers that September that he intended to accelerate the closure programme whether the NUM consented or not. He now proposed to shut 75 pits by the end of 1985 (cutting 64,000 jobs and shrinking the workforce from 202,000 to 138,000). This was agreed at a meeting with the Prime Minister, the Chancellor (now Nigel Lawson), Employment Secretary Tebbit and Energy Secretary Peter Walker, notwithstanding vigorous denials at the time and subsequently of claims from Scargill that 70 pits were to be closed.[82]

The strike began in early March 1984, when miners at Cortonwood colliery in Yorkshire walked out in protest after the NCB announced that it was one of six pits scheduled for 'accelerated closure'. The NUM declared a national strike a few days later. No ballot of all members was ever run, leading to legal action against the NUM and to the attempted sequestration of its assets. Scargill, the NUM General Secretary Peter Heathfield and the striking miners were frequently accused of tactical errors. It was said they should have called a national ballot and that it was a mistake to start the dispute in the spring, when coal stocks were high (it had been a mild winter and the government had been stockpiling coal in anticipation of the strike) and summer was only three months away. Yet the case for a ballot was not straightforward, thanks to the highly regional nature of the industry.[83] Moreover there were widespread local ballots in favour of action while opinion polls showed well over 60 per cent of miners in favour of the strike.[84] Within a fortnight of it starting, 80 per cent of them had ceased working, the majority of these staying out for a year.[85] As far as the timing was concerned, recognition of the walkout at

Cortonwood amounted to acknowledgement of a *fait accompli* and an attempt by the NUM to gain control of developments on the ground. Perhaps the most serious blunder made by the leadership was the failure to court opinion in Nottinghamshire, where the majority of miners had come out against the action and continued to work throughout the dispute.[86]

Despite the split within the NUM caused by Nottinghamshire's refusal to join the strike, the miners came close to achieving a negotiated settlement which would have returned the closure programme to the consensual approach followed by MacGregor's predecessor Sir Derek Ezra.[87] Retreat on the pit closures would have committed the Conservatives to a form of accountancy based on broad social and economic costs rather than the narrow profit and loss calculations which were central to the commercialization of the coal industry and indeed to the entire free market project.[88] It would have emboldened the trade union movement and threatened to turn the tide of legislation curtailing the rights of organized labour. Finally it would have represented yet another setback for a Conservative government at the hands of the miners. The government was therefore determined not to give way to the NUM, seeing the conflict as a crucial test both of its strength and of its credibility as an administration committed to the transformation of Britain. It turned to the deployment of covert State agencies and the armed forces, as well as of important sections of the media, against the miners. Its mobilization of these forces, reflecting the origins of Thatcherism in the network of right-wing factions within private industry, the City and the military-intelligence establishment which had coalesced in the mid-1970s, was testimony to the high stakes involved in the outcome of the dispute.

It followed that the 'concentrated power of the state' was brought to bear on the striking miners: there were 11,000 arrests, the movement of pickets across the country was subject to disruption by roadblocks and there was nationwide deployment of the police force.[89] On occasion army units, dressed in police uniform, were used to face the miners. Tony Benn reports two examples: in the Nottinghamshire coalfield, where pickets were endeavouring to turn back working miners; and in Felixstowe, where striking miners were picketing the docks in an attempt to prevent the movement of imported coal.[90] Communications between members of the NUM leadership (as well as between striking miners) were monitored by the intelligence and security services; agents provocateurs provoked violent incidents intended to discredit the NUM; and Special Branch informers in pit villages earned between £30 and £40 per week passing information to the authorities.[91] Running in parallel with these actions was a sustained media offensive against the miners and their leaders which lasted throughout the strike and beyond. As late as 1990 Scargill and Heathfield were subject to a sensational and entirely fictional set of allegations in the press and on television about their handling of the NUM's finances during the strike.[92] Former *Times* editor Simon Jenkins described newspaper coverage of the dispute as 'ludicrously biased', a position indicating not only government encouragement and briefings but the politics of the media conglomerates which owned most of the British press.[93] Even the BBC contributed to the smears. Its broadcast of one of the most infamous episodes in the history of the strike, a clash between pickets and the police at the British Steel Orgreave coking coal plant in June 1984, showed mounted police charging in response to missile-throwing on the part of the striking miners. This was not simply a distortion but a complete – and deliberate – reversal of what had actually happened.[94]

In the end the government and the NCB won. The miners returned to work, in good order, in March 1985. This could not however disguise the scale of the defeat: there had been no retreat on the closure programme, which was in fact accelerated after the strike. Over the next decade 200,000 jobs were lost. The Kent coalfield closed in 1989. Only 11 of the 56 pits operating in Yorkshire in 1985 were running a decade later. Mining in Durham ceased in 1994. By the mid-1990s there were just two deep mines remaining in south Wales. The rump of the industry was privatized in 1994.[95] In 2013 there were three deep coal pits in operation out of the 170 in 1984. Many former mining communities were unable to find viable economic alternatives and were afflicted by social deprivation and high rates of unemployment.[96] Yet the implications of the dispute went well beyond the mining community. The outcome of the strike represented a fatal blow to the post-war consensus. The Thatcher administration had never accepted the philosophical argument behind the 1944 settlement, namely that government, industry and the unions were partners in the construction of a society committed to full employment and the construction of a welfare state. Now, the pragmatic case for co-operation with the unions had been demolished. As Thatcher herself argued in her memoirs,

> From 1972 to 1985 the conventional wisdom was that Britain could only be governed with the consent of the trade unions…Even as we were reforming trade union law and overcoming lesser disputes…many on the left and outside it continued to believe that the miners had the ultimate veto and would one day use it. That day had now come and gone.[97]

The government's triumph over the NUM, which was not only at the core of the British trade union movement but arguably its most powerful member, represented a historic defeat for organized labour. From this point it was unable to offer sustained resistance to the Thatcher government's neo-liberal reconstruction of labour relations and industrial policy.

These now became increasingly characterized by 'flexible accumulation'. This was a new world for labour. Its arrival was signalled by the publication of the 1985 White Paper, *Employment: The Challenge for the Nation,* which saw long-term unemployment as more a product of institutional constraints, notably within the labour market, than of weak demand. It therefore advocated a range of remedies, such as limiting the duration of unemployment benefit and tougher job search requirements for those out of work.[98] For those in work flexible accumulation meant a reduction in the level of employment protection, changes to working hours and practices, the introduction of part-time work and the growth of outsourcing (the transfer of work from in-house providers to outside suppliers) by public and private institutions. Apologists for the change argued that in fact it had the potential to provide workers with more freedom in the labour market than they had enjoyed as members of the workforce in large factories operating on the basis of mass production. Whatever the advantages for individual workers, however, the new system was more beneficial for employers and it both strengthened the power of and increased rewards to capital. It weakened job security, tended to lower wage levels and led to the dilution of employee benefit schemes (over time pensions proved to be the most vulnerable of these).[99] Labour's share of national income dropped from its peak of 61 per cent in the mid-1970s to 47 per cent in 1988–89 while the private sector's net rate of return grew from a post-1945 low point of 5 per cent in 1977–78 to between 13 and 14 per cent by the late 1980s, close to its post-1945 peak of 15 per cent.[100]

For capital, especially for large corporations, flexible accumulation involved an acceleration of the tendency to internationalization of production and finance, with firms tending to transfer industrial plant and labour resources to green-field sites where unions were weak or non-existent. This development, which was to spread across much of the industrialized world over the next generation, was perhaps most strikingly visible first in the UK. Here, the government was true to its liberal views and offered no serious national industrial strategy (beyond limited funding for information technology and more generous support for the defence export sector). Wilsonian corporatism and Bennite *dirigisme* were alike discarded in favour of the encouragement of inward investment by multinational corporations, often headquartered in Japan, attracted by tax incentives, government subsidies and compliant workers. It was a regime which, initially at least, reduced large parts of the British electronics and automobile industries to assembly plants for companies such as Panasonic, Nissan and Toyota, eager to use the UK as a springboard into the European market.[101]

The defeat of the NUM had cleared away the most serious obstacle in the way of Thatcher's struggle to regenerate British capitalism. But the term 'enemy within' was quickly extended to include not simply trade unions but local authorities, universities (especially departments of sociology) and even the Anglican Church. The government became involved in a long-running showdown with left-leaning Labour authorities such as the Greater London Council (GLC) and Sheffield City Council. Mobilizing coalitions of trade unionists, ethnic minorities, and new social movements such as those seeking to advance gay rights, these had attempted to run varieties of municipal socialism. The most commonly pursued policies involved support for local enterprise, council house building, job creation schemes, subsidized public transport and the promotion of the arts. The Conservatives refused to accept this attempt to turn localities into centres of an alternative political economy. The Prime Minister referred to the Labour groups in charge of these authorities as 'loony lefties', a term which was to enter the discourse of popular politics through her supporters in the press,[102] and launched a series of assaults on the freedom of local authorities. The GLC was abolished in 1986. Local authorities saw their functions stripped away, with councils obliged to put services out to competitive tendering on the part of private providers. Legislation was passed allowing schools to opt out of local authority control. Finally, councils' financial autonomy was restricted, with the introduction of 'rate-capping' to limit the amount they could raise from householders and businesses. Thatcher was determined to go further and favoured the introduction of a 'poll tax' (the term 'community charge' was used by the scheme's supporters) to replace the rates altogether, on the basis that nothing less would ensure that councils were restricted to funding basic services such as highway maintenance rather than wasting rate-payers' money on inefficient practices and political experiments.

Universities found themselves under attack, mainly on two fronts. First of all, the study of 'class', 'class formation' and 'class inequality', a long-standing and fundamental component of degree schemes and research programmes run in university sociology departments throughout the country, was deeply unpopular with the Prime Minister and her supporters. They suspected it to be at the intellectual core of Marxist-inspired movements aiming at the overthrow of capitalism. The budget of the Social Science Research Council, responsible for funding work in the social sciences, was halved.[103] Secondly, the difficulties experienced by sociology departments came as part of a more general assault on higher education. In 1981 universities were given four weeks to plan for three years of cuts to the State funding they received annually through the University Grants Committee. Further reductions in support, worth 2 per cent, were announced in 1983. The government called for higher education to shift its teaching and research away from the arts and social sciences towards 'enterprise', business and vocational studies. Staffing was cut, appointments were frozen and spending on books and journals fell by 33 per cent in real terms between 1980–88 while student numbers climbed by 45,000 from 1984 to 1989, putting the entire system under growing pressure.[104] Painful and dramatic rationalizations became common, and were especially acute at Aston, Bradford and Salford Universities in the first years of the 1980s, while in 1986–88 University College, Cardiff only escaped bankruptcy as a result of a merger with its neighbour, the University of Wales Institute of Science and Technology (UWIST).

The row with the Anglican Church developed out of the same clash of philosophies underlying the conflict with the universities. Disturbed by the impact of cuts in local government services and rising joblessness, the Archbishop of Canterbury, Robert Runcie, established a Commission on Urban Priority Areas, which produced a report, *Faith in the City*, in the autumn of 1985.[105] The document noted the growth of material and spiritual poverty in Britain's inner cities, attributing much of this to the effect of government policies. It called for more support for disadvantaged groups and, in essence, argued for higher social welfare spending as well as State and local authority housing and employment programmes designed to regenerate run-down areas. The government's response was to accuse the Church of promoting 'Marxist theology' and to lament the absence in the document of any focus on self-help on the part of individual citizens. It was a foolish and ignorant response (which ironically helped to spread the message of the report and give it a fame it might not otherwise have enjoyed)[106] but indicated the gulf that had now arisen between supporters of the government and its critics. The document was not Marxist but was, however, drafted by a team including prominent exponents of the post-war consensus Thatcher wished to demolish, such as Sir Richard O'Brien (former Chairman of the Manpower Services Commission, established by the Heath government in 1973 to promote training and employment), the Right Reverend David Sheppard (Bishop of Liverpool), Professor A.H. Halsey (Nuffield College, Oxford) and Ron Keating (Assistant General Secretary, National Union of Public Employees). The showdown with the Anglican Church was therefore part of what Middlemas, quoting the Italian Marxist philosopher Antonio Gramsci, refers to as Thatcher's 'wars of position' with the key institutions of the post-war settlement.[107] These wars, whether against the miners, the local authorities, the universities or the Anglican Church, were conflicts fought to promote a new political, economic and cultural hegemony, replacing the values of social democracy with those of neo-liberalism.

Neo-liberal values had penetrated the Conservative Party through think tanks such as the IEA, the Selsdon Group and the CPS as well as through the efforts of senior politicians such as Sir Keith Joseph and Margaret Thatcher herself. These values also found expression, however, in a popular discourse, or 'common sense', Thatcher did much to endorse. This was rooted in her belief that 'there is no such thing as society. There are individual men and women, and there are families. And no government can do anything except through people, and people must look to themselves first.'[108] In this world the encouragement of self-help took priority over collective action; individuals and their families counted for more than class; the obligation of the State to ensure full employment was replaced by the duty of governments to keep markets free; the rights of trade unionists to protection from long hours and low pay were eclipsed by the rights of citizens as consumers to enjoy freedom of choice, whether of privately provided goods or of public services; reducing personal and business taxation took priority over the levying of sufficient resources from the community to fund a generous welfare state; and enterprises which were not commercially viable were not to be rescued but allowed to disappear. Although the battle with the Church was not one of the government's more successful wars of position there is no doubt that its other engagements ended victoriously. By 1986, following the victories over the Cabinet 'wets' and the opposition in civil society there were no significant political or intellectual obstacles left to the particular reinvention of Britain sought by Margaret Thatcher and her allies.

U-turn

Absence of sustained opposition to neo-liberalism would not have been enough to guarantee its status as the hegemonic discourse in British politics and economics from the mid-1980s. Consent was essential. Although Thatcher's own ability to tap into popular cultural values helped to make the case, neo-liberalism would never have become so attractive to many in the electorate if the economy had failed to escape from the recession of the early 1980s. Ironically it became apparent that the long contraction of the economy had ended almost at the very moment that the 364 economists published their warning about the likely consequences of the 1981 Budget. Real GDP growth averaged 3.5 per cent per annum between 1983 and 1989, rising by as much as 4.4 per cent in 1987 and by 4.7 per cent in 1988.[109] Having continued to mount to its peak level of 3.4 million (12.2 per cent) in 1986 unemployment fell rapidly thereafter, down to 1.55 million in June 1990 (5.4 per cent of the workforce, its lowest level since the spring of 1976).[110] For those in work the 1980s became years of great prosperity, an affluence experienced especially by company directors, senior managers, middle managers and skilled workers. Living standards improved faster than at any time since 1945, with average personal *incomes* increasing by 20 per cent between 1983 and 1987 while over the 1980s as a whole personal *wealth* climbed by 80 per cent, a process in large part driven by rising asset values.[111]

Given this expansion, the most sustained since the first half of the 1950s, and the low rate of inflation (the RPI briefly tumbled to less than 3 per cent in 1986 before picking up at the end of the year),[112] it was unsurprising that the Conservative election outlook began to improve. Judging by the opinion polls, during the course of 1982 voters came to view the British triumph in the Falklands war and the improving economy as indications that the Conservatives had indeed drawn a line under the Suez legacy and were on their way to transforming the nation's prospects at home and abroad for the better: the national 'decline' which had so depressed Margaret Thatcher was now being reversed.[113] Buoyed by the recovery and by military victory, and with the Labour Party weakened by splits and infighting (and by the defection of many of its members as well as a considerable number of MPs to the SDP), the Conservatives won a landslide in the 1983 General Election, confounding all the dire predictions of the 1980–81 period. In 1987 the triumph was repeated, albeit in less spectacular fashion.

By the late 1980s Chancellor Lawson was claiming that he would like to be remembered for presiding over the same kind of 'economic miracle' in Britain as the one which had transformed the Federal Republic of Germany into the powerhouse of Western Europe in the 1950s.[114] The 364 economists found themselves under heavy criticism. The apparent magnitude of their blunder served to discredit the Keynesian argument that spending should be increased and taxes cut during a recession. The government had done the reverse, and the outcome appeared to have validated the determination of Thatcher and Howe to eschew any U-turn. Yet the course of events did not prove the economists wrong. To begin with, the rise in output during 1981 was so small that it made no impact on the rapidly increasing rate of unemployment. Secondly, from late 1981 there was what the Cambridge economist and former Treasury official Wynne Godley called 'a colossal U-turn',[115] although he could have added that the abrupt shift in macroeconomic policy was accompanied (and facilitated) by firm adherence to the neo-liberal agenda. In any event, the government started to pull every lever in its possession to revive the economy. The PSBR targets were relaxed. Far from reducing public expenditure the government increased it by an average (in real terms) of 2.5 per cent a year from 1981–82.[116] In 1982 the Cabinet agreed that nationalized industries and local authorities should be provided with the means to increase capital spending in order to stimulate the construction industry.[117] During Nigel Lawson's period as Chancellor, from 1983 until 1989, there was a *de facto* reinstatement of demand management.[118]

Lawson abandoned the use of sterling M3 as the operational measure of the money supply (it increased by 17 per cent in 1985 and 19 per cent in 1986)[119] and stressed the importance of using monetary policy to promote the expansion of employment and of the nominal level of national output. Although there was to be no attempt to hit a specific annual percentage target for GDP growth he now argued that it was right to use macroeconomic policy to sustain a rising level of national income.[120] To this end the Chancellor repeatedly cut the MLR (especially in the wake of the short-lived but dramatic Stock Market crash of October 1987), which in turn encouraged a downward float of sterling (already set in motion by a sharp decline in the price of oil) against other currencies. Between January 1981 and January 1985 the sterling-dollar rate slipped from $2.41 to $1.38, a devaluation of almost 43 per cent, while over the same period it fell against the deutschmark from DM4.85 to DM3.3265, a decline of 31.5 per cent. Lawson was willing to see the pound fall in order to encourage exports and reduce import penetration, especially given North Sea oil's falling contribution to export income.[121] The stimulus resulting from changes to the MLR and sterling was reinforced by budgetary policy: public spending was increased especially on infrastructure, employment and training programmes and on the National Health Service,[122] whose funding rose by 31.8 per cent between 1979 and 1990. This investment outstripped the growth of GDP over the period (23.3 per cent) and included a 4.5 per cent real terms boost, the largest annual injection of cash in its history, for 1989–90.[123] There were reductions in personal taxation, with the basic rate falling to 27p in the pound in 1987.[124] In the 1988 Budget it was cut to 25p while the top rate was slashed from 60p to 40p.

The expansionary impact on activity resulting from fiscal and monetary policy was strengthened by two other features of the government's economic strategy. The first was liberalization of the credit markets. Controls on consumer credit were removed, with all restrictions on hire purchase being abolished in the summer of 1982; ongoing reforms to the housing market led to the evaporation of the distinction between building societies and banks.[125] Once, building societies had rationed mortgages to would-be borrowers; this system now collapsed. Mortgage finance became easily available. Many building societies demutualized while banks competed with them to provide funds to house buyers and for home improvement.[126] All this in turn fed an abundant supply of credit to the growing numbers demanding it thanks to rising wages and salaries and the availability of tax relief on mortgages. Many of the new borrowers were council tenants, given the right to purchase their homes under the 1980 Housing Act: 1.5 million were sold to private owners under this legislation during the decade, transactions which undoubtedly helped to drive up the number of mortgages from 5.5 million in 1981 to 8 million in 1990.[127] The result was a rise in the total of housing loans, amounting to £16 billion in 1978 and to £63 billion in 1988, while non-housing loans grew from £7 billion to £28 billion over the same period.[128] Net lending to the personal sector on the part of banks and other financial institutions rose by a factor of three between 1984 and 1987; between 1987 and 1989 it amounted to 10 per cent of the national income. Personal savings fell by a similar amount and their ratio to personal income slumped from 12 per cent in 1979 to 5.5 per cent in 1988.[129]

The rising demand generated by this combination of credit, tax cuts and buoyant personal incomes began to feed inflationary forces, first seen in the property market. By 1988 house prices were 40 per cent above what they had been in 1986, taking them from 3 to 4.5 times the level of average incomes since the start of the decade.[130] This differential stimulated the flow of credit. By 1989 net household debt was 2.5 times higher than it had been in 1982.[131] The commercial sector joined in the borrowing spree, its net lending up by a factor of four between 1983 and 1990.[132] This was privatized Keynesianism: the government was delivering economic expansion through higher spending, based on an increase in borrowing, with the risk transferred from the State to individuals, private firms, financial institutions and banks. The escalating value of property assets offset the deflationary impact stemming from labour's falling share of national income. Apparently a one-way ticket to greater individual wealth, they appeared to guarantee the financial security of debtors and a healthy return to lenders.

Secondly, the privatization of State-owned industries facilitated increases in public spending whose impact on government accounts could be offset by the money brought into the Exchequer by the sales. Indeed the PSBR diminished after 1983 despite Lawson's combination of spending increases and tax giveaways: by 1986–87 it was down to 2 per cent of GDP and set to fall further.[133] Privatization had been an objective of the economic liberals around Thatcher from the start, but only relatively small steps had been taken, such as the sale of BP and BNOC assets and of the telecommunications firm Cable and Wireless, in its first term. It was not until after the landslide General Election victory of 1983 that the government had felt confident enough to proceed with a major programme, starting with the sale of British Telecom in 1984. This was followed by privatization of the public utilities (gas, water and electricity) as well as British Aerospace, BNOC (now slimmed down and known as Enterprise Oil), British Steel, British Shipbuilding, BL (known as the Rover Group from 1986 and sold to British Aerospace in 1988) and a wide range of smaller enterprises. The public responded enthusiastically, attracted by the windfall gains to be made when they found that shares in privatized industries purchased at low (indeed undervalued) prices could be sold on at a handsome profit. Along with the sale of council houses this radical departure transferred public property to private ownership, helping to fuel a spectacular increase in the share of the public owning shares, which grew from 7 per cent to 29 per cent during the 1980s.[134] For many Conservatives this was genuine progress towards the ideal of a 'property-owning democracy' and to what Thatcher and her allies termed 'popular capitalism'. It also delivered purchasing power into public hands and helped to feed the rise in asset prices which encouraged owners to increase their borrowing.

It was ironic that Thatcher, for whom the free market was identified with personal virtues such as individual responsibility, financial prudence and frugality, should have presided over a government which had produced an old-fashioned credit-driven boom. In October 1986, noting the fall of sterling, a deteriorating current account balance and a PSBR projection of £7 billion, she queried the Chancellor's policy. Lawson, however, ignored the Prime Minister's misgivings and did not change course.[135] Yet the Prime Minister's concern that the government might be engineering another version of the Barber boom was not misplaced. By 1989, after all the sacrifices inflicted on the economy between 1979 and 1981 in the name of reducing inflation, the RPI was threatening to reach an annual rate of 10 per cent. Gilmour records that from 1982–89 personal consumption grew at an annual average rate of 4.6 per cent, double its rate of growth in the twenty years to 1979. At the end of the 1980s the share of GDP taken by consumer spending stood at 39.5 per cent, some seven points above its 1979 level.[136] Much of the new spending occurred in the service sector of the economy, whose share of GDP grew from 57 per cent in 1980 to 63 per cent ten years later.[137] The expanding property market stimulated demand for estate agents, solicitors and accountants as well as electricians and plumbers. Higher disposable personal income led not only to the growth of private education and private medical treatment for the salariat but to a rapid increase in the number of enterprises operating at the mass consumption end of the market. Spending on fast food outlets grew from £1.8 billion to £2.9 billion in the four years from 1985 to 1989[138] and by 30 per cent in real terms on sport over the decade from 1985 to 1995[139] (most of this increase occurring before 1991). The increasingly wide range of consumer requirements was reflected in the continuing rise of self-employment, a trend encouraged by a series of tax concessions for small businesses. By 1990 this was accounting for just over 13 per cent of the workforce.[140]

It was, however, a different story in manufacturing. The damage done in 1980–81 took its toll. Manufacturing output failed to exceed its 1979 level until 1987–88 and declined as a percentage of GDP to less than 20 per cent by 1990;[141] until the last years of the decade spending on new plant and equipment, training and research and development was unimpressive.[142] Investment in manufacturing rose by just 12.8 per cent over the 1980s as a whole; the comparable figure for services – notably finance, insurance, property, distribution and communications along with the accompanying infrastructure of office blocks and information technology – was 10.3 per cent.[143] It followed that serious shortages of skills and capacity developed once demand started its rapid acceleration: as in the latter stages of the Maudling and Barber booms, rapid economic expansion sucked in a rising volume of imports. Services, which are less widely traded than manufactured goods, were unable to come near bridging the gap: in the second half of the 1980s the country slid into deficit, which by 1989 was equivalent to 3.5 per cent of GDP. This was close to the 4 per cent level it reached at the end of Barber's period as Chancellor but its magnitude in 1974 could be partly explained by reference to rising commodity prices, a factor largely absent during the second half of the 1980s.

Lawson, along with leading economists including the influential commentator Samuel Brittan, argued that the combination of floating exchange rates with the volume and availability of finance in the global economy, most of it no longer subject to restrictions on movement, had made balance of payments deficits unimportant. Countries in the red no longer needed to look to the IMF or central banks for funds to cover their external imbalances. To begin with they could allow their exchange rates to sink. This would cause imports to become more expensive and exports to be cheaper, thereby setting in motion an adjustment to the current account deficit. Should the fall in the rate required to achieve this effect be of a magnitude liable to enhance inflation, then it would be possible to attract an inflow of foreign capital large enough to cover the deficit through upward manipulation of the MLR. In these circumstances it would be up to individuals and companies to limit their borrowing to what they could afford to repay: if they failed to do this they would become insolvent. Either way indebtedness would fall. The correction of the deficit would be automatic.[144] There would be what Lawson called 'a soft landing'.[145]

By late 1988 the Chancellor had come to the conclusion that it was time to engineer a soft landing. The pressures of inflation and the credit boom were now causing concern; debt could not be allowed to continue rising relative to income.[146] Unwilling to let the exchange rate fall because of anxiety about the impact of this on the RPI Lawson increased the MLR in a series of stages during 1988–89 until it stood at 14.8 per cent in the autumn of 1989. His observations about how individuals and firms should react to this were made to look somewhat *insouciant* by the results. The return of high borrowing rates brought an end to the boom, but there was no soft landing. Spending on consumption and investment as well as on property and other assets fell as debt repayment took an increasing share of personal and company income. House prices, rising at an annual rate of 32 per cent in the first quarter of 1989, increased by just 0.1 per cent in the last quarter. They then fell until October 1993: by this time the house price index stood at 2700 as against its high point of 3152 at the end of 1989, a decline of 14.3 per cent (1952=100).[147] The London FTSE index of 100 leading shares dropped by 11.3 per cent in 1990.[148] Lower asset prices meant a fall in the value of the collateral available to borrowers, whether this was in the form of property or shares, and an increase in the burden of debt. Many homeowners were now confronted by the disturbing phenomenon of 'negative equity', whereby the amount of the mortgage outstanding on their house exceeded its value. This left large numbers of borrowers unable to discharge their obligations: in consequence property repossessions rose sharply, from 14,580 in 1988 to 75,540 in 1991.[149] In the business sector companies now struggled to repay loans; many failed, causing them to close. There was a surge in company insolvencies, from just under 50,000 in 1989 to 120,000 in 1992.[150] This, in turn, fed rising unemployment, which grew from its low point of 5.4 per cent in June 1990 to 10.5 per cent of the workforce (just over 3 million) by January 1993.[151] The resulting collapse in demand provoked a recession, with falls in the national output every quarter from the summer of 1990 until the end of September 1991.[152]

Lawson had gambled that the external constraint which had frustrated so many of his predecessors would be much weakened in the new world of abundant credit and floating exchange rates: this time sustained expansion, underpinned by a tamed workforce and a generous regime of personal and corporate taxation, would lead to rising investment. This would facilitate rising exports of goods and services, by volume and value, generating the profits which would provide for higher employment along with increased company spending on plant and equipment. Britain would finally have achieved the virtuous economic circle seen throughout most of the leading west European economies in the post-1945 era. And indeed, the Thatcher governments' many supporters in the mainstream media, especially in print journalism, have maintained that the era from 1979–90 saw Britain's long-term economic prospects transformed for the better. Yet the evidence does not support them. Notwithstanding the rapid expansion of output between 1985 and 1989 the annual average level of growth during the Thatcher years was just 1.8 per cent, less than the 2.6 per cent reached by Labour and Conservative social democracy between 1968 and 1979.[153] Sympathetic commentators pointed to a manufacturing 'productivity miracle'[154] but the signs of this are elusive. Output per person and person hour was said to have increased at an annual average rate of 4.7 per cent between 1979 and 1989, against 4.2 per cent for the years 1960–73 and just 1.7 per cent for 1973–79, a performance which exceeded what had been achieved by the economies of Federal Germany and the USA over the same period. Yet over half of this increase was a function of falling employment in manufacturing, where the workforce shrunk by 26 per cent: the other key component, output, rose by just 12 per cent.[155] The reality was different: the Thatcher era had started and finished with two severe recessions, punctuated by a boom straight out of the 'Stop-Go' era. Its legacy was rapid industrial contraction on the one hand and fast growth of services on the other, while the years of financial deregulation destabilized the economy, leaving it vulnerable to volatile international capital flows and speculative shocks.

Breakout

Thatcherism may not have led to an economic miracle but it certainly facilitated the transformation of contemporary Britain. Under the Conservatives Britain broke out of social democracy into a new era based on deregulation and a firm belief that free markets, including the freedom of capital to move anywhere in the world in search of a good rate of return, were more efficient at allocating resources than managed ones. The greatest beneficiaries of this change were to be found in the City of London and the financial sector. If the most representative visual image of early Thatcherism's impact on the economy was the derelict factory, the iconic picture of its later years was the 1986 Lloyd's building in Lime Street, at the heart of London's financial centre.

Deregulation and internationalization of the economy were central to the great expansion in the City's power and wealth after 1979. First of all, the abolition of exchange controls in 1979 was followed by a dramatic exodus of capital. Net overseas assets rose from £32.6 billion in 1981 to £103.6 billion in 1986.[156] In 1985 Britain briefly returned to being the world's leading creditor nation, a position it had not held since 1914. The rapid expansion of overseas investment and the vast turnover of foreign currency business transacted in London, larger than in any other comparable centre,[157] were evidence of the Square Mile's increasing detachment from the fortunes of manufacturing industry in Britain: as this suffered and shrank after 1979 the City increasingly took on the form of an offshore island, handling a growing volume of mobile global capital (£1 trillion in 1985, three times the national income).[158] This churn of footloose funds through the City provided the resources which allowed British multinationals to expand direct investment, both overseas (a turn which became especially noticeable in the mid- to-late 1980s when it was encouraged by a wave of cross-border mergers and takeovers) and inward. Notable examples involved the Hanson Trust's takeover of the Imperial Group, Nestlé's purchase of Rowntree and the Guinness acquisition of the Distillers Company.[159] Many of the transactions falling into this category were not designed to improve productivity but to capture fashionable brands and expand market share.[160]

Secondly, the reforms to the London Stock Exchange in October 1986, known as the 'Big Bang', sought to enhance the international role played by the Exchange, which had been losing business to its rivals on Wall Street and in Tokyo. Old practices and traditions were swept aside: the distinction between brokers and jobbers was abolished, leading to the replacement of floor trading by computerization and screen-based trading. Fixed commissions for services were scrapped, and entry to the Stock Exchange was opened up to permit corporate membership. Commercial bank subsidiaries, many of them foreign, entered the equity market, attracted by the absence in London of the restrictions in New York and Tokyo which prevented them from dealing in equities. Mergers and takeovers followed as banks and broking firms joined forces in order to establish businesses buying and selling in both the equity and bond markets. Demand for expertise and experience pushed up both the cost of these transactions as well as the price of labour in the City. Barclays paid £150 million, a sum equivalent to the estimated capitalization of all the brokers on the London Stock Exchange in 1983, for their 1986 purchases of broker De Zoete and Bevan and of jobber Wedd Durlacher Mordaunt. The average income of a Morgan Grenfell director rose from £40,000 in 1979 to £225,000 by 1986;[161] there was a growing differential between the rewards available in the financial sector and elsewhere in the economy. The combination of reforms succeeded in boosting the competitive position of the Stock Exchange: none of its rivals could approach the level of its turnover; by the early 1990s, of all the major financial centres, London was home to the largest number of branches or subsidiaries of foreign banks.[162]

Thirdly, the government's privatization programme brought real benefits for London. Thatcher and her Ministers were determined to make the process work and therefore provided State support for the whole process of transferring nationalized enterprises to private ownership and the free market. Some £15 billion of the Exchequer debts of publicly owned industries were written off by the Treasury, and initial share values were kept below the market price.[163] This ensured both that the share issues were well subscribed by the public, fuelling the move towards popular capitalism, and that the transactions were virtually risk-free and well-rewarded in terms of the fees and commissions paid to the City firms underwriting them. The National Audit Office calculated that the expenses incurred in privatizing £3.86 billion of British Telecom shares amounted to £263 million (6.8 per cent of the transaction's value).[164] Moreover, this transfer of so large a volume of public wealth into private hands fuelled both the internationalization of the British economy and the securities market: shares of utilities were increasingly traded globally. It was a process which generated further revenue for City firms and contributed to the multiplying business opportunities for those working within the Square Mile.

The new business opportunities stemmed from the expansion of the financial sector, services, property speculation and the wave of merger activity in the USA and the UK. Permissive regulatory regimes in both countries, along with the falling cost of communication and information worldwide thanks to the fax, computing and automated teller machines (ATMs) accelerated the free movement of capital and the creation of a global securities market in which a growing volume of exchangeable goods and services (including the privatized utilities and mortgages on council houses) were converted into tradable financial assets: the process was known as financialization. Financial transactions became the fastest growing area of international economic activity, with the result that funds in search of the best rates of profit tended to flow into this sector rather than into industry.[165] In 1992 the National Manufacturers' Council, established by the CBI during the recession at that time in order to promote policies likely to help reconstruct British industry, reported that in the past decade the financial system had increased its lending to sectors such as real estate by 800 per cent in real terms but by just 50 per cent to manufacturing.[166] Meanwhile dividends grew three times more rapidly than both profits and investment on average during the 1980s; this was another factor in suppressing the level of capital spending in these years.

In general financialization fed an increasing tendency in the UK (and in the USA) for the flow of funds to be driven by the search for short-term profit. This reflected the changing nature of capitalism in the later twentieth century. The era of corporate autonomy, in which firms had been run by a class of salaried managers quite separate from the numerous (and largely inactive) shareholders who owned them, was fading rapidly into the past. The 1980s saw a rise in shareholder power, driven by the expansion of institutional investors such as pension funds and insurance companies. The rise of 'popular capitalism' notwithstanding, the volume of assets owned by these organizations eclipsed individual share ownership, which actually fell as a proportion of all shares during the 1980s, from 28 per cent in 1981 to 21 per cent in 1989.[167] Institutional investors placed more emphasis on share value and dividends than on investment in building up the labour and capital resources of the firm, a longer and less immediately rewarding process which involved a corporatist approach based on co-operation between both sides of industry and possibly a role for government. This development led to the rise of a new term, 'corporate governance', essentially a set of rules designed to ensure that owners and managers worked together. Senior managers increasingly internalized the values of the shareholder-investor, a trend encouraged by the transformation of the corporate executive into a manager-owner, rewarded not by salary but by share options and contractual interest payments, on the basis that a system of remuneration like this would prevent managers from 'wasting' shareholders' money.[168] A synthesis of the mid-century 'managerial revolution', which had underpinned Crosland's seminal 1956 analysis of how capitalism had evolved into a proto-social democratic form, with financialization and the return of shareholder power had been created. It left management increasingly under pressure to distribute rather than retain profits (a practice encouraged by Chancellor Lawson's reduction of corporation tax from 52 per cent to 35 per cent in his 1984 Budget) and more comfortable in a deregulated business environment where capital was free to move at short notice to areas where it fetched the best returns.

This transformation of the British economy during the Thatcher years, in which the City figured so prominently, could not have occurred in the absence of two exogenous developments. One was a deepening of the 'special relationship' with the USA. This had of course operated at the level of defence technology (including the nuclear deterrent), strategic security, and intelligence sharing since the 1940s. During the 1980s it extended to finance. Anglo-American financial collaboration was not new: it had existed during and after World War Two and remained close throughout the Bretton Woods era. What made the Thatcher years different was the extension of this from co-operation between governments and central banks to an alliance between US and UK private capital, especially the two nations' financial sectors. By 1988 aggregate investment by British firms in the USA was worth £43 billion (just under 5 per cent of the GDP), twice its level in the European Community, while the Big Bang of 1986 opened up the London Stock Exchange to US investment banks, Goldman Sachs and Morgan Stanley being two leading examples. Already well known in the City as a result of their activities in the Eurodollar market, these firms now established themselves on the Stock Exchange, enhancing London's ability to promote corporate financial business on a global scale.[169] This convergence of US and UK capital was itself propelled not only by the financial opportunities available in the post-Big Bang City but also by the ideological similarities between the administrations in London and Washington. US President Reagan shared Thatcher's commitment to liberal individualism and the neo-liberal revolution and their two nations became partners in the struggle to construct a new world order based on the hegemony of free markets.[170] It was a relationship Thatcher found a good deal more congenial than Britain's membership of the European Community. This she increasingly came to regard as a bastion of corporatism and socialism on a journey to political union and therefore quite incompatible with her faith in the British national sovereignty.[171]

The second key development was the exploitation of Britain's North Sea oil resources. By the late 1970s it was clear that Britain was well on the way to becoming one of the world's leading oil producing countries. The extent of the reserves, actual and potential, on the UK North Sea Continental Shelf was so vast that, as Harold Wilson once said, any government in power once they were being produced and sold on the world market would have the chance to stay in power for a generation. In the late 1970s this prospect led to the emergence of different strategic options concerning the future of the national economy. On the Left Tony Benn, Energy Secretary from 1975–79, argued that the revenues earned in the sale of oil could be used to facilitate a State-led modernization programme designed to refurbish British social democracy and free it from the external shocks which had created difficulties for recent Labour governments. One portion could be used to support the current account so that it did not lurch into deficit while Britain's industrial structure was being re-equipped. Another could be re-cycled through the taxation system into a national investment fund to finance infrastructural renewal, new technology and support for firms producing goods in the faster growing knowledge-based, advanced industrial sectors such as pharmaceuticals, computing, electronics and aerospace.[172] A different, but related vision was proposed by the corporatists of the CBI, in a 1977 manifesto, *Britain Means Business*, arguing the case for the use of tax income deriving from the export of oil in the improvement of industrial training and skills as well as in the nation's transport and communications network.[173]

This vision was paralleled by a neo-liberal strategy. On the Right both the Bennite and the CBI approaches were regarded with hostility. Here, the prospect of a British oil surplus was welcomed because it provided a historic opportunity for changing the balance of political and economic power in the UK. The argument was set out by Lawson: the market was far superior to the State at the allocation of investment for the benefit of the whole economy. What was required was a non-interventionist and deflationary macroeconomic programme involving deregulation (notably the scrapping of exchange controls), tax cuts, public spending reductions and a willingness to allow sterling to rise on the foreign exchange markets as the proceeds from oil exports drove the current account into substantial annual surpluses. This would bring substantial returns to the City and create a reservoir of assets overseas whose yield would help to sustain a healthy external balance not only while the economy was being restructured but when Britain's oil resources started to shrink (or the price of oil fell).[174]

Taking this path involved a repudiation of the post-war settlement and the corporatist, social-democratic British State. These would be undermined by what Woolfson, Foster and Beck described as 'one massive "market clearing" operation in which the income from North Sea oil provided a safety net' while governments applied shock therapy to the economy. Industrial contraction and mass unemployment would be likely, accompanied by a massive outflow of capital. The short-term pain involved would be outweighed by the benefits likely to follow for capital in Britain: large-scale joblessness would reduce wage levels and weaken the bargaining power of the trade unions. Oil could be used to replace coal in power stations, thereby strengthening the hand of a Conservative administration in the event of a showdown with the miners. Profits would start to rise and a political environment congenial to legislation designed to swing the balance of power away from labour towards employers and managers would be created. Britain would be safe for 'a truly entrepreneurial capitalism'.[175]

It was, of course, the Right's strategy which was chosen. In 1977–78 Labour considered using oil wealth to promote national development but the combination of an approaching General Election with concern to lower taxes and thereby reduce rising trade union frustration with frozen living standards led the Callaghan government to put the proposal into cold storage. Once the Conservatives had won the 1979 General Election it was inevitable that the neo-liberal path would be taken, given the inclinations of Thatcher and her close economic advisers. There was no Cabinet discussion dedicated to the question of how the North Sea oil wealth could be used. From the start the Treasury took the line advocated by Howe and Lawson. UK oil production climbed as industrial output collapsed and unemployment mounted. In 1982 revenue from the UK Continental Shelf amounted to £20 billion, approximately 7 per cent of the GDP.[176] In each year from 1980 to 1982 Britain ran a larger current account surplus than any other member of the OECD,[177] facilitating its dramatic accumulation of overseas assets. By the mid-1980s Britain was one of the largest oil producing nations in the world, responsible for between 2.5 and 2.6 million barrels a day and 20 per cent of all OPEC output.[178] Just as the neo-liberals had wanted, the tax revenue was used to cut public borrowing (while also contributing to unemployment benefit). Even with the assistance provided by the proceeds of North Sea oil Britain was shaken by the inner city riots of 1981 and the bitter conflict of the miners' strike in 1984–85: had there been no such bounty it is hard to see how the Thatcherite project could have been politically sustainable.

The course of electoral politics was a necessary condition of using North Sea oil to underpin the transformation of Britain into a free market economy but it was not the only one. Britain may have become a major oil producer in the 1980s but there had been a British oil industry since the early twentieth century. Its two leading representatives had been Anglo-Iranian, known as the British Petroleum Company (BP) from 1954, and Royal Dutch Shell. These corporations, exploiting the oil resources to be found within the Empire as well as within the nations which had fallen under British influence such as Iran, Iraq and the states of the Persian Gulf, had long been contributing to the country's overseas earnings and therefore to the international role played by the pound sterling as a trading and reserve currency. They were, in short, rooted at the heart of the British establishment, where the interest of finance and capital merged with those of imperial security. The boards of both companies had for decades interlocked with those of the leading merchant banks: examples were F. C. Tiarks (1874–1952), a director not only of Anglo-Iranian but of the Bank of England and of the merchant bank J. Henry Schroder, and Walter Samuel (Lord Bearsted: 1882–1948), Chairman of the Nineteen Twenty-Eight Investment Trust, the merchant bank Samuel's and of the Shell Transport and Trading Company.[179] The historic location of the oil industry within the financial-imperial fraction of British capital identified by J. A. Hobson as being at the heart of 'Consumer's England' back in 1910 made it a natural ally of a government like Thatcher's, intent on promoting both a domestic and overseas free market revolution and the global projection of British power. There were no calls from senior levels within the oil industry for its profits to be deployed in the modernization of British industry.

In these circumstances it was no surprise that the only portion of manufacturing industry given sustained assistance by the State after 1979 was the military-industrial sector, with a generous use of subsidies and credits to support corporations such as British Aerospace to manufacture and export complex weapons systems and aircraft, especially to the Middle and Near Eastern countries in which British interests had traditionally been strong.[180] During the Thatcher era Britain became the world's second largest arms' exporter, rising from the position of fourth or fifth when the Conservatives came to power. The most lucrative deal was the Al-Yamamah (meaning 'the dove' in English) agreement between Britain and Saudi Arabia, the principal contractor being British Aerospace (now BAE systems). The company has been responsible since the mid-1980s for supplying multirole strike aircraft (Tornados),[181] military trainers (Hawks) and missiles to Saudi Arabia; the arrangement continues up to the time of writing and the hardware is paid for in deliveries of crude oil (up to 600,000 barrels a day) to the UK government.[182]

There is no doubt that the Thatcher governments successfully asserted the interests of Consumer's over those of Producer's Britain. This is apparent both in the profile of the economy, marked by the rapid expansion of finance and services, and in the appearance of increasingly uneven development across the United Kingdom. Regional disparities between the green and affluent south and much of industrial Britain were exaggerated by industrial contraction and the advent of mass unemployment across large parts of Wales, Scotland, northern England and the West Midlands. By the start of the 1990s 41 per cent of all individual shareholders lived in the south-east of the country.[183] The fifteen most prosperous towns in Britain were all to be found in the Home Counties, with a spur out to East Anglia, while the fifteen least prosperous were all old industrial centres apart from Pembroke and Cardigan in the rural south-west and west of Wales.[184] True to its free market philosophy the government dismantled the regional policy framework established to reduce this gulf.[185] This was replaced by 'Enterprise Zones'. These were established with much fanfare to promote new business, sometimes in areas hardest hit by the recession at the start of the 1980s, such as the Black Country and South Yorkshire. They were designed on the neo-liberal assumption that private investment would be attracted to areas characterized by low business rates and taxes and few regulations; government and local authorities provided funds to improve the local infrastructure, especially with road improvement, land reclamation, the clearance of derelict sites and the construction of business parks and retailing facilities. The bill for this amounted to £300 million between 1981 and 1986. It was a modest expense and the results were underwhelming. Only 13,000 net jobs were created and the most spectacular developments, Merry Hill near Dudley and London Docklands, were in the service and financial sectors: little industrial regeneration resulted from the scheme and its impact on the widening regional imbalances of the time was minimal.[186]

In the words of David Thomson, until the 1980s successive governments had sought to honour the commitment made by British people at the end of World War Two to 'ensuring greater social justice, less extreme economic inequality and a continued economic growth compatible with these social purposes'.[187] The Thatcher governments did seek economic growth, but now the purposes had changed. Poverty increased after 1979. In that year 13.4 per cent of the population lived below median incomes (before housing costs); by 1992 the figure had risen to 22.2 per cent. Over the same period the Gini coefficient measuring inequality rose from 0.253 to 0.339 (the scale running from 0, denoting complete equality, to 1, a score indicating the most extreme inequality).[188] The divide in income and wealth was replicated in politics: as the 1980s progressed the Conservatives continued to win large majorities of Parliamentary seats in England but lost ground in Wales and Scotland. In 1987 the swing to Labour was just 1.2 per cent across the UK as a whole but it exceeded 7 per cent in Scotland and Wales, both of which clung to the politics of social democracy and sent large numbers of Labour MPs to Westminster.

The Britain which emerged from the Thatcher revolution was a nation whose political centre of gravity had swung to the Right: it was more tolerant of inequality than any of its predecessors since 1945 (arguably since 1906), committed to the political economy of the free market, militantly supportive of the USA in the Cold War, not unafraid to project its power on the world stage, sometimes formally (as with the Falklands War of 1982 and the Gulf War of 1991) and sometimes informally (as it did in the Middle East). It was able to generate support for this dramatic new turn in British history by encouraging individual enterprise and championing policies which delivered rising living standards for those in work as well as by its positive encouragement of property ownership. The liberal ideal of 'equality of opportunity', now replaced the social-democratic aspiration to greater social and economic equality of outcome. This was a remarkable transformation and a notable political triumph for Thatcher along with the coterie of economic liberals, Right of centre Conservatives and supporters within the UK's 'Deep State', which had supported her from the start of her bid for the Tory leadership back in 1975. Yet as the 1980s drew to a close it appeared that this new political and economic settlement was under threat from the Prime Minister herself.

Downfall

In 1989–90 the Conservative government and the nation itself were rocked by instability, resulting from two political crises. Both stemmed from Thatcher's increasing tendency to trust her own judgement more than that of her colleagues. First there was a growing rift between Thatcher and Chancellor Lawson and Foreign Secretary Geoffrey Howe concerning policy towards Europe. This had already come close to destabilizing the government in 1986, when Michael Heseltine had resigned as Defence Secretary. He had quarrelled with the Prime Minister and the Trade and Industry Secretary Leon Brittan over the rescue of Westland, an ailing West Country firm which was the UK's last manufacturer of helicopters. Heseltine favoured a rescue led by a consortium of British Aerospace and French and Italian firms. This would be given a commitment by the relevant national governments, and by West Germany, that they would only purchase helicopters made in Europe. Thatcher and Brittan regarded this as protectionist and statist, and supported a bid by the US corporation Sikorski, arguing (correctly) that this was what the Westland Board wanted. Thatcher's position squared with her pro-Americanism and enthusiasm for the free market. It also revealed her growing distrust of 'Europe'. The Sikorski bid was accepted, but not before the conflict had shaken the government, provoking the resignations of Heseltine and Brittan and briefly threatening Thatcher herself.

Some of the same tensions now resurfaced, thanks on this occasion to Lawson's handling of sterling. From late 1987 Lawson had been following a managed exchange rate policy, intervening in the markets when necessary to keep sterling close to the level of DM3, a rate he believed compatible with expanding exports and the reduction of domestic inflation. Aware that the Prime Minister was a believer in freely floating rates he had not openly admitted to this strategy of 'shadowing the deutschmark'. When Thatcher discovered what he had been doing there was a row between them, but he was able to stick to his approach. Thatcher refused to leave the subject alone, however, antagonizing Lawson and Geoffrey Howe, who believed that sterling should enter the European Exchange Rate Mechanism (ERM), established in the late 1970s. Under the ERM member currencies were pegged against each other but adjustable when it became evident that there was serious deviation between official and market rates. It was part of the European Monetary System (EMS), designed to end exchange rate instability in the European Community and prepare the ground for movement to a single currency and European Monetary Union. The ERM was therefore seen by many advocates of European integration as a crucial stage on the road to full-blown political and economic union. This did not apply to Lawson, who favoured membership of the ERM on pragmatic rather than idealist grounds because he believed it would help to lock in the gains to competitiveness and counter-inflationary policy which in his view would follow from shadowing the deutschmark. For Howe and the Foreign Office, on the other hand, joining the ERM was seen as a way of maximizing British influence in the European Community.

By now, however, Thatcher was becoming increasingly hostile to the European project, seeing in it a threat to national sovereignty and to the free market. Speaking at Bruges in September 1988 she made clear her determination to prevent ongoing membership of this proto-European superstate from reversing her reforms, proclaiming that 'We have not successfully rolled back the frontiers of the state in Britain, only to see them re-imposed at a European level'.[189] The speech was given a warm reception by many in the Conservative Party, inside and outside Parliament; it appealed particularly to the nationalist tendency originally mobilized by Enoch Powell, who backed the Prime Minister's line. Seeking to bolster her own position Thatcher moved Howe from the Foreign Office to become Lord President of the Council and Leader of the House of Commons in July 1989, replacing him with John Major. She hoped that Major would be more sympathetic to her opinion about the ERM and the whole question of European Union. In fact, the new Foreign Secretary shared Lawson's favourable attitude to sterling's participation in the ERM. Faced with this strong Foreign Office and Treasury axis the Prime Minister now undermined her own Chancellor, refusing to condemn comments critical of his policy on sterling by her personal economics adviser, Sir Alan Walters.[190] Lawson resigned and was replaced by Major, who persuaded an exceedingly reluctant Prime Minister to back sterling's move into the ERM in October 1990, at £1 = DM 2.95 (with a lower limit of DM 2.78: if the pound fell beneath this it would be necessary for the Bank of England to intervene).[191] The defeat on this issue did not prevent Thatcher making a powerful assault on what she saw as the ambitions of the European Commission and its President, Jacques Delors, to create a federal state with a single currency and a single government. Howe then resigned from the Cabinet, publicly attacking the Prime Minister's good faith in the process. His speech triggered a leadership contest. Heseltine ran against Thatcher but although he gained enough votes to weaken her fatally he was unable to win himself: the eventual victor was John Major, a compromise candidate who, it was hoped, would return unity to the government.

This was an essential task, since the Conservatives were now facing electoral defeat. The 1989 European elections had gone badly for them and well for Labour: it seemed that Labour was poised to win the next General Election and that its leader, Neil Kinnock, would be Prime Minister by the spring of 1992 at the latest. By 1990 the opinion polls were giving Labour a commanding lead: a Harris poll in March put them 28 per cent ahead of the Tories (57 per cent to 29 per cent); a Gallup poll at the start of June had them in front by 23.5 per cent (53 per cent to 29.5 per cent).[192] Although the Lawson boom was now finished, this collapse in the government's standing was not mainly the result of the nation's economic problems. It was more a function of the disarray over Europe and of public hostility to the poll tax, which Thatcher had persuaded the Cabinet to endorse, powerful objections from Chancellor Lawson notwithstanding. This was first introduced in Scotland, in 1989–90, and then in England and Wales in 1990–91. The tax, which was a fixed charge payable by every resident, was extensively criticised on the grounds of its injustice. It favoured small, affluent families while creating serious problems for those on low incomes. It was meant to bring simplicity and accountability to the collection of funds by local government; it achieved the reverse. In many cases authorities struggled to collect the money, especially from those living in rented property. In order to keep the tax bills at a level which allowed people to pay them without endangering the ability of local authorities to provide the range of services communities required it became necessary to increase central government support. In the end this amounted to 80 per cent of local government finance. The new regime became increasingly expensive: quite apart from costing £1.5 billion to establish, it led to the transfer of £20 billion in costs to the national taxpayer by the time of its replacement by Council Tax, a levy similar to the old rating system, in 1993–94.[193]

The tax was widely disliked. It inflicted serious (possibly long-term) damage on the Conservatives in Scotland, where their position was already weak. Many people all over Britain refused to pay. This was another problem for the local authorities, who were obliged to chase the defaulters. Mass protest movements developed, co-ordinated by the All-Britain Anti-Poll Tax Federation. There was a series of riots, the most dramatic coming after a mass demonstration of at least 200,000 in central London on 31 March 1990. The government stepped up its surveillance of the protestors, on occasion resorting to tactics reminiscent of its approach to the miners' strike.[194] This time it was unable to defeat the forces ranged against it: the unpopularity of the poll tax ran too wide and deep. Many members of Parliament from all parties found their mail overwhelmed by letters from constituents denouncing the charge; resolutions urging its abolition were regularly tabled even at successive Conservative conferences.[195] There was no doubt that the Conservatives would lose the coming General Election unless they scrapped the poll tax. The problem was, however, that Margaret Thatcher was committed to it: it had achieved her old ambition, expressed as long ago as October 1974, of ending the system of rates. Only when Thatcher was no longer Prime Minister would it become possible for the Conservatives to extricate themselves from this position.

The rows over Europe destabilized the government; the unpopularity of the poll tax deprived it of popular legitimacy. By the summer of 1990 it had become clear to a growing number of Conservative activists, MPs and Ministers that the replacement of Thatcher by a more consensual figure was essential if the Party was to have any chance of remaining in power beyond 1992 and if the Thatcherite reinvention of Britain was to be made safe. Labour was now more united than at any time in the previous generation. Finally, it posed a formidable threat. It had abandoned support for the controversial causes such as unilateralism, State-led planning and the extension of public ownership which had characterized it in the first half of the 1980s. After taking over the leadership following the defeat in 1983 Neil Kinnock had led the Party on a long march to the Right. Yet even though it now embraced a version of social democracy that both Hugh Gaitskell and Harold Wilson might have considered mild, it was still not trusted in the City or in the board rooms of industry. Kinnock's history as an admirer of Aneurin Bevan and one-time supporter of the Campaign for Nuclear Disarmament (CND), enabled his enemies in the press as well as in Parliament to depict him as an old-fashioned 'tax and spend' socialist who would turn back the clock to before 1979. There was a good deal of caricature in this image: yet there was genuine fear on the Right that a Labour government would embark on a comprehensive deconstruction of the Thatcherite settlement. John Major's task was therefore to preserve the settlement by restoring popular legitimacy to the government and give Thatcherism a human face, the sacrifice of the eponym herself notwithstanding.

Notes

1. En route every Tuesday, just for the day, to give a course of history lectures at Crewe and Alsager College of Higher Education (now part of the University of Staffordshire).
2. David Smith, *North and South: Britain's Economic, Social and Political Divide* (London: Penguin Books, 1988), Table 6.5, p. 145.
3. See Charles Moore, *Margaret Thatcher: The Authorised Biography: Volume One* (London: Penguin, 2014), pp. 517–518; Margaret Thatcher: *The Downing Street Years* (London: Harper Collins 1993), pp. 115–120; David Bowen, Terry McCarthy and John Eisenhammer, 'How Honda Let BL Go to Strangers', *The Independent*, 6 February 1994, http://www.independent.co.uk/news/business/how-honda-let-rover-go-to-strangers-belief-in-its-partners-independence-was-only-one-reason-that-the-1392300.html (accessed 24 February 2016).
4. Ellen Wilkinson, *The Town That Was Murdered* (London: Victor Gollancz, 1939). Of the insured workforce in Jarrow 67.8 per cent were on the dole by 1934.
5. See Tony Kearney, *Painted Red: A Social History of Consett, 1840–1990* (Consett, Durham: DCA, 1990); 'Quaker Family's Corby Legacy', *Northamptonshire Telegraph*, 21 April 2013.
6. The unemployment statistics are taken from Smith, *North and South*, Table 6.5, p. 145.
7. Andy Wightman, 'From the Hillman Imp to Tescotown', 3 May 2013, http://bellacaledonia.org.uk/2013/05/03/from-the-hillman-imp-to-tescotown/ (accessed 2 February 2016).
8. See http://hansard.millbanksystems.com/written_answers/1981/nov/26/unemployment-statistics (accessed 2 February 2016).
9. Newton and Porter, *Modernization Frustrated*, pp. 194–195.
10. Ibid.
11. Ian Gilmour, *Dancing with Dogma: Britain under Thatcherism* (London: Simon and Schuster, 1992), p. 35.
12. Ibid., pp. 35–40.
13. See Smith, *North and South*, Table 6.5, p. 145.
14. See James Denman and Paul McDonald, 'Unemployment Statistics from 1881 to the Present Day',*Labour Market Trends*, January 1996. The annual average for 1986 was 3.2 million. It was pointed out that had the government not changed the way the unemployment statistics were collected in 1982 (from counting the numbers of registered unemployed to counting those claiming benefit) the number would have been 3.6 million (13 per cent of the workforce): see Middlemas, *Power, Competition and the State*, vol. III, p. 336.
15. Middlemas, *Power, Competition and the State*, vol. III, p. 336; see also fn. 40, p. 556.
16. Ibid.
17. Newton and Porter, *Modernization Frustrated*, p. 197.
18. Ken Coutts and Wynne Godley, 'Does Britain's Balance of Payments Matter any More?', in Jonathan Michie (ed.), *The Economic Legacy 1979–1992* (London: Academic Press, 1992), p. 63.
19. Newton and Porter, *Modernization Frustrated*, p. 197.
20. David Parker and Hsueh Liang Wu, 'Privatisation and Performance: A Study of the British Steel Industry under Public and Private Ownership', *Economic Issues*, Vol. 3, Part 2, (September 1998), pp. 31–51.
21. Gilmour, *Dancing with Dogma*, p. 35.

22 Ibid.
23 William Keegan, *Mrs Thatcher's Economic Experiment* (Harmondsworth: Penguin, 1984), p. 203.
24 William Keegan, *Britain without Oil: What Lies Ahead?* (Harmondsworth: Penguin, 1985), pp. 70–71.
25 Following the Brixton riots, Lord Scarman, a senior member of the judiciary, was appointed by Home Secretary William Whitelaw to chair an inquiry into their causes. His report, published in November, emphasised the part played by provocative policing and by racial discrimination and disadvantage. See Lord Scarman, *The Brixton Disorders, 10–12 April 1981* (London: HMSO, 1981).
26 Richard Vinen, *Thatcher's Britain: The Politics and Social Upheavals of the 1980s* (London: Pocket Books, 2009), p. 130.
27 John Hoskyns, *Just in Time: Inside the Thatcher Revolution* (London: Aurum Press, 2000), p. 318.
28 Hoskyns, *Just in Time*, p. 357.
29 Ciaran Driver and Paul Temple, *The Unbalanced Economy: A Policy Appraisal* (Basingstoke: Palgrave, 2012), p. 16; Nigel Lawson, *The View from No. 11: Memoirs of a Tory Radical* (London: Corgi, 1993), pp. 29–30.
30 All quotations in this and the preceding paragraph are from the *Conservative General Election Manifesto 1979*, launched on 11 April 1979.
31 See Adam Curtis, 'The Living Dead: The Attic', first broadcast on BBC2, 13 June 1995.
32 Moore, *Margaret Thatcher*, p. 295.
33 Thatcher, *The Downing Street Years*, p. 10.
34 Ibid., pp. 8–9.
35 Middlemas, *Power, Competition and the State*, vol. III, pp. 305f.
36 Camilla Schofield, 'A Nation or No Nation?, Enoch Powell and Thatcherism', in Ben Jackson and Robert Saunders (eds), *Making Thatcher's Britain* (Cambridge: Cambridge University Press, 2012), p. 98.
37 See Margaret Thatcher Foundation, 1978 Margaret Thatcher, TV Interview for Granada *World in Action*, Friday 27 January 1978, http://www.margaretthatcher.org/document/103485 (accessed 8 February 2016).
38 Schofield, 'A Nation or No Nation?', p. 100.
39 Jon Lawrence and Florence Sutcliffe Braithwaite, 'Margaret Thatcher and the Decline of Class Politics', in Jackson and Saunders, *Making Thatcher's Britain*, p. 133. See also the comments of John Vincent, that 'to vote Liberal was closely tied to the growing ability of whole new classes to stand on their own feet and lead independent lives'; and that the working class (in the 1860s) 'was genuinely liberal', *The Formation of the Liberal Party 1857–1868* (London: Collins, 1966), pp. xiv and 77.
40 Andrew Gamble, *The Free Economy and the Strong State* (Basingstoke, Palgrave 1994), p. 250.
41 John Ross, *Thatcher and Friends: The Anatomy of the Tory Party* (London: Pluto Press, 1983), p. 78.
42 Newton and Porter, *Modernization Frustrated*, p. 191; Lawrence and Sutcliffe Braithwaite, 'Margaret Thatcher and the Decline of Class Politics', in Jackson and Saunders, *Making Thatcher's Britain*, pp. 143–144.
43 Nigel Lawson, *The View from No. 11*, pp. 20–21.
44 Lawson was Financial Secretary of the Treasury from 1979–81, Energy Secretary from 1981–83 and Chancellor of the Exchequer, 1983–89.
45 See Lawson, *The View from No. 11*, p. 64.
46 See Gamble, *The Free Economy and the Strong State*; Stuart Hall, 'The Great Moving Right Show', *Marxism Today*, January 1979, pp. 14–21.
47 Lawson, *The View from No. 11*, pp. 46–57.
48 Ibid., p. 33.

49 'The 1981 Budget – Background & Documents', aide-memoire of economic policy from May 1979 to March 1981, Margaret Thatcher Foundation, http://www.margaretthatcher.org/archive/1981_budget.asp (accessed on 9 February 2016).
50 Newton and Porter, *Modernization Frustrated*, pp. 188, 193; Gamble, *The Free Economy and the Strong State*, p. 99.
51 Wynne Godley, 'Economic Policy and Performance under Mrs Thatcher' (2007), 446/12, papers of Sir Bryan Hopkin, Arts and Social Studies Library, Cardiff University, p. 5.
52 Lawson, *The View from No. 11*, pp. 68–69.
53 Moore, *Margaret Thatcher*, p. 524.
54 Robin Ramsay, 'Mrs Thatcher, North Sea Oil and the Hegemony of the City', *Lobster*, 27 (1994), p. 4; Hoskyns, *Just in Time*, pp. 163–164; 226–227.
55 See Ramsay, 'Mrs Thatcher, North Sea Oil and the Hegemony of the City', p. 3.
56 'External Flows and Broad Money', *Bank of England Quarterly Bulletin*, December 1983, p. 525.
57 'The Development of the Building Societies Sector in the 1980s', *Bank of England Quarterly Bulletin*, November 1990, p. 503.
58 Lawson, *The View from No. 11*, p. 72.
59 Gilmour, *Dancing with Dogma*, p. 26.
60 'The 1981 Budget – Background & Documents', aide-memoire of economic policy from May 1979 to March 1981, Margaret Thatcher Foundation.
61 The price of crude oil rose from $14 per barrel at the start of 1979 to $35 two years later, before stabilizing.
62 It should be pointed out that the Swiss economist Jürg Niehans argued that the monetary base had in fact been kept too tight and should be expanded, since its growth had fallen well behind that of national output since 1979. His argument reinforced the belief held by the influential financial commentator C. Gordon Pepper and by two of the Prime Minister's advisers, Alan Walters and John Hoskyns, that attempts to manage sterling M3 should be replaced by monetary base control. The argument was not accepted by the Treasury and the Bank, nor was it widely shared in the City. See Hoskyns, *Just in Time*, pp. 255–257; Ramsay, 'Mrs Thatcher, North Sea Oil and the Hegemony of the City', pp. 4–5.
63 Derek H. Aldcroft and Steven Morewood, *The European Economy since 1914* (Routledge: London, 2013) p. 277.
64 Keegan, *Britain without Oil*, p. 38. The real exchange rate amplifies the nominal one quoted in the markets every day by the rise in the price of British exports relative to the price of goods and services in foreign countries.
65 Philip Stevens, *Politics and the Pound: the Conservatives' Struggle with Sterling* (Basingstoke: Macmillan, 1996), pp. 30–31.
66 Newton and Porter, *Modernization Frustrated*, p. 193.
67 Pollard, *The Wasting of the British Economy*, p. 176.
68 Newton and Porter, *Modernization Frustrated*, p. 194.
69 Ibid., pp. 198–199.
70 Michael White, 'Supermac was Right in 1980 and He's Right Today', *The Guardian*, 30 December 1980, http://www.theguardian.com/uk/blog/2010/dec/30/supermac-was-right-1980-and-right-now (accessed 12 February 2016).
71 Hugo Young, *The Hugo Young Papers* (London: Penguin, 2009), pp. 152–157, interviews with Jim Prior on 15 July 1980, with Ian Gilmour on 5 November 1980 and with Francis Pym on 8 November 1980.
72 The arguments are covered in Moore, *Margaret Thatcher*, chs 18 and 19; see pp. 532–533 for the conference speech episode.
73 Figures from Middleton, *The British Economy since 1945*, Table II.1, pp. 146–147.
74 See TNA CAB 128/72, 'Public Expenditure Survey', 23 July 1981.
75 Hoskyns, *Just in Time*, p. 321.

76 Gill Dix, John Forth and Keith Sisson, *Conflict at Work: The Pattern of Disputes in Britain since 1980*, figure 1, p. 5, ACAS Research Paper 03/08, p. 5.
77 'Self-employed Workers in the UK 2014', Office of National Statistics, 20 August 2014, p. 2; http://webarchive.nationalarchives.gov.uk/20160105160709/http://www.ons.gov.uk/ons/rel/lmac/self-employed-workers-in-the-uk/2014/rep-self-employed-workers-in-the-uk-2014.html (accessed 3 March 2016).
78 Thatcher, *The Downing Street Years*, p. 339.
79 Thatcher's view was not shared by MI5. See Christopher Andrew, *The Defence of the Realm: The Authorized History of MI5* (London: Allen Lane, 2009), pp. 676–680.
80 See Keith Boyfield, *Put Pits into Profit*, Centre for Policy Studies, Policy Study no. 73 (London, 1985), table 2. p. 21. Boyfield's figures are from the NCB.
81 Seumas Milne, *The Enemy Within* (London: Verso, 2004 edition), p. 9.
82 Seumas Milne, 'Now We See What Was Really at Stake in the Miners' Strike', *The Guardian*, 12 March 2014.
83 Milne, *The Enemy Within*, p. 17.
84 Donald Macintyre, 'How the Miners' Strike of 1984–85 Changed Britain For Ever', *New Statesman*, 16 June 2014.
85 Milne, *The Enemy Within*, p. 17.
86 See Tony Benn, *The End of an Era: Diaries 1980–90* (London: Arrow, 1992), pp. 340–341; and p. 387, entry for 1 December 1984.
87 Milne, *The Enemy Within*, p. 19.
88 Ibid., p. 18.
89 Ibid., p. 24.
90 Benn, *The End of an Era*, p. 346, entry for 4 May 1984; and entry for 4 November 1986, pp. 479–480. The second entry recorded a conversation with a former soldier, who told Benn that, 'At Nottingham, of the sixty-four policemen in our group, sixty-one were soldiers....We didn't wear any numbers.' The soldiers were 'from the Military Police, the SAS and the Green Jackets'.
91 Milne, *The Enemy Within*, pp. 317–318.
92 Roy Greenslade, 'Sorry, Arthur', *The Guardian*, 27 May 2002.
93 Milne, *The Enemy Within*, pp. 364–365.
94 Ibid., pp. 365–366.
95 'Pit closures, year by year', BBC News, 5 March 2004, http://news.bbc.co.uk/1/hi/uk/3500979.stm (accessed 17 February 2016).
96 The UK economy continued to use coal: in 2012 consumption totalled 64 million tonnes, 55 million of which were used for electricity generation. But the vast bulk of this was imported, with Russia, Columbia and the USA the leading exporters to the British market.
97 Thatcher, *The Downing Street Years*, pp. 377–378.
98 Driver and Temple, *The Unbalanced Economy*, pp. 42–43.
99 Harvey, *A Brief History of Neo-liberalism*, pp. 75–76; Chris Gifford, *The Making of Eurosceptic Britain* (Aldershot: Ashgate, 2008), pp. 86–87.
100 Office of National Statistics, 'Compensation of Employees as % of Gross Domestic Product 1955–2015: CP SA', released 31 March 2017, https://www.ons.gov.uk/economy/grossdomesticproductgdp/timeseries/ihxp (accessed 3 April 2017); Driver and Temple, *The Unbalanced Economy*, figure 1.8, p. 16.
101 Harvey, *A Brief History of Neo-liberalism*, p. 59; Newton and Porter, *Modernization Frustrated*, p. 202.
102 Harvey, *A Brief History of Neo-liberalism*, p. 60.
103 Lawrence and Sutcliffe-Braithwaite, 'Margaret Thatcher and the Decline of Class Politics', in Ben Jackson and Robert Saunders (eds), *Making Thatcher's Britain* (Cambridge: Cambridge University Press, 2012), p. 146.
104 Gilmour, *Dancing with Dogma*, pp. 147–148.
105 *Faith in the City: A Call for Action by Church and Nation* (London: Church House Publishing, 1985).

106 John Campbell, *Margaret Thatcher, Volume Two: The Iron Lady* (London: Jonathan Cape, 2003), p. 390; See also David Sheppard, *Steps along Hope Street: My Life in Cricket, the Church and the Inner City* (London: Hodder and Stoughton, 2002), ch. 17.
107 Middlemas, *Power, Competition and the State*, vol. III, chs. 9 and 10; see Antonio Gramsci, *Selections from Prison Notebooks*, edited by Quintin Hoare and Geoffrey Nowell-Smith (London: Lawrence and Wishart, 1971), pp. 238–239.
108 The comments were published in an interview given by Thatcher to *Women's Own*, 31 October 1987. The full, unedited text can be found in 'Interview for *Woman's Own* ("no such thing as society")', http://www.margaretthatcher.org/document/106689 (accessed 18 February 2016).
109 Lawson, *The View from No. 11*, p. 1086; Gilmour, *Dancing with Dogma*, p. 75.
110 Denman and McDonald, 'Unemployment Statistics from 1881 to the Present Day'.
111 Gilmour, *Dancing with Dogma*, pp. 75–76; pp. 81ff.
112 Simon Rogers, 'How Britain Changed under Margaret Thatcher. In Fifteen Charts. *The Guardian*, 8 April 2013, http://www.theguardian.com/politics/datablog/2013/apr/08/britain-changed-margaret-thatcher-charts (accessed 24 February 2016).
113 See 'UK Polling Report 1979–83' by Anthony Wells of YouGov, http://ukpollingreport.co.uk/voting-intention-1979-1983 (accessed 24 February 2016): support for the Conservatives passed the 40 per cent mark at the end of April 1982 and remained there for most of the next year, even exceeding 50 per cent on occasion.
114 William Keegan, 'The Miracle Worker', *The Tablet*, 4 June 1988.
115 Godley, 'Economic Policy and Performance under Mrs Thatcher', p. 6.
116 Middlemas, *Power, Competition and the State*, vol. III, p. 274.
117 Lawson, *The View from No. 11*, p. 282.
118 Stevens, *Politics and the Pound*, pp. 50–51.
119 Godley, 'Economic Policy and Performance under Mrs Thatcher', p. 6.
120 Lawson, *The View from No. 11*, p. 422.
121 Stevens, *Politics and the Pound*, pp. 54f.
122 Gilmour, *Dancing with Dogma*, p. 75.
123 Lawson, *The View from No. 11*, pp. 301 and 649.
124 Stevens, *Politics and the Pound*, p. 90.
125 Vinen, *Thatcher's Britain*, p. 205.
126 Gilmour, *Dancing with Dogma*, p. 76.
127 Coakley and Harris, 'Financial Globalisation and Deregulation', p. 52.
128 Vinen, *Thatcher's Britain*, p. 206.
129 Gilmour, *Dancing with Dogma*, pp. 76 and 81; Godley, 'Economic Policy and Performance under Mrs Thatcher', p. 6.
130 See Gilmour, *Dancing with Dogma*, p. 76.
131 Ibid., p. 81.
132 Coakley and Harris, 'Financial Globalisation and Deregulation', p. 52.
133 Lawson, *The View from No. 11*, pp. 660–661.
134 Vinen, *Thatcher's Britain*, p. 199.
135 Lawson, *The View from No. 11*, pp. 660–661.
136 Gilmour, *Dancing with Dogma*, p. 81; Lawson, *The View from No. 11*, p. 1083.
137 DeAnne Julius, 'Inflation and Growth in a Service Economy', *Bank of England Quarterly Bulletin*, November 1998, p. 339, Chart 2.
138 Richard Thomson, 'Fast Food's Chain Reaction', *Independent*, 30 April 1994.
139 Dilwyn Porter, 'British Sport Transformed: Sport, Business and the Media since 1960', in Richard Coopey and Peter Lyth, *Business in Britain in the Twentieth Century* (Oxford: Oxford University Press, 2009), p. 332.
140 Srdan Tatomir, 'Self-Employment: What can we Learn from Recent Developments?', *Bank of England Quarterly Bulletin*, March 2015, Chart 3, p. 59.
141 Gilmour, *Dancing with Dogma*, p. 81; Coutts and Godley, 'Does Britain's Balance of Payments Matter Any More?', p. 64.

142 Driver and Temple, *The Unbalanced Economy*, p. 17.
143 Andrew Glyn, '"The Productivity Miracle", Profits and Investment', in Michie (ed.), *The Economic Legacy*, pp. 84–85.
144 Coutts and Godley, 'Does Britain's Balance of Payments Matter Any More?', pp. 64–65.
145 Gilmour, *Dancing with Dogma*, p. 77.
146 Coutts and Godley, 'Does Britain's Balance of Payments Matter Any More?', p. 65.
147 Nationwide Building Society, *UK House Prices since 1952*. See http://www.nationwide.co.uk/about/house-price-index/download-data#xtab:uk-series (accessed 3 April 2017).
148 See FTSE All-Share index and FTSE-100 index since 1985, % change and total return, http://swanlowpark.co.uk/ftseannual.jsp (accessed 29 February 2016).
149 Chris Hamnett, *Winners and Losers: Home Ownership in Modern Britain* (London: UCL Press, 2004), p. 37.
150 See Jeremy Franks, *Coping with the Credit Crunch? A Financial Appraisal of UK Farming*, University of Newcastle Centre for Rural Economy Discussion Paper Series no. 25, Figure 7, p. 19.
151 Denman and McDonald, 'Unemployment Statistics from 1881 to the Present Day', *Labour Market Trends*, January 1996.
152 Office of National Statistics, 'UK GDP since 1955'. See http://www.theguardian.com/politics/datablog/2013/apr/08/britain-changed-margaret-thatcher-charts (accessed 24 February 2016).
153 Gilmour, *Dancing with Dogma*, p. 88.
154 See for example Tim Congdon, 'Miracle versus Mirage: the Conservatives' Economic Record', *Economic Affairs*, vol. 16, no. 4 (1996), pp. 27–31.
155 Glyn, '"The Productivity Miracle", Profits and Investment', pp. 78–79.
156 Coakley and Harris, 'Financial Globalisation and Deregulation', p. 45.
157 Ibid., p. 47.
158 Newton and Porter, *Modernization Frustrated*, p. 201; Perry Anderson, 'The Figures of Descent', *New Left Review*, 161 (1987), p. 69.
159 'Takeover Activity in the 1980s', *Bank of England Quarterly Bulletin*, March 1989, Table B, p. 2.
160 Driver and Temple, *The Unbalanced Economy*, p. 110; Coakley and Harris, 'Financial Globalisation and Deregulation', p. 44.
161 See the discussion of the reforms in Vinen, *Thatcher's Britain*, pp. 183–184.
162 Coakley and Harris, 'Financial Globalisation and Deregulation', pp. 45–47.
163 Ibid., p. 51.
164 Ibid., p. 50.
165 Newton, *The Global Economy*, p. 135.
166 Driver and Temple, *The Unbalanced Economy*, p. 112.
167 Coakley and Harris, 'Financial Globalisation and Deregulation', p. 50.
168 Driver and Temple, *The Unbalanced Economy*, p. 128.
169 Geoffrey Ingham, 'Shock Therapy in the City', *New Left Review*, 14 (2nd series, 2002), p. 155.
170 Gifford, *The Making of Eurosceptic Britain*, p. 87; Harvey, *A Brief History of Neo-liberalism*, ch. 2.
171 Gifford, *The Making of Eurosceptic Britain*, p. 89.
172 See for example, Tony Benn, *Conflicts of Interest: Diaries 1977–80* (London: Arrow, 1991), p. 280, entry for 12 February 1978.
173 Charles Woolfson, John Foster and Matthew Beck, *Paying for the Piper: Capital and Labour in Britain's Offshore Oil Industry* (London: Mansell, 1997), p. 33.
174 Lawson, *The View from No. 11*, p. 186.
175 See the discussion in Charles Woolfson, John Foster and Matthew Beck, *Paying the Piper: Capital and Labour in Britain's Offshore Oil Industry* (London: Mansell, 1997), pp. 31–33.

176 Ibid. p. 35.
177 Keegan, *Britain without Oil*, p. 45.
178 Ibid., p. 42.
179 Woolfson, Foster and Beck, *Paying the Piper*, pp. 8–9. Tiarks was an ardent supporter of the appeasement of Nazi Germany both before and during World War Two. See Scott Newton, *The Profits of Peace: The Political Economy of Anglo-German Appeasement* (Oxford: Oxford University Press, 1996).
180 See for example TNA PREM 19/413, 'Defence Sales', covering correspondence between the Prime Minister's Private Office and the Ministry of Defence, concerning British defence sales to countries in the Persian Gulf and Thatcher's close interest in the matter. This became a controversial political issue in the 1990s following revelations that support from the taxpayer for the construction of the Pergau Dam in Malaysia had been tied to the purchase by that country of British-made weapons and that British companies had been supplying arms and arms-related equipment to Iraq during the Iran–Iraq war (1980–88), with discreet government approval. See Sir Richard Scott, *Report of the Inquiry into the Export of Defence Equipment and Dual-Use Goods to Iraq and Related Prosecutions* (London: HMSO, 1996). The whole subject is explored at length in Gerald James, *In the Public Interest* (London: Warner Books, 1996). It is also given compelling fictional treatment by John Le Carre in *The Night Manager* (London: Hodder and Stoughton, 1993).
181 The manufacturing of Tornados was shared with Aeritalia and the West German firm MBB; the resulting consortium was called Panavia Aircraft GmbH, based and registered in West Germany.
182 BBC News, 'Arms Sales Fuel BAE's Profits', 25 February 1999, http://news.bbc.co.uk/1/hi/business/the_company_file/285963.stm (accessed 9 March 2016). See also James, *In the Public Interest*, esp. pp. 104–108 and 117–119; David Pallister, 'The Arms Deal they Called the Dove: How Britain Grabbed the Biggest Prize', *The Guardian*, 15 December 2006.
183 Coakley and Harris, 'Financial Globalisation and Deregulation', p. 50.
184 Smith, *North and South*, table 5.3, p. 115.
185 See Ibid., ch. 4.
186 See Peter Hall and Mark-Tewdr-Jones, *Urban and Regional Planning*, 5th edition (London: Routledge, 2011), pp. 102ff.; pp. 138–143. Government enthusiasm for the Enterprise Zones waned after the 1987 General Election, when they tended to become superseded by the urban development corporations. These had first appeared in the early 1980s and were established with a mission to revive run-down inner cities: the majority of them, however, were created after Thatcher's resignation.
187 Thomson, *England in the Twentieth Century*, p. 288.
188 http://www.theguardian.com/politics/datablog/2013/apr/08/britain-changed-margaret-thatcher-charts (accessed 24 February 2016).
189 Thatcher, *The Downing Street Years*, pp. 742–746.
190 See Lawson, *The View from No. 11*, pp 747–748.; Thatcher, *The Downing Street Years*, pp. 713–718.
191 John Major, *The Autobiography* (London: Harper Collins, 2000), p. 161.
192 UK Polling Report for 1992, http://ukpollingreport.co.uk/historical-polls/voting-intention-1987-1992 (accessed 8 March 2016).
193 Major, *The Autobiography*, p. 170.
194 An acquaintance of this author who was involved in the anti-poll tax campaign found that some of his post was being opened and resealed with sellotape; on one occasion the police burst into his house looking for 'documents related to a serious crime'.
195 Major, *The Autobiography*, p. 170.

6

MAJOR INTERLUDE, 1990–97

'At the very heart of Europe'

John Major became Prime Minister at the end of November 1990, inheriting a legacy of recession, rising unemployment, double digit inflation and large-scale popular resentment about the poll tax. A General Election was due in eighteen months; there was every chance this would be a short-lived and uneasy administration. Major himself was well aware of his government's fragile position but had clear ideas about how to make it more secure. His main objective was to rehabilitate the 'One Nation' Conservatism which he felt had been increasingly marginalized during the Thatcher years.[1] Although he was still something of an unknown quantity to much of the electorate those familiar with his political progress pointed to his service as a Conservative councillor in Lambeth during the 1970s. For a time he had chaired the housing committee, acquiring a progressive reputation even among political opponents such as Labour's Ken Livingstone (who took over the position when the Council changed hands).[2]

A man from humble beginnings himself, Major had never been comfortable with the more robust expressions of individualism characteristic of some of Thatcher's supporters. He did however strongly back two aspects of Thatcher's political economy. One was the commitment to reduce inflation, which he viewed as a threat to the aspirations of the very people the Conservatives should be defending: responsible, hard-working members of the electorate, living in modest circumstances and dependent on fixed incomes, by wiping out their 'hard-earned savings'.[3] Secondly, he backed the free market revolution. Indeed the new Prime Minister favoured further reductions in the size of the nationalized sector and ensured that the return of the coal industry and the railways to private ownership featured in the Conservative Manifesto for the 1992 election.[4] Major's brand of Conservatism did, however, involve a changed approach to the poll tax and the welfare state. He was clear that the former would have to go as soon as possible. He was, furthermore, a strong supporter of the welfare state and of the idea that Conservatives should be prepared to support collective action, notably through spending on health, education and social benefits, to protect the living standards and improve the opportunities of the less affluent. Two early decisions were evidence of this commitment: the new government unfroze child benefit payments (frozen in 1989, to reduce welfare spending) and agreed on compensation for haemophiliacs infected with the HIV virus as a result of transfusions with contaminated blood.

The shift away from Thatcher became apparent quickly as Major's Cabinet saw the promotion of Ministers whose political sympathies (and loyalties) tended towards Ted Heath rather than Margaret Thatcher. Thus Douglas Hurd became Foreign Secretary while Kenneth Baker took over the Home Office.[5] The unapologetically interventionist Michael Heseltine was appointed Secretary of State for the Environment, with the mission of scrapping the poll tax and replacing it with a settlement more acceptable to the public, a commitment announced as early as April 1991. Chris Patten, a critic of Thatcherite policies in the early 1980s and keen to shift British Conservatism towards the pro-welfare and social market political outlook of the German Christian Democrats, became Party Chairman with a seat in Cabinet (as Chancellor of the Duchy of Lancaster). The only significant exception to this changing of the guard was Norman Lamont, from the centre-right of the party: he had run Major's successful campaign for the leadership and was elevated from Chief Secretary to the Treasury to Chancellor.

Lamont's period as Chancellor did not prevent the emergence of other differences with the Thatcher years, relating to the composition of the macroeconomic policy and Britain's relationship with the European Community (EC). As the economy headed into recession, rather than follow the deflationary route taken by Howe and Thatcher a decade earlier, Lamont and Major allowed public expenditure to rise (higher education, transport and health were identified as in need of more investment)[6] and cut taxes (reducing the basic rate to 20p in the 1992 Budget). This pushed the borrowing requirement up to 6 per cent of the GDP by April 1992.[7] At the same time Major sought to replace Thatcher's increasing scepticism about the value of Britain's role in the EC by insisting that his administration wanted Britain to be 'at the very heart of Europe'.[8]

Major's approach was driven by two separate arguments. The first was linked to his vision of Britain's place in the world. He strongly believed membership of the EC to be in Britain's national interest. It provided Britain with a place within a powerful political and economic bloc. This not only absorbed almost 50 per cent of all the country's exports but amplified its voice on a series of key international issues, embracing the Palestinian question, East–West relations, international development and trade negotiations with the rest of the world. Furthermore, given that decisions taken by the EC concerning commercial, regional and environmental policy were bound to affect Britain itself, it made little sense to Major for Britain to be anywhere except 'at the very heart' of the institution.

Developments in the EC made this imperative. The Rome Council of December 1990 had agreed that member states should prepare for an intergovernmental conference, to be held at Maastricht in the Netherlands a year later. The objective was a treaty establishing the framework for a new phase of European co-operation: the EC was to be transformed into the European Union (EU). The EU was to have its own structure of government, composed of the European Commission, the Council of Ministers and the European Parliament. Its aim was the establishment of economic and monetary union, including a single currency managed by a European Central Bank (ECB), a 'Cohesion Fund' to transfer resources to the union's less developed regions, a Social Chapter to promote common standards regarding social security, labour relations and conditions of employment, and investment in the creation of a pan-EU transport network. There was to be common citizenship for the populations of all member states. All countries in the EU would automatically belong to the single market, whose establishment had already been agreed (via the signature of the Single European Act in 1986). Due to come into existence at the start of January 1993, this guaranteed the free movement of goods, services, people and capital between members.

Major's government supported much of this agenda but was concerned about the supranational aspects, above all the single currency, and about what many Conservatives saw as the unwelcome corporatism of the Social Chapter. Many backbenchers, as well as Margaret Thatcher, saw in Maastricht evidence for their belief that continuing participation in the European project would leave Britain as one region within a continental super-state. Given, however, that the government had no intention of leaving the EC/EU, it was essential to negotiate terms acceptable to Conservative supporters. The upshot of this effort were two opt-outs, one from the single currency and the other from the Social Chapter. Major regarded the achievement as one of his most substantial,[9] and Britain signed the Maastricht Treaty along with its partners in the EC on 7 February 1992.

The second argument governing Major's pro-European outlook concerned economic policy and British membership of the ERM. The new Prime Minister was uncomfortable with the industrial contraction and increasing reliance on services which had become apparent since 1979. He aimed to promote a rebalancing of the economy in favour of a sustainable expansion characterized by low inflation and grounded in manufacturing and a healthy current account based on increasing exports. He saw participation in the ERM as the key to achieving this objective: in guaranteeing exchange rate stability it would eliminate the danger that a falling pound would add to inflationary pressures. Stable prices would facilitate reductions in the MLR, in the process helping both industry and hard-pressed homeowners struggling to pay their mortgages. At the same time the need to ensure that sterling remained close to £1 = DM 2.95 (there were fluctuation bands of 6 per cent on either side of the central parity) would impose an obligation on both sides of industry to pursue higher productivity and ensure that costs did not move out of line with those operating elsewhere in the ERM. Senior economic commentators such as William Keegan of *The Observer* repeatedly argued that given the size of Britain's external deficit, which had peaked at 4.5 per cent of GDP in 1989–90 (and remained at 2 per cent of GDP in 1991–92), the rate was too high: neither industrialists nor unions would be able to reduce prices and wages enough to eliminate the deficit in the absence of unsustainable deflation.[10] But for Major and Lamont membership of the ERM became the lynch-pin of the government's political and economic strategy, and a symbol of the distance Major wished to place between his administration and that of his predecessor.

Despite the recession and rising joblessness, which seemed to bear out the warnings of Keegan, Major's attempt to refurbish One Nation Toryism made a favourable impression on the electorate. Labour's lead in the polls, so emphatic in the last year of the Thatcher government, narrowed dramatically. By the time the General Election started in March 1992 it was generally running at less than 5 per cent. Labour remained slightly ahead throughout the campaign and most informed commentators expected a minority government led by Neil Kinnock. The result, on 9–10 April, therefore came as a surprise: the Conservatives were returned with a small (21 seat) overall majority. They had taken 42 per cent of the vote, a figure which represented only a very small fall from what they had achieved in 1987, while Labour's share was just over 35 per cent (the figures exclude votes in Northern Ireland, where neither party ran candidates). Although this represented a 3.8 per cent improvement in Labour support over 1997 the outcome came as a huge disappointment to Kinnock and his team.

Many commentators suggested that the key issue had been taxation: the Conservatives had promised higher public expenditure and reductions in taxation, whereas Labour were committed to increases in national insurance contributions and income tax, albeit only on those earning over £40,000 a year (the average annual wage at the time was just over £20,000). Later studies suggested that other factors were more significant. One was the declining share of the electorate taken by the working class, falling from 60 per cent in 1964 to 40 per cent in 1992; another was the revelation that the polls had consistently underestimated the strength of support for the Conservatives.[11] In any event, Major's success (under his leadership the Conservatives attracted the largest number of votes ever given to a political party at a British General Election) was seen by him and his supporters as evidence of popular endorsement for the neo-liberal course taken by the nation since 1979, modified by pro-Europeanism along with the 'One Nation' element of backing for the welfare state and investment in public services.

Sterling crisis

The Conservatives did not have long to enjoy their unexpected victory. Within weeks of Major's triumph the government was facing a crisis resulting from sterling's membership of the ERM. The German Bundesbank had been increasing interest rates at intervals from 1989 until 1993 out of anxiety that the expenditure made necessary by reunification (to support social security and the public finances in East Germany) might lead to overheating.[12] During 1992 short-term rates in Germany reached almost 10 per cent. This led to constant pressure on the pound in the markets, which were selling it in favour of deutschmarks. The UK MLR, which had been gradually reduced from 13.9 per cent in November 1990 to just under 10 per cent in May 1992 now became stuck, resulting in a real interest rate of over 5 per cent.[13] Clearly, in the circumstances MLR could not be reduced further: indeed the logic of ERM membership pointed in the direction of increases. Yet these would place deflationary pressures on an economy struggling to escape from recession, with unemployment now at 2.7 million. Lamont was therefore reluctant to raise the MLR and persuaded the Treasury to consider a unilateral sterling devaluation or even a suspension of British participation in the ERM, but these options were rejected by his civil servants and by Major, who all took the view that such action would undermine the credibility of the government's commitment to a strong pound and low inflation.[14]

The markets were unimpressed by the government's refusal to act, taking the view that no sustained recovery could occur until sterling's value had fallen against the deutschmark, facilitating lower interest rates and an expansion of exports. Major and Lamont's response was to make the best of the situation, pointing to the dramatic fall in inflation (now below 4 per cent). But speculation against sterling grew: in July large-scale selling caused it to sink to DM 2.778, the bottom of its lower fluctuation band. Ongoing reluctance to increase the MLR to protect the parity now left only one option: sanction Bank of England intervention and hold on in the hope that the Bundesbank would cut rates in Germany.

This approach led nowhere: German officials argued that the real problem was sterling's overvaluation, invoking the current account deficit worth 2 per cent of GDP at a time when the economy was scarcely growing at all.[15] Bank of England intervention failed to calm the situation: over $1 billion was lost to the foreign exchange reserves at the end of August in the face of intense speculation. By Wednesday 16 September, with sterling still marooned at DM 2.778, confidence had collapsed. By this time only central banks (notably the Bank of England, the Bundesbank and the Banque de France) were prepared to buy sterling, and they did not possess the resources to hold back the tidal wave of selling on the part of commercial banks. During the morning losses to the Bank of England's resources of dollars and deutschmarks were so severe that its reserve position turned negative for a short time. The MLR was raised two percentage points, from 10 per cent to 12 per cent: the move was ineffectual, so another increase was announced, to 15 per cent, to take effect from 17 September.[16] Major and Lamont hoped this would persuade the markets that the government was unshakeable in its determination to keep the currency in the ERM. If that drastic announcement made any difference, however, it was only to confirm the opposite of what was intended. The implications of a 15 per cent MLR for the British economy were so grave that the markets were now convinced that the government was in a state of panic, and that sterling's rate in the ERM was indefensible. The lesson was not lost on the government: following an emergency meeting of senior Ministers, the Chancellor announced, at 7 p.m., that sterling was leaving the ERM. The second MLR increase was aborted and the pound immediately slumped on the foreign exchanges (down to DM 2.69 in New York that evening and to DM 2.67 in Tokyo the next morning).[17] It continued to slide until the end of the year, reaching a low point of DM 2.35 in early 1993. There was a limited rally which saw it rise back up to between DM 2.50 and DM 2.60 in the second half of the year; thereafter it slipped to DM 2.40 and remained there in 1994–95. This amounted to a substantial devaluation of almost 20 per cent.

The 16 September quickly became known in the media as 'Black Wednesday'; sterling's time in the ERM had ended in humiliating fashion for the Conservatives. Given the economic fundamentals applying at the time such a denouement was always likely, but its arrival had perhaps been accelerated by the process of financialization which had been unleashed by the deregulation of markets in the previous decade. During the late 1980s and early 1990s the City 'extended its lead as the world's largest centre for foreign exchange trading'. By 1992 the average daily turnover of transactions in this field had reached $300 billion, some 30 per cent of overall global volume.[18] This growing volume of business attracted mobile international capital, much of it handled by hedge funds, which tended to profit by speculating with borrowed capital. One of the largest and most successful of these was George Soros's Quantum Fund. Convinced that sterling's position in the ERM was doomed, Soros bet $10 billion – more than the entire value of his fund – on a devaluation, borrowing pounds to buy deutschmarks at the parity of £1 = DM 2.95, and then paying his creditors back at a lower rate after sterling had crashed out of the ERM.[19] He made £1 billion through these transactions; it was ironic that the *coup de grâce* for sterling had been administered by an institution which now flourished thanks to the neo-liberal revolution driven forward by the Thatcher governments.

In placing ERM membership at the heart of its economic strategy and then abandoning the institution in what appeared to be chaotic circumstances, the Major government had very publicly failed to meet the exact criteria it had deemed essential to its success. Although it quickly replaced the discredited strategy with an alternative one, and stuck by this for the rest of its time in office, its reputation for economic competence never fully recovered from the ERM fiasco. This now became an embarrassment for the Prime Minister in the same way as devaluation had been for Harold Wilson and his administration after November 1967.

The ERM experience also fed the increasing hostility within the Conservative Party to Britain's position in the European Union which had become apparent at the end of the 1980s. It was used by a significant fraction of Tory backbenchers who became known as 'Eurosceptics'. These were encouraged by Margaret Thatcher (now in the House of Lords as Baroness Thatcher of Kesteven), and championed a series of positions ranging all the way from opposition to further European integration to open backing for British withdrawal from the European Union. Most of the Eurosceptics were staunch Thatcherites: their outlook stemmed from a fusion of economic liberalism with a commitment to the preservation of

British national sovereignty. The Eurosceptics maintained that the politico-economic changes delivered by the Thatcher governments could only be guaranteed by an independent Britain pursuing free market policies within a open global economy. Departure from the ERM marked the beginning of a civil war in the Conservative Party which had been brewing for at least four years.

New economic policy

Sterling's exit from the ERM in fact provided the opportunity for a shift towards a more expansionary economic policy, given that there was now no need to use the MLR to defend sterling. Lamont hailed the chance to construct 'a British policy', indicating that freedom from ERM rules allowed the government to construct a strategy for national recovery. Major, along with Lamont and Heseltine (now President of the Board of Trade and responsible for the Department of Trade and Industry), was determined to ensure that this would be sustainable and therefore built on the generation of real wealth, reflected in an improved external position, rather than via a credit-based stimulation of demand. They developed a new approach, which was continued by Kenneth Clarke after Lamont left the government in the spring of 1993 following a series of public relations gaffes which undermined his credibility as Chancellor.[20]

The new strategy established a target for the annual increase in the rate of inflation, to assure the markets that there would be no departure from the commitment to price stability. However, the pursuit of this objective was now characterized by some flexibility, with any one of a range of outcomes varying between 1 per cent and 4 per cent being seen as acceptable. This in turn permitted freedom to reduce interest rates, which would (it was hoped) encourage private investment, while allowing the Treasury and the Bank to take a reasonably relaxed attitude to the lower rate for sterling as long as this did not jeopardise the government's ability to meet its inflation targets. There was to be no crackdown on public expenditure although projections for the borrowing requirement indicated that by 1993–94 it was likely to amount to £50 billion (7.5 per cent of GDP). In a marked shift away from the Thatcher–Howe obsession with cutting back government programmes, Major and Lamont took the broadly Keynesian line that the high levels of public spending and borrowing would assist growth and provide a counterweight to the deflationary forces which had driven joblessness so high.[21] Although there was agreement that the impact of infrastructure projects on the public purse could be offset by encouraging an element of private funding, capital investment projects in the public sector were to be protected. Borrowing was to be reduced gradually, with the emphasis falling on tax increases (a flat contradiction of the Conservative 1992 General Election manifesto).

Concrete evidence that the government was committed to what Major called a 'strategy for growth' was provided in the 1992 Autumn Statement, when Lamont unveiled a modest stimulus package which in his estimation would add £4 billion to borrowing up to 1994–95.[22] The measures included a cut in the MLR, now down to 7 per cent; increases in spending on education and health; a pay limit of 1.5 per cent for workers in the public sector, to create room for capital investment programmes; £750 million for housing associations so that they could purchase up to 20,000 empty homes (and therefore help to boost the property market); the relaxation of financial controls on local authorities so that they would be able to use the receipts from selling council houses to fund capital programmes worth £1.75 billion; a £700 million expansion of export credit; and the scrapping of taxation on new car purchases.[23] Lamont announced a series of direct and indirect tax increases designed to bring down borrowing in his 1993 Budget (his last), but these were deferred until 1994. They included higher national insurance contributions, increases in duties on cigarettes, beer and petrol and a rise in VAT on fuel, currently zero-rated, to 8 per cent in 1994 and 17.5 per cent in 1995. In November Clarke introduced the year's second Budget, which tightened the forthcoming squeeze: the new Chancellor announced further tax rises and trimmed government spending projections by £10 billion for the 1994–97 period. The blow was, however, softened by a 1.5 per cent real terms increase in spending on the NHS and the first rise in the value of pensions above the rate of inflation since the 1970s. All the same, the combined effect of the two 1993 Budgets was to deliver the largest package of tax rises seen in peacetime.[24]

Clarke's careful management of the public finances lasted all the way to 1997. It facilitated a gradual reduction in borrowing, which had fallen to £1 billion by the time the government left office.[25] This led to the development of increasing strains within the public sector but did not have a deflationary impact on the economy, and output rose throughout the period from 1993–97, averaging just over 3 per cent per annum.[26] Unemployment, which had peaked at almost 3 million (10 per cent of the workforce) in 1993, fell to just over 1.5 million in 1997 (5.7 per cent).[27] The expansion of the Major years was not checked by Clarke's fiscal caution because this did not start to take effect until recovery was already established.

What caused this revival? The RPI sank to just 1.9 per cent in 1993 (it had not been down at that level since 1963) and never exceeded 3.5 per cent during the remaining years of the government's lifetime.[28] Given only modest pay increases in the public and private sectors (earnings grew by just 3.4 per cent in 1993–94 while the share of national output taken by wages and salaries fell from 55 per cent of GDP in 1990 to 51 per cent in 1997)[29], the tax and national insurance increases following the two Budgets of 1993, and extensive deleveraging from the 115 per cent ratio of personal debt to income reached at the end of the Thatcher years, there was little prospect either of inflation reviving or of demand being stimulated by private spending.[30] On the other hand the conjunction of low income growth and weak domestic demand with stable industrial costs (including wages), a pound generally fluctuating between 20 and 25 per cent below its central rate in the ERM and an MLR varying between 5 per cent and 6 per cent throughout 1993–99, led to a transfer of resources into the production of goods for the export market. Britain's external position was transformed as businesses responded well to the improvement in industry's international competitiveness generated by austerity, cheap money and lower sterling. Following sterling's exit from the ERM the current account followed a classic J-curve as the deficit rose from just over £10 billion to £10.6 billion in 1992–93 and then narrowed rapidly. In 1997 it achieved a surplus of £8 billion.[31] This was the first (and the last) time Britain has been in the black since 1984. The economic recovery after 1992 was therefore driven by exports, which grew twice as fast as GDP, stimulating the sustainable rise in output and employment Major had aimed for since becoming Prime Minister and in the process generating the tax receipts which had largely wiped out the borrowing requirement by the time the Conservatives left office.

The government's macroeconomic strategy after 1992 continued the shift away from the monetarism and credit-fuelled expansion of the Thatcher era which started when Major became Prime Minister. This departure was underlined by the work of Michael Heseltine at the Board of Trade. Heseltine had never supported Thatcher and Lawson's hostility to 'corporatism' and dialogue between government and industry. His resignation from Thatcher's Cabinet in 1986 had stemmed from his firm view that the modern State should act to support key industries and assist business to exploit opportunities in global markets. He had backed key aspects of the Thatcher revolution – the drive to reduce inflation, privatization, the encouragement of competition, the reform of industrial relations legislation and the curtailing of trade union influence – but argued that these measures on their own would not raise the level of Britain's national economic performance.[32] He looked not to the USA for examples of good economic practice but West European states such as Germany and France, characterized by higher wages and taxes than the UK and by partnership between the public and private sectors. These were societies which were able to finance their high living standards and well-funded welfare systems through productivity growth and a focus on quality as well as through higher output. Heseltine therefore attempted to construct at the Department of Trade and Industry (DTI) what he considered to be the features of the state–industry relationship responsible for the success of Britain's partners in the European Union.[33]

The new approach concentrated on government dialogue with industry concerning education and training, design and quality, marketing, overseas trade and public sector procurement. Although the NEDC had been abolished by Lamont (with Major's agreement) in 1992 in a symbolic repudiation of corporatism (in fact its role had been minimal for some years), Heseltine reinvented many of its functions (though not, of course, the tripartite approach) within the DTI. Here he worked closely with the CBI, the Engineering Employers' Federation, Chambers of Commerce and Trade Associations in a bid to boost British industrial strength through measures which focused on competitiveness. From 1994 the DTI produced an annual Competitiveness White Paper, combining assessment of the strengths and weaknesses of leading sectors such as pharmaceuticals, aerospace and ceramics with detailed suggestions about how these could be addressed.[34] To this end a Competitiveness Division was established in the DTI, run by a mixed public and private sector team; support for small and medium businesses (SMEs) was expanded and reorganized; and there was increased funding for apprenticeships and R and D.

Under Heseltine, backing for export promotion was given particular priority: 80 individual country units were established, one for each of the UK's main export markets.[35] These were staffed by civil servants and managers on secondment from private industry and their main areas of responsibility involved organizing and supporting trade exhibitions, marketing and the provision of commercial intelligence to firms producing for overseas.

After May 1997 many of these initiatives were continued by the new Labour government, but it is hard to say what impact they had during the Major years. Heseltine's industrial strategy did not involve a return to the interventionism of the 1960s and 1970s but it did take up many of the issues felt by the CBI to have been neglected during the Thatcher era, and was further evidence of the government's determination to take a more consensual approach to economic policy than had been evident between 1979 and 1990. Certainly, the British trade performance improved. It is also clear that the trend to deindustrialization, so marked during the 1980s, was checked during the Major years. The declining share of GDP taken by manufacturing was stabilised (at between 18 and 19 per cent).[36] It is likely that this owed something to Heseltine's reforms; but the funding he was able to wring out of the Treasury for many of his initiatives was disappointing,[37] while pursuit of his programme was constantly buffeted by a series of crises which engulfed the government from sterling's exit from the ERM all the way to the end of its time in office.

Terminus

Black Wednesday seriously compromised the government's standing with the electorate but its reputation was perhaps irretrievably ruined by the crisis caused by its handling of the coal industry. This was caused by the desire of the now privatized electricity generating industry, responsible no longer to the public but to its shareholders, to switch from dependence on supplies of coal to the cheaper energy source of gas. The move looked good from the view point of profits and dividends but the implications for the coal mining industry were very serious: 31 pits faced closure, with a loss of 30,000 jobs. Heseltine at the DTI decided not to oppose this development but concentrated instead on persuading the Treasury to finance a reasonably generous redundancy scheme which would provide £23,000 per head to the redundant miners as long as they left work in the 1992–93 financial year. The Cabinet approved the proposals, which were announced on 13 October 1992.

The public reaction was dramatic. There was great dismay at the prospect that so many mining communities were to be shut down. Following as it did the very bruising and sometimes tragic divisions experienced across the country during the 1984–85 strike, the decision was seen by many as sheer vindictiveness, intended to stamp out the potential for any further working-class resistance to the free market economy and society established after 1979.[38] These sentiments extended all the way from the trade unions and the Labour Party to a significant fraction of Conservative Party members and MPs, who were appalled at the prospect that those who had refused to join the strike (concentrated in the Nottinghamshire coalfields) now faced abandonment. There were demonstrations across the country and so great was the public anger that the government decided to execute a partial U-turn. This led to agreement on more money for the miners, a review procedure for 21 of the pits, a subsidy for British Coal (which had replaced the NCB in 1987), and assistance worth £200 million for areas affected by pit closures.[39] The review procedure slowed the closure programme without making any significant difference to the run-down of the industry, with 25 pits being shut down between 1993–97 rather than 31 inside a year; in 1994 the newly privatized UK Coal inherited just 15 collieries. The opinion polls had started to turn against the Conservatives after Black Wednesday. Now they swung dramatically towards Labour, which established a double-digit lead.

The episode reinforced the lessons to be drawn from the closure of Ravenscraig steelworks in Motherwell, Scotland, in June 1992, which caused the loss of 1,200 jobs.[40] It revealed the limits to Major's One Nation Conservatism, which sought to modify Thatcherism rather than challenge the assumptions which underpinned it. Indeed the neo-liberal revolution marched on, even if its progress was more muted and less abrasive than under Thatcher. By 1994 London's share of the European equity markets amounted to 44 per cent, triple the portion taken by Paris and Frankfurt. The government, the Treasury, the Bank of England and the City all continued to advertise the attractions of Britain's low tax, low pay, industrially quiescent and deregulated economic environment to mobile international capital, corporate as well as financial.[41] Attempts to revive the Welsh economy revolved around the encouragement of inward direct investment on the part of multinationals such as Panasonic, Sony and the Korean firm LG Electronics.[42] Rejection of the Social Chapter had made it clear that there would not even be a small step back towards the institutionalized co-operation between the State and both sides of industry which had disappeared from the UK after 1979.[43] Further evidence of Britain's liberal economic trajectory was provided by the privatization of the railways, the continuation of compulsory competitive tendering and school opt-outs and the introduction (albeit limited) of an internal market into the NHS.[44]

Many voters who had been attracted by Major's brand of Conservatism became disenchanted, and drifted away from supporting the Conservatives. They were not persuaded back by the economic recovery, which was not accompanied by widespread experience of rising living standards thanks to ongoing pay restraint. In 1994, 37 per cent of all full-time workers and 76.7 per cent of all part-time workers were earning less than 68 per cent of average full-time income (the level defined by the Council of Europe as the 'decency threshold').[45] The proportion of the population in poverty, identified in terms of those living on less than 60 per cent of median household income, up from 13.7 per cent in 1979 to 23.8 per cent in 1990, continued to grow, to 25.3 per cent, by 1996–97.[46] Both health and education were affected by the financial squeeze, notwithstanding government efforts to sustain real term increases in resources. In the NHS there were growing waiting lists and mounting prescription charges. The provision of dental care contracted dramatically, as did long-term care for the elderly.[47] Schools and universities struggled with shortages of staff and equipment.[48] The steady growth of the 1993–97 era brought with it no 'feel-good factor'.

The government's difficulties were compounded by a series of scandals affecting a small number of Tory MPs and Ministers. Some of these revolved around the private lives of the people concerned but others were more serious, revealing actions which brought into question the integrity of the accused. Two, Neil Hamilton (a junior Minister) and Tim Smith, were found to have accepted substantial cash payments from Harrods owner Mohammed Al-Fayed, in return for asking Parliamentary Questions on his behalf.[49] Allegations of improper financial dealings with the Saudi Arabian royal family swirled around the head of another, Jonathan Aitken, forcing him to resign from his position as Chief Secretary to the Treasury in 1995.[50] The damage done by these affairs, while serious, was surpassed by the impact of the Conservative party's split over Britain's relationship with the European Union. The Eurosceptics, supported by Margaret Thatcher and emboldened by the ERM fiasco, continued to harass the government. Major attempted to placate them by negotiating what Gifford calls 'policy exits'. The Maastricht opt-outs over the single currency and the Social Chapter were followed in 1995 by another one, concerning the Schengen Agreement, which largely abolished internal borders within the EU. Major also promised that no Conservative government led by him would take Britain into EU monetary union without a referendum on the subject first. These concessions simply encouraged the Eurosceptics to demand more: they rebelled over the UK financial contribution to the EU, demanded a renegotiation of the Maastricht Treaty and, by 1996–97 were calling for a referendum on whether Britain should remain part of a federal European Union.[51]

The differences between those who favoured closer engagement with the European Union and the Eurosceptics were expressed in arguments about national sovereignty but they stemmed from the economic changes wrought by the Thatcher revolution. Thatcher and her allies on the Tory backbenches and in the Bruges Group, formed to make the case for Euroscepticism in the wake of Thatcher's Bruges speech in 1988, saw EU regulations as a threat to free market capitalism in Britain. They argued this could best be sustained in a partnership between the USA and the UK committed to the worldwide expansion of political and economic liberalism, in the form of national self-determination, free trade and the free movement of capital. There was a real basis for these aspirations. Economists and historians have observed how the successful exploitation of global opportunities by financial institutions based in London in the years since 1979, especially after the 'Big Bang' of 1986, had created a new rentier class whose wealth was dependent on income from significant investments in the USA, Canada, Latin America and the Far East.[52] Indeed it was Thatcher herself who pointed out that in 1993 80 per cent of Britain's £1.3 trillion portfolio of overseas assets was held outside the EU, driving a rebalancing of the country's pattern of trade towards relatively more commerce with the Pacific Rim countries in particular and relatively less with Europe.[53]

The Eurosceptics were convinced that membership of the European Union threatened this continuing internationalization of British finance, a process which generated what Gifford has called a 'reactionary British exceptionalism' not seen since the heyday of British financial imperialism in the early twentieth century. Here, the national interest was identified with the welfare of overseas-oriented economic interests whose goal was integration into a 'global market society'.[54] The strategy was sustained internationally through the Atlantic alliance and at home by a populist fusion of consumerism and national chauvinism, encouraged and exploited by print and broadcasting outlets belonging to wealthy and powerful media proprietors with world-wide interests such as Rupert Murdoch and Conrad Black. It was an end of the century version of the phenomenon noted by Hobson in 1902 when he commented that 'cheap booze and Maffeking'[55] were blinding many British citizens to the realities in which they lived: a society increasingly dominated by financiers and rentiers whose wealth, derived more from assets abroad than in the UK, allowed them to employ 'great tame masses of retainers no longer engaged in the staple industries of industry and agriculture' in 'the performance of personal or minor industrial services'.[56]

The profundity of the fracture over the future strategy for British capitalism as it had been reformed after 1979, witnessed in the battle between Major and the Eurosceptics, ensured that the normal imperatives governing the conduct of political parties ceased to apply to the Conservatives. The split within their ranks endured throughout the government's life. Major's bitterness over this, and his anger with the Eurosceptic colleagues whose obsessions he deemed irrational and backward looking, came through in his autobiography as well as in his off-the-record description of them to a political journalist as 'bastards'.[57] This row, which even continued into the General Election, undermining the credibility of the Conservative campaign in a spectacular way, reinforced the public impression of disorganization, incompetence and indeed sheer unpleasantness which had been growing since 1992.

Despite all the confusion and the disappointing (if predictable) outcome of Major's attempt to revive One Nation Conservatism in a neo-liberal context, the government did have achievements to its name. These included not only its successes on the economic front but real progress in establishing a peace process in Northern Ireland and an enlightened approach to freedom of information. But they counted for little in the public mind. Conservative standing in the polls never recovered from its collapse in the autumn of 1992. By 1995–96, with the Labour Party reinvigorated under the new leadership of Tony Blair, the divided and tainted Conservative administration seemed to have very little that was either new or attractive to offer the electorate. Its appeal was shrinking, in terms both of popular appeal and of its geographical reach across the nation. British Conservatism had long defended the Union and indeed in the 1992 General Election campaign Major had opposed the devolution of power to Edinburgh and Cardiff because of the danger that it might lead to an unravelling of the United Kingdom. But now the Conservatives had shrunk to being an English party, their position in Wales in retreat after the collapse of the coal industry while in Scotland they faced crisis, with the Ravenscraig closure compounding the political damage caused by the poll tax and the long industrial contraction of the 1980s. North of the border

Conservative support had fallen below 20 per cent: the party was heading for electoral oblivion there.

Unsurprisingly the May 1997 General Election saw the Conservatives defeated in humiliating fashion. Labour was returned with 418 seats (13.5 million votes and 43 per cent of the vote) against just 165 for the Conservatives (whose public support slumped to 9.6 million votes and 30.7 per cent of the vote). Conservative representation in Scotland collapsed from 12 MPs to zero; the result was paralleled in Wales, where it dropped from 6 to none. Even the Liberal Democrats (created in 1988 from a merger of the Liberals and the SDP) increased their representation from 20 to 46 MPs, thanks to tactical voting against the sitting members in Conservative seats. The result of the General Election revealed a public in a state of quiet and determined revolt against the Conservative Party, and looking to Labour to chart a new course for the nation, away from Thatcherism.

Notes

1 See John Major, *John Major: The Autobiography*, (London: Harper Collins, 2000), pp. 202–205.
2 See Ken Livingstone, *You Can't Say That* (London, Faber and Faber, 2011), pp. 84–85.
3 Stevens, *Politics and the Pound*, p. 219.
4 Major, *The Autobiography*, p. 300.
5 Hurd, a former diplomat, had worked for Heath before becoming an MP in February 1974. After the 1970 election victory he had become Heath's Political Secretary. See John Campbell, *Edward Heath: A Biography* (London: Pimlico, 1994), pp. 219ff. In 2013 Baker admitted that 'I was always a Heathite. Strangely enough, though, I came to like Margaret the more I got to know her'. See Decca Aitkenhead, 'Kenneth Baker: "People told me to abandon Thatcher but I stood by her"', *The Guardian*, 20 January 2013.
6 Major, *The Autobiography*, p. 664; Kenneth O. Morgan, *The People's Peace: British History 1945–1990* (Oxford: Oxford University Press, 1992), p. 507.
7 Stevens, *Politics and the Pound*, p. 197.
8 Major, *The Autobiography*, p. 269; also see Major's speech to the Conservative Central Council, 23 March 1991, http://www.johnmajor.co.uk/page2017.html (accessed 18 July 2016).
9 Major, *The Autobiography*, p. 288.
10 Stevens, *Politics and the Pound*, p. 177.
11 Anthony Heath, Roger Jowell and John Curtice, 'Exclusive: How Did Labour Lose in '92?', *The Independent*, 28 May 1994.
12 Eric Owen Smith, *The German Economy* (London: Routledge, 1994), Figures 4.4b and 4.4c, pp. 158–159.
13 See Will Hutton, *The State We're In* (London: Vintage, 1995), pp. 75–76.
14 Stevens, *Politics and the Pound*, p. 210; Lamont, 'Out of the Ashes', p. 157.
15 Stevens, *Politics and the Pound*, p. 225.
16 Bank of England, 'Changes in Bank Rate, Minimum Lending Rate, Minimum Band 1 Dealing Rate, Repo Rate and Official Bank Rate', http://www.bankofengland.co.uk/statistics/Documents/rates/baserate.pdf (accessed 22 July 2016), p. 3.
17 Larry Elliott, Will Hutton and Julie Wolf, 'Pound Drops Out of ERM', *The Guardian*, 17 September 1992.
18 'The Foreign Exchange Market in London', *Bank of England Quarterly Bulletin*, 1992, pp. 408–410; Noel Thompson, *Political Economy and the Labour Party*, 2nd edition (London: Routledge, 2006), p. 250.
19 Niall Ferguson, *The Ascent of Money* (London: Penguin, 2008), pp. 317–318.

20 See Major, *The Autobiography*, pp. 679–680. Major offered Lamont the Department of the Environment, but this was refused.
21 Jim Tomlinson, 'Tale of a Death Exaggerated: How Keynesian Policies Survived the 1970s', *Contemporary British History*, vol. 21 (2007), pp. 429–448.
22 See 'Autumn Statement, 1992', http://www.publications.parliament.uk/pa/cm199293/cmhansrd/1992-11-12/Debate-1.html (accessed 25 July 2016).
23 Major, *The Autobiography*, p. 673; Stevens, *Politics and the Pound*, pp. 275–276.
24 Stevens, *Politics and the Pound*, p. 289.
25 Major, *The Autobiography*, p. 689.
26 See United Kingdom National Accounts (London: The Stationery Office, 2000), p. 24.
27 Middleton, *The British Economy since 1945*, Table II.2, p. 149.
28 For MLR see Bank of England, 'Changes in Bank Rate, Minimum Lending Rate, Minimum Band 1 Dealing Rate, Repo Rate and Official Bank Rate', p. 3; for RPI see ONS, 'RPI All Items: Percentage Change over 12 Months', https://www.ons.gov.uk/economy/inflationandpriceindices/timeseries/czbh/mm23 (accessed 26 July 2016).
29 Stewart Lansley and Howard Reed, *How to Boost the Wage Share:* Touchstone Pamphlet no. 13 (London: TUC, 2013), Figure 1, p. 6; Stevens, *Politics and the Pound*, p. 290.
30 Stevens, *Politics and the Pound*, pp. 281 and 288.
31 Middleton, *The British Economy since 1945*, Table II.3, pp. 150–151.
32 Michael Heseltine, *Life in the Jungle: My Autobiography* (London: Hodder and Stoughton, 2001), p. 415.
33 Ibid.
34 'Outlook: Tough Decisions ahead but a Better Class of Deficit', *The Independent*, 27 January 1995.
35 Michael Heseltine, *Life in the Jungle*, p. 425.
36 World Bank, 'Manufacturing, Value Added (% GDP)', http://data.worldbank.org/indicator/NV.IND.MANF.ZS?locations=GB (accessed 28 July 2016).
37 See for example David Bowen, 'DTI Given Muscle to Help Industry: White Paper to Focus on Manufacturing', *The Independent*, 21 May 1994.
38 Milne, *The Enemy Within*, pp. 12–13.
39 Major, *The Autobiography*, pp. 669–671.
40 Brian McIver, 'Closure of Ravenscraig Steelworks still Causing Pain Twenty Years on', *Daily Record*, 23 June 2012.
41 Gifford, *The Making of Eurosceptic Britain*, p. 113.
42 See Leon Gooberman, *Government Intervention in the Welsh Economy, 1974 to 1997*, unpublished PhD thesis, Cardiff University, 2013.
43 Gifford, *The Making of Eurosceptic Britain*, p. 113.
44 Ibid.
45 Julia Lourie, *A Minimum Wage*, House of Commons Research Paper 95/7 (1995).
46 The Poverty Site, United Kingdom: Numbers in Low Income, http://www.poverty.org.uk/01/index.shtml (accessed 29 July 2016).
47 Timmins, *The Five Giants*, pp. 503–504.
48 Ibid., pp. 516–517; pp. 548–549.
49 Hamilton was forced to resign his Ministerial post and lost his seat (Tatton in Cheshire) at the 1997 election. After a period in disgrace he achieved TV celebrity status, joined the United Kingdom Independence Party and in May 2016 became leader of their group in the Welsh Assembly.
50 Aitken was found guilty of perjury and attempting to pervert the course of justice and given an 18 month jail sentence in 1999.
51 See for example Major, *The Autobiography*, pp. 697–698, 705–706.
52 Gifford, *The Making of Eurosceptic Britain*, p. 107.
53 Thatcher quoted in Gifford, *The Making of Eurosceptic Britain*, p. 108.
54 Gifford, *The Making of Eurosceptic Britain*, p. 109.

55 See J. A. Hobson, *Imperialism: A Study* (London: George Allen and Unwin, 1902), p. 101. 'Maffeking' referred to an episode in the Boer War of 1899–1902: the outburst of popular celebrations and patriotic sentiment, encouraged by the press, following the 1899 relief of Mafeking following a six month siege. The phrase was an update of the comment made in the early second century CE by the Roman satirist Juvenal when he said that his fellow citizens were only bothered about 'panem and circenses' (bread and circuses).
56 Hobson, *Imperialism: A Study*, p. 364.
57 See Major, *The Autobiography*, ch. 15.

7

NEW LABOUR IN POWER, 1997–2010

New Labour

The Labour Party which won the 1997 General Election was very different, in terms of policies and organization, from the Labour Party of Wilson and Callaghan, and even of Kinnock. Indeed Tony Blair and those who worked closely with him in this transformative project – Gordon Brown, Alistair Campbell, Peter Mandelson and Jonathan Powell[1] – spoke of 'New' Labour, a name which caught on and has since become common currency in political discourse, even though there was no formal change of nomenclature. As Blair and his supporters intended, the use of this term automatically established a distance from 'Old' Labour.

Blair had become Labour leader in May 1994 following the sudden death of John Smith, who had replaced Kinnock after the 1992 election defeat. Though still young (he was 42) he had successfully held a series of front bench positions under both of his predecessors. At the time of Smith's demise he was Shadow Home Secretary and had acquired a reputation for competence and a willingness to approach problems pragmatically. He had supported the efforts of Kinnock and Smith to make Labour more attractive to business and finance as well as to middle-ground, uncommitted voters. His youth, articulacy and evident ability to handle hostile questions, along with his role as father and family man with two growing children, made him a very attractive figure to many in the electorate. He was classless and seemed to understand the problems of ordinary people who were doing their best to provide a good life for themselves and their families.

Blair was the ideal leader for a party attempting to widen its appeal beyond its traditional sources of support in the trade unions and the old working class to those in the professions and small and medium-sized businesses. His apparent normality, approachability and empathy with the public made it virtually certain that he would be elected leader ahead of his more cerebral Parliamentary Labour Party colleague Gordon Brown, the Shadow Chancellor. Brown, along with Mandelson, had been involved in Labour's gradual repositioning of itself under Kinnock and Smith, but was not seen to have Blair's presentational and public relations skills. These limitations ruled him out of the leadership contest and he withdrew in favour of Blair. In exchange Blair acknowledged that Brown would have suzerainty over economic and social policy and promised to step down in his favour at some date in the future.[2]

The decision to draw a line under Labour's history emerged from a process which had started after the 1992 General Election defeat, the fourth in succession. This had in many ways been the hardest to take, since there had been a general expectation of victory throughout the party. The result was attributed to public reaction against Labour's willingness to increase taxes to fund its spending commitments as well as to continuing memories, frequently stirred by the Conservative Party and its supporters in the press, of the high inflation and industrial disputes associated with the Wilson–Callaghan governments of 1974–79.[3] It was taken as confirmation that Kinnock's leadership had not succeeded in liberating Labour from its depiction in Tory publicity ever since the 1970s as wedded to irresponsible financial policies and penal levels of taxation while being controlled by the unions and the radical left.

Rather than contest this version of history, the new leadership embarked on a process of radical change designed to alter the identity of the Labour Party. Its ability to strike out on this path was facilitated by independence from the traditional sources of financial and intellectual support, namely the trade unions and the Fabian Society. Instead, the Blair leadership deliberately sought to raise money from private industry and the City. The resulting donations, from organizations such as Enron, ICI, Northern Foods and Sainsbury's, along with 'blind trusts', gave Blair and his team access to substantial funds not only large enough to support election campaigns but also a private political office owing the old Party establishment no favours.[4] This gave the leadership the space which enabled it to side-step Labour opinion and accept the hostile Conservative presentation of what had happened to Britain under the Labour governments of the 1960s and 1970s, in order to neutralize its impact on the party's future electoral prospects. A 'new' Labour party committed to a complex of policies distinct from those pursued under past leaders would leave the Tory accusations mired in the same past as Old Labour, in consequence appearing misdirected and irrelevant. This was, at one level, a form of political ju-jitsu in which Labour's opponents found that their strength was not directly confronted but turned against them. But the refurbishment of Labour's image was not just tactical: it was accompanied by a profound ideological shift in which the party embraced the political economy of neo-liberalism and did indeed become a new political organization as a result. Willingness to go along with the highly misleading Conservative interpretation of the recent past stemmed not just from pragmatism but from a conviction that it was, in fact, broadly accurate.

Blair and his associates started from the position that traditional social democracy had failed in the 1970s: its reliance on the corporatist alliance with the unions and collectivist policies (it was argued) had neither revived the economy nor stabilized an increasingly volatile society. On the other hand Thatcher's support for private enterprise, through deregulation, tax cuts and privatization, along with her governments' commitment to reforming industrial relations and the encouragement of a more individualist popular culture, had generated growth, employment and economic expansion. Keen to secure Labour's support for this new economic model, Blair and his colleagues determined to bring the party's aims and values into line with the Thatcher revolution.[5] They called this 'modernization' and determined to go about it in the most public way, by changing the clause in Labour's constitution which was most identified with the ambition to create a democratic socialist society. That was Clause IV, which had historically committed the party to 'the common ownership of the means of production, distribution and exchange'.

The phrase's enemies identified it with State ownership of the entire economy, although no Labour government had ever expressed this ambition and in any case the full wording was open to many different interpretations.[6] The only aspiration which did seem clear was the supercession of production for private profit by unspecified and quite possibly diverse forms of collectively owned enterprises whose profits were shared between those who worked for them and the communities they serviced. Hugh Gaitskell had unsuccessfully attempted to amend the Clause in 1959 on the grounds that it misleadingly implied public ownership to be an end in itself rather than a means of promoting democratic socialism and had caused Labour to lose votes at the recent General Election.[7] His successors had left well alone, sharing Harold Wilson's view that the phrase reflected an ideal and that its removal or replacement made about as much sense as taking the Book of Genesis out of the Bible.[8]

This relaxed attitude was not shared by the Labour modernizers, who were keen to establish that the party's objective was no longer a different model of society from capitalism but the encouragement of 'social-ism'. This amounted, first, to an appreciation that human beings lived socially interdependent lives and secondly to the commitment by government, in recognition of this, that policies should promote equality of opportunity; greater political accountability via reforms to the House of Lords and constitutional change to devolve decision-making to elected Scottish, Welsh and Northern Irish assemblies in Edinburgh, Cardiff and Belfast; protection of the environment; and investment in health, education and skills.[9] To this end Blair proposed a new Clause IV, which aimed at the creation, 'by the strength of our common endeavour', of

> the means to realize our true potential and for all of us a community in which power, wealth and opportunity are in the hands of the many, not the few, where the rights we enjoy reflect the duties we owe, and where we live together, freely, in a spirit of solidarity, tolerance and respect.

The leader found the membership of the party, all the way across the trade unions, constituency parties and MPs, to be more sympathetic to a new Clause IV than they had been in Gaitskell's time. The four election defeats had eroded resistance to change and Blair's version was adopted by Labour at a Special Conference in April 1995.

The new Clause IV was little more than a set of good-natured aspirations which many Conservatives and Liberals could endorse. This was not accidental, since New Labour's quarrel with Thatcherism was not about its philosophy and objectives but simply about aspects of it which were not essential to its central project. These included low pay, increasing poverty, unnecessarily tough anti-trade union legislation and inadequate investment in the public services, though not the widening inequality evident in contemporary Britain. New Labour's objective was to humanize Thatcher's neo-liberal revolution, succeeding where John Major had failed, and the transformation of Clause IV was a clear sign of this dramatic shift in the party's priorities. It was all summed up in Peter Mandelson's 1998 observation that he was 'intensely relaxed about people getting filthy rich'.[10]

Third Way

New Labour's commitment to neo-liberalism was reinforced by developments on the other side of the Atlantic and conclusions drawn from the process of globalization at work in the international economy. The critical event was the victory of the Democrats in the 1992 US Presidential Election; their candidate, Bill Clinton, defeating Republican incumbent George Bush.[11] The Democratic Party, admired by many in the British Labour Party for its commitment to progressive reform, had since the Franklin Delano Roosevelt's New Deal in the 1930s been a champion of using the power and the resources of the Federal Government to attack poverty, unemployment and racial discrimination. But, like Labour, it had fallen on hard times in the 1980s. Jimmy Carter, the last Democrat President before Clinton (he was in office from 1977–81) had struggled to sustain the interventionist tradition in the face of the gathering strength of the neo-liberal revolution led by Ronald Reagan, which duly swept him and the Democrats out of office for over a decade.

Clinton's victory returned the Democrats to power, but they were not promoting the policies and philosophy of the era from Roosevelt to Carter. Instead they compromised with the liberal individualism of the neo-liberals: they promoted freedom of trade and capital movements and repealed the 1933 Glass-Steagall Act, a New Deal reform which had separated high street and investment banking by preventing commercial banks from dealing in securities.[12] Clinton pursued a balanced Federal Budget, achieving this through a combination of revenue raising measures and spending cuts, notably on defence and on social security programmes. Deregulation extended from the banking sector to agriculture and telecommunications. Middle-class Americans saw their taxes being reduced while those on low incomes or without jobs were hit by reforms to welfare provision. These included the introduction of time limits on assistance for struggling families, restrictions on the provision of food stamps and a requirement that recipients of support find work (an approach to the provision of benefits for the unemployed known in the USA as 'workfare'). Such measures were balanced by others more in keeping with the traditions of the Democratic Party, notably strong backing for civil rights and Federal investment in education, training and skills and in the nation's infrastructure.[13]

Clinton's success in 1992, repeated in 1996, impressed key figures in the British Labour establishment. Their admiration increased as they watched the US economy grow in the 1990s, with falling unemployment, low inflation and successful new corporations such as Microsoft, Netscape and Oracle expanding rapidly in response to the opportunities for innovation in information technology provided by the arrival of the world-wide web. It seemed that these firms had emerged not thanks to any State-led industrial strategy (although in fact the internet had grown out of ARPANET, established by the US Department of Defense to promote research and development in advanced technology back in the 1970s), but out of the entrepreneurial activities of highly mobile networks of researchers, engineers and scientists able to access abundant resources of capital.[14]

Blair and Brown made frequent visits to the USA and developed contacts with important members of the Clinton administration such as Treasury Secretary Larry Summers and Labour Secretary Robert Reich. Brown met Alan Greenspan, Chair of the Federal Reserve Bank since 1987 and a key figure in the neo-liberal revolution.[15] Philip Gould, adviser to Labour on strategy and polling during the 1987, 1992 (and 1997) General Elections, studied the Clinton campaign of 1992 at first hand and was later responsible for organizing a series of meetings between full-time workers for the Democrats and their Labour opposite numbers so that Blair's team could learn from Clinton's triumphs.[16]

The main lessons Labour absorbed from the Clinton experience were that a *soi-disant* centre-left political party could succeed at the polls if it appealed to non-traditional supporters in the middle class, dropped what had been fundamental policy aspirations and embraced the free market. Blair and Brown accordingly endorsed the Atlanticism of the Thatcher era, a position which led to British participation in the hugely controversial invasion of Iraq in 2003. The commitment implied continuity with the drive to project political and economic liberalism world-wide which had started during the Thatcher era. It dictated abandonment of the historic commitment to the post-war consensus that governments should seek to sustain the economy at a level of demand capable of maintaining full employment or something close to it.[17] During the period from 1994 to 1997 New Labour committed itself to a series of policies which exchanged this for the pursuit of 'economic stability', in other words low inflation and a business-friendly tax climate. Most dramatically, Blair and Brown anticipated Tory attempts to revive Labour's image as a party committed to the politics of 'tax and spend', stating that if they won power they would not increase either the basic or the top rates of taxation (though there would be a windfall tax on the former public utilities) and would abide by Chancellor Kenneth Clarke's public expenditure plans for at least their first two years in office.[18]

These pledges were accompanied by an approach intended to guarantee improvement on the economic record of the Thatcher years and raise national output over the long-term. This result was expected to follow not from Keynesian policies designed to produce full employment of resources but from the application of 'post neo-classical endogenous growth theory'.[19] In practice this amounted to supply-side reforms targeted at the removal of imperfections in the market. These would include modernization of the country's transport and communications (including information technology and computing networks), and spending on health. An increase in investment in the nation's infrastructure was to be paralleled by spending on education, training and skills (as in the USA). Improving the areas of the economy linked to knowledge would both raise Britain's growth potential and create an 'employable' workforce adaptable enough to take advantage of all the job opportunities provided by the labour market.[20]

Alongside these commitments were proposals designed to deliver a (limited) correction of the balance between capital and labour as it had developed after 1979. New Labour agreed to a strengthening of collective bargaining arrangements through legislation to provide workers with protection against unfair dismissal, the introduction of statutory procedures for trade union recognition and adoption of the Social Chapter of the Maastricht Treaty. These steps were to be complemented by the introduction of a 'national minimum', to be achieved by a Minimum Wage and tax credits for the working poor. On the other hand Blair promised the unions 'fairness not favours': the key reforms to industrial relations legislation introduced in the Thatcher era, concerning strike ballots, picketing, secondary action and the closed shop, were to remain.[21]

There was little empirical support for neo-classical endogenous growth theory.[22] In essence this amounted to an endorsement of the flexible accumulation model which had emerged during the 1980s, albeit on a broader and more generous basis.[23] If the political catalyst for this transformation had been Clinton's electoral successes, the economic driver had been globalization. The scale and mobility of international financial flows, with the daily turnover of foreign exchange transactions reaching $1trillion during the first half of the 1990s and doubling by the last year of the decade,[24] meant (it was argued) that governments needed to ensure their economic strategies were friendly to capital if their countries were to prosper. It followed that the most effective policies would have to deliver low taxes, weak unions, a flexible workforce and a modern infrastructure. Leftist administrations which pursued traditional social and economic goals such as higher welfare spending, greater social equality and full employment via a *dirigiste* industrial strategy, foreign exchange controls and high corporate taxes now faced the real prospect of capital flight. The experience of the socialist administration of France's President François Mitterrand during the first half of the 1980s was taken as a demonstration of this: it had been forced to abandon its radical policies and adopt economic orthodoxy in order to restore confidence to the French franc after speculation had led to a series of devaluations. The failure of this experiment was seen to be evidence that social-democratic governments seeking to promote economic growth now had no alternative but to adopt a macroeconomic strategy which not only attracted an inflow of mobile international capital but in addition sustained an environment congenial enough to keep it.[25]

The distinguished sociologist Anthony Giddens termed the synthesis of neo-liberalism and progressive policies which characterized the political economy of New Labour's modernization project the 'Third Way'. The term had a long history, being used over the years by disparate political groups from the Right and Left; it was now taken up by New Labour as a name for its version of social democracy. Indeed, proponents of the Third Way, such as Giddens and the Labour leadership, took the view that there was no workable alternative political economy available to the Left: this was the new face of social democracy.

This conviction was, however, challenged by the distinguished commentator and journalist Will Hutton, in his book *The State We're In*, published in 1995. Hutton rejected the neo-liberal analysis and argued that politics and philosophy of the free market had damaged British society. The unregulated capitalism of the 1980s had caused both fund and corporate managers to become fixated on favourable stock market price movements and high dividends rather than company growth, which took second place to keeping shareholders happy. During the 1980s manufacturing investment had risen (on average) by 2 per cent per annum, profits by 6 per cent and dividends by 12 per cent.[26] This form of 'short-termism' led both to the late 1980s wave of mergers and acquisitions, with company growth generated by takeovers rather than by investment in new capacity, and to unbalanced social development (for example cities with surpluses of office blocks and shops but short of housing and public space).[27] Good firms had disappeared and the British economy had become increasingly vulnerable to speculative financial movements, leading to the shrinking of the manufacturing sector, de-skilling and the growth of part-time labour: by the mid-1990s only 40 per cent of the workforce was in either tenured full-time or secure self-employment. No British equivalent of Honda, Apple or Microsoft emerged: instead the most dynamic concerns were financial, such as the Hanson Trust, which grew by takeover, a process which reached a climax with its purchase of the Imperial Group in 1990.[28]

Hutton's remedy involved a raft of proposals starting with the reform of the financial system so that it was able to guarantee firms stable, long-term funding. He called for a 'public agency' (later identifying this as a National Investment Bank) to collect long-term bank deposits and channel them to lending institutions, including a new network of regional investment banks.[29] There should be a 'penal, short-term capital gains tax' for shareholders taking early profits, 'tapering to near zero for long-term shareholders'.[30] He argued for tighter control of takeovers and for the democratization of the corporate environment through the establishment of an institutional framework accommodating a firm's 'stakeholders', identified not simply as the management and the shareholders but also as workers, customers, suppliers and local communities. Reform of corporate governance to ensure representation of these interests on company boards would militate against shareholder influence in the direction of short-termism. Hutton's project, with its interventionism, backing for the opening up of company boardrooms and willingness to use the power of the State to curtail corporate power, repudiated the prevailing free market orthodoxy. The objective was to limit and democratize the 'irresponsible power of British financial capital',[31] in order to achieve the social-democratic objective of rebalancing the relationship between capital and society. This would embed a commitment to social justice and the promotion of the community, rather than simply the private interest, at the heart of the nation's economic system.

Hutton's call for 'stakeholder democracy' or 'stakeholderism' attracted many on the Left but Shadow Chancellor Gordon Brown was unhappy with it.[32] He suspected that it would conflict with his commitment to 'business-friendly' policies[33] and continued to look to the USA for inspiration. All the same, the concept of stakeholder democracy had made such a favourable impression on the British liberal-left that it could not be easily discarded. Blair and close advisers such as Geoff Mulgan and Roger Liddle therefore proceeded to appropriate the terminology while emptying it of any meaning consistent with the ideas which Hutton had been promoting. Rather than focus on reforming the nation's industrial and financial structure, they now spoke about 'giving every individual a stake in society'. As Thompson has observed, individualistic aspirations and endeavour were now placed 'centre-stage'; the stakeholder society, for New Labour, was 'about giving individuals the opportunity … to earn and get on'. Hutton's ideas for the reform of corporate governance were brushed aside by the argument that people wanted 'real shares' in the companies they worked for rather than some 'ill-defined role' in decision-making. Companies were responsible first and foremost to their shareholders and were obliged to deliver 'shareholder value'.[34] It was hard to see how any Thatcherite could have disagreed with these views, which amounted to an endorsement of the crusade for shareholder democracy and popular capitalism led by the Conservative administrations after 1979.

Clearly, the Third Way did not involve a radical rebalancing of the relationship between capital and society. It did, however, amount to a historic fracture with the history and development of socialism and social democratic movements. Throughout western Europe, these had become politically formidable, as mass organizations and Parliamentary parties, from the late nineteenth century. As the historian David Thomson has argued, this had been the era when nationalism became socialized and socialism became nationalized. Prior to that conjuncture, socialism, its intellectual roots in liberalism, had been internationalist largely because liberalism was internationalist: but 'in an era of nation-states, it was bound to become more nationalistic'.[35] Parliamentary socialist movements, including the Labour Party, were inevitably nationalist in character. They were, after all, accountable to national electorates. The resulting political formations were highly successful. The reformist programmes they pursued in the era up to the 1980s, centring on the construction of welfare states, the reduction of social and economic inequality, public ownership of key industries and State-led planning to deliver full employment and economic growth, could not have been delivered in the absence of reliance on the power and resources of the modern nation-state. In Britain this connection was severed thanks to New Labour's embrace of the economic liberalism of the Third Way, creating a version of social democracy incapable of challenging the power of domestic or global capital since its objectives could not be achieved without the co-operation of either.

The size of the electoral landslide in 1997, combined with a respectable turnout of 72 per cent, indicates that the magnitude of what had happened to the British Left was not at first wholly apparent. Blair succeeded in rebuilding the coalition embracing working-class voters and the professions (lawyers, doctors, teachers, university and college lecturers, research and applied scientists) which had helped Labour win in 1945, 1964 and 1966. Many of them were voting out of a dissatisfaction with the Conservatives and Thatcherism more profound than that which was felt by the New Labour establishment, and they were more willing than Blair and Brown to see substantial increases in public spending even if this meant higher taxation.[36] On the surface it is perhaps surprising that there could have been such expectations following the fairly comprehensive ideological refurbishment of Labour for which the Blair leadership had been responsible. But it is quite possible that those who were uneasy with the commitment to neo-liberalism and with the repudiation of many policies and much of the philosophy which had characterized Old Labour were reassured by the insistence that New Labour was committed to the 'traditional (Labour) values in a modern setting',[37] especially when this claim was made by totemic figures rooted in the Party's working-class base such as Deputy Leader John Prescott. Yet disenchantment grew over the subsequent years, leaving Tony Benn to claim, with some plausibility, that 'it could truthfully be said for the first time in history that the public was to the left of a Labour government'.[38]

Blair's Britain

The new administration rapidly embarked on its programme of constitutional modernization. It reduced the number of hereditary peers entitled to sit in the House of Lords by over 600 and passed legislation which enabled public votes to be held on the establishment of locally accountable decision-making institutions in Edinburgh, Cardiff and Belfast. Referendums were held in 1997 and 1998, resulting in the creation of the Scottish Parliament, the National Assembly for Wales and the Northern Ireland Assembly. All were up and running by the start of the new century, although the extent of the powers wielded by the new institutions has remained a subject for political debate ever since.

The Blair government also lost no time in the implementation of its economic and social programme. It quickly signed up to the Social Chapter and established a Low Pay Commission, with members drawn from business, the unions and the academic world, to determine an appropriate level for a National Minimum Wage (finally introduced in 1999). The government was true to its word on industrial relations reforms, leaving most of the Conservative legislation in place but introducing procedures for statutory recognition. New Labour also stuck by the commitment to retain the Conservatives' spending projections. The period from 1997 up to 2000 saw fiscal austerity, notwithstanding that Kenneth Clarke called the plans 'eye watering' and admitted that he would never have kept to them himself.[39] Brown repeatedly made it clear that he was determined to avoid any return to 'Tory boom and bust'[40] and eschewed attempts to increase demand, arguing that the existence of near full employment meant the economy was threatened by inflationary pressures.

Brown moved quickly to put in place policies intended to provide long-term macroeconomic stability, providing the private sector with the confidence to raise levels of investment in new plant and equipment, raising output and improving competitiveness so that the economy would achieve sustainable expansion over the long term. The rationale was neo-liberal and had been fundamental to economic policy in both the Thatcher and the Reagan administrations. To this end he established a new framework of monetary and fiscal policy. This framework included price stability, based on an inflation target of 2.5 per cent per annum, and a rules-based approach to the public finances. There were two of these rules. First was the 'golden rule', which required governments to balance current expenditure over the cycle out of tax and other income, with borrowing permitted only for capital investment programmes. Secondly, there was the 'sustainable investment rule', which required that public sector debt should remain at 'a stable and prudent level', defined as 40 per cent of the GDP.[41] Running in parallel with these fiscal rules was a change to the way monetary policy was to be formulated. This involved granting the Bank of England independence over the setting of interest rates. The task of managing what now became known as the 'official Bank rate' or 'Bank of England base rate' in order to ensure that inflation stayed close to its target became the responsibility of a Monetary Policy Committee (MPC), composed of nine members, five from the Bank and four outsiders distinguished by their experience as economists and bankers. The removal of the Chancellor's discretion over the setting of rates and the transfer of this duty to a group of experts was a clear sign that New Labour regarded low inflation as a higher priority than low unemployment. There was no doubt that Brown genuinely regarded this reform as conducive to macroeconomic stability; but it was also calculated to win the confidence of the financial markets – global, not just British – so that the new government did not suffer from the shocks and sterling crises experienced by Old Labour.[42]

The attempt to win the confidence of the markets was successful. Sterling appreciated on the foreign exchanges. This process was driven by the relatively high official Bank rate, which was raised after New Labour's victory and reached 7.5 per cent by June 1998. Rates in the EU were lower, and the European Central Bank (ECB), responsible for managing the new single currency (the euro, due to start operating from 1 January 1999) set the rate for the euro area at just 3 per cent between 1998 and 2000; it never exceeded the level of 4.5 per cent reached in 2001. The attractiveness of sterling to currency traders was enhanced by low inflation: indeed this undershot the target at times, falling below 2 per cent in 1999. The impact on the economy was mildly deflationary: there was a check to export growth, and the current account deficit, virtually eliminated by 1997, started to expand once again, reaching £6 billion in 1999 (2.4 per cent of GDP).[43] Manufacturing exports were hit especially hard, and by July 1998 the sector had slipped back into recession, with underlying output contracting for the first time since 1992.[44]

Despite calls in the press and within industry itself for a less hawkish approach to price stability, the Treasury was unmoved. Output in the financial and service sectors remained buoyant.[45] Cheap import costs resulting from the strong pound and falling global prices were sustaining consumer activity. Growth in 1998 fell just short of 3 per cent and then reached 3.8 per cent in 1999.[46] Unemployment continued to fall until it dropped just below 5 per cent in 2000, at which point it stabilized. It all led the Treasury to welcome the appreciating exchange rate on the grounds that in the prevailing economic circumstances it helped to contain inflation by restraining 'the net export contribution to demand'.[47] Over-performance on inflation trumped a healthy current account: the implication was that 'persistent current account deficits do not matter'.[48] This was the same position as had been taken in the Lawson years, a period which had not ended well. New Labour's political economy had led it to follow a similar set of priorities. These, too, were to prove very damaging to the economy, although their effect took a good deal longer to become apparent than during the Lawson boom.

Confidence in New Labour on the part of the markets was enhanced by its very cautious fiscal policy. As he had promised, Brown did not deviate from the Conservative spending projections, with government spending as a proportion of GDP falling to 36 per cent, its lowest level in forty years. The impact on the public sector was severe, especially in schools and hospitals, which continued to experience growing waiting lists.[49] The squeeze was, however, offset by revenue raising measures such as the windfall tax on public utilities, an increase in employers' national insurance contributions, and the auctioning of the next generation of mobile phone licenses, which provided the Treasury with £25 billion. The income was used to support the NHS and fund the establishment of two reforms central to New Labour's Third Way project. One was Britain's own version of workfare, called (somewhat disingenuously) the 'New Deal' and welcomed by Brown as offering the 'most ambitious programme of employment opportunities our country has seen'.[50] Initially focusing on 18–25 year olds, its range was extended to cover older workers, single parents and the disabled. Its aim was to provide those who had been out of work and in receipt of unemployment benefit (called Jobseeker's allowance since 1995) with training, subsidized employment and voluntary work placements. Those deemed guilty of refusing work opportunities faced the withdrawal of their benefit. The second was the Working Families' Tax Credit (WFTC), introduced to ensure that families with one child or more, in which one or both parents worked over sixteen hours per week, received a guaranteed minimum income of £200 per week.[51]

On one level the tax credit policy was entirely in the tradition of the social-democratic reforms passed by previous Labour governments. It was part of a range of measures intended to reduce child poverty in Britain. With 3.4 million children living in poverty by the end of the 1990s, Britain had the third highest level of child poverty among developed nations and the highest in Europe.[52] The government's ambition was to eliminate this altogether by 2020. The WFTC worked in conjunction with a set of other initiatives, all intended to deliver this result. The most significant of these were the Sure Start programme, designed to provide support for poor families with very young children; the National Childcare Strategy, established to ensure that access to affordable and good child care was available in every neighbourhood; and investment targeted on ethnic minorities, many of which suffered from lack of opportunity and social disadvantage.

In other ways, however, the overall trajectory of these reforms distanced the government from social democracy: they represented a break with its tradition that all citizens had universal rights linked to needs. They were more evidence of New Labour's common ground with the Clinton Democrats and were based on the conviction that 'the poor must work' and that if they did so they would receive support, but if they failed to play by these rules they 'must accept individual responsibility' for their poverty and exclusion from society.[53] The measures reverted to the distinction between the 'deserving' and the 'undeserving' poor which had been common in Victorian Britain. They were inspired by 'the political economy of the independent individual fired by the ideals of self-help, self-improvement, thrift and upward social mobility' and revealed the depth of New Labour's debt to the nineteenth-century liberal tradition rediscovered by Thatcher and the Right.[54]

Pursuit of more orthodox social-democratic policies in conjunction with the enthusiasm for inflation targeting, low taxes and workfare did not start until 1999–2000. At this point, with the two-year moratorium on spending having lapsed and the government running a budget surplus (worth 1.9 per cent of national income in 2000–2001)[55], the Chancellor launched what he called an 'unprecedented programme of public investment'. This gathered momentum over the next two years, and in his 2002 Budget, Brown unveiled plans to invest £100 billion in the public services, especially on education and the NHS (where the objective was to raise the level of expenditure as a proportion of GDP from 6.8 per cent to 8 per cent, the European average).[56] A genuine refurbishment of the public sector followed as all public spending rose in real terms by 2.75 per cent between 2002 and 2005, investment in health and education increasing by 5.5 per cent over the same period. There were major programmes of hospital and school construction and renewal of university buildings and infrastructure, along with an expansion of recruitment covering doctors, nurses, teachers and university staff. Between 1998 and 2003 more than 500,000 jobs were created in the public sector.[57]

New Labour's modernization of the public sector outstripped the best efforts in this field of previous administrations and amounted to a real break with the Thatcher era, when private affluence had taken priority over the renewal of the public sector even if this order of precedence had sometimes (notably regarding the NHS) been more rhetorical than real. The share of GDP taken by public spending increased, reaching 44 per cent of national output by 2005.[58] The motivation for the timing of this rise in spending was not Keynesian, but a function of electoral politics: there was a General Election in 2001 and the robust condition of the government finances facilitated electorally attractive spending programmes which did not require significant tax increases. It was therefore consistent with the political economy of the Third Way and achieved without any need to break the government's own fiscal rules.

All the same the impact of the spending was impeccably counter-cyclical, making Brown, in William Keegan's words, an 'accidental Keynesian'[59] (he was later to convert to a much more deliberate version). It offset the deflationary impact of the collapse of the dotcom boom in 2000. This had led to sharp falls of share prices along with a wave of bankruptcies and company restructurings, mostly in new firms linked to the internet and electronic communications. Growth between the first quarters of 2000 and 2001 fell back to 2.5 per cent; the following year saw this figure slip to 2.2 per cent, while unemployment, having fallen steadily to 4.9 per cent of the workforce in early 2001, now stabilized and rose to over 5 per cent. The injection of spending checked any further decline in the growth of national output while joblessness started to fall, albeit slowly, dropping beneath 5 per cent once again in 2005.[60]

There was, however, another dimension to this programme which did not reflect orthodox social democratic political economy. It opened up the public sector to private enterprise, first achieved through the use of the Private Finance Initiative (PFI) started by Kenneth Clarke when he was at the Treasury. Many of the projects commissioned by New Labour in Brown's programme were executed under the PFI, which established partnerships between the private sector and the State. PFI deals had been somewhat limited during Clarke's time but Brown relied heavily upon them. In March 2000 Labour announced that public projects worth £20 billion were to be privately financed by 2003.[61] These arrangements were in conformity with Blair and Brown's neo-liberal view that the private sector was inherently more efficient than the public because of its accountability to shareholders and the market, while keeping the up-front costs of public projects off government books by transferring their construction to consortia of private firms. This practice therefore left the private sector with the debt, expenditure and risk associated with the work. In return, each contract governing these deals would specify that the private consortium responsible for a given project would then receive funding from the State, usually over a 25 to 30 year period (after which time the project would come under public ownership), while providing agreed services which would otherwise have remained in the public sector. By 2004 there were 86 PFI schools projects in England, covering some 500 schools. Much of their new IT hardware (such as interactive whiteboards) was supplied by private corporations such as Hitachi and SMART, who also provided training and technical support.[62] Other agreements with private companies covered grounds maintenance, professional development and supply teaching.

PFI projects proved controversial and expensive. First, public sector unions protested that they created two-tier workforces as staff working in PFI-built hospitals and schools, or in other services formerly provided by local authorities, now found themselves employees of a private company or consortium. Contractual arrangements which could have disturbing implications for workers' conditions of service (often leading to unpaid overtime) and future security resulted as the employers sought to increase profit margins by reducing the pressure of labour costs and backing away from supporting workers' pension schemes.[63] Secondly, private firms tended to inflate the long-term cost of PFI deals to the State (and therefore the taxpayer) because they were often unable to raise funding for them as cheaply as the government. As early as April 2000 34 PFI-financed hospitals had been commissioned at a cost of £3.5 billion – while the bill for 6 publicly funded developments authorized at the same time amounted to £217 million.[64]

Blair's response to protests from the workforce was unsympathetic. He regarded public sector unions as organizations which saw their duty as beginning and ending with the protection of their members' pay and conditions of service, not as working with the State and local authorities to provide the best possible service to the public. 'Try getting change in the public sector and the public services. I bear the scars on my back after two years in government', he told the Venture Capitalists Association (many of whose members would tender for PFI contracts) in July 1999, echoing the Thatcherite view that the public sector and those who worked in it were among the last bastions of the corporatist (and therefore, according to this discourse) inefficient structures which governments after 1979 had sought to dismantle.[65]

The second major example of government enthusiasm for bringing private capital into the public sector was provided by its approach to education and the NHS. In 2000 the government passed the Learning and Skills Act, under which it became possible to establish new secondary schools known as 'academies'. These required private sponsors to provide £2 million of the £25 to £30 million needed to finance construction of a new school, which would then be administered not by the local authority but by a private trust such as the United Learning Trust or a corporation such as the construction firm Amey plc. The establishment of the programme reflected the conviction of Blair and of his (unelected) Education Minister Andrew Adonis[66] that schools would be more likely to flourish and achieve high academic standards if they had both the flexibility and the freedom to innovate which, it was argued, they did not possess while under the control of local education authorities. By 2010 there were over 200 academy schools in England.[67] Moreover, New Labour's faith in private providers even led to a limited number of cases in which they were employed to run local education authorities and schools deemed to be 'failing', in terms of their educational performance: by 2005 14 local authorities had seen their educational responsibilities contracted out to private sector or not-for-profit trusts.[68]

The government's reliance on the market was even more evident when it came to the NHS. John Major's administration had taken some limited steps towards the creation of an internal market in the health service, in which the roles of purchaser and provider were separated. District Health Authorities (DHAs) became main purchasers, able to buy hospital and community health services from a range of public, private or voluntary providers (though in practice most providers were in the public sector). In 2002 New Labour replaced the DHAs with Primary Care Trusts (PCTS), which took over their predecessors' function as commissioning bodies. In the same year private treatment centres, undertaking routine surgery and diagnostic work, were allowed to compete with NHS providers. This was an indication of the government's conviction that only competition between providers would drive up standards, lead to more rapid and effective treatment for patients and ensure that the new resources it was injecting into the system would not be wasted. A system of payment by results was introduced, with money following the patients, so that the most heavily used providers received the heaviest financial support; it was a reform under which patients were seen as customers, with the democracy of individual choice intended to determine the most efficient allocation of resources throughout the NHS.

Labour's investment and the pro-market innovations accompanying it did achieve changes. There was more rapid treatment of patients and a shrinking of waiting lists. Recruitment of nurses and doctors increased and there was a much-needed modernization of the nation's hospitals, in terms of buildings and medical and research facilities. On the other hand the turn to the market, in which care for patients – especially those with long-term conditions – was often shared between a variety of different suppliers, could undermine 'continuity of multidisciplinary care'.[69] It also tended to reinforce inequalities within the system: money flowed to areas already well resourced rather than to parts of it struggling with funding problems, threatening to destabilize local health economies in the process.[70] It was, therefore, not invariably evident that the marketization of public services delivered optimum results.

Despite these problems, New Labour's public spending programme did lead to a substantial refurbishment of the public sector. At the same time the government's social policy measures, focused on Sure Start, the National Childcare Strategy and tax credits, made a real impact on child poverty: statistics from the Child Poverty Action Group showed a net reduction of 600,000 by 2008–09. These achievements owed much to the government's ability to sustain uninterrupted economic growth, untroubled by inflation (the annual rate remained below 4 per cent until the end of 2006) or recession throughout the period up to 2007. There were occasional quarters which saw low growth (and one of zero in 2004) but economic output rose each year between 1997 and 2007, reaching an annual average level of 2.89 per cent.

This record was not matched by any other European country (although the US economy expanded at an average 3 per cent per annum over the same period).[71] It represented an improvement on the growth performance of all governments since 1964 and generated high levels of employment along with a private sector net rate of return worth 15 per cent of GDP by 2006–07, as high as it had been in the affluent 1950s.[72] This in turn led to buoyant tax revenues which were ploughed back into the modernization of the welfare state and ensured that the government met its fiscal rules. Living standards rose, with real household disposable incomes increasing by an average 2 per cent each year between 1996–97 and 2007–08.[73] The prosperity of these years, combined with ongoing splits over Europe in the Conservative party, ensured Labour was returned to power in 2001 and 2005, achieving not just its longest ever period in office but three successive Parliamentary majorities. When Brown succeeded Blair as Prime Minister he enjoyed a high reputation at home and abroad as the author of what Bank of England Governor Mervyn King termed Britain's 'NICE' (non-inflationary, consistently expansionary) decade. The political economy of the Third Way had, indeed, been a period free from 'boom and bust'; the evidence suggested that Britain was a better country to live in than it had been in 1997.

Fracture

New Labour's record was in fact a good deal more problematic than appearances suggested. The geographic, social and economic fracture which had opened up between Producer's and Consumer's Britain after 1979 continued to widen throughout the decade after 1997. The 2005 General Election confirmed the Conservatives' position as mainly an English party; they won 189 of their 198 seats in that country and (narrowly) won a larger share of the popular vote there. In 2007 the impression that the component parts of the UK were heading in very different political directions found expression in two significant political developments, neither of which could have occurred in the absence of New Labour's constitutional reforms. Elections to the Scottish and Welsh Assemblies saw the Scottish National Party (SNP) take power within the Scottish Assembly, albeit as a minority government, while in Cardiff the polls delivered a Labour-Plaid Cymru (PC: the Party of Wales) Coalition in the Welsh Assembly Government.

These developments shook the Labour Party, which had enjoyed uninterrupted power in both Scotland and Wales since the first devolved elections in 1999. But now the nationalists, especially in Scotland, had brought this period of dominance to an end and in doing so had drawn a line under an era of Labour political and cultural hegemony which dated back to before the First World War. Given that both the SNP and PC advocated independence within the EU for their respective nations the outcomes in Edinburgh and Cardiff suggested that the future of the Union itself had now become uncertain. There was clear evidence from the results in Scotland that working-class voters were turning away from Labour and towards the SNP in large numbers. Labour's retreat was less dramatic in Wales, but the result was a serious setback. Its core vote weakened, with losses in what had once been safe seats such as Blaenau Gwent and Llanelli, both characterized by large working-class populations rooted in the old coal fields and in the steel industry.

A number of factors accounted for the rise of the nationalist vote. Weak leadership, a donations scandal, personality clashes and party in-fighting were often cited to explain the defeat in Scotland, while it was suggested that the Welsh setback was partly the result of political indifference on the part of voters and partly a function of the disillusionment caused by the invasion of Iraq four years earlier. These may have been influential, but in Scotland at least a deeper process was at work. The SNP was starting to replace Labour as a party of the Left. Under the leadership of Alex Salmond the SNP entered the 2007 elections committed to a programme likely to appeal to many in the Labour Party. It advocated indicative planning led by the government in Edinburgh, support for environmental improvement, the rejection of nuclear power in favour of alternatives such as hydro-electric and wind power, spending on the country's infrastructure, greater public investment in health (to abolish prescription charges and avert the closure of Accident and Emergency Departments) and an end both to PFI deals and to private sector involvement in the provision of NHS services. It also opposed the stationing of Britain's submarine-launched nuclear deterrent, the Trident missile system, on the Scottish west coast.

The SNP's turn to the Left made it attractive not just to Labour voters but to public intellectuals such as the historian Christopher Harvie (who had historically helped to develop Labour's policies and philosophy) and Neal Ascherson who had not been sympathisers in the past. Once known as the party of 'tartan Tories', given its strong position in the rural Highlands, the SNP had moved since the 1970s to promote what its supporters called 'progressive nationalism'. Separatism, fuelled by the poll tax fiasco and industrial decline, became increasingly appealing to a growing section of the Scottish electorate. It steered clear of xenophobia and preoccupation with ethnicity and 'made a reverse takeover of the social democratic consensus that Labour presided over for the past half century'[74], until its conversion to neo-liberalism and the Third Way under Blair and Brown. The SNP's strategy bore even more spectacular fruit in 2011, when the party won an extra 23 seats and formed a majority government pledged to offer the Scottish people a referendum on whether or not the nation should become independent or remain in the UK. The commitment was honoured in 2014, when the separatist option was defeated after a hard fought campaign by 55 per cent to 45 per cent (on an 84 per cent turnout).

The advance of the SNP, along with Labour's retreat in Wales, signalled growing disillusionment with the results of New Labour's neo-liberal policies within Producer's Britain. Given New Labour's record on the economy, public spending and social justice, this may seem surprising. The reality, however, is that New Labour's economic strategy was in its essentials a continuation of the one introduced after 1979 and therefore simply accelerated many of the structural changes which had become apparent in the Thatcher era. Since the effects of these changes were most dramatic in Britain's old industrial heartlands it is not surprising that a political reaction against Labour began to develop there. By 2008–10 this was becoming apparent not only in Scotland and Wales but in parts of England as well, with evidence that a significant minority of working-class voters there were defecting to the populist and anti-EU UK Independence Party (UKIP): in the 2009 European elections UKIP, with 16.5 per cent of the vote, came second to the Conservatives while Labour dropped to third, with 15.7 per cent.[75]

The British economy grew during the New Labour era but the growth was unbalanced. Labour policies encouraged the bias towards the financial and service sectors and away from industry which had become pronounced since the 1980s (apart from during the short interlude during Major's premiership when this process had been checked). Indeed, right from the start the Blair governments had taken the liberal economic view that Britain should no longer attempt to compete with the newly industrialized nations in Eastern Europe or East Asia (such as China, Korea or Malaysia) in the large-scale manufacturing of products such as cars (the government did not intervene to save Rover, the country's last high volume car producer, after its collapse in 2004), electronics, ships and steel. The ability of these nations to mass produce such items at low cost made competition with them impossible for developed economies where capital, labour and overheads were relatively expensive. The government believed this to be another reason why the party needed to turn its back on Old Labour, with its commitment to industrial modernization and strategies to improve the range and quality of British manufacturing.

Indeed the Blair governments displayed less interest in manufacturing than in 'the knowledge economy', defined as 'Production and services based on knowledge-intensive activities that contribute to an accelerated pace of technical and scientific advance, as well as rapid obsolescence', with the 'key component' being 'greater reliance on intellectual capabilities than on physical inputs or natural resources'.[76] It followed that Blair and Brown placed a high priority on creating a congenial environment for the financial sector and backed government assistance, mainly through support for research and development, for areas such as biotechnology and pharmaceuticals. This was paralleled by willingness to assist 'cool Britannia', namely the cultural industries, notably films, sport and music, through tax concessions. Indeed by 2006 sport, along with merchandising, income associated with television coverage of sporting events, travel and gambling, took 3 per cent of the nation's GDP.[77] As in the Thatcher era, the one exception to this pro-market approach was the aerospace industry. This was protected, for three main reasons. First of all its links to the defence sector ensured its importance as a crucial part of the British military contribution to the Atlantic alliance. Secondly, its exports provided significant amounts of foreign exchange (£5 billion in 1998) and, under the Al Yamamah agreements with Saudi Arabia, helped to sustain the inflow of cheap oil. Thirdly, it supported 440,000 jobs: not even a government committed to free market policies could ignore the economic, social (and political) benefits of employment generation on this scale.[78]

Above and beyond the knowledge economy and 'cool Britannia', it was the financial sector of the economy which benefited most from New Labour. Banks, finance firms and insurance companies dominated the list of Britain's 40 largest public companies. The Royal Bank of Scotland (RBS), Barclays and Halifax Bank of Scotland (HBOS) and the Hong Kong and Shanghai Banking Corporation (HSBC) were all in the top ten. The leader was HSBC, also the fourth largest global banking group.[79] These organizations, dealing not only in traditional high-street banking but in the global investment and securities market, helped the City attract lucrative business, enhancing its position as one of the world's most important international financial centres. By 2007 over 40 per cent of the world's foreign equities were traded in the City of London, more than on Wall Street, along with almost one-third of the world's foreign exchange transactions, a larger fraction than the combined share of New York and Tokyo.[80]

Government policies encouraged this commerce: its approach was based on a permissive culture known as 'light-touch regulation' designed to facilitate both an expansion of business in London and an inflow of overseas capital. One example of this was Brown's 'Better Regulation' plan, announced in 2005 and intended to cut by one million the number of company inspections by government departments, including those conducted by HM Revenue and Customs (HMRC) and the Financial Services Authority (FSA), the latter established to supervise the banking industry after the collapse of Barings in 1995. The approach to be followed was 'risk based', in other words based on the assumption that banks and businesses if left unregulated would behave responsibly, and subject to scrutiny only upon evidence of malpractice or failure.[81] This was supplemented by the conviction that regulators should not attempt to rule on the economic value or security of financial innovations, but leave this to the market.[82] Another example of 'light-touch regulation' was the replacement of the standard relationship between HMRC and large corporations. First, staff cutbacks reduced the numbers responsible for these organizations, so that by 2009 HMRC's Large Business Service was employing just 600 members to cover '700 groups of companies' (a large multinational had the resources to employ one hundred lawyers for just one tax case).[83] Secondly, the government insisted that multinationals and banks were now to be seen as 'customers'. Once the responsibility of 'case directors' they were assigned to 'customer relations managers' seeking to promote a happy relationship in which businesses would pay their taxes voluntarily, with threats (and cases) of litigation relegated to history.

This business-friendly strategy encouraged the development of tax evasion on a spectacular scale. Shaxson records how a UK Parliamentary Committee found in October 2008 that 25 per cent of all British multinational firms paid no corporation tax at all in 2005–06.[84] The £200 billion held in London by 'non-resident domiciled' billionaires yielded just £20 million for the Inland Revenue in 2006.[85] Banks used 'Special Purpose Vehicles' (SPVs) to reduce their tax liabilities. By April 2009 Barclays had 315 of these, which were essentially legally independent subsidiaries, established in tax havens, borrowing money and then re-lending it at a profit. Thanks to their location and status under the law SPVs were able to conduct their operations off balance sheet, leaving the parent institution free from the obligation of paying tax on them. Much of the capital held by the SPVs and other financial institutions based in tax havens, along with the business involved in handling it, was channelled to the City of London. In the second quarter of 2009 there was a net flow of funds to the City worth $332.5 billion from the three Crown Dependencies of Guernsey, Jersey and the Isle of Man; in 2007 it was estimated that *these islands alone* were home to $1 trillion 'of potentially tax evading assets', with the scale of tax evasion on these funds amounting to $30 billion each year (twice the size of the UK's overseas aid budget).[86] Other leading tax havens were the British Overseas Territories of Bermuda, the Bahamas and the Cayman Islands. Indeed, by 2009 37 per cent of all the world's banking assets were located in this network of tax havens based in the Crown Dependencies, the remaining parts of the British Empire and former colonies such as Hong Kong; given that the City held another 11 per cent, Britain's financial empire accounted for almost half of the global total.[87]

Money flooded into London, swelling the balance sheets of UK banks as a result. In 1970 these had amounted to 50 per cent of the nation's GDP; by 2000 they exceeded it by a multiple of five.[88] This vast reservoir of capital could be drawn on for investment in the domestic economy or recycled through Britain's network of offshore satellites to finance luxury hotels and office blocks in the Gulf States, condominiums in Brazil and the expansion of the housing market in the USA.[89] Very little of this money was invested in industry. Some 75 per cent of net lending by banks to domestic enterprise was destined for mortgages and commercial property, helping to create an asset bubble in the process, while just 3 per cent went to manufacturing.[90] The profits from this activity financed huge bonuses for bankers, which increased from an annual average of £10 billion between 2000 and 2007 to £14 billion in 2010–11. This trend was accompanied by the ongoing rise of rentier capital, characterized in particular by mounting real returns from investment in commercial and household property (through renting, leasing and speculation) driven by rising real estate values,[91] along with the development of a small group of the ultra rich: the 1,000 wealthiest Britons owned wealth worth £335 billion in 2010, a marked increase over the 1997 figure of £99 billion.[92]

New Labour's policies sustained the revival of Consumer's Britain, rooted in the old financial heart of British imperialism, which had started in 1979, generating extraordinary wealth for the financial sector and for many who worked within it. It was a development which reflected the rising profitability of financial sector firms in the UK over the previous decade, their share of total UK profits having steadily increased from 1 per cent in the 1950s and 1960s to 15 per cent by 2008.[93] Rather than attempt to redress this bias by developing strategies to encourage manufacturing industry, the government celebrated the expansion of the financial sector as an example of entrepreneurial capitalism at its most dynamic[94] and used the tax revenue it did collect from this area of the economy (in 2006–07 this had a net worth of £12.7 billion)[95] to finance its public spending and welfare policies. Although real domestic spending on manufacturing rose by 3.4 per cent between 1997 and 2005, domestic manufacturing production failed to rise at all during these years. Over the same period employment in manufacturing continued the rapid fall which had started in the Thatcher era, dropping by 3.5 per cent.[96] By 2011 it had fallen to 2.5 million (having been 6 million in 1979).[97] The share of GDP taken by manufacturing, slightly under 19 per cent in 1997, fell to 10.1 per cent by 2009.[98]

This shift away from manufacturing towards greater specialization in services was not, of course, unique to the UK: it was evident in most developed economies during the second half of the twentieth century and after. It reflected both the tendency of populations in the more affluent parts of the world to spend an increasing proportion of their incomes on services and the impact of competition with low-cost manufactured goods produced in the newly industrializing nations, estimated to have led to the loss of some 300,000 jobs in manufacturing in the UK between 1997 and 2005.[99] All the same, the scale of deindustrialization in the UK was greater than in most advanced economies, and the rate at which the process developed accelerated under New Labour. The trend was reflected in the deteriorating current account; having fallen back into the red in 1999 it stayed there thanks to the combination of rising home demand with a declining manufacturing base. This helped to suck in imports, and by the early 2000s the current account deficit was averaging 2 per cent of GDP, although this was a somewhat flattering figure given the favourable terms of trade (low import prices relative to export prices) enjoyed by the UK at this time.[100] The trade gap was covered by an inflow of foreign capital, purchasing UK assets such as the British Airports Authority (sold to the Spanish) and historic companies such as Pilkington Glass (sold to the Japanese) and ICI (sold to the Dutch), a process which brought more business to the City even as it reflected the decline of manufacturing.[101]

The evidence is clear: New Labour's policies neither slowed down (let alone reversed) deindustrialization nor reduced regional imbalances. The south of the UK, especially London and the Home Counties, enjoyed prosperity in the New Labour years. House building was concentrated here. There was significant investment in the transport infrastructure, with the construction of the high speed link from London to the Channel Tunnel, modernization of the London Tube and the Crossrail project.[102] New Labour might have derived its political support from the Labour Party's historic roots in Producer's Britain but its policies tended to favour middle class, professional and higher paid sections of the community in Consumer's Britain rather than the old working class and the areas where this was most concentrated.[103] Overall the Blair governments advanced the economic project of their Conservative predecessors in office, intensifying the social and regional divisions which these had created.

The impact of ongoing deindustrialization was most evident in Scotland, Wales, northern England and the Midlands. It exacerbated joblessness and social problems in these regions and was responsible for a shift in Britain's regional demographic balance. From the late 1980s up to 2000 the working age population of southern Britain had grown by 0.4 per cent but had fallen by 0.1 per cent in the old industrial regions. After 2000 there had been a 0.4 per cent rise in the size of the working age population of northern Britain; but the demographic decline of this area relative to the south continued, with the working age population here rising by 0.8 per cent. The difference between the two regions was especially evident when it came to employment opportunities for unskilled male workers, who were 20 per cent less likely to find work in the North East than in the South East.[104] The incidence of poverty and social deprivation increased away from southern England; single women with children found work difficult to find in Wales, the

Midlands and northern Britain. Overall, 33 per cent of them were unemployed by 2010.[105]

Neither the current account deficit nor regional imbalances led the government to deviate from its relaxed attitude to deindustrialization. A Treasury statement of 2004 argued that 'changes in the structure of employment and production are a necessary part of economic development', resulting from open trade, technological innovation and changing consumer choices.[106] A DTI paper on Manufacturing Strategy in 2002 offered little beyond a reassertion of New Labour's conviction that a prosperous manufacturing sector depended on macroeconomic stability, low inflation, tax incentives to encourage entrepreneurial activity and inward investment, and spending on education, skills, and R and D.[107] Although the government established Regional Development Agencies these had modest resources. Their work was dominated by a supply-side approach which looked for solutions to unemployment in training and skills initiatives and reforms to the labour market. They were not especially effective. There were no incentives to investment and employment typical of initiatives such as Regional Employment Premium in the 1960s and 1970s. In the end it was the government's public spending programme which achieved the best results in bringing jobs to the less prosperous parts of the UK.[108]

Quite apart from the geographic fractures scarring Britain, the country was divided by pronounced inequality, with 1 per cent of the population owning 13 per cent of its wealth, a pattern of distribution similar to the one found in the USA, where the richest 1 per cent owned 17 per cent of its wealth.[109] By 2009 the proportion of the labour force on low pay (in other words those receiving less than two-thirds of median earnings) was 20.6 per cent, second only to the USA (24.8 per cent) among leading economies.[110] The Blair years saw no restoration of labour's share of national output to what it had been before 1979. By 2007 it stood at just 53 per cent, held down by deindustrialization and falling trade union membership, which by 2007 was 7.6 million (just over 25 per cent of the workforce), and still declining, having peaked at 13.2 million (45 per cent of the workforce, in 1978).[111] Over the same period the portion of GDP taken by profits (the 'gross operating surplus') had risen from little more than 20 per cent to 28 per cent.[112] It is true there had been some redistribution towards the least well off 40 per cent of the population during the New Labour era, largely thanks to tax credits and in-work benefits which partially offset low pay; but comparisons with northern Europe revealed that during these years the UK remained 'one of the most inegalitarian of countries'.[113]

Bust

Unemployment remained low in the decade after 1997, the diminishing availability of jobs in industry being offset not just by more opportunities in finance and in the service sector, public as well as private, but by an expansion of self-employment. This was to be found especially in taxi-driving, construction, carpentry and fast-food outlets, whose number rose by 45 per cent between 1996 and 2014.[114] By 2008 there were 3.9 million self-employed workers in the UK, this proportion of the workforce having increased from 8.75 per cent in 1975 to 15 per cent in 2008.[115]

Conditions of high or full employment are normally associated with rising wage and salary levels. This did not happen to any great extent in the UK after 1997. Wages tended to be held down, for a number of reasons. First, there was the impact of de-unionization, which reduced the bargaining power of labour. Secondly, large numbers of public sector workers, notably those providing services such as cleaning, catering and rubbish collection for local government and the NHS, were subject to strict pay controls. Thirdly, the labour supply increased considerably over these years, thanks more to the government's encouragement of large-scale immigration (notably from east European countries such as Poland, which had recently joined the EU) than to an increasing birth rate. By 2010, 8 per cent of the labour force was foreign and there was evidence of social tension developing between locals and immigrants in some parts of the country.[116] Many of the immigrant workers were prepared to work for lower wages than their British counterparts, largely because relatively ungenerous remuneration in the UK still provided a higher standard of living than pay at home.[117] Fourthly, an increasing amount of the work people did tended to be casual, insecure and part-time. There was a tendency on the part of employers, especially in catering, agriculture, accommodation and support services (often in health and social care) to turn to zero hour contracts, in other words contracts which guaranteed staff no shifts but simply called upon them as and when businesses needed them.[118]

Downward pressure on pay and conditions went hand in hand with an acceleration of the neo-liberal revolution after 2000, a trend encouraged by the government. Notwithstanding its backing for British participation in the EU Social Chapter, it resisted subsequent efforts on the part of Brussels to improve working conditions, notably its efforts to protect part-time workers and the Working Time Directive which established maximum hours. In the end New Labour signed up to these reforms, but not before negotiating exemptions covering millions of workers.[119] It fought against initiatives which aimed at the regulation of the European labour market, advocating 'flexibility' and non-intervention, focusing instead on measures to improve competitiveness and the operations of the single market.

Alongside its defence of flexible accumulation, New Labour continued to support the participation of the private sector in secondary education and in the provision of health and social care in the NHS, along with pro-market reforms to higher education. Both Old Labour and One Nation Conservatism (of the type followed between 1951 and 1964 and 1970 and 1974) had taken the view that there were important areas of social and economic life which had no place in the private sector (although they disagreed on the scope of such an immunity). In rejecting this philosophy and identifying 'modernization' of the public sector with its subjection to the laws of the market, the government was working with the grain of mobile international capital, which in the developed world has tended to seek remunerative rates of return outside industrial production. Given the continuing low rate of return in this sector and aggregate global growth rates of little more than 1 per cent per annum after the 1970s, the Thatcher and Reagan revolutions notwithstanding,[120] it was looking to the rewards to be made from finance and from investment in new frontiers. These included not only music, culture and sport but history, heritage, health, sexuality, and personal 'life-style' (ranging all the way from personal trainers and bespoke holidays to tanning centres and nail bars). Seen in this light even marriage could appear as 'a short-term and contractual arrangement rather than as a sacred and unbreakable bond'.[121] All forms of human activity were ripe for commodification, and by the time Tony Blair stepped down from the Prime Ministership, it was clear that New Labour was comfortable with this process.

This turn in the nature of capitalism led to the shrinking of common rights in the face of advancing private ownership and the imperative of short-term profitability to satisfy shareholders. David Harvey has called this 'accumulation by dispossession'. In developing countries such as Brazil and Indonesia this can cover the illegal seizure of land from self-sufficient indigenous cultures so that it can be converted to intensive farming in order to produce crops for the world market. In developed nations such as the UK it has led, characteristically, to the transfer of public assets to the private sector and the erosion of rights won by workers after long struggles, including paid holidays and pensions.[122] In both the USA and the UK the first decade of the 21st century saw the disappearance of many final salary pension schemes, which were initially closed to new entrants prior to 'reforms' that reduced both their cost to the employers and the level of the benefits received by the workers who had been paying into them.[123] Notable examples were British Airways, HSBC and Sainsbury's. By 2002, 10 out of the 20 largest UK listed companies had closed their schemes to new employees.[124]

This process was given an unintentional helping hand by the government, which withdrew tax exemption from pension funds in 1997, but it became associated with one of the by-products of financialization, namely the rise of new financial intermediaries, such as private equity firms, commanding large pools of capital (typically drawn from sources such as public and corporate pension funds, insurance companies, wealthy individuals, endowments, foundations and sovereign wealth funds). These often invested in leveraged buyouts in which borrowed funds were used to purchase a company, with the assets of the corporation to be acquired being taken as collateral.[125] The need to repay debt in turn provided an incentive for the private equity firm to increase the return on its investment, leading to corporate rationalization including the closing of pension schemes. One such example was purchase of the pharmaceutical corporation Alliance Boots by Kohlberg Kravis Roberts in 2007, followed in 2010 by the winding up of the company's final salary pension scheme, covering 15,000 employees, 'to ensure the long-term sustainability of retirement savings'.[126]

The assault on pensions along with labour's falling share of output might have been expected to have generated deflationary pressures, resulting from loss of purchasing power across a large section of the community. This did not occur, with the economy remaining buoyant throughout the early years of the new century, thanks in part to the rise in public spending. However, the main reason for Britain's relatively robust growth after 2000 was a boom in property prices. Taking 1970 as a base of 100, these had reached 250 by 1990. They fell during the 1990s before climbing back to 250 by the end of the century. Thereafter they rose sharply, reaching a figure of 400 by 2005.[127] One explanation for this was the expansion of commercial activity in major cities, especially in London, where it received a shot in the arm from overseas investors keen to exploit the rising value of both commercial and residential accommodation and from profits made by firms in the City. A second was failure to build many new houses. This stemmed from planning regulations which inhibited private development and from a collapse in local authority house-building.

During the 1960s and 1970s over 300,000 houses had been built each year. The number slipped during the following decades, falling to less than 200,000 between 1991 and 2004. Councils had been responsible for over 100,000 new homes each year throughout the post-war period but made little contribution to new building after 1979. This was an effect of the tight controls on local authority spending stemming from the Thatcher government's determination to encourage private ownership and distrust for what it considered municipal socialism. When Brown succeeded Blair in 2007 he set a target of 240,000, but neither he nor subsequent governments came near this total: in fact housing construction under New Labour peaked in 2007 at 219,070. This was not enough to meet the requirements of a rising population, which went from just under 59 million in 2000 to 62.7 million in 2010.[128] With demand exceeding supply, local authority housing lists increased by 73 per cent between 1997 and 2007[129] and the average UK house price increased in real terms by 238 per cent, while average earnings (adjusted for inflation) rose by just 22 per cent over the same time.[130]

This tendency for property prices to increase much faster than incomes encouraged a dramatic expansion of credit, just as it had done in the 1980s. Once again household debt rather than income was used to finance the purchase of property. Confident that property prices would carry on rising, banks and building societies such as Northern Rock offered customers loans worth 125 per cent of the house which was acting as security.[131] Obtaining mortgages became extremely simple, with the development of 'self-certification', by which borrowers could take out home loans without having to verify their income. Between 2007 and 2010 almost half of all new mortgages fell into this category.[132] By 2007 lenders were offering first-time buyers, keen to start climbing the property ladder, mortgages six times the size of annual salary.[133] Rapidly rising asset values fed a substantial growth in borrowing, with debtors confident that the capital gains to be made from their property would more than compensate for modest pay and disappointing pension prospects. UK household debt in 2005 exceeded the nation's GDP and amounted to 180 per cent of annual disposable income; it remained high for the rest of the decade, falling only a few percentage points to 173 per cent by 2009.[134] The process drove a consumer boom as banks, supermarkets, building societies and charities all piled into the credit market.

There was widespread confidence that there would be no crash and re-run of what had happened at the end of the Lawson boom. This stemmed largely from the development of financial innovations which, it seemed, had taken risk out of capitalism. These were known as 'derivatives' and were contracts between two (or more) parties whose value was derived from an underlying asset. Derivatives covering property assets were very popular. This was a function of the securitization of property assets which had become noticeable after the sale of council houses during the 1980s. Banks were able to transfer their portfolio of mortgages to the SPVs established during the previous decade, a transaction which would apparently free them from the risk of default. The SPVs would then bundle these portfolios into collateralized debt obligations (CDOs), a range of securities which could be turned into bespoke packages and sold to other investors at different interest rates, reflecting different levels of risk (high risk paid high interest and low risk was less rewarding) in a process known as 'tranching'. The investors could then protect themselves by taking out an insurance policy, known as a credit default swap (CDS), in which international insurance corporations such as American International Group (AIG) would underwrite the CDOs against the possibility that they might turn bad.

All parties seemed to gain. The banks earned a fee by selling the mortgages to their own shell companies. The SPVs made a profit on the sale of the securitized loans and mortgages (with SPVs subject to zero, or minimal tax on the transactions thanks to their location in tax havens). The financial institutions which bought these assets could be confident that they were protected from any damage likely to arise from the failure of some borrowers to continue servicing their debts. They considered themselves covered not only by insurance in the form of the CDS but also simply because risk had been spread so widely thanks to the process of securitization and tranching. The insurance companies profited from the sale of CDSs; even though by the summer of 2008 AIG was insuring CDOs worth $440 billion without the collateral to cover them all, its confidence in the property market led it to continue looking for more business opportunities.[135]

The housing boom which drove so much of the trade in these novel financial arrangements had originated in the USA. There, the market for the extension of domestic mortgages was dramatically enlarged by the simple expedient of making them available to people lacking the financial means or job security which guaranteed they could keep paying them. This was not a healthy development. By 2007, with CDSs and CDOs being traded as securities on the global financial markets, there were many counterparties holding contracts exposed to the danger that the loans might turn very bad. On top of this nobody could be sure which institutions and individuals were likely to be worst hit in the event of a crash. Yet the existence of these 'sub-prime' mortgages was not regarded as a serious threat, partly because the element of risk seemed to have been eliminated and partly because of the continuing rise in property prices, which was becoming marked not just in the USA and the UK but also in western Europe. The prospects of profit, combined with easy access to credit, generated a dramatic escalation in the size of this business, which in June 2008 was estimated by the International Swaps and

Derivatives Association (ISDA) to have reached $54 trillion, not far from the sum total of the planet's GDP and considerably larger than the entire value 'of all the stocks and shares traded in the world'.[136]

A good part of this lucrative business was based in the City of London. Indeed it was the centre of the global trade in derivatives: Lanchester records that the average daily turnover in London in 'over-the-counter' derivatives (those directly traded between two counterparties without going through an exchange or other intermediary) reached an all-time high of $2.105 trillion every day in 2007, while the equivalent figure for all derivatives in New York was $959 billion.[137] AIG preferred 'light-touch' London to New York, establishing the office which wrote out all the company's CDSs there.[138] British banks such as Barclays, HSBC, Lloyds TSB and RBS expanded dramatically, making large profits and acquiring extensive assets through the trade in securities. By 2008 the leverage ratio (defined by Lanchester as the multiple by which assets exceeded equity, with equity representing net worth)[139] in these organizations was 61.3:1 (Barclays), 20:1 (HSBC), 34:1 (Lloyds TSB) and 18.8:1 for RBS. In the same year the total assets held by RBS amounted to £1.9 trillion. This figure not only exceeded the UK GDP (£1.7 trillion) but made RBS larger (in terms of its assets) than any other company in the world. It all meant that only a rather modest fraction of the assets held by each bank (a very modest one of 1/61.3 in the case of Barclays) needed to turn bad for the institution to become insolvent.[140]

Those who argued that there was no reason why this merry-go-round should stop were ignoring a fundamental problem which had caused the collapse of the Lawson boom at the end of the 1980s: it was not possible for debt to continue growing faster than income. Signs of strain in the housing market were becoming evident, with increasing numbers of borrowers struggling to repay their mortgages. By 2007–08 there was evidence that a shift in the international economic climate was putting consumers under further pressure. Commodity prices started to increase sharply as a result of rising global economic activity. Oil, just $10 per barrel in 1999, had risen to $150 per barrel in 2008, with escalating fuel costs helping to push the annual rate of inflation over 4 per cent for the first time since 1991. UK housing repossessions jumped from 25,900 in 2007 to 40,000 in 2008.[141] By 2007–08 sales of new homes in the USA, which had peaked in 2005, were in decline. Growing numbers of sub-prime borrowers were unable to meet the rising energy costs, and defaulted on their mortgages. Property prices started to fall. In the USA they dropped by 5 per cent between the second quarter of 2007 and the second quarter of 2008;[142] in the UK they slid by 10.3 per cent between the third quarter of 2007 and the third quarter of 2008.[143] By the start of autumn 2008 experts were predicting that property values could fall by as much as 30 per cent.[144]

Falling property prices led to turbulence in the international financial system. This spread across the markets thanks to the very innovations, notably the CDSs and CDOs, which were supposed to prevent such a contingency; these were now exposed as massive liabilities. A number of major US companies announced losses from exposure to sub-prime loans. In August 2007 the French bank Paribas suspended trading in three asset-backed securities funds as a result of 'The complete evaporation of liquidity in certain market segments of the US securitization market'.[145] In Britain, Northern Rock was the first major financial institution to feel the impact of this rapid slowdown in the property market. As asset values started to slide it found raising money from other financial institutions to fund its mortgage business increasingly difficult.[146] The Bank of England, acting as lender of last resort, pumped liquidity into the company. When news about what was happening leaked out there was a run on the bank, with depositors queuing in the streets to retrieve their savings, a phenomenon not seen in Britain since the failure of the City of Glasgow Bank in 1878.[147] The government tried to find buyers willing and able to rescue Northern Rock but no bank would take it on unless the government took over all its liabilities first. No market-led solution to Northern Rock's problems was in fact feasible, and early in 2008 the government agreed to take it into public ownership (the bailout cost £25 billion) to prevent a bank failure which would have left depositors ruined and spread rising fear throughout the financial system.[148] The deed marked the start of a dramatic return to the interventionism of Old Labour which the government only undertook with very considerable reluctance. However, its hand was forced by the rapidly deepening crisis, which initially seemed to be at its most severe in the USA.

During the spring of 2008 the investment bank Bear Stearns collapsed. In September the US Federal Government took over Fannie Mae and Freddie Mac, the government-sponsored mortgage finance corporations which owned or guaranteed over half of all home loans on the American housing market.[149] AIG, now facing a flood of CDS claims, was unable to cover all the bad assets it had insured: it collapsed. It was rescued at the cost of $173 billion to the American taxpayer. On 15 September the investment bankers Lehman Brothers failed. Lehmans conducted 50 per cent of its trade through its London subsidiary and had become heavily exposed to the property market, a fact disguised by accounting practices legal in the City but not in New York.[150] There was no Federal rescue package for Lehmans: the failure of one to appear brought the crisis to a head. Inter-bank lending had been slowing throughout the year, largely on account of (justifiable) anxieties on the part of banks that any credit they provided might end up in the hands of an institution holding asset-backed securities which had become toxic, leaving it unable to repay any loans. The freezing up of inter-bank lending accelerated after the failure of Lehmans thanks to fear throughout the financial community that the US government had now decided to take no action if any more banks followed it into bankruptcy. There was an increasing danger that credit would dry up, leaving banks and businesses unable to continue.

The fate of Northern Rock had illustrated that British banks could not be insulated from the crisis. Chancellor of the Exchequer Alistair Darling warned that the nation was facing 'arguably the worst' economic downturn in 60 years.[151] By the spring and summer the effects of this downturn were becoming evident. Given that inter-bank lending is central to the flow of liquidity around the financial system and economic activity in general, its marked deceleration in 2008 was bound to affect national output. Indeed, this ended 2008 at 0.6 per cent down on its level the previous year, bringing a conclusion to sixteen successive years of growth. Investment and consumption fell back sharply from the second quarter of the year, as easy access to credit disappeared and deleveraging grew. Fund managers switched their lending away from banks into government bonds and national debt. In an effort to recycle this money back into circulation the Bank of England announced on 9 October a £250 billion guarantee for short and medium term debt issued by the banks.

This was not enough to prevent a development which threatened to bring about the collapse of the entire financial system. Leading banks, notably HBOS, Barclays and RBS were now in great difficulty. HBOS launched a £4 billion rights issue in July in an effort to boost its capital but the operation failed. The setback left HBOS dependent on the increasingly sclerotic wholesale banking market, especially in the USA, which it had already drawn on for support earlier in the year. It proved close to impossible to repeat this after the collapse of Lehmans: on 16 September the price of HBOS shares collapsed, losing 33 per cent of their value in a single day.[152] The government drafted in the smaller Lloyds TSB group, hoping that a rapid merger might rescue HBOS by increasing its capital, creating a giant bank holding 33 per cent of all UK mortgages.[153] The merger went ahead but HBOS's liabilities were so large that the rescue failed: by early October it was borrowing £16 billion per night just in order to survive into the following day.[154] Barclays, rumoured to be highly exposed to bad debts in the USA, also attempted an unsuccessful rights issue but in November 2008 managed to secure funding from Abu Dhabi and Qatar.

Meanwhile the plight of RBS was exacerbated by its purchase of the large Dutch bank ABN-AMRO late in 2007. The transaction put considerable pressure on the bank's reserves, which was intensified by severe losses resulting from the deteriorating mortgage finance and credit markets in the UK, USA and beyond. They forced RBS into a £5.9 billion write-down of its assets and the announcement of a £12 billion rights issue in April 2008 (the largest in British history at the time)[155] in an attempt to offset these losses. This venture failed and by October 2008 RBS, like HBOS, was on the point of failure. The price of its shares fell by 50 per cent, from £1.75 to £0.80, and dealing in them was suspended twice on the morning of 13 October. This was a clear indication that the bank itself was about to fail, a position confirmed when the RBS chairman Sir Tom McKillop told Darling that the bank would be forced to cease trading within hours. 'It's going bust this afternoon', said Darling to his officials.[156]

This was a dire prospect. The failure of a major bank like RBS would paralyse the financial system. All deposits held by RBS would become inaccessible. It would be unable to extend loans. The size of the bank meant that its collapse would lead to the drying-up of credit and liquidity throughout the economy. HBOS would quickly follow RBS into insolvency. Cash machines would soon cease to operate, 'cheques would not be honoured, people would not be paid'. How would shops be able to continue trading once they had run down their stocks? What would happen to the availability of food and fuel supplies? In any case how would consumers be able to purchase these if they had no money? What would be the implications for social stability? Moreover, given the size and international reach of RBS there was every chance that 'the banking system would freeze, not just in the UK but around the globe'.[157] Clearly, this situation had to be avoided. This crisis was the most serious one faced by the global economy since the onset of the Slump in 1929. For Britain it was even graver than this, since throughout the depression of the late 1920s and early 1930s there had at least been no anxiety that the banking system was in danger of collapse. Yet this was now the upshot of thirty years of neo-liberalism.

The free market revolution started by the Thatcher governments in 1979 and embraced by New Labour in the 1990s had produced an economy characterized by growing social inequality and a rapidly shrinking manufacturing sector while finance and services expanded. By 2007–08 the current account was running a deficit worth 3.5 per cent of the GDP, not much less than what had been recorded at the peak of the Lawson boom in 1989.[158] Inflows of foreign capital had allowed the economy to evade the adjustment (and concomitant deflationary shock) otherwise unavoidable if it was to resume living within its means, while generous consumer credit arrangements and public spending had sustained demand and therefore growth. Just as in the 1980s, all this had been based largely on the belief that asset prices, notably property, would continue to rise indefinitely. With asset prices falling, however, money and credit started to disappear from the banks, leading to the crises at Northern Rock, Barclays, HBOS and RBS (as well as at a small number of building societies). As deleveraging replaced lending and output continued to drop (by the end of 2009 it was almost 6 per cent below its pre-crash peak in 2007), unemployment rose, from 5 per cent in 2007 to 8 per cent early in 2010. Government tax receipts declined and at the same time the foreign banks, funds, corporations and individuals whose money had covered Britain's external position began to sell their assets: sterling plunged on the foreign exchange markets, falling from £1 = 1.28 euros at the end of September to near parity by the end of the year. The economic correction had started.

Redux[159]

The government now moved very fast in order to prevent the situation precipitating a catastrophic breakdown of the financial system along with a collapse in output and employment. First of all it authorized the Bank of England to act as lender of last resort to keep RBS open, whatever the cost.[160] This was followed by more radical steps: the government injected £37 billion into RBS and HBOS, taking a 58 per cent share in RBS and 43 per cent in Lloyds TSB and HBOS (known as Lloyds Banking Group after the completion of the merger) in order to guarantee the banks' survival. Over the next year the public stake in both organizations increased, to 84 per cent in the case of RBS and 65 per cent with the Lloyds Banking Group, as a result of government concern that both would need additional capital to survive a recession which was expected to be severe and prolonged. It was feared that the trend of annual rates of growth would not be resumed until 2012, that unemployment would rise to 12 per cent and property prices would fall by 50 per cent.[161] By 2010 Northern Rock, the Bradford and Bingley and Dunfermline Building Societies and most of RBS and the Lloyds Banking Group were in public ownership. It all amounted to the most sweeping extension of nationalization since 1945 and, in practice at least, a complete repudiation of the neo-liberal political economy whose breakdown had ended up making a mockery of Brown's pledge to avoid any return to 'boom and bust'.

The nationalizations did not mark the government's conversion to the kind of radical socialist policies being advocated by the Labour left in its Alternative Economic Strategy of the mid 1970s, which called for public control of the financial system including an investment fund and public ownership of the four largest clearing banks.[162] Neither Brown nor Darling were interested in using the powers the State now possessed over the financial sector to direct investment into the reconstruction of manufacturing industry. Rather, their concern was recapitalization of the broken banks with State support, prior to their return to private ownership.[163] Yet the autumn of 2008 did mark a watershed in the life of the 1997–2010 Labour governments. From this point until the 2010 General Election the Brown administration turned back towards the social-democratic political economy of Old Labour; Keynesianism was back in fashion. Darling admits in his memoirs that he 'became hugely influenced' by the insight developed during *The General Theory of Employment, Interest and Money* that spending needed a stimulus if the risk of recession turning into profound and long-lasting depression was to be averted.[164]

This return to Old Labour was evident in two areas. One was macroeconomic strategy. The course was set by the 2008 Autumn Statement. With the Treasury forecasting a fall of 1.25 per cent in output over the coming year, the Chancellor abandoned New Labour's fiscal rules and determined to sustain economic activity via tax reductions (notably a 2.5 per cent cut in VAT) and the bringing forward of capital projects worth £3 billion (especially road building, school refurbishment and council house repairs). These measures were supplemented by monetary policy, which became increasingly expansionary. First of all the official bank rate was cut from 4.5 per cent to 3 per cent early in November 2008, before a series of further reductions saw it fall to 0.5 per cent by April 2009 (where it remained until August 2016). Given the gloomy outlook for the period from 2009–12 and the impossibility of any more substantial cuts in interest rates, it became necessary to reinforce this attempt to stimulate activity. The method chosen was quantitative easing (known as QE), by which the Bank of England increased the volume of money circulating in the economy by purchasing financial assets from the banks in return for cash. The banks were then expected to re-cycle this money into the real economy via loans to businesses and individuals. QE opened with a £200 billion asset purchase programme (most were UK government securities) in November 2009.[165]

Fiscal policy paralleled this expansionary approach, in the short term at least. The 2008 Autumn Statement announced a mild injection of public spending, worth £20 billion (slightly over 1 per cent of GDP) and a shift back towards the cautious industrial interventionism pursued by the Wilson–Callaghan governments in 1974–79. In July 2009 Brown announced a £1.1 billion railway electrification scheme.[166] Peter Mandelson, Secretary of State for Business, Innovation and Skills (the old DTI), admitted that New Labour had placed too much faith in the capacity of the financial sector to generate an increasing proportion of the nation's wealth, and that it was necessary to increase State support for manufacturing. The new, activist approach to industrial strategy was illustrated in the summer of 2009 with a £150 million package backing innovation in the aerospace industry (concentrated mostly on work to develop greener aircraft engines by Rolls Royce) and nuclear power.[167]

These initiatives were all set against a sharp increase in the government's borrowing requirement, expected to rise to £178 billion (12 per cent of GDP) in 2010[168] and in the national debt, predicted to shoot from 40 per cent of GDP before the crisis to 80 per cent by the end of the decade.[169] The 2009 budget saw more action to counter the recession, with a car scrappage scheme intended to boost car manufacturing, by which consumers received cash for trading in their old vehicles for new models; a job creation scheme for those in the 18–21 age bracket; and the extension of a stamp duty holiday announced in September of the previous year. Darling aimed to finance this in part from increases in national insurance contributions and in the top rate of taxation on incomes over £150,000 per annum (first to 45 per cent and then to 50 per cent),[170] leaving substantial fiscal tightening to reduce the budget deficit until after growth had resumed.[171]

The second area indicative of a return to the political economy of the post-1945 consensus was international economic policy. Britain was due to host a summit meeting for the governments and central bank governors of the world's twenty major economies in April 2009. Brown and Darling were keen for all parties to agree on a commitment to stimulate global economic activity via a substantial injection of liquidity into international financial institutions, so providing nations in deficit with the means to continue with economic expansion rather than turn to tariffs and deflation. This, in turn, would stimulate world trade, offset the powerful downward pressure on activity set off by the banking crisis and generate flows of capital which would begin to replenish reserves lost in the crash. The strategy was based on the Keynesian insight, basic to the establishment of the post-war global financial architecture agreed at Bretton Woods in 1944, that sustained national economic expansion required a congenial international environment. The era of free markets, deregulation and floating exchange rates which had flourished since the 1980s had led to the eclipse of efforts at co-ordinated international expansion;[172] the reassertion of this approach now was designed to avert the downward spiral of output, commerce and employment which had characterized the Slump some eighty years before.

The outcome was very positive. With Brown receiving the support of the new US President, Barack Obama, and the Chinese government, the summit agreed on a $1.1 trillion stimulus for the global economy.[173] This was to be composed of a $750 billion increase in the resources at the disposal of the IMF, along with $250 billion in finance to promote trade and $100 billion to fund economic development in the world's poorest nations. A 4 per cent increase in global output was expected to result from these measures. Alongside the financial commitments there was agreement on the need to introduce tighter regulation of bank capital requirements and on co-operation between governments to improve oversight of tax havens, private equity funds and hedge funds.

This was a triumph for Brown and led to a boost in Labour's standing in the opinion polls, which had fallen as the crisis intensified during 2007–08. The government had shown decisiveness and a clear sense of direction and had implemented a strategy which both addressed the fundamental problems raised by the crisis and was in tune with Old Labour's social-democratic traditions. Darling noted that 'we were beginning to develop a good story on the role of modern government in promoting growth';[174] from outside, Tony Benn commented that 'the Labour Party was being awakened by the crisis'.[175] Clear evidence that the government's strategy had worked emerged when the output figures for the third quarter of 2009 revealed that the economy had begun to grow again. Between then and the equivalent stage in 2010 it expanded by just under 2.6 per cent. A recovery had started.

Labour's revival was short-lived. The handling of the financial crisis notwithstanding, the government's reputation for competence and plain dealing suffered a series of shocks. These stemmed from the somewhat unsavoury conduct of certain members of the Prime Minister's entourage, a botched reshuffle, stories of dissension in the Cabinet and, above all, from revelations that many MPs were in the habit of making extravagant expenses claims. The impact of all this on public opinion was intensified by anxiety about the economic position, especially the government's deficit. Before and during the 2010 General Election campaign the Conservatives developed a narrative of the crisis in which the crash had been caused by Labour's fiscal irresponsibility. Opposition leader David Cameron and his Shadow Chancellor George Osborne claimed that Labour had 'maxed out Britain's credit card'. The accusation gained credibility in May 2009 when the distinguished US financial services company Standard and Poor's (S and P) placed the UK on 'negative watch'.[176] This meant that S and P considered there was a 50 per cent chance of the country's credit rating being downgraded, an eventuality which would result in an increase to the cost of government borrowing in the financial markets and one unlikely to be reversed in the absence of substantial public sector economies.

There certainly was reason to apportion some responsibility for the crisis to Labour, but its faults stemmed more from the party's conversion to neo-liberalism and the resulting cultivation of a non-interventionist, light touch approach to the financial sector and the management of the economy than from its public spending. However the Conservatives were never likely to lay the blame for the crash at the feet of neo-liberalism: to have done so would have involved a recantation of the ideology they had adopted over thirty years before and with which they had reinvented Britain so successfully that even Labour had bought into the project. For the Conservatives it made political sense to draw attention to the state of the public finances. During 2009–10 they warned that Britain was heading into the same territory as Greece, whose central government deficit had reached 15 per cent of GDP. That country was now in the midst of a sovereign debt crisis and finding it increasingly difficult to borrow money on the markets, except at increasingly prohibitive rates of interest. The warning legitimized Conservative leader Cameron and Shadow Chancellor Osborne's determination to embark on a course of fiscal austerity, reversing Britain's move back towards social democracy in the process. They argued that if Britain was going to avoid the fate of Greece it needed to retrench: the borrowing requirement had to be reduced, with cuts in government spending rather than tax increases the way to achieve this.

There was little basis for the comparisons between Britain and Greece. The British government was not having trouble raising funds while Greece's difficulties had been worsened by low growth since 2007–08 (a function of the crash, which hit receipts from tourism and shipping), and by low tax receipts (a problem intensified by widespread avoidance) combined with high government spending over decades.[177] During the election campaign the Tories made headway with their Greek parallel and criticisms of Labour's approach to public spending. Labour's retort, that it was too early in the recovery to embark on a radical approach to reducing government borrowing, made economic sense but proved hard to communicate to voters persuaded by the simplicity and directness of the Conservative message. Disenchantment with Labour was compounded by widespread press stories about 'social security scroungers' and by rising hostility to immigration in some English towns where the party had traditionally been able to rely on a strong working-class vote.

The evident unpopularity of Labour did not translate into a Conservative victory at the polls. Cameron had sought to modernize British Conservatism. The party remained committed to neo-liberalism but now took a socially liberal position on gender issues, committed itself to protecting spending levels on the NHS and overseas aid so they did not fall in real terms, and promoted a somewhat vague 'Big Society' programme (implying a rejection of Thatcher's comment that there was 'no such thing' as society) of encouraging greater voluntary participation in the delivery of public services. It was all intended to communicate the impression that the party had purged itself of the doctrinaire individualists and xenophobes who had caused it so many difficulties during the Major years and that it was prepared to work with the legacy of New Labour. This was not quite persuasive enough, possibly because of confusion over what was meant by 'Big Society' and because Conservative as well as Labour MPs had been implicated in the row over expense claims. No doubt the existence of 'unsavoury far right European associates' did not help.[178] Although the Tories made very substantial gains in the 2010 election they failed to win a majority of seats in Parliament. The result left the nation with a hung Parliament, with the Conservatives the largest party on 307 seats, Labour second with 258 and the Liberal Democrats, led by the youthful and popular Nick Clegg, on 57. After negotiations between the parties lasting the best part of a week a coalition government – Britain's first since World War Two – was established, composed of the Conservatives and the Liberal Democrats. Cameron was Prime Minister and Osborne the Chancellor, while Clegg became Deputy Prime Minister.

Gordon Brown quickly retired to the back benches and was succeeded as Labour leader by Ed Miliband in October. Miliband had worked for Brown before becoming an MP and then Minister, but he quickly made it clear that he was not likely to take the party back to the 1990s. The year 2010 was the end of New Labour, defeated at the polls and ideologically discredited by the crash, in two fundamental ways. First of all the events of 2007–09 had been a crisis of the neo-liberal system Labour had embraced and promoted under Blair and Brown. Secondly, the intellectual foundations of New Labour had lacked both the philosophy and the economic techniques needed to manage the crash and prevent it from turning into a depression more profound than any downturn over the preceding century. The means had indeed been found, but by returning to the Keynesian roots of British social democracy; perhaps Labour's finest hours in the period from 1997–2010 only occurred in 2008 and after, when, up to a point, it became Old Labour Redux.

Notes

1 Robin Ramsay, *The Rise of New Labour* (Harpenden: Pocket Essentials, 2002), pp. 64–65.
2 This was known as 'the Granita pact', so-called because it was said to have been made in the restaurant of that name in Islington.
3 Ramsay, *The Rise of New Labour*, p. 52.
4 See Ramsay, *The Rise of New Labour*, pp. 64–65; David Hencke, 'A Straight Sort of Guy?', *The Guardian*, 11 May 2007.
5 Speaking to the BBC on the occasion of Lady Thatcher's death in 2013 Blair explained that 'I always thought my job was to build on some of the things she had done rather than reverse them.' http://www.bbc.co.uk/news/uk-politics-22073434 (accessed 4 August 2016).
6 The key part of the Clause reads:

> To secure for the workers by hand or by brain the full fruits of their industry and the most equitable distribution thereof that may be possible upon the basis of the common ownership of the means of production, distribution and exchange, and the best obtainable system of popular administration and control of each industry or service.

This could cover not just nationalized corporations but also (for example) municipal ownership, social enterprises and co-operatives of workers, producers and consumers.
7 See Philip Williams, *Hugh Gaitskell* (London: Jonathan Cape, 1979), pp. 553–571.
8 E. Cashmore, *Race, Class and Gender since the War* (London: Unwin Hyman, 1989), p. 21.
9 See Michael Freeden, *Liberal Languages: Ideological Imaginations and Twentieth-Century Progressive Thought* (Princeton: Princeton University Press, 2004), p. 198.
10 John Kampfner, *The Rich from Slaves to Super-Yachts: A Two-Thousand Year History* (London: Little Brown, 2014), p. 315.
11 Clinton's cause had been very greatly assisted by a split in Republican ranks: a populist Right wing candidate, the Texan businessman Ross Perot, fought as an independent, on a Reform Party platform, and received 19 per cent of the vote.
12 Joseph Stiglitz, *Freefall: Free Markets and the Sinking of the Global Economy* (London: Penguin, 2010), pp. 162–163.
13 James Max Fendrich, Jamie Miller and Tim Nickel, 'It's the Budget, Stupid: A Policy Analysis of Clinton's First Budget', *The Journal of Sociology and Social Welfare*, vol. 21, no. 4 (2015), p. 16.

14 Thompson, *Political Economy and the Labour Party*, second edition (London: Routledge, 2006), p. 268.
15 See Adam Curtis, *All Watched Over by Machines of Loving Grace*, part 1, 'Love and Power', first broadcast on BBC2, 23 May 2011.
16 See Ramsay, *The Rise of New Labour*, p. 59.
17 Ramsay, *The Rise of New Labour*, p. 75.
18 Alastair Campbell and Richard Stott (eds), *The Blair Years: Extracts From the Alastair Campbell Diaries* (London: Arrow Books, 2007), pp. 148–150; Fran Abrams, 'Labour to Pledge Two-year Public Spending Freeze', *The Independent*, 20 January 1997.
19 The term was given unexpected and somewhat unlikely prominence as a result of a speech made by Brown's adviser Ed Balls in 1994.
20 See Michael Kitson and Frank Williamson, 'The Economics of New Labour: Policy and Performance', *Cambridge Journal of Economics*, vol. 31 (2007), pp. 807–808.
21 Eric Shaw, *Losing Labour's Soul? New Labour and the Blair Government 1997–2007* (London: Routledge, 2007), p. 123.
22 Kitson and Williamson, 'The Economics of New Labour', p. 808.
23 Shaw, *Losing Labour's Soul?*, p. 123.
24 Thompson, *Political Economy and the Labour Party*, p. 250.
25 Thompson, *Political Economy and the Labour Party*, p. 251. The 'lesson' drawn from the Mitterrand experience was based on a misreading of the episode. Mitterrand's U-turn was provoked by fear that the repeated devaluations of the franc were damaging the prospects of creating a single European currency and in consequence undermining the Franco-German alliance, a cornerstone of French national strategy since 1950. See Newton, *The Global Economy*, pp. 131–132.
26 Will Hutton, *The State We're In* (London: Vintage, 1996), p. 8.
27 Ibid. pp.157–163; 217–218.
28 Ibid., pp. 14–15; 163–164.
29 Ibid., p. 300.
30 Ibid., p. 303.
31 Thompson, *Political Economy and the Labour Party*, p. 262.
32 Campbell and Stott, *The Blair Years*, pp. 99–100, entries for 15 and 18 January 1996.
33 See Thompson, *Political Economy and the Labour Party*, p. 274.
34 Ibid., pp. 268–269.
35 See David Thomson, *Europe Since Napoleon* (London: Penguin, 1966), pp. 425–427; and *World History, 1914–1968* (Oxford: Oxford University Press, 1969), p. 99.
36 Ross McKibbin, 'Why The Tories Lost', *London Review of Books*, vol. 19, no. 13, 3 July 1997.
37 Ramsay, *The Rise of New Labour*, p. 92.
38 Tony Benn, *More Time For Politics: Diaries 2001–2007* (London: Arrow Books, 2008), p. xi.
39 Kenneth Clarke, 'The Quest for the Holy Grail', in Howard Davies (ed.), *The Chancellors' Tales: Managing the British Economy* (London: Polity Press, 2006), p. 207.
40 Deborah Summers, 'No Return to Boom and Bust; What Brown Said when he was Chancellor', *The Guardian*, 11 September 2008.
41 See Robert Chote, Carl Emmerson and Gemma Tetlow, 'The Fiscal Rules and Policy Framework', in Robert Chote, Carl Emmerson, David Miles and Jonathan Shaw, *The IFS Green Budget January 2009* (London: Institute for Fiscal Studies, 2009), pp. 81–83.
42 Aimee Oakley, 'New Labour and the Continuation of Thatcherite Policy', *POLIS Journal*, vol. 6 (2011–12), pp. 9–10.
43 Office of National Statistics, 'Balance of Payments: Current Account Balance as per cent of GDP', *The Pink Book* time series dataset, https://www.ons.gov.uk/economy/nationalaccounts/balanceofpayments/timeseries/aa6h/pb (accessed 11 August 2016).
44 'Manufacturing Industry Heading for Recession', BBC News, 6 July 1998, http://news.bbc.co.uk/1/hi/business/127274.stm (accessed 11 August 2016).

45 Ken Coutts, Andrew Glynn and Bob Rowthorne, 'Structural Change Under New Labour', *Cambridge Journal of Economics*, vol. 31 (2007), pp. 846–847.
46 See 'UK GDP since 1955', *The Guardian Datablog*, https://www.theguardian.com/news/datablog/2009/nov/25/gdp-uk-1948-growth-economy (accessed 11 August 2016).
47 Coutts, Glynn and Rowthorne, 'Structural Change Under New Labour', p. 858.
48 Ibid.
49 Florence Faucher-King and Patrick Le Galès, *The New Labour Experiment: Change and Reform under Blair and Brown* (Stanford: Stanford University Press, 2010), p. 20.
50 Andrew Hindmoor, *New Labour at the Centre: Constructing Political Space* (Oxford: Oxford University Press, 2011), p. 109.
51 Ibid., p. 116.
52 David Piachaud and Holly Sutherland, 'Child Poverty in Britain and the New Labour Government', *Journal of Social Policy*, vol. 30 (2001), p. 96.
53 Faucher-King and Le Galès, *The New Labour Experiment*, pp. 30–31.
54 Thompson, *Political Economy and the Labour Party*, pp. 282–286.
55 Robert Chote, Rowena Crawford, Carl Emmerson and Gemma Tetlow, *The Public Finances 1997–2010* (London: Institute for Fiscal Studies Election Briefing Note No. 6, 2010), p. 4.
56 Faucher-King and Le Galès, *The New Labour Experiment*, p. 22.
57 Ibid., pp. 22–23.
58 Ibid.
59 Tomlinson, 'Tale of a Death Exaggerated: How Keynesian Policies Survived the 1970s', *Contemporary British History*, vol. 21 (2007), p. 429.
60 Office of National Statistics, 'Unemployment Rate' (Labour Market Statistics time series dataset), https://www.ons.gov.uk/employmentandlabourmarket/peoplenotinwork/unemployment/timeseries/mgsx (accessed 12 August 2016).
61 George Monbiot, *Captive State: The Corporate Takeover of Britain* (London: Pan Macmillan, 2000), p. 62.
62 Rick Muir, *Not for Profit: The Role of the Private Sector in England's Schools* (London: Institute for Public Policy Research, 2012), p. 6.
63 Oliver Morgan and Nick Mathiason, 'Public-Private Discord', *The Observer*, 6 October 2002.
64 Monbiot, *Captive State*, p. 79.
65 Nicholas Watt, 'Blair Berates Old Labour's "Snobs"', *The Guardian*, 7 July 1999.
66 Adonis was a one-time Liberal Democrat activist who became one of Blair's team of advisers in the 1990s, specializing in education and constitutional reform. He was awarded a life peerage in 2005, becoming Minister of State at the Department for Education, with responsibility for schools.
67 'Q & A: Academies and Free Schools', BBC News 22 July 2010, http://www.bbc.co.uk/news/10161371, accessed 15 August 2016.
68 Muir, *Not for Profit*, p.7.
69 This was not an uncommon experience for elderly patients and their families. See Nicholas Mays, Anna Dixon and Lorelei Jones, 'Return to the Market: Objectives and Evolution of New Labour's Market Reforms', in Nicholas Mays, Anna Dixon and Lorelei Jones (eds), *Understanding New Labour's Market Reforms of the NHS* (London: King's Fund, 2011), p. 13.
70 Mays, Dixon and Jones, 'Return to the Market', pp. 4–8.
71 Dan Corry, Anna Valero and John Reenan, *UK Economic Performance since 1997* (London School of Economics: Centre for Economic Performance, 2011), Table 1, p. 2.
72 Driver and Temple, *The Unbalanced Economy*, Figure 1.8, p. 16.
73 Mike Brewer, David Phillips and Luke Sibieta, *Living Standards, Inequality and Poverty: Labour's Record* (London: Institute for Fiscal Studies, 2010), p. 1.
74 'Salmond's Bold New Era of Progressive Nationalism', *The Herald*, 22 December 2007.

75　See BBC News: Elections 2009, http://news.bbc.co.uk/1/shared/bsp/hi/elections/euro/09/html/ukregion_999999.stm (accessed 17 August 2016).
76　See Walter W. Powell and Kaisa Snellman, 'The Knowledge Economy', *Annual Review of Sociology*, vol. 30 (2004), pp. 199–220. The quotation is from p. 199.
77　Christopher Harvie, *Broonland: The Last Days of Gordon Brown* (London: Verso, 2010), p. 23.
78　See David Edgerton, 'Tony Blair's Warfare State', *New Left Review*, 238/1 (1999), p. 128.
79　Paul Maidment, 'The UK's 40 Largest Companies', *Forbes*, 12 May 2006, http://www.forbes.com/2006/12/02/forbes40-hsbc-hbos-biz-cx_pm_1205uk40_intro.html (accessed 19 August 2016).
80　'Speech by the Chancellor of the Exchequer, the Rt Hon Gordon Brown MP, to the Mansion House', 20 June 2007, http://webarchive.nationalarchives.gov.uk/+/http:/www.hm-treasury.gov.uk/2014.htm (accessed 19 August 2016).
81　Nicholas Shaxson, *Treasure Islands: Tax Havens And The Men Who Stole the World* (London: Vintage, 2012), p. 273.
82　John Lanchester, *Whoops! Why Everyone Owes Everyone Money and No One Can Pay* (London: Penguin, 2011), p. 135. This excellent book provides a witty, pellucid and indispensable guide to the crash of 2007–08.
83　Shaxson, *Treasure Islands*, p. 274. This section relies heavily on the evidence presented by Shaxson in his highly illuminating work.
84　Ibid., p. 274.
85　Harvie, *Broonland*, p. 60.
86　Shaxson, *Treasure Islands*, pp. 16–17.
87　Ibid., p. 15.
88　Ibid., p. 278.
89　Ibid., pp. 278–279.
90　Ibid., p. 277.
91　See *Understanding UK Commercial Property Investments: A Guide for Financial Advisers* (London: Investment Property Forum, 2015), especially Figures 7 and 9, pp. 5–6.
92　Shaxson, *Treasure Islands*, p. 277.
93　Lansley and Reed, *How to Boost the Wage Share*, p. 16.
94　See for example Brown's Mansion House speech of 2007, in which he congratulated the City on its 'remarkable achievements' and celebrated 'an era that history will record as the beginning of a new golden age for the City of London'. See http://webarchive.nationalarchives.gov.uk/+/http:/www.hm-treasury.gov.uk/2014.htm (accessed 19 August 2016).
95　Harvie, *Broonland*, p. 83.
96　Coutts, Glynn and Rowthorne, 'Structural Change Under New Labour', Table 2, p. 849.
97　Shaxson, *Treasure Islands*, p. 277.
98　World Bank, 'Manufacturing, Value Added (% of GDP): United Kingdom', http://data.worldbank.org/indicator/NV.IND.MANF.ZS?locations=GB (accessed 19 August 2016).
99　See Coutts, Glynn and Rowthorne, 'Structural Change Under New Labour', p. 849.
100　Ibid., p. 850. These economists estimated that the current account deficit would have grown to 3 per cent of GDP in the early 2000s had it not been for the improvement in the terms of trade.
101　Harvie, *Broonland*, p. 70.
102　Faucher-King and Le Galès, *The New Labour Experiment*, p. 39.
103　Ibid., p. 38.
104　Coutts, Glynn and Rowthorne, 'Structural Change Under New Labour', Table 3, p. 856.
105　Faucher-King and Le Galès, *The New Labour Experiment*, pp. 38–39.

New Labour in power, 1997–2010 239

106 Quoted by Coutts, Glynn and Rowthorne, 'Structural Change Under New Labour', p. 857.
107 See DTI, 'The Government's Manufacturing Strategy' (London, 2002) http://webarchive.nationalarchives.gov.uk/+/http:/www.dti.gov.uk/manufacturing/strategy.htm (accessed 19 August 2016).
108 See Coutts, Glynn and Rowthorne, 'Structural Change Under New Labour', pp. 858–860.
109 Faucher-King and Le Galès, *The New Labour Experiment*, p. 39.
110 Lansley and Reed, *How to Boost the Wage Share*, p. 19.
111 See Department for Business, Innovation and Skills, *Trade Union Membership 2014: Statistical Bulletin* (London, June 2015), p. 20, Table 1.1.
112 See Lansley and Reed, *How to Boost the Wage Share*, Figure 3, p. 8, for the wage share of GDP and Figure 4, p. 16 for the proportion taken by profits.
113 Faucher-King and Le Galès, *The New Labour Experiment*, p. 38.
114 See Angela Monaghan, 'Self-employment in UK at Highest Level since Records Began', *The Guardian*, 20 August 2014; Chris Green, 'Fast Food Britain: The Number of Takeaways Soars across the Nation's High Streets', *The Independent*, 1 April 2015.
115 See Monaghan, 'Self-employment in UK at Highest Level since Records Began'.
116 Faucher-King and Le Galès, *The New Labour Experiment*, p. 27.
117 Len McCluskey, 'A Brexit Won't Stop Cheap Labour Coming to Britain', *The Guardian*, 20 June 2016.
118 Oscar Williams-Grut, 'There are now 120,000 more Zero-hours Contracts in the UK than Last Year', *Business Insider UK*, 31 March 2015.
119 Faucher-King and Le Galès, *The New Labour Experiment*, p. 28.
120 Aggregate global growth rates were 3.5 per cent in the 1960s and 2.4 per cent in the 1970s but just 1.4 per cent and 1.1 per cent, respectively, during the 1980s and 1990s. See Harvey, *A Brief History of Neoliberalism*, p. 154; Figure 6.2, p. 158.
121 Ibid., p. 166.
122 Ibid., pp. 160–165.
123 See TUC, *Pensions in Peril: The Decline of the Final Salary Pensions Scheme* (London: TUC, 2002). This development received a stimulus from the fall in the stock market following the collapse of the dotcom boom. Sliding share prices reduced company asset valuations, with the result that employers sometimes found themselves unable to demonstrate that they could fund pension schemes (as they were required to do by accounting regulations) unless they themselves increased their inputs. This was liable to upset the shareholders, causing further pressure on shares. The most favoured solution was to close the scheme.
124 Robert Peston, *Who Runs Britain?* (London: Hodder and Stoughton, 2008), p. 230.
125 See Steven N. Kaplan and Per Stromberg, 'Leveraged Buyouts and Private Equity', *Journal of Economic Perspectives*, vol. 22, no. 4 (2008), p. 1.
126 Heath Aston, 'Alliance Boots Deals Pensions Blow to 15,000 Staff', *This is Money*, 29 January 2010, http://www.thisismoney.co.uk/money/article-1247176/Alliance-Boots-deals-pension-blow-15-000-staff.html (accessed 23 August 2016).
127 Faucher-King and Le Galès, *The New Labour Experiment*, p. 39.
128 David Beckett, *Trends in the UK Housing Market, 2014*, Office of National Statistics, 22 September 2014, p. 12.
129 Faucher-King and Le Galès, *The New Labour Experiment*, p. 145.
130 See Nationwide House Price Index, 'UK House Prices Adjusted for Inflation'; Office of National Statistics, *Annual Survey of Hours and Earnings, 2015*, Figure 1, Median full-time gross weekly earnings in current and constant (2015) prices, UK, April 1997 to 2015.
131 Faucher-King and Le Galès, *The New Labour Experiment*, p. 144.
132 Jill Insley, 'FSA to Ban Fast-track and Self-certified Mortgages', *The Guardian*, 13 July 2010.

133 Faith Archer, 'Mortgages on Offer for Six Times Salary', *Daily Telegraph*, 11 April 2007.
134 Faucher-King and Le Galès, *The New Labour Experiment*, p. 40.
135 Lanchester, *Whoops!*, pp. 55–61; Adam Davidson, 'How AIG Fell Apart', *Reuters*, 18 September 2008, http://www.reuters.com/article/us-how-aig-fell-apart-idUSMAR85972720080918 (accessed 6 September 2016).
136 Lanchester, *Whoops!*, p. 64.
137 Ibid., p. 173.
138 Ibid.
139 See the discussion of 'equity' in Ibid., pp. 19–21.
140 See Ibid., pp. 21–26.
141 The repossession figures are all taken from The Poverty Site, 'Mortgage Repossession', graph 1 (1990–2010), http://www.poverty.org.uk/84/index.shtml (accessed 26 August 2016).
142 See *The Economist*, 'American House Prices: Realty Check', http://www.economist.com/blogs/graphicdetail/2016/08/daily-chart-20, accessed 26 August 2016.
143 Nationwide Building Society, 'UK House Prices since 1952'.
144 Harvie, *Broonland*, p. 165.
145 'BNP Paribas Suspends Funds because of Subprime Problems', *New York Times*, 9 August 2007.
146 Alistair Darling, *Back From The Brink* (London: Atlantic Books, 2011), p. 17.
147 Harvie, *Broonland*, p. 157.
148 See Darling, *Back From The Brink*, pp. 64–68; Lanchester, *Whoops!*, p. 28.
149 Darling, *Back From The Brink*, p. 114.
150 Lanchester, *Whoops!*, p. 209.
151 Nicholas Watt, 'Economy at 60-year Low, says Darling. And It Will Get Worse', *The Guardian*, 30 August 2008.
152 Darling, *Back From The Brink*, p. 126.
153 BBC News, 17 September 2008, 'Lloyds TSB Seals £12bn HBOS Deal', http://news.bbc.co.uk/1/hi/business/7622180.stm (accessed 30 August 2016).
154 Darling, *Back From The Brink*, p. 141.
155 Ibid., p. 114.
156 Ibid., pp. 12 and 152–154. Interestingly Darling dates the conversation with McKillop to 'Tuesday morning, on 11 October 2008' (p. 12). But 11 October was in fact on a Saturday. Was this dating error an accident? On the morning of Sunday 12 October the author and his wife had a chance meeting with a retired colleague, who said that he had just been on the telephone to his broker and had been told that two major British banks would close on Monday (13 October). A moment's questioning brought the answer that these institutions were RBS and HBOS.
157 Ibid., p. 154.
158 Office of National Statistics, 'BoP: UK Current Account Balance as per cent of GDP' (time series data).
159 Redux: 'brought back' or restored; from the Latin verb '*reducere*' (to bring back) – *Oxford English Dictionary*.
160 Darling, *Back from the Brink*, p. 154.
161 Lloyds Banking Group, 'Proposed Alternative to the Government Asset Protection Scheme Comprising a Rights Issue and Liability Management Exercise by way of Exchange Offers', 3 November 2009, p. 11.
162 Kevin Theakston, *The IMF Crisis of 1976 and British Politics* (London and New York: Tauris Academic Studies, 2005), p. 51.
163 This was made clear to the author very early in 2009 by a senior member of the TUC Economic and Social Affairs Department.
164 Darling, *Back from the Brink*, p. 154.
165 Ibid., p. 204.

166 'Gordon Brown Unveils £1 Billion Rail Electrification', *Daily Telegraph*, 23 July 2009.
167 Heather Stewart and Emily Martin, 'Labour Put too much Faith in City, admits Mandelson', *The Guardian*, 28 July 2009.
168 Darling, *Back from the Brink*, p. 216.
169 Faucher-King and Le Galès, *The New Labour Experiment*, p. 150.
170 Ibid., p. 150.
171 Darling, *Back from the Brink*, pp. 177 and 182.
172 See Newton, *The Global Economy 1944–2000*, ch. 6.
173 Darling, *Back from the Brink*, p. 208.
174 Ibid., p. 219.
175 Tony Benn, *A Blaze of Autumn Sunshine: The Last Diaries* (London: Arrow Books, 2013), p. 279.
176 Darling, *Back from the Brink*, p. 235.
177 Much of it on defence – Greek military spending as a proportion of GDP was second only to the USA among NATO members: see Judy Dempsey, 'Military in Greece is Spared Cuts', *New York Times*, 7 January 2013.
178 Harvie, *Broonland*, p. 173.

8
ENVOI

The Cameron Coalition government frequently expressed a determination to 'rebalance' the economy towards manufacturing and away from its growing dependence on finance and services. It made some important changes to financial regulations and took an increasingly rigorous approach to the closing of tax loopholes previously exploited by banks and large corporations. These steps indicated that it was aware of some of the issues which had led to the crisis. But it did not seek to resolve this by continuing with Labour's approach. Instead it sought to make 2010 an inflection point whereby the road back towards Keynesian social democracy was abandoned and replaced by a return to neo-liberalism. To achieve this it continued to exploit the (unjustified) anxieties that government borrowing was now so large that Britain risked experiencing its own version of the Greek crisis. Cameron and Osborne claimed that if the nation was to avert this eventuality it was essential to rein in public expenditure. They aimed to reduce its share of the GDP, driven by the crisis to its current level of 47 per cent, to under 40 per cent by 2015 (and 36 per cent by 2019–20), using superficially pragmatic arguments to mask an ideological project. The Liberal Democrats, who had entered the 2010 election on a Keynesian platform some way to the left of the other two major parties and were now part of the government, were persuaded: they rapidly performed a volte-face on key pledges in their manifesto and embraced the fiscal austerity advocated by the Conservatives.

Cameron and Osborne quickly made it clear that their aim was to eliminate the budget deficit by 2015. True to their comments before and during the election campaign they determined to set about this by a fiscal contraction worth £110 billion by 2014–15, £81 billion of which was to come from public spending cuts and £29 billion from higher taxes (with VAT, which was raised to 20 per cent, responsible for the lion's share of this). The contraction was accompanied by the continuation of low interest rates and QE. Bond purchases by the Bank of

England rose to £375 billion by the start of 2013, with another £60 billion being made in August 2016. The assumption behind this combination of measures was that austerity would achieve a dramatic fall in government borrowing, increasing investor confidence in the process, while monetary expansion offset the deflationary side-effects of the fiscal tightening. Labour's Shadow Chancellor, Ed Balls, accused the government of taking 'an unprecedented gamble with the future of the economy', implementing measures likely to curtail demand and hold back growth just as expansion was returning after the recession of 2008–09. These anxieties were shared by critical economists such as David Blanchflower, a member of the Bank of England MPC from 2006–09, and Nobel Prize for Economics winner Joseph Stiglitz.

Osborne rejected the charge, arguing that the spending cuts were essential to 'take the country back from the brink of bankruptcy'. The strategy would work (he said) because it would bring stability to the country's finances, create space for domestic investment previously 'crowded out' by public expenditure, and help 'rebalance' the economy in favour of manufacturing and exports. Ministers forecast that the outcome would be output growth of 2.7 and 2.9 per cent per annum by 2013 and after, leading to higher tax revenues and the steady disappearance of the deficit. They expressed confidence that the expansion would be driven by private investment, exports and import substitution rather than by domestic consumption and public spending, as it had been between 1997 and 2008. The external deficit would close as import growth fell from its high levels under New Labour (7.1 per cent in 2005 and over 8 per cent in 2006) to 4 per cent by 2014–15.[1]

The Coalition quickly set about its task. Headline measures included the VAT increase and public spending cuts featuring the scrapping of Labour's £1 billion school building programme, reductions in housing benefit, child benefits and help for industry (notably the axing of an £80 million loan to Sheffield Forgemasters to assist the company's investment in equipment designed to manufacture parts for the civil nuclear industry). These were followed by the abolition of the Education Maintenance Allowance, which had provided financial support for 16–19 year olds from families on below average incomes so they could pursue further education. Corporation tax was cut and the top marginal rate of income tax brought back down from 50 to 45 per cent.

The programme did not fulfil the expectations of the government and its supporters. The recovery of 2009–10 did not continue. Instead there was a marked deceleration of activity, with the economic impact of domestic deflation intensified by stagnation in the EU (the nation's largest market) resulting from a crisis surrounding the future of the euro. UK unemployment rose above 8 per cent in 2011–12. The slowdown of activity and rising joblessness led to disappointing tax revenues, with the result that the government consistently failed to meet either its deficit reduction or growth targets. Indeed output growth fell back from its levels in 2010 to just over 1 per cent by 2013. With the Coalition's strategy failing on its own terms there were growing calls for a reflationary 'Plan B'. Keen to emulate Mrs Thatcher's distaste for U-turns (although this had not of course been reflected in practice during her time as Prime Minister) government Ministers sternly rejected these demands in public. All the same, Osborne quietly shifted his strategy by allowing spending to rise in 2012–13, bringing forward capital projects and taking steps to stimulate the housing market; the deadline for deficit reduction was extended. These measures, along with easy credit, permitted growth to resume, and the economy expanded more rapidly than that of any other EU member in the period up to the 2015 General Election, by which time it was growing at an annual rate of over 3 per cent. Unemployment dropped smartly, from its peak of 8.3 per cent in 2011–12 to less than 6 per cent by 2015.

The burst of expansion after 2012–13 wrong footed Labour, which had made much of what Balls and Miliband liked to call the 'flatlining economy' produced by Osborne's policies after 2010. In response to the approach taken by the Coalition Miliband attempted to construct a post-New Labour political economy, characterized by 'responsible capitalism'. This agenda featured not just familiar Labour policies such as more investment in the public services and infrastructure but a larger role for the State as guardian of the public interest.[2] The Labour leader suggested restrictions on the level of executive pay, with worker representatives on major companies' remuneration boards 'to keep salaries in check', measures to support small businesses and reforms to the voting rights of shareholders. These were to be focused on preventing investors from prioritizing short-term profits over the longer development process often required in the manufacturing of new products. Miliband's modest attempt to rehabilitate the form of productionist interventionism developed by Will Hutton in the 1990s (assisted by Hutton himself, with a new manifesto for progressive change which built on his earlier ideas)[3] was not well received in all quarters of the Labour Party. Many MPs and former Ministers reckoned it was too sharp a departure from the political economy of New Labour.[4] The efforts of Miliband and his supporters to capture the Party for their ideas were frustrated and Labour found itself mired in a political no man's land, half way between neo-liberalism and a refurbished social democracy.[5] This was not the basis for a coherent and convincing alternative to Osborne's pragmatism.

Labour's weakness, combined with economic expansion, delivered a surprise result at the 2015 Election. Another hung Parliament was widely anticipated but instead the Conservatives were returned to power with a small overall majority of 12 seats. They benefited from the collapse of the Liberal Democrats, punished for abandoning commitments in their 2010 manifesto (notably their opposition to increases in student university fees) after entering the Coalition. 27 Liberal Democrat seats fell to the Tories as their support dwindled to 7.9 per cent of the vote, bringing them just 8 MPs, a spectacular decline from 23 per cent of the vote and 57 seats in 2010. Labour, by contrast, made modest advances in England but these counted for little thanks to the Party's electoral collapse in Scotland, where its representation fell from 41 seats to 1. All the losses were to the SNP, which increased its representation by 50 seats, ending with 56 out of the 59 MPs sent to Westminster from Scotland. Led now by Nicola Sturgeon, the SNP capitalized on its record in government since 2007 and its high profile in the 2014 referendum campaign, underlining its dedication to a progressive and social-democratic variety of nationalism. It consciously positioned itself as anti-austerity, advocating higher taxes for the wealthy, annual public spending increases 0.5 per cent above the rate of inflation, the abolition of zero hours contracts and the extension of the Living Wage (which at that time paid £7.85 an hour to workers, a higher rate than the Minimum Wage of £6.50). Labour's economic programme, founded on deficit reduction (albeit at a slower pace than proposed by the Coalition) and tax increases, implied that, at root, the Labour leadership shared Cameron and Osborne's long-term ambition of reducing public spending. Labour's inability to come to terms with the failure of neo-liberalism and the SNP's adoption of an unambiguous centre-left strategy seems to have accelerated the former's retreat: it lost its position as the hegemonic political force in Scotland and was marginalized there. This was a development which threatened to reduce the Labour Party to the status of permanent opposition while leaving the Conservatives continuously in office, either in the UK or (were Scotland to opt for independence in a second referendum) in a shrunken state composed (for how long?) of England, Wales and Northern Ireland.

Conservative political success owed a good deal, therefore, to Labour's breakdown as well as to Cameron and Osborne's modest boom, which recreated the conditions responsible for the economic growth of the 2000s and the 1980s – a consumer and credit driven expansion underpinned by a rise in the price of housing. Having fallen from their peak of 367.7 at the end of 2007 (first quarter of 1993 = 100) to an index of 324.9 in third quarter of 2012, UK house prices began to escalate briskly in 2013 and after, surpassing 2007 levels to reach 404.1 by 2016.[6] During the year from February 2015 they rose by 7.6 per cent, with the market being driven by movement in the South East (11.4%), the East (10.3%) and London (9.7%).[7] Rising property prices provided collateral for more private borrowing, with a 30 per cent growth in mortgage lending between February 2015 and February 2016.[8] Household debt remained high at over 140 per cent of income.[9] Unsurprisingly, given the parallels with the recent past, the expansion of the 2013–16 period came without any significant rebalancing of the economy. By 2015 manufacturing accounted for 10.3 per cent of the GDP[10] and the current account had lurched dramatically further into the red, the deficit amounting to 5.6 per cent of GDP.[11]

The return to neo-liberalism was accompanied by many of the divisive features associated with this form of political economy. The country was suffering from a housing crisis,[12] with all forms of social house-building still regarded with disfavour by leading Conservatives[13] while private development remained sluggish. Inadequate supply helped to push up both house prices and the cost of rental accommodation. Homelessness increased, a problem made more acute by changes to housing benefit. In England 114,790 households applied to their local authority for homelessness assistance in 2015–16, an 11 per cent rise since 2010–11.[14]

The number of people on zero hours contracts went from 190,000 in 2011 (0.6 per cent of those employed) to 744,000 (2.4 per cent) by the second quarter of 2015.[15] Inequality in Britain grew, with wage and salary increases remaining low for most of the workforce[16] but reaching stratospheric levels for executives. In

2014–15 the richest 10 per cent of all households owned 45 per cent of all the nation's wealth while the poorest 50 per cent of the population owned just 8.7 per cent of it. By the summer of 2016 incomes at the highest levels of Britain's largest public companies were 'typically 129 times greater – including pensions and bonuses – than those of their employees'.[17] In 2015 the Gini co-efficient revealed that the distribution of income in the UK left it the sixth most unequal nation in the OECD.

As had been increasingly evident since the 1980s the fracture in British society was geographic as well as social, with the South East of England enjoying considerably superior levels of income and wealth to the rest of the nation. According to the Office of National Statistics in 2014–15, 'an average household in the South East has almost twice (183%) the amount of wealth of an average household in Scotland'.[18] The highest regional unemployment figures in 2016 were to be found in the North East, with 7.6 per cent of all in the 16–64 age group out of work (the national figure was 4.9 per cent). The next highest rates were to be found in the West Midlands (6.1 per cent) and Northern Ireland (6.0 per cent). East and South East England had the lowest rates, at 3.3 per cent and 3.7 per cent respectively.[19]

The politico-economic strategy pursued since 2010 had preserved neo-liberal Britain. Yet there was a high price to pay for salvaging a system which had been responsible for financial crisis, unbalanced economic development and growing regional and social inequality. The social and economic dislocation exploded in the summer of 2016, when the country narrowly voted to leave the EU. Studies of this referendum indicated that the strongest support for 'Brexit' was to be found in some of the least affluent parts of England and Wales, where the stability, confidence and culture associated with long-term employment in prosperous and large-scale industry had collapsed along with the economic structure which had sustained them.[20] This had left large areas of the nation not only relatively poor and deprived but open to a xenophobic and chauvinistic form of popular politics manipulated by ambitious and unscrupulous politicians in alliance with the media barons and editors who had given the Major government such a hard time. The EU became a scapegoat for the failings of neo-liberalism, even as those running the campaign to take the UK out did so as part of a bid to entrench the system and complete Thatcher's reinvention of Britain. Half a century earlier British membership of the EEC had been seen by many of its advocates as central to a social-democratic modernization of the country. Now, withdrawal from the EU was seen by leading Conservative 'Brexiteers' such as Michael Gove,[21] Boris Johnson[22] and former Chancellor Nigel (now Lord) Lawson as fundamental to the nation's transformation into a free market society fully integrated into a global economy characterized by the unrestricted movement of goods and capital. Domestic living standards would be under continual pressure to adjust to costs and prices in the wider world, with the welfare state and vestigial attempts to protect the regions from the consequences of *laissez-faire* largely consigned to history.[23]

Such an outcome would mark the complete hegemony of Consumer's Britain, with its roots in the City and the social and economic dominance of the South East and the Home Counties, over the rest of the nation. Although Britain had not yet reached this point by the end of 2016 it is clear that the period since 1979 has seen a long counter-revolution against British social democracy. Far from attempting to reverse this the party of Producer's Britain, the Labour Party, had embraced it, seeking only to humanize its impact on society. A shift back to the politics and economics of the Wilson–Callaghan years after 2008 had been incomplete and short-lived; it was aborted by the Coalition. Both Ed Miliband and his successor as Labour leader after the 2015 debacle at the polls, Jeremy Corbyn, had attempted to rehabilitate ideological currents and traditions predating the New Labour takeover of the Party. In doing so, however, they encountered fierce resistance. Labour's internal conflicts, along with the outcome and aftermath of the 2015 Election, left the political forces committed to a reversal of the neo-liberal revolution enfeebled and fragmented.

The long counter-revolution has led to the erosion of much of what had characterized post-war Britain. Above all, this society had possessed a common set of values. These had prized the dignity and worth of all individuals and had stemmed from a sensitivity to social and political injustice first nurtured by over a century of humanistic and religious teaching before flourishing in the hothouse of total war and shared national suffering. During the era from 1945–79 successive governments, of both main parties, sought to build a society in which those values could be realised, with all citizens enjoying the opportunity to lead the good life free from anxiety about joblessness, homelessness, inability to afford medical care and insecurity in old age. If post-war Britain can be said to have had a 'mission statement', that was it. It underpinned reconstruction after 1945 and the effort to reinvent the nation as a social democracy after 1960. This was the heyday of Producer's Britain, when all parts of the Union, the regions of England as well as the different nations of the UK, recognised a shared commitment to 'Britishness' and an understanding, however vague, of what this meant.

By 2016, after thirty-seven years of neo-liberalism, this was no longer clear. The disappearance of a political economy sustaining a Union which for all its faults had been social, economic and cultural as much as it had been political, now threatened to lead to the disintegration of the country. Within much of England and Wales there was a noticeable turn to the politics of xenophobia and a home-grown version of *Poujadisme*. Local petty nationalisms replaced an acceptance that all the citizens of these islands shared a common home. North of the border, the rejection of independence in 2014 notwithstanding, elections to the Scottish Parliament in 2016 saw the SNP returned to power, albeit just short of a majority, while Labour's decline continued: it was replaced by the Conservatives as second party. Not only did approaching 50 per cent of the Scottish electorate continue to support the progressive nationalism of the SNP, seeing in it perhaps a vehicle for the preservation of those 'British' values which were becoming so etiolated in England and Wales: the Scots also voted emphatically to remain in the EU, by 62 per cent to 38 per cent, in the 2016 referendum.

By 2016 the component parts of the United Kingdom were fracturing. Producer's Britain was in eclipse along with the Union itself. It was not implausible to think that the UK itself might break up within the next generation. Britain had been reinvented as a welfare state in 1945, a social democracy in the 1960s and 1970s and as a neo-liberal society after 1979. By 2016 it was arguable that Britain was overdue for another reinvention; but would there be a Britain left to reinvent?

Notes

1 These points are based on a discussion of the Coalition's economic strategy by Peter Cain and Scott Newton, 'Crisis and Recovery: Historical Perspectives on the Coalition's Economic Policies', paper for *History and Policy*, 2 March 2011, http://www.historyandpolicy.org/policy-papers/papers/crisis-and-recovery-historical-perspectives-on-the-coalitions-economic-poli (accessed 2 September 2016).
2 Tim Ross, 'Ed Miliband Calls for "More Responsible" Capitalism in Attack on Bankers' Pay', *Daily Telegraph*, 17 November 2011.
3 Will Hutton, *How Good We Can Be: Ending the Mercenary Society and Building a Great Country* (London: Little Brown, 2015).
4 Nicholas Watt, Rowena Mason and Toby Helm, 'Miliband Made "Terrible Mistake" in Ditching New Labour, Says Mandelson', *The Guardian*, 11 May 2015.
5 Eunice Goes, 'The Labour Party under Ed Miliband', *Renewal: A Journal of Social Democracy*, vol. 24, no. 1 (2016), pp. 29–40.
6 See Nationwide House Price Index, Seasonally Adjusted (Q1 1993= 100).
7 Office of National Statistics, *Statistical Bulletin*, 'House Price Index, February 2016'.
8 Hilary Osborne, 'Demand for Homes Fuels 30% Rise in Mortgage Lending', *The Guardian*, 17 March 2016.
9 Office for Budgetary Responsibility, *Economic and Fiscal Outlook* (London: Stationery Office, November 2016), pp. 70–74. The November 2016 reports forecast that household debt would reach 148 per cent of GDP by 2021, a revision of its March estimate of 164 per cent.
10 See World Bank, 'Manufacturing, Value Added (% of GDP)', http://data.worldbank.org/indicator/NV.IND.MANF.ZS?locations=GB (accessed 7 September 2016).
11 Office of National Statistics, 'BoP: Current Account Balance as Percentage of GDP', https://www.ons.gov.uk/economy/nationalaccounts/balanceofpayments/timeseries/aa6h/pb (accessed 5 September 2016).
12 Hilary Osborne, 'Home Ownership in England at Lowest Level in 30 Years as Housing Crisis Grows', *The Guardian*, 2 August 2016.
13 Tory objections were ideological and also based on electoral calculation. Former Liberal Democrat leader Nick Clegg commented that Cameron and Osborne saw social housing 'as a Petri dish for Labour voters. It was unbelievable.' See Simon Hattenstone, 'Nick Clegg: "I Did Not Cater for the Tories' Brazen Ruthlessness"', *The Guardian*, 3 September 2016.
14 Crisis: the national charity for single homeless people, 'About Homelessness', http://www.crisis.org.uk/pages/homeless-def-numbers.html (accessed 5 September 2016).
15 Williams-Grut, 'There are Now 120,000 more Zero-hours Contracts in the UK than Last Year', Business Insider UK, 2 September 2015, http://uk.businessinsider.com/ons-uk-zero-hours-contracts-latest-data-2015-9 (accessed 3 April 2017).
16 See 'Employers' Plan to Rein in Pay Increases in 2016', *Reuters Business News*, 15 February 2016.
17 Juliette Garside, 'UK's Top Bosses Received 10% Pay Rise in 2015 as Average Salary Hit £5.5m', *The Guardian* 8 August 2016.

18 Quoted by The Equality Trust, 'The Scale of Economic Inequality in the UK', https://www.equalitytrust.org.uk/scale-economic-inequality-uk (accessed 5 September 2015).
19 Statistics from Office of National Statistics, 'Regional Labour Market Statistics in the UK: August 2016'. The North East had also been the region with the highest rate in 2015, at 8.2 per cent, http://www.ons.gov.uk/employmentandlabourmarket/peopleinwork/employmentandemployeetypes/bulletins/regionallabourmarket/august2016#unemployment (accessed 5 September 2016).
20 Anushka Asthana, 'People who Felt Marginalised Drove Brexit Vote, Study Finds'. *The Guardian*, 31 August 2016.
21 A journalist turned politician, Gove was Secretary of State for Education from 2010 to 2014 and Secretary of State for Justice from 2015 to 2016.
22 Johnson, like Gove, had built a career in journalism before entering politics. He had been Mayor of London from 2008 to 2016 before taking the post of Foreign Secretary after the EU referendum.
23 See for example John Hulsman, 'A Global Free Trade Alliance Should be Britain's Stunning Post-Brexit Future', *City A.M.*, 22 August 2016, http://www.cityam.com/247909/global-free-trade-alliance-should-britains-stunning-post (accessed 18 January 2017).

BIBLIOGRAPHY

Primary sources: unpublished

National Archives (Public Record Office, Kew, London)
Cabinet (CAB)
Prime Minister (PREM)
Treasury (T)
Margaret Thatcher Foundation (http://www.margaretthatcher.org)
Sir Bryan Hopkin Papers, Arts and Social Studies Library, Cardiff University

Primary sources: published

HM Government, Department of Economic Affairs, *The National Plan* (Cmnd 2764, London: HMSO, 1965)
HM Government, Department of Economic Affairs, *The Task Ahead: Economic Assessment to 1972* (Cmnd 2764, London: HMSO, 1969)
HM Government, Department of Industry, *The Regeneration of British Industry* (Cmnd 5710: HMSO, London, 1974)
Bank for International Settlements, *Annual Reports*, 1964–70
United States Government, Department of State, *Foreign Relations of the United States* (Washington: United States Government Printing Office)

Newspapers, journals and periodicals

Bank of England Quarterly Bulletin
The Banker
The Daily Telegraph
The Guardian
The Independent
New Left Review
The Times

Diaries

Tony Benn, *Arguments for Socialism* (Harmondsworth: Penguin, 1980)
Tony Benn, *Out of the Wilderness: Diaries 1963–67* (London: Arrow, 1988)
Tony Benn, *Office without Power: Diaries 1968–72* (London: Arrow, 1989)
Tony Benn, *Against the Tide: Diaries 1973–76* (London: Arrow, 1990)
Tony Benn, *Conflicts of Interest: Diaries 1977–80* (London: Arrow, 1991)
Tony Benn, *The End of an Era: Diaries 1980–90* (London: Arrow, 1992)
Tony Benn, *A Blaze of Autumn Sunshine: The Last Diaries* (London: Arrow Books, 2013)
Tony Benn, *The Best of Benn* (ed. Ruth Winston: London: Arrow Books, 2015)
Alastair Campbell and Richard Stott (eds), *The Blair Years: Extracts From the Alastair Campbell Diaries* (London: Arrow Books, 2007)
Barbara Castle, *The Castle Diaries 1964–76* (Basingstoke: Macmillan, 1990)
Richard Crossman, *The Diaries of a Cabinet Minister, Volume 1: Minister of Housing 1964–1966* (London: Jonathan Cape, 1975)
Bernard Donoughue, *Downing Street Diary: With Harold Wilson in No. 10* (London: Jonathan Cape, 2005)
Bernard Donoughue, *Downing Street Diary, Volume Two: With James Callaghan* (London: Cape, 2008)
Cecil King, *The Cecil King Diaries 1965–70* (London: Jonathan Cape, 1972)
Hugo Young, *The Hugo Young Papers: A Journalist's Notes from the Heart of Politics* (London: Penguin, 2009)

Memoirs

George Brown, *In My Way* (London: Gollancz, 1971)
James Callaghan, *Time and Chance* (London: Collins, 1987)
Barbara Castle, *Fighting all the Way* (London: Macmillan, 1993)
Esme Cromer, *From this Day Forward* (Stoke Abbot: Thomas Harmsworth, 1991)
Brian Crozier, *Free Agent: The Unseen War 1941–1991* (London: Harper Collins, 1993)
Alistair Darling, *Back from the Brink* (London: Atlantic Books, 2011)
Howard Davies (ed.) *The Chancellor's Tales: Managing the British Economy* (London: Polity Press, 2006)
Denis Healey, *Time of My Life* (London: Michael Joseph, 1989)
Edward Heath, *The Course of my Life: My Autobiography* (London: Hodder and Stoughton, 1998)
Peter Hennessy, *Distilling the Frenzy: Writing the History of One's Own Times* (London: Biteback, 2012)
Michael Heseltine, *Life in the Jungle: My Autobiography* (London: Hodder and Stoughton, 2001)
John Hoskyns, *Just in Time: Inside the Thatcher Revolution* (London: Aurum Press, 2000)
Jack Jones, *Union Man: An Autobiography* (Collins: London, 1986)
Norman Lamont, 'Out of the Ashes', in Howard Davies (ed.) *The Chancellor's Tales: Managing the British Economy* (London: Polity Press, 2006), pp. 147–166
Nigel Lawson, *The View from No. 11: Memoirs of a Tory Radical* (London: Corgi, 1993)
Donald MacDougall, *Don and Mandarin: Memoirs of an Economist* (London: John Murray, 1987)
John Major, *The Autobiography* (London: Harper Collins, 2000)
Margaret Thatcher, *The Downing Street Years* (London: Harper Collins 1993)

Harold Wilson, *The Labour Governments, 1964–1970: A Personal Record* (London: Weidenfeld and Nicolson, 1971)
Harold Wilson, *Final Term: The Labour Governments 1974–76* (London: Weidenfeld and Nicolson and Michael Joseph, 1979)
Harold Wilson, *Memoirs: The Making of a Prime Minister 1916–1964* (London: Weidenfeld and Nicholson, 1986)
Peter Wright, *Spycatcher: The Candid Autobiography of a Senior Intelligence Officer* (New York: Viking, 1987)

Secondary sources

Christopher Andrew, *The Defence of the Realm: The Authorized History of MI5* (London: Allen Lane, 2009)
Michael Artis and David Cobham, *Labour's Economic Policies 1974–1979* (Manchester: Manchester University Press, 1981)
Michael Artis, David Cobham and Mark Wickham-Jones, 'Social Democracy in Hard Times: The Economic Record of the Labour Government, 1974–1979', *Twentieth Century British History*, vol. 3 (1992), pp. 32–58
Stuart Ball and Anthony Seldon (eds), *The Heath Government 1970–74* (London: Longman, 1996)
Andy Beckett, *When the Lights Went Out: Britain in the Seventies* (London: Faber and Faber, 2009)
Frank Blackaby (ed.), *British Economic Policy, 1960–74* (Cambridge: Cambridge University Press, 1978)
Samuel Brittan, *The Treasury under the Tories 1951–64* (London: Penguin, 1964)
P. J. Cain, 'J. A. Hobson, Financial Capitalism and Imperialism in Late Victorian and Edwardian Britain', in A. N. Porter and R. F. Holland (eds), *Money, Finance and Empire 1790–1969* (London: Frank Cass, 1985)
P. J. Cain and A. G. Hopkins, *British Imperialism 1688–2000* (London: Pearson Education, 2002)
Alec Cairncross and Barry Eichengreen, *Sterling in Decline: The Devaluations of Sterling 1931, 1949 and 1967* (Oxford: Blackwell, 1983)
John Campbell, *Edward Heath: A Biography* (London: Pimlico, 1994)
Michael Charlton, *The Price of Victory* (London: BBC, 1983)
Alan Clark, *The Tories: Conservatives and the Nation State 1922–1997* (London: Phoenix, 1998)
Jerry Coakley and Laurence Harris, *The City of Capital: London's Role as a Financial Centre* (Oxford: Blackwell, 1983)
Jerry Coakley and Laurence Harris, 'Financial Globalisation and Deregulation', in Jonathan Michie (ed.), *The Economic Legacy 1979–1992* (London: Academic Press, 1992), pp. 60–74
Richard Cockett, *Thinking the Unthinkable: Think-Tanks and the Economic Counter-Revolution, 1931–83* (London: Harper Collins, 1995)
John Cooper, *A Suitable Case for Treatment: What to do about the Balance of Payments* (London: Penguin, 1968)
Richard Coopey, Steven Fielding and Nick Tiratsoo (eds), *The Wilson Governments 1964–1970* (London: Pinter, 1993)
Richard Coopey, 'Industrial Policy in the White Heat of the Scientific Revolution', in Coopey, Fielding and Tiratsoo, *The Wilson Governments 1964–1970*, pp. 104–126
Ken Coutts and Wynne Godley, 'Does Britain's Balance of Payments Matter Any More?', in Michie, *The Economic Legacy 1979–1992*, pp. 37–59

Ken Coutts, Andrew Glynn and Bob Rowthorne, 'Structural Change Under New Labour', *Cambridge Journal of Economics*, vol. 31 (2007), pp. 845–861

James Cronin, *New Labour's Pasts: The Labour Party and its Discontents* (London: Routledge, 2004)

Anthony Crosland, *The Future of Socialism* (London: Cape, 1956)

Anthony Crosland, *Socialism Now* (London: Jonathan Cape, 1974)

James Denman and Paul McDonald, 'Unemployment Statistics from 1881 to the Present Day', *Labour Market Trends*, January (1996)

Peter Dorey (ed.), *The Labour Governments 1964–1970* (London: Routledge, 2006)

Ciaran Driver and Paul Temple, *The Unbalanced Economy: A Policy Appraisal* (Basingstoke: Palgrave, 2012)

David Edgerton, *Warfare State: Britain 1920–1979* (Cambridge: Cambridge University Press, 2005)

David Edgerton, 'The "White Heat" Revisited: The British Government and Technology in the 1960s', *Twentieth Century British History*, vol. 7 (1996), 53–82

Florence Faucher-King and Patrick Le Galès, *The New Labour Experiment: Change and Reform under Blair and Brown* (Stanford: Stanford University Press, 2010)

Ilaria Favoretto, '"Wilsonism" Reconsidered: Labour Party Revisionism 1952–64', *Contemporary British History*, vol. 14 (2000), pp. 54–80

Paul Foot, *The Politics of Harold Wilson* (London: Penguin, 1968)

Andrew Gamble, *The Conservative Nation* (London: Routledge & Kegan Paul, 1974)

Andrew Gamble, *The Free Economy and the Strong State* (Basingstoke: Palgrave, 1994)

Chris Gifford, *The Making of Eurosceptic Britain* (Aldershot: Ashgate, 2008)

Ian Gilmour, *Dancing with Dogma: Britain under Thatcherism* (London: Simon and Schuster, 1992)

Andrew Glyn, '"The Productivity Miracle", Profits and Investment', in Michie, *The Economic Legacy 1979–1992*, pp.77–90

Wynne Godley, 'Economic Policy and Performance under Mrs Thatcher', *papers of Sir Bryan Hopkin, Arts and Social Studies Library, Cardiff University*, vol. 446/12 (2007)

E. H. H. Green, *Ideologies of Conservatism: Conservative Political Ideas in the Twentieth Century* (Oxford: Oxford University Press, 2002)

Stuart Hall, Edward Thompson and Raymond Williams, *New Left: May Day Manifesto* (London: Goodwin Press, 1967)

David Harvey, *A Brief History of Neoliberalism* (Oxford: Oxford University Press, 2005)

Christopher Harvie, *Broonland: The Last Days of Gordon Brown* (London: Verso, 2010)

Andrew Hindmoor, *New Labour at the Centre: Constructing Political Space* (Oxford: Oxford University Press, 2011)

J. A. Hobson, *Imperialism: A Study* (London: Cosimo, 1902)

J. A. Hobson, 'The General Election: A Sociological Interpretation', *Sociological Review*, vol. 3 (1910)

Stuart Holland, 'The Industrial Strategy', in Kevin Theakston and Anthony Seldon, *New Labour, Old Labour: The Wilson and Callaghan Governments 1974–79* (London: Routledge, 2004), pp. 296–302

Martin Holmes, *The Labour Government 1974–1979: Political Aims and Economic Reality* (London: Palgrave Macmillan, 1985)

David Horner, 'The Road to Scarborough: Wilson, Labour and the Scientific Revolution', in Coopey, Fielding and Tiratsoo, *The Labour Governments 1964–1970*, pp. 48–71

Mike Hughes, *Spies at Work* (Bradford: One in Twelve Publications, 1995)

Will Hutton, *The State We're In* (London: Vintage, 1995)

Geoffrey Ingham, *Capitalism Divided: The City and Industry in British Social Development* (London: Macmillan, 1984)

Ben Jackson and Robert Saunders (eds), *Making Thatcher's Britain* (Cambridge: Cambridge University Press, 2012)

Gerald James, *In the Public Interest* (London: Little, Brown, 1995)

Kevin Jeffreys, *Retreat from New Jerusalem* (Basingstoke: Macmillan, 1997)

Wolfram Kaiser, *Using Europe, Abusing the Europeans: Britain and European Integration, 1945–73* (Basingstoke: Palgrave Macmillan, 1996)

William Keegan, *Mrs Thatcher's Economic Experiment* (Harmondsworth: Penguin, 1984)

William Keegan, *Britain without Oil: What Lies Ahead?* (Harmondsworth: Penguin, 1985)

Michael Kitson and Frank Williamson, 'The Economics of New Labour: Policy and Performance', *Cambridge Journal of Economics*, vol. 31 (2007)

John Lanchester, *Whoops! Why Everyone Owes Everyone Money and No One Can Pay* (London: Penguin, 2011)

Stewart Lansley, *Life in the Middle: The Untold Story of Britain's Average Earners*, TUC: Touchstone Pamphlet no. 6, 2009

Stewart Lansley and Howard Reed, *How to Boost the Wage Share*: TUC: Touchstone Pamphlet no. 13, 2013

Jon Lawrence and Florence Sutcliffe Braithwaite, 'Margaret Thatcher and the Decline of Class Politics', in Jackson and Saunders, *Making Thatcher's Britain*, pp. 132–147

Andrew Marr, *A History of Modern Britain* (London: Pan Books, 2007)

Nicholas Mays, Anna Dixon and Lorelei Jones, 'Return to the Market: objectives and evolution of New Labour's market reforms', in Nicholas Mays, Anna Dixon and Lorelei Jones (eds), *Understanding New Labour's Market Reforms of the NHS* (London: King's Fund, 2011), pp. 1–15

John Medhurst, *That Option No Longer Exists* (London: Zero Books, 2014)

Keith Middlemas, *Power, Competition and the State, Vol. 2: Threats to the Post-war Settlement 1961–74* (Basingstoke: Macmillan, 1990)

Roger Middleton, *The British Economy since 1945* (Basingstoke: Macmillan, 2001)

Roger Middleton (ed.), *Inside the Department of Economic Affairs: Samuel Brittan, the Diary of an 'Irregular', 1964–66* (Oxford: Oxford University Press, 2012)

Seumas Milne, *The Enemy Within* (London: Verso, 2004)

Alan S. Milward, *The Reconstruction of Western Europe 1945–51* (London: Methuen, 1984)

Alan S. Milward, *The European Rescue of the Nation-State* (2nd edn, London: Routledge, 2000)

George Monbiot, *Captive State: The Corporate Takeover of Britain* (London: Pan Macmillan, 2000)

Charles Moore, *Margaret Thatcher: The Authorised Biography, Volume 1: Not for Turning* (London: Allen Lane, 2013)

Michael Moran, *The Politics of Banking* (London: Macmillan, 1986)

Kenneth O. Morgan, *The People's Peace: British History 1945–1990* (Oxford: Oxford University Press, 1992)

Kenneth O. Morgan, *Callaghan: A Life* (Oxford: Oxford University Press, 1997)

Rick Muir, *Not for Profit: The Role of the Private Sector in England's Schools* (London: Institute for Public Policy Research, 2012)

Michael Newman, *Socialism and European Unity: The Dilemma of the Left in Britain and France* (London: Junction Books, 1983)

Scott Newton, *Profits of Peace: The Political Economy of Anglo-German Appeasement* (Oxford: Oxford University Press, 1996)

Scott Newton, *The Global Economy 1944–2000* (London: Arnold, 2004)

Scott Newton, 'The Two Sterling Crises of 1964', *The Economic History Review*, vol. 62 (2009), pp. 73–98

Scott Newton, 'The Sterling Devaluation of 1967, the International Economy and Post-War Social Democracy', *The English Historical Review*, vol. CXXV, no. 515 (2010), pp. 912–945

Scott Newton, 'Sterling, Bretton Woods and Social Democracy, 1968–70', *Diplomacy & Statecraft*, vol. 24 (2013), pp. 427–455

Scott Newton and Dilwyn Porter, *Modernization Frustrated: The Politics of Industrial Decline in Britain since 1900* (London: Unwin Hyman, 1988)

Glen O'Hara, *From Dreams to Disillusionment: Economic and Social Planning in the 1960s* (Basingstoke: Macmillan, 2007)

Glen O'Hara, 'Dynamic, Exciting, Thrilling Change': The Wilson Government's Economic Policies, 1964–70', *Contemporary British History*, vol. 20 (2006), 383–402

Richard Parker, *John Kenneth Galbraith* (New York: Farrar, Strauss, Giroux, 2005)

Helen Parr, *Britain's Policy towards the European Community: Harold Wilson and Britain's World Role, 1964–1967* (Abingdon: Routledge, 2005)

Henry Pelling, *A Short History of the Labour Party*, 5th edn (Basingstoke: Macmillan, 1976)

Barrie Penrose and Roger Courtiour, *The Pencourt File* (London: Secker and Warburg, 1978)

Leo Pliatzky, *Getting and Spending: Public Expenditure, Employment and Inflation* (Oxford: Blackwell, 1984)

Sidney Pollard, *The Wasting of the British Economy* (Beckenham: Croom Helm, 1984)

Sidney Pollard, *The Development of the British Economy 1914–1990* (London: Edward Arnold, 1992)

Clive Ponting, *Breach of Promise: Labour in Power 1964–70* (London: Penguin, 1990).

Dilwyn Porter, 'British Sport Transformed: Sport, Business and the Media since 1960', in Richard Coopey and Peter Lyth (eds), *Business in Britain in the Twentieth Century* (Oxford: Oxford University Press, 2009), pp. 330–355

Robin Ramsay, 'Mrs Thatcher, North Sea oil and the Hegemony of the City', *Lobster*, 27 (1994), pp. 1–7

Robin Ramsay, 'Back to the Future: The British Political Economy of the 1970s Re-examined', *Lobster*, 34 (1998), pp. 26–30

Robin Ramsay, *The Rise of New Labour* (Harpenden: Pocket Essentials, 2002)

Robin Ramsay and Stephen Dorril, *Smear! Wilson and the Secret State* (London: 4th Estate, 1991)

Chris Rogers, 'The Labour Government, the Treasury and the £6 Pay Policy of July 1975', *British Politics*, vol. 5 (2010), pp. 224–236

John Ross, *Thatcher and Friends: The Anatomy of the Tory Party* (London: Pluto Press, 1983)

Paul Routledge, *Public Servant, Secret Agent: The Elusive Life and Violent Death of Airey Neave* (London: Fourth Estate, 2003)

Dominic Sandbrook, *Never Had It So Good: A History of Britain from Suez to the Beatles* (London: Abacus, 2005)

Dominic Sandbrook, *White Heat: A History of Britain in the Swinging Sixties* (London: Abacus, 2006)

Dominic Sandbrook, *Seasons in the Sun: The Battle for Britain, 1974–76* (London: Penguin, 2012)

Camilla Schofield, 'A Nation or No Nation?, Enoch Powell and Thatcherism', in Ben Jackson and Robert Saunders (eds), *Making Thatcher's Britain* (Cambridge: Cambridge University Press, 2012), pp. 95–110

Eric Shaw, *Losing Labour's Soul? New Labour and the Blair Government 1997–2007* (London: Routledge, 2007)

Nicholas Shaxson, *Treasure Islands: Tax Havens and the Men Who Stole the World* (London: Vintage, 2012)

David Smith, *North and South: Britain's Economic, Social and Political Divide* (London: Penguin Books, 1988)

Philip Stevens, *Politics and the Pound: The Conservatives' Struggle with Sterling* (Basingstoke: Macmillan, 1996)

Robert Taylor, 'The Heath Government, Industrial Policy and the "New Capitalism"', in Ball and Seldon, *The Heath Government 1970–74*, pp. 139–160

Kevin Theakston, *The IMF Crisis of 1976 and British Politics* (London and New York: Tauris Academic Studies, 2005)

Catherine Schenk, *The Decline of Sterling: Managing the Retreat of an International Currency 1945–1992* (Cambridge: Cambridge University Press, 2010)

Michael Stewart, *The Jekyll and Hyde Years: Politics and Economic Policy since 1964* (London: Dent, 1977)

D. R. Thorpe, *Supermac: The Life of Harold Macmillan* (London: Chatto and Windus, 2010)

Nicholas Timmins, *The Five Giants: A Biography of the Welfare State* (London: Harper Collins, 2001)

Noel Thompson, *Political Economy and the Labour Party*, 2nd edn (London: Routledge, 2006)

David Thomson, *England in the Twentieth Century* (London: Penguin, 1965)

David Thomson, *Democracy in France since 1870* (Oxford: Oxford University Press, 1969)

Jim Tomlinson, *The Labour Governments 1964–1970, Volume 3: Economic Policy* (Manchester: Manchester University Press, 2004)

Jim Tomlinson, 'Tale of a Death Exaggerated: How Keynesian Policies Survived the 1970s', *Contemporary British History*, vol. 21 (2007), pp. 429–448

Gianni Toniolo (with the assistance of Piet Clement), *Central Bank Cooperation at the Bank for International Settlements, 1930–1973* (Cambridge: Cambridge University Press, 2005)

Kees Van der Pijl, *The Making of an Atlantic Ruling Class* (London: Verso, 1984)

Richard Vinen, *Thatcher's Britain: The Politics and Social Upheavals of the 1980s* (London: Pocket Books, 2009)

Richard Wade, *Conservative Economic Policy: From Heath in Opposition to Cameron in Coalition* (London: Palgrave Macmillan, 2013)

Douglas Wass, *Decline to Fall: The Making of British Macro-Economic Policy and the 1976 IMF Crisis* (Oxford: Oxford University Press, 2007)

Nicholas Woodward, *The Management of the British Economy, 1945–2001* (Manchester: Manchester University Press, 2004)

Charles Woolfson, John Foster and Matthew Beck, *Paying for the Piper: Capital and Labour in Britain's Offshore Oil Industry* (London: Mansell, 1997)

INDEX

Note: page numbers in italic type refer to Tables; those in bold type refer to Figures.

10 Downing Street, bugging of 117
1944 settlement 2–3, 7, 18, 93, 149

Abel-Smith, Brian 25
ABN-AMRO 229
abortion laws 68
academy schools 214
'accumulation by dispossession' 224
Act of Union 1707 3
Adamson, Campbell 90, 92
Addison, Paul 1
Adonis, Andrew 214
Advisory, Conciliation and Arbitration Service 102
AEA *see* Atomic Energy Authority
aerospace industry 65, 114, 173; Labour government 1997–2010 (New Labour) 218, 232; privatisation of 148, 164
AES *see* Alternative Economic Strategy
AEU *see* Amalgamated Engineering Workers Union
Africa, decolonization of 14
AIG *see* American International Group
Aims of Industry 121
Airwork 118
Aitken, Jonathan 196
Al-Fayed, Mohammed 196
Al-Yamamah agreement 173, 218
All-Britain Anti-Poll Tax federation 177

Alliance Boots 224
Alternative Economic Strategy (AES) 105–8, 110, 115, 231
Amalgamated Engineering Workers Union (AEU) 91, 112
ambulance drivers, strike action 132
American International Group (AIG) 226, 227, 228
Amey plc 214
Andrew, Christopher 116, 136n108
Anglican Church 159, 160–1
Anglo-Eastern Bank 118
Anglo-Iranian 172
Angola 119
apprenticeships 36
Approach to an Industrial Strategy (White Paper 1975) 113, 114
Arab-Israeli War, 1973 87
ARAMCO 101
aristocracy, and Macmillan 19
arms exports 173
Armstrong, Sir William 83, 92
Ascherson, Neal 217
ASLEF 81, 90, 91
Asquith, H. H. 5
Associated Electrical Industries 65
Association of British Chambers of Commerce 21
Aston University 160
Atkinson, Fred 59
Atomic Energy Authority (AEA) 46

Atomic Weapons Research Establishment (AWRE) 65, 66
Attlee, Clement 7, 8, 18, 20, 35, 98; *see also* Labour government 1945–1951
austerity policies 242, 243
Australia 8, 13
Austria 20
automotive industry 36, 65, 97, 113–14, 144, 164
AWRE *see* Atomic Weapons Research Establishment

BAE Systems 173; *see also* British Aerospace
Bahamas 220
Baker, Kenneth 186
balance of payments: 1964 37–8; Conservative government 1970–1974 87; Conservative government 1979–1990 (Thatcher) 166; and the Labour government 1964–1970 48, 59, 61, 62–3
Baldwin, Stanley 154
Ball, James 84, 86
ballistic missiles 14–15
Balls, Ed 143, 244
Balogh, Thomas 51
Bank for International Settlements (BIS) 63, 103–4, 124, 128
Bank of England 63; and the 1944 settlement 2; 1957 sterling crisis 16, 17; 2008 financial crisis 230, 231; bank rescues 1973 87; and CCC (Competition and Credit Control) 85; independence 210; and Northern Rock 228
Bank Rate changes: 1964 49; 1966 58, 59; 1968 61; 1971 80, 84; *see also* MLR (Minimum Lending Rate)
banks: and mortgage lending 163–4; secondary 85, 86, 109; *see also* financial sector
Barber, Tony 76, 79, 80, 95n89, 165, 166
Barclays 85, 168, 218, 219, 227, 229, 230
Barings bank 219
Barnett, Corelli 1–2
Barnett, Joel 102
BBC, and the miners' strike 157–8
BCS *see* British and Commonwealth Shipping
Bear Stearns 228
Beaver, Sir Hugh 29, 30
Beck, Matthew 171–2
Beckett, Andy 1
Beckett, Sir Terence 154
Benn, Tony 65, 66, 91, 111, 113, 120, 127, 157, 171, 209, 233; AES (Alternative Economic Strategy) 105–8, 110, 115, 231

Berlin 15
Bermuda 220
Bernstein, George 2
Bevan, Aneurin 177
Beyond the Fringe 19
Big Bang reforms 168–9, 196
Big Society 234
Birch, Nigel 17, 18
Birmingham pub bombs 118
Birmingham riots, 1981 146
BIS *see* Bank for International Settlements
BL *see* British Leyland
Black Country: deindustrialisation 143–4; *see also* West Midlands
Black Wednesday 190, 194, 195
Black, Conrad 197
Blair, Tony 197; background and party leadership 201–2; and the Clinton Administration 205; and public sector unions 213–14; *see also* Labour government 1979–2010 (New Labour)
Blanchflower, David 243
BLMC *see* British Leyland Motor Corporation
Blue Streak missile 14, 15, 38
BNOC *see* British National Oil Corporation
Board of Trade 35, 76
Boyson, Rhodes 121
BP *see* British Petroleum
Bradford and Bingley 231
Bradford University 160
Brandt, Willy 81
Bretton Woods system 51, 86, 98, 170, 232
Brexit referendum 2016 246
Britain in Europe campaign, 1975 EEC referendum 111
British Aerospace 164, 173, 175
British Airports Authority 221
British Airways 224
British and Commonwealth Shipping (BCS) 104
British Coal 195
British Empire 3–4, 8
British Leyland (BL) 65, 144, 164
British Leyland Motor Corporation (BLMC) 97, 113–14
British Motor Corporation 65
British National Oil Corporation (BNOC) 151, 164
British Petroleum (BP) 106, 164, 172–3
British Shipbuilding 164
British Steel 164
British Telecom 164, 169
British United Industrialists 121
Brittan, Leon 175

Brittan, Samuel 166
Brixton riots, 1981 146, 197n25
Brown, George 46, 48, 58, 67; and Britain's second bid to join the EEC 59–60
Brown, Gordon 201, 216, 225, 232, 233, 235, 321; Chancellor of the Exchequer 208, 210, 212, 213, 219; and the Clinton Administration 205, 208; *see also* Labour government 1997–2010 (New Labour)
Bruges Group 196
Budgets: of 1962 33; of 1963 33; of 1965 54; of 1966 57; of 1968 63; of 1970 76; of 1971 76, 79; of 1974 100, 103; of 1979 151; of 1981, March 154, 162; of 1988 163; of 1992 (Autumn Statement) 191–2; of 1993 (March) 192; of 1993 (November) 192; of 2008 (Autumn Statement) 231–2; of 2009 232; People's Budget 1909 5
Bullock Report 114
Butler, R. A. 17
Byers, Lord 117

Cable and Wireless 164
Callaghan, James: Chancellor of the Exchequer, 1964–1967 46, 58, 61, 122; Foreign Secretary, 1974–1976 109, 111, 122; Home Secretary, 1967–1970 12; and the IMF 115, 124–30; political background 122; Shadow Foreign Secretary 91; *see also* Labour government 1974–1979
Cameron, David 233, 234, 242, 245; *see also* Coalition government 2010–2015
Campaign for Nuclear Disarmament (CND) 15, 177
Campbell-Bannerman, Henry 5
Campbell, Alistair 201
Canada 8, 13
car production 36, 65, 97, 113–14, 144, 164
Carr, Robert 91
Carrington, Lord 117, 147
cartels 106
Carter, President Jimmy 204
Castle, Barbara 62, 67–8, 71n24
Cater Ryder 118
Cayman Islands 2220
Cayzer, Sir Nicholas 104, 118
Cazenove's 118
CBI (Confederation of British Industry) 133; and the 1944 settlement 2; Conservative government 1970–1974 76, 78, 84, 89, 90; Conservative government 1979–1990 (Thatcher) 154, 169; Conservative government 1990–1997 (Major) 193, 194; Labour government 1964–1970 48, 66–7; Labour government 1974–1979 114; monetarism 89; North Sea oil revenues 171; *see also* FBI (Federation of British Industries)
CCC *see* Competition and Credit Control
CDOs *see* collateralized debt obligations
CDS *see* credit default swaps
Cedar Holdings 87
censorship laws 68
central banks, and monetarism 103–4
Central Policy Review Staff (CPRS) 76
Centre for Policy Studies (CPS) 77–8, 79, 80–1, 83, 88, 104, 118, 120
Ceylon (Sri Lanka) 8
Chambers of Commerce 89, 193
Channel Tunnel 221
Chatsworth House 19
child poverty: Labour government 1997–2010 (New Labour) 212, 215
Chrysler 113, 114
Churchill, Winston 7, 13, 15, 148
City of London: 1944 settlement 2; 1957 sterling crisis 16, 17; 2008 financial crisis 227; Conservative government 1979–1990 (Thatcher) 167–71; early twentieth century 5–6; Labour government 1997–2010 (New Labour) 219–20, 227; as nineteenth-century financial centre 4; sterling crises, 1960s 53, 54–61, **56, 60**; Wilson's views on 109
Civil Assistance 117, 121
Clarke, Kenneth 191, 192, 205
Clarke, Peter 1, 2
Clarke, R. W. B. 29
Clause IV (Labour Party) 203–4
Clegg, Nick 234; *see also* Coalition government 2010–2015
Clinton, President Bill 204–5
Clockwork Orange operation 117
CND *see* Campaign for Nuclear Disarmament
co-operatives 106
coal industry: miner's strike 1984–1986 155–8; *see also* NCB (National Coal Board); NUM (National Union of Mineworkers)
Coalition government 2010–2015 234, 242–4
Cockerell, Michael 120
Cold War 15, 19
collateralized debt obligations (CDOs) 226, 227
Commission on Industrial Relations 68
commodification 224

commodity price rises, 1973–1974 99–100
Common Market *see* EEC (European Economic)
Commonwealth 8, 20, 23, 38; and the Suez crisis 13, 14
Competition and Credit Control (CCC) 84–6, 87, 88
competitive tendering 160
comprehensive education 56
computing industries 48, 65, 66
Concorde airliner 66, 74n115
Conditions Favourable to Growth (NEDC) 32
Confederation of British Industry *see* CBI (Confederation of British Industry)
Confrontation with Indonesia, 1966 56, 71n34
Conservative government 1951–1955 7
Conservative government 1955–1959 7; sterling crisis 1957 16–17
Conservative government 1959–1964 13–39; dash for growth 31–9; economic policy 18–19; and the EEC 20–3; foreign policy 15, 23; planning modernization 24–31; regional policy 35–6
Conservative government 1970–1974 75–93; 'whirlpool' period, 1973 84–8; breakdown, 1973–1974 88–93; disengagement policy 75–9, 82, 83, 90; industrial relations 77, 79, 81–2, 90–2; industrial strategy 78, 82–3, 84; policy change, 1971–72 79–83; public spending 76, 80
Conservative government 1979–1990 (Thatcher) 143–78; conflict 155–61; downfall 175–8; financial deregulation 167–71; industrial policy 148, 158–9, 173; industrial relations 148, 155–9; money policy 151–5; North Sea oil resources 171–3; policy changes 161–7; public spending 151, 153–4.163; Thatcherism 146–50
Conservative government 1990–1997 (Major) 185–98; coal industry 194–5; decline and end of 194–8; and Europe 186–7; industrial policy 193–4; new economic policy 191–4; public spending 186, 191, 192; sterling crises 187–91
Conservative Party: 2005 General Election 216; 2010 General Election 233–4; and the EEC 22; Eurosceptics 190–1, 196–7; mid-twentieth century 6; and plots against the Labour government 1974–1979 118, 120–1; Scottish Parliament 247; *see also* Coalition government 2010–2015
Consett steel works 144
Consolidated Goldfields 118
constitutional reform: Labour government 1997–2010 (New Labour) 209; *see also* devolution
Consumer's Britain 25, 93, 220, 221, 246–7
Consumer's England 5, 120, 173
Cook, Chris 48
Corby steel works 144
Corbyn, Jeremy 247
Corn Laws, repeal of 4
corporate governance 170, 207
corporation tax evasion 219–20
Cortonwood colliery 156–7
council houses 192; right to buy 148, 164; *see also* housing provision
Council of Ministers 187
Council Tax 177
Courtaulds 21
Cousins, Frank 34, 45, 58
CPRS (Central Policy Review Staff) 76
CPS *see* Centre for Policy Studies
credit *see* CCC (Competition and Credit Control)
credit default swaps (CDS) 226, 227, 228
credit markets, liberalization of 163–4
Cromer, Lord 37, 49, 54
Crosland, Anthony 24, 75, 78–9, 88, 170; Environment Secretary 109; Foreign Secretary 127–8
Crossman, Richard 55
Crossrail 221
Crown Agents 85
Crozier, Brian 116–17, 120–1, 150
Cuba 15
cultural industries: Labour government 1997–2010 (New Labour) 218

Darlaston 143
Darling, Alistair 228, 229, 231, 232, 233
dash for growth 31–9, 48, 87
Davie, Grace 1
Davies, John 67, 78, 91
de Gaulle, President Charles 23, 35, 60, 77
De Havilland Comet 8
de Zulueta, Philip 15
de-unionization 223
DEA (Department of Economic Affairs) 45, 46, 57. 58, 61, 64, 83
'declinism' 1–2, 24
decolonization 8, 14, 38, 119
Deedes, Bill 117
'Deep State' 117, 174

defence policy: 1950s to early 1960s 14–15; Conservative government 1979–1990 (Thatcher) 148; Labour government 1964–1970 54, 55, 63, 64, *64*, 66, 68
deflation 37, 49
deindustrialisation 194, 221–2; Conservative government 1979–1990 (Thatcher) 143–6
Delors, Jacques 176
Democratic Party, USA 204–5
Denmark 20
DEP (Department of Employment and Productivity) 67, 69
Department of Economic Affairs (DEA) 45, 46, 57, 58, 61, 64, 83
Department of the Environment 76
Department of Trade and Industry (DTI) 76, 78, 82, 83, 193
derivatives 226–7
deutschmark, German 16, 17, 18
devaluation of sterling 49–51, 59; 1957 fears of 16; 1976 123; *see also* sterling
Development Districts 35–6
devolution 197, 203, 209
DHAs (District Health Authorities) 214–15
Distillers Company 168
divorce laws 68
dock strikes 61
docks modernisation 36
dollar 51, 99; *see also* Eurodollars
Donoughue, Bernard 111, 116, 135n86
Donovan, Lord 67, 68
Douglas-Home, Sir Alec 34, 35, 43; *see also* Conservative government 1959–1964
DTI (Department of Trade and Industry) 76, 78, 82, 83, 193
Duffy, Terry 131
Dulles, John Foster 13–14
Duncan, Sir Val 117
Dunfermline Building Society 231

EC (European Community): Conservative government 1990–1997 (Major) 186–7, 190–1, 196–7; Maastricht Treaty 187; *see also* Common Market); EEC (European Economic Community; EU (European Union)
ECB (European Central Bank) 210
Economic Development Committees (EDCs) ('little Neddies') 36, 46, 57, 69
Economic Prospects to 1972: A Revised Assessment 69
economy: 1950s 7, 15–16; Conservative government 1970–1974 84, 88; Conservative government 1979–1990 (Thatcher) 162–7, 170; Labour government 1964–1970 48, **56**, 56–7, 68–9; Labour government 1974–1979 97, 98–9, 103, 129, 130; Labour government 1997–2010 (New Labour) 211, 213, 215–16, 218, 224–5; mid-twentieth century 6
EDCs *see* Economic Development Committees
Eden, Anthony 7, 8, 14, 15; *see also* Conservative government 1955–1959
Edgerton, David 2
education: academy schools 214; early 1960s 22–3, 24, 27; expansion of tertiary education 27; and industrial policy 36; Labour government 1964–1970 56; Labour government 1966–1970 64, *64*; Labour government 1997–2010 (New Labour) 206, 212, 213, 214, 223; post-15 22–3; *see also* higher education; universities
Education Maintenance Allowance 243
Edward VII, King 3
EEC (European Economic Community; Common Market): Britain's early relationship with 15, 19, 26; Britain's first application 20–3, 35; Britain's second application 59–60, 61; Britain's third application and accession to 76–7, 83; Conservative government 1979–1990 (Thatcher) 171, 175–6; economic growth, 1955–1960 15; and the Labour government 1975–1979 108–9, 110–11; *see also* EC (European Community); EU (European Union)
EFTA *see* European Free Trade Area
Egypt 4
Eisenhower, President Dwight D. 13, 14
electrics industry 65
electronics industry 65
Elizabeth II, Queen, coronation, 1953 8
Employment Protections Act 102
Employment: The Challenge for the Nation (White Paper, 1985) 158–9
EMS *see* European Monetary System
'enemy within' 150, 155, 159
Engineering Employers' Federation 193
English Electric 65
Enron 202
Enterprise Oil 164
Enterprise Zones 173–4
ERM (Exchange Rate Mechanism): Conservative government 1979–1990 (Thatcher) 175–6; Conservative government 1990–1997 (Major) 187–91, 193

ethnic minorities, urban riots 1981 146
EU (European Union) 187; Brexit referendum 2014 246; Conservative government 1990–1997 (Major) 196–7; *see also* Common Market); EC (European Community); EEC (European Economic Community)
euro 210; crisis 243; *see also* European Monetary Union
Eurodollars 51, **52**, 53, 57, 86, 99, 106, 170
European Central Bank (ECB) 210
European Commission 176, 187
European Elections: 2009 217
European Free Trade Area (EFTA) 20–1
European Monetary System (EMS) 175
European Monetary Union 175, 187, 196; *see also* euro
European Parliament 187
Eurosceptics 190–1, 196–7
Evans, Moss 131
Everest, first ascent 7
Exchange Rate Mechanism (ERM) *see* ERM (Exchange Rate Mechanism)
Export Council for Europe 22
Ezra, Sir Derek 157

Fairey 114
Faith in the City (Anglican Church) 160–1
Falklands War 150, 162, 174
Fannie Mae 228
FBI (Federation of British Industries) 48; and the EEC 21, 22; and the NEDC (National Economic Development Council) 31, 32, 33; and planning 27–8, 29; *see also* CBI (Confederation of British Industry)
Feather, Vic 68
Federal Reserve Bank of New York (FRBNY) 53, 99
Federation of British Industries (FBI) *see* FBI (Federation of British Industries)
Felixstowe docks 157
Ferranti 114
final salary pension schemes 224
financial crisis 2008 228–31; global stimulus package 232–3; roots of 225–8
financial deregulation: Conservative government 1979–1990 (Thatcher) 163–4, 167–71
financial sector: and CCC (Competition and Credit Control) 84–6; Conservative government 1970–1974 85–6, 87–8; Conservative government 1979–1990 (Thatcher) 163–4, 167–71; Labour government 1997–2010 (New Labour) 218–20; post-war period 2
Financial Services Authority (FSA) 219
financialization 169–70, 190, 224
Fisher, Alan 131
'flexible accumulation' 158–9, 223
Foot, Michael 102
Foot, Paul 48
Ford 131
Foreign Office 76
foreign policy: 'three circles' doctrine 13; Conservative government 1959–1964 15
Foster, John 171–2
France 8, 206–7; planning 28–9
FRBNY *see* Federal Reserve Bank of New York
Freddie Mac 228
free trade, nineteenth-century 4, 5
freedom of information 197
Friedman, Milton 89, 124
FSA (Financial Services Authority) 219

G10 (Group of Ten) 124, 125, 128
Gaitskell, Hugh 44, 99, 177
Galbraith, J. K. 25
Gamble, Andrew 150
GATT: Kennedy Round 99
GB75 117
GEC (General Electric Company) 22, 65, 66
General Elections: of 1945 98; of 1951 7; of 1955 7; of 1959 18; of 1964 37–8, 43, 45; cf 1966 50, 55; of 1970 50; of 1974 (February) 92, 115, 118; of 1974 (October) 103, 115; of 1979 120, 132, 133, 146–7, 149, 172; of 1983 162, 164; of 1987 205; of 1989 176; of 1992 188, 201, 202, 205; of 1997 198, 205, 209; of 2001 213, 216; of 2005 216; of 2010 231, 233–4, 242; of 2015 244–5, 247
General Electric Company (GEC) 22, 65, 66
Geneva Accords 8
Germany 6; *see also* deutschmark, German
Get Britain Out campaign, 1975 EEC referendum 111
Giddens, Anthony 207
Gilmour, Sir Ian 147, 154
Gini coefficient: 1977 132; 2015 246; Conservative government 1979–1990 (Thatcher) 174
GKN (Guest, Keen and Nettlefolds) 89, 143
Glass-Steagall Act 1933 204
GLC *see* Greater London Council
globalization 206

Godley, Wynne 59, 162–3
'golden rule' 210
Goldman Sachs 170
Gormley, Joe 91, 156
Gould, Philip 205
Govan Shipbuilders 82
Gove, Michael 246
Gramsci, Antonio 161
Greater London Council (GLC) 159–60
Greece: sovereign debt crisis 234, 242
Greenspan, Alan 205
Group of Ten (G10) 124, 125, 128
Growth of the UK Economy to 1966, The (NEDC) 32
Grunwick Film Processing Laboratories 137n136
Guernsey 219
Guinness 168
Gulf War, 1991 174

Haines, Joe 135n56
Halifax Bank of Scotland *see* HBOS
Hall, Robert 29
Hall, Stuart 150
Halsey, A.H. 161
Hambros 85
Hamilton, Neil 196
Hanson Trust 168, 207
Harvey, David 224
Harvie, Christopher 217
HBOS (Halifax Bank of Scotland) 218, 229, 230
Healey, Denis: Chancellor of the Exchequer 100, 102, 103, 109, 112, 113, 123; and the IMF 115, 124–30
Health and Safety Executive 102
Heath, Edward: at the Board of Trade 35; economic policy 80; and the EEC 22, 76–7; industrial relations policy 77, 79, 81–2, 90–2; and monetarism 89–90; 'quiet revolution' strategy 74–5; *see also* Conservative government 1970–1974
Heathcoat Amory, Derick 18
Heathfield, Peter 156, 157
Heseltine, Michael: and the coal industry 194; leadership challenge 176; President of the Board of Trade 191, 193–4; Secretary of State for the Environment 186; Westland crisis 175
higher education: Conservative government 1979–1990 (Thatcher) 159, 160; early 1960s 23, 24; Labour government 1964–1970 56; Labour government 1966–1970 64, *64*; Robbins Report 27
Hillary, Edmund 7

hire purchase controls 80, 84
HMRC (HM Revenue and Customs) 219
Hobson, J. A. 5, 117, 173, 197
Hogg, Quintin 147
Hoggart, Richard 25–6
Holland, Stuart 106–7, 108, 109, 110
homelessness 245
homosexuality laws 68
Honda 144
Hong Kong 220
Hong Kong and Shanghai Banking Corporation *see* HSBC
Hoskyns, John 154
hospital staff: strike action 132
House of Lords reform 209
house prices: Coalition government 2010–2015 245; Conservative government 1970–1974 84, 86, 87; Conservative government 1979–1990 (Thatcher) 164, 166; Labour government 1997–2010 (New Labour) 225–6, 227–8
Housing Act 1980 164
housing provision: 1950s 7; Conservative government 1990–1997 (Major) 192; early 1960s 25, 26–7; Labour government 1964–1970 56; Labour government 1966–1970 64, *64*; Labour government 1997–2010 (New Labour) 221, 225
Howe, Sir Geoffrey 151; Chancellor of the Exchequer 147, 152, 154; Foreign Secretary 165; sacking from Foreign Office 176; Shadow Chancellor 126
HSBC (Hong Kong and Shanghai Banking Corporation) 218, 224, 227
Hungary 14
Hunt, John 7
Hurd, Douglas 186
Hutton, Will 207–8, 244
hyperinflation 112

ICI (Imperial Chemical Industries) 22, 202, 221
ICL (International Computers Ltd) 65, 106
IEA (Institute for Economic Affairs) 78, 88, 161
IMF (International Monetary Fund) 49, 52, 54, 59, 61, 98, 99, 100, 232; and the Labour government 1974–1979 97, 121, 124–9; and monetarism 103–4; and petrodollars 101
immigration 149, 223, 234
Imperial Chemical Industries *see* ICI
Imperial Group 168, 207
In Place of Strife 67–8, 122
India 8, 13

indigenous cultures 224
Indochina 8
industrial democracy 106, 114
Industrial Development Executive 83
Industrial Expansion Act 1968 65–6667
industrial policy: Conservative government 1959–1964 35–6; Conservative government 1970–1974 78, 82–3, 84; Conservative government 1979–1990 (Thatcher) 148, 158–9, 173; Conservative government 1990–1997 193–4; Labour government 1964–1970 36, 45–7, 57, 65–9; Labour government 1974–1979 105–8, 110, 113–15, 122, 125; Labour government 1997–2010 (New Labour) 218
industrial relations: Conservative government 1970–1974 77, 79, 81–2, 90–2; Conservative government 1979–1990 (Thatcher) 148, 155–9; Labour government 1964–1970 67–8; Labour government 1974–1979 97, 99, 102, 105, 112, 119, 123, 129, 130–2; Labour government 1997–2010 (New Labour) 206, 209–10, 213–14
Industrial Relations Act 1971 77, 79, 81–2, 89, 90, 92, 102, 148
Industrial Reorganisation Corporation *see* IRC
Industrial Training Act 1964 36
Industrial Training Boards (ITBs) 36
industrialization: social impacts of 4–5
Industry Act 1972 82, 83
inequality: Coalition government 2010–2015 245–6; Gini coefficient, 1977 132; Gini coefficient, 2015 246
inflation: 1957 sterling crisis 17, 18; 1971 80–1; 1973 87; Conservative government 1979–1990 (Thatcher) 147, 149, 151, 153, 162, 164, 165, 166; Conservative government 1990–1997 (Major) 185, 191, 192; Labour government 1974–1979 102–3, 111–12, 122–3, 131; Labour government 1997–2010 (New Labour) 210, 211; and monetarism 89; and the Phillips curve 88
infrastructure development: Conservative government 1970–1974 83; early 1960s 24–5; Labour government 1964–1970 **64,** 64–5; Labour government 1997–2010 (New Labour) 206, 221
Inmos 114
insecure employment 223
Institute for Economic Affairs (IEA) 78, 88, 161

insurance companies 169–70
intelligence agencies: and the miners' strike 157; and plots against the Labour government 1974–1979 116, 117, 118, 120–1
International Bank for Reconstruction and Development 98; *see also* World Bank
International Computers Ltd (ICL) 65, 106
International Monetary Fund (IMF) *see* IMF (International Monetary Fund)
International Swaps and Derivatives Association (ISDA) 226–7
internment without trial 116
invisible trade, early twentieth century 4
Iran 101, 172
Iraq 172, 205, 217
IRC (Industrial Reorganisation Corporation) 65, 76, 107, 110, 113–14
Ireland 20; Potato Famine 133; *see also* Northern Ireland
IRI (*Istituto per la Riconstruzione Industrialei*) 107
ISDA (International Swaps and Derivatives Association) 226–7
Isle of Man 219
Italy 119

Japan 6, 159
Jarrow 144
Jay, Peter 125, 131
Jenkins, Roy: Chancellor of the Exchequer 61–2, 63; Home Secretary 109
Jenkins, Simon 157
Jersey 219
Johnson, Boris 246
Johnson, President L. B. 54, 56
Jones, Harriet 1
Jones, Jack 81, 112, 122, 123, 131
Joseph, Sir Keith 77–8, 79, 80–1, 83, 88, 104, 120; Secretary of State for Industry 144, 147, 154

Kahn, Lord Richard 62, 73n99
Keating, Ron 161
Keegan, William 213
Kennedy Round of GATT talks 99
Kennedy, President John F. 14–15
Keynes, J. M. 2–3, 20, 73n99, 86, 98
Keynesian economics 18, 80, 103, 125
'Keynesian plus' policies 44
King, Cecil 68, 69, 117
King, Mervyn 216
Kinnock, Neil 176, 177–8, 188, 201, 202
Knight, Jill 121
knowledge economy 2, 218

Koestler, Arthur 24
Kohlberg Kravis Roberts 224
Kuwait 110, 112

Labour government 1945–1951 7, 8, 98–9
Labour government 1964–1970 43–69, 99; 'hard slog' period 61–4; industrial and technology policy 36, 45–7, 57, 65–9; modernization policies 44–9, 64; public investment **64,** 64–5; sterling crises 49–59, **52, 56, 60,** 63–4
Labour government 1974–1979 97–133; alternative strategy 104–9, 110; external environment and context 97–102; and the IMF crisis 97, 121, 124–9; industrial policy 105–8, 110, 113–15, 122, 125; industrial relations 97, 100, 102, 105, 112, 119, 123, 129, 130–2; North Sea oil revenues 172; plans to overthrow 116–21, 122; public spending 97, 115, 123, 124, 125–6, 127, 128; 'winter of discontent' 98, 132–3
Labour government 1997–2010 (New Labour) 198, 201–35; decline and defeat 233–5; economic and social programme 209–16; financial crisis 222–30; fractures in 216–22; New Labour 201–4; public spending 205, 206, 209, 212–13, 214, 215, 220, 222, 232; recovery policies 2008–2010 230–3; Third Way policies 204–9
Labour Party: 2010 General Election 234, 235; Clause IV 203–4; electoral collapse in Scotland 244, 245, 247; funding under Blair's leadership 202; mid-twentieth century 6; in opposition 2010–2016 244, 245, 247; in opposition, 1979–1990 162, 176, 177–8; in opposition, 1990–1997 188, 195, 197; in Scotland 216–17; and working class voters 5
Lamont, Norman 193; Chancellor of the Exchequer 186, 188, 189, 191, 192
Lawson, Nigel 150, 246; Chancellor of the Exchequer 156, 162, 163, 164, 165, 166, 167, 170, 171, 175, 176; Energy Secretary 154; Financial Secretary 151, 152; resignation 176
Lazard's 118
Learning and Skills Act 2000 214
Lee, Sir Frank 21
Leeds riots, 1981 146
Leese, Peter 1
Lehman Brothers 228, 229
Lewis, Jane 1
Leyland 65

LG Electronics 195
Liberal Democrats 198, 242; 2010 General Election 234; 2015 General Election 244; *see also* Coalition government 2010–2015
Liberal Government: People's Budget 1909 5
Liberal Party 5, 23, 198
Liddle, Roger 208
light touch regulation of the financial sector 219, 227
Linwood car plant 144
little Neddies *see* EDCs (Economic Development Committees)
Liverpool riots, 1981 146
Living Wage 245
Livingstone, Ken 185
Lloyd George, David 5, 6, 44
Lloyd, Selwyn 18, 30, 31, 32, 33
Lloyds Banking Group 230–1
Lloyds TSB 227, 229, 230
local authorities: Conservative government 1979–1990 (Thatcher) 159–60
Lockheed 66, 82
London *see* City of London
London and Counties Securities Group 87
London Docklands 174
London Stock Exchange: 'Big Bang' reforms 168–9, 196; Stock Market crash, October 1987 163
London Tube 221
Low Pay Commission 209
Lucas Aerospace 105

M0 (monetary base) 152
Maastricht Treaty 187, 196
MacGregor, Ian 156, 157
Mackie, David 48
MacLeod, Ian 76
Macmillan, Harold 16, 38–9, 154; and the 1957 sterling crisis 16, 17–18; background and politics 19–20; Chancellor of the Exchequer 14; and the EEC 19; foreign policy 14, 15; and housing provision 7; and the NIC 33–4; resignation, 1963 34; *see also* Conservative government 1955–1959; Conservative government 1959–1964
Major, John 178, 204; background and politics 185–6; Chancellor of the Exchequer 176; defeat of Thatcher 176; and the Eurosceptics 196–7; Foreign Secretary 176; *see also* Conservative government 1990–1997 (Major)
management training 48
Manchester riots, 1981 146

Manchester School 3
Mandelson, Peter 201, 202, 204, 232
Manpower Services Commission 161
manufacturing sector: Coalition government 2010–2015 242, 245; Conservative government 1979–1990 (Thatcher) 143–6, 165, 173; Labour government 1997–2010 (New Labour) 207, 218, 220–1, 222, 232; post-war period 2; *see also* deindustrialisation; industrial policy
Marconi 65
Marr, Andrew 1, 48
Marshall Plan 51, 98
Marx, Karl 3
Matthews, Robin 84, 86
Maudling, Reginald 33, 34–5, 37, 38, 43, 48, 49, 52, 87
McAlpine 121
McFadzean, Sir William 22
McKillop, Sir Tom 229
media: and the miners' strike 157–8; proprietors 197
Medium Term Financial Strategy (MTFS), Conservative government 1979–1990 (Thatcher) 151–3
mercantilism 3–4
mergers 65; Conservative government 1979–1990 (Thatcher) 168; Labour government 1997–2010 (New Labour) 207; Labour government, 1964–1970 46
Merry Hill, Dudley 174
MI5: plots against the Labour government 1974–1979 116, 117, 118, 120–1
MI6 (Secret Intelligence Service) 116
Middlemass, Keith 2, 27, 55, 69, 114, 161
Middleton, Roger 2
Midlands: deindustrialization 221–2; *see also* West Midlands
Miliband, Ed 235, 244, 247
military-industrial manufacturing sector 173
military, the: Conservative Government 1979–1990 (Thatcher) 150; miners' strike 157; plots against the Labour government 1974–1979 116–17, 118
Milward, Alan 26
miner's strike 1984–1986 155–8
Minimum Lending Rate (MLR) *see* MLR (Minimum Lending Rate)
Minimum Wage 206, 209, 245
Ministry of Housing and Local Government 76
Ministry of Overseas Trade 76
Ministry of Public Buildings and Works 76
Ministry of Transport 76

MinTech (Ministry of Technology) 45–6, 57, 65, 66, 67, 69, 76, 83, 105, 107
Mitterand, President François 206–7
mixed economy 75
MLR (Minimum Lending Rate) 85, 87; Conservative government 1979–1990 (Thatcher) 152–3, 154, 163, 166; Conservative government 1990–1997 (Major) 187, 189, 191–2
monetarism 89, 103–4, 121, 125
Monetary Policy Committee (MPC) 210
monopolies and merger legislation 26, 35
Monopolies Commission 35
Morgan Grenfell 168
Morgan Stanley 170
Morgan, Kenneth 2
mortgage lending: and the 2008 financial crisis 225–8; liberalization of 152, 163–4
Moss, Robert 121
motorway construction 27
Mountbatten of Burma, Earl 68, 116, 117
Mozambique 119
MPC (Monetary Policy Committee) 210
MPs' expenses scandal 233, 234
MTFS (Medium Term Financial Strategy), Conservative government 1979–1990 (Thatcher) 151–3
Mulgan, Geoff 208
multinational companies 106, 109, 159
Murdoch, Rupert 197

NAFF (National Association for Freedom) 121
Nasser, President Gamal Abdel 13
National Assembly for Wales 209, 216
National Assistance 25
National Board for Prices and Incomes (NBPI) 47, 55, 67, 76, 81, 82
National Childcare Strategy 212, 215
National Coal Board (NCB) *see* NCB (National Coal Board)
National Economic Development Council (NEDC) *see* NEDC (National Economic Development Council)
National Enterprise Board (NEB) 106–7, 110, 113–14, 148
National Government 116, 117
National Health Service (NHS) *see* NHS (National Health Service)
National Income Commission (NIC) 33, 34
National Industrial Relations Court (NIRC) 77
National Insurance, introduction of 5
National Investment Bank 109
National Manufacturers' Council 169

Index 267

National Plan 69, 99; Labour government 1964–1970 46, 47–9, 50, 54, 55, 56–7, 58, 61, 64
National Union of Mineworkers (NUM) see NUM (National Union of Mineworkers)
National Union of Public Employees (NUPE) 131, 132, 161
National Union of Railwaymen (NUR) 111–12
National Union of Seamen (NUS) 124
nationalism 208
nationalization 105, 106–7, 109, 114; see also AES (Alternative Economic Strategy)
NATO, and Northern Ireland 118
NBPI (National Board for Prices and Incomes) 47, 55, 67, 76, 81, 82
NCB (National Coal Board) 81, 91, 113, 195; miner's strike 1984–1986 155–8
Neave, Airey 118, 120, 121
NEB see National Enterprise Board
NEDC (National Economic Development Council) 31–3, 36, 69, 79, 113, 123, 193; and the Labour Government, 1964–1970 45, 46
negative equity 166
neo-liberalism 104, 121, 150, 161–2, 171–2, 247; Coalition government 2010–2015 242, 246; Labour government 1997–2010 (New Labour) 204, 210, 223
Nestlé 168
New Deal (Labour government 1997–2010) 211
New Deal (USA) 204
New Labour see Labour government 1997–2010 (New Labour)
New Zealand 8, 13
NHS (National Health Service): Conservative government 1979–1990 (Thatcher) 163; Conservative government 1990–1997 (Major) 195; early 1960s 25, 27; internal market 214–15; Labour government 1966–1970 64, *64*; Labour government 1997–2010 (New Labour) 212, 214–15, 223
NIC (National Income Commission) 33, 34
Nigeria 101, 112
NIRC (National Industrial Relations Court) 77
Nissan 159
non-classical endogenous growth theory 206
non-resident domiciles 219
North East England: Coalition government 2010–2015 246
North Sea oil resources 100; Conservative government 1979–1990 (Thatcher) 145, 151, 153, 163, 171–3; Labour government 1974–1979 172
Northern England: Conservative government 1979–1990 (Thatcher) 173; deindustrialization 144, 221–2
Northern Foods 202
Northern Ireland 118; Coalition government 2010–2015 246; devolution 203, 209; internment without trial 116; peace process 197
Northern Ireland Assembly 209
Northern Rock 225, 228, 230, 231
Norway 20
Nott, John 126
nuclear powers, 1950s to early 1960s 8, 14–15
NUM (National Union of Mineworkers): and the Conservative government 1970–1974 81, 82, 90, 91, 92; and the Labour Government 1974–1979 100, 102, 111, 112, 118; miner's strike 1984–1986 155–8
NUPE see National Union of Public Employees
NUR (National Union of Railwaymen) 111–12
nurses, strike action 132
NUS (National Union of Seamen) 124

O'Brien, Sir Leslie 87
O'Brien, Sir Richard 161
O'Hara, Glen 30, 32
Obama, Barack 232
OECD (Organisation for Economic Cooperation and Development) 60, 63, 64
oil industry 172–3; see also North Sea oil resources
oil price rise, 1973–1974 99–100
old age pensions, introduction of 5
Old Labour 98; see also Labour Party
One Nation Conservatism 93, 154, 185, 188, 195, 197, 223
OPEC (Organisation of the Petroleum Exporting Countries) 100–1
Open University 69
Organisation for Economic Cooperation and Development see OECD
Orgreave coking plant 158
Osborne, George 233, 234, 242, 244, 245
outsourcing 159

Paish, F. W. 30
Pakistan 8
Panasonic 159, 195

PAR (Programme Analysis Review) 76
Paribas 227–8
Paris Summit, 1960 15, 23
Parkinson, Cecil 154
part-time employment 207, 223
Patent Shaft Steelworks 143
Patten, Chris 186
pay bargaining: Conservative government 1959–1964 32, 33–4, 34–5, 37; Conservative government 1970–1974 81–2; early 1960s 30–1; Labour government 1964–1970 67; Labour government 1974–1979 102, 110–13, 122–3, 130–1
Pay Board 82, 92
Pay Pause 30–1, 32, 33, 34
pay restraint: Conservative government 1959–1964 32, 33, 34; Conservative government 1970–1974 81–2; Conservative government 1990–1997 (Major) 195; Labour government 1964–1970 47, 55, 62, 67, 68
PCTs see Primary Care Trusts
peak institutions: and the 1944 settlement 2–3; and the EEC 22
Peel, Sir Robert 133
pensions: final salary pension schemes 224; introduction of old age pensions 5; pension funds 169–70, 225
People's Budget 1909 5
Persian Gulf 172
petrodollars 101
PFI (Private Finance Initiative) 213–14, 217
Phillips curve 88
picketing 155
Pilkington Glass 221
PIRA see Provisional IRA
Plaid Cymru (PC: the Party of Wales) 216
planning: Conservative government, 1959–1964 27–31; France 28–9; USSR 28
planning agreements 107–8, 110, 113
Poland 223
Polaris missile system 15, 23
police, and the miners' strike 157
poll tax (community tax) 160, 176, 185, 186
Pollard, Sidney 1
Pompidou, President Georges 77
Ponting, Clive 48, 55
port development 36, 83
Porter, Dilwyn 2, 66
Portugal 20, 119
post-war Britain: declinism 1–2; overview of 7–8

Poujadisme 38–9, 247
poverty: Conservative government 1979–1990 (Thatcher) 174; Conservative government 1990–1997 (Major) 195; *see also* child poverty; inequality
Powell, Enoch 17, 18, 27, 88, 111, 148, 149, 176
Powell, Jonathan 201
Pratt and Whitney 66
Prescott, John 209
Price Commission 82
Primary Care Trusts (PCTs) 215
Prior, Jim 147, 154, 155
Private Eye 19
Private Finance Initiative (PFI) 213–14, 217
privatization of state-owned businesses 148, 164–5, 169
Producer's Britain 25, 34, 93, 145, 173, 217, 221, 247, 248
Producer's England 5, 6
Profumo affair 19, 34
Programme Analysis Review (PAR) 76
Pronunciamento against the Labour government 1974–1979 116–21, 122
property prices *see* house prices
property-owning democracy 148, 165
Provisional IRA (PIRA) 118, 120
Prudential 85
PSBR (Public Sector Borrowing Requirement): Conservative government 1979–1990 (Thatcher) 151, 154, 163, 164; Labour government 1974–1979 100, 123, 124, 125–6, 127, 128, 130; Labour government 1997–2010 (New Labour) 232
public sector strikes, 1979 131–2
public sector workers: Labour government 1997–2010 (New Labour) 213–14, 223
public services: charges for 79
public spending: 1950s 7, 17; Coalition government 2010–2015 242, 243, 244, 245; Conservative government 1970–1974 76, 80; Conservative government 1979–1990 (Thatcher) 151, 153–4.163; Conservative government 1990–1997 (Major) 186, 191, 192; early 1960s 26–7; EEC countries 26; Labour government 1964–1970 47, 48, 55, 56–7, 63, 64, 64–5, 69; Labour government 1974–1979 97, 115, 123, 124, 125–6, 127, 128; Labour government 1997–2010 (New Labour) 205, 206, 209, 212–213214, 215, 220, 222, 232
purchase tax 80
Pym, Francis 154

QE (quantitative easing) 231, 242
Quantum Fund 190

R and D (research and development): and the Labour Government, 1964–1970 45, 48, 57, 66
race relations laws 68
rationing 7
Ravenscraig steelworks 195, 197
RB 211 aero-engine 66, 82
RBS *see* Royal Bank of Scotland
Reagan, President Ronald 170–1, 204
recession, 1979–1982 145, 167
recession, global, 1974–1976 100
Regeneration of British Industry, The (White Paper, 1974) 110
Regional Development Agencies 222
Regional Employment Premium (REP) 59
regional policy: Conservative government 1959–1964 35–6; Conservative government 1979–1990 (Thatcher) 173–4; Labour government 1964–1970 46, 65; Labour Government 1974–1979 113; Labour government 1997–2010 (New Labour) 222
Reich, Robert 205
REP (Regional Employment Premium) 59
Resale Price Maintenance 26, 35
Retail Price Index (RPI) 80, 85, 87
Ridley, Nicholas 118, 121
right to buy, council tenants 148, 164
Rio Tinto Zinc (RTZ) 117
riots: Conservative government 1979–1990 (Thatcher) 146, 154; poll tax 177
road haulage industry 131–2
Robbins Report 27
Robens, Lord 116, 117
Rolls Royce 66, 82, 106, 114, 232
Roosevelt, Franklin Delano 204
Rootes factory, Linwood 36
Rosen, Andrew 1
Round Oak Steelworks 143–4
Rover group 164
Rowntree 168
Royal Bank of Scotland (RBS) 218, 227, 229–30, 231
Royal Commission on Industrial Relations 67
Royal Dutch Shell 172–3
Royal Navy 4
Royal Radar Establishment (RRE) 65, 66
RPI (Retail Price Index) 80, 85, 87
RRE *see* Royal Radar Establishment
Rubery Owen 143
Runcie, Robert 160

S and P *see* Standard and Poor's
Sainsbury's 202, 224
Salford University 160
Salmond, Alex 217
Sampson, Anthony 24
Samuel, Walter 173
Sandbrook, Dominic 1, 48
Saudi Arabia 101, 112, 173, 196
scandals, in Major's government 196
Scanlon, Hugh 91, 112, 131
Scargill, Arthur 156, 157
Scarman, Lord 197n25
Schengen Agreement 196
Schonfield, Andrew 1
school milk 78
Schroder, J. Henry 173
science and technology policies: Labour government 1964–1970 45–7, 65–7, 69
Scotland: 2015 General Election 244–5; Coalition government 2010–2015 246; Conservative government 1979–1990 (Thatcher) 173, 174; Conservative government 1990–1997 (Major) 195, 197–8; deindustrialization 144, 221–2; devolution 197, 203, 209; EU referendum 2016 216; independence referendum 2014 217; poll tax (community tax) 176–7
Scotstoun Marine 82
Scott, Peter Dale 117
Scottish Development Agency 113
Scottish National Party (SNP) *see* SNP (Scottish National Party)
Scottish Parliament 209, 216; 2016 elections 247
SDP (Social Democratic Party) 146, 162, 198
SDR (Special Drawing Rights) 99
seamen's strike, 1966 57, 58
secondary banks 85, 86, 109
secondary picketing 148, 155, 206
Secret Intelligence Service (SIS, MI6) *see* SIS
Selective Employment Tax (SET) 57, 69, 76
self-certification of mortgages 225
self-employment 155, 222–3
Selsdon Group 77–8, 79, 80–1, 83, 88, 161
service sector: Conservative government 1979–1990 (Thatcher) 145, 165–6; Labour government 1997–2010 (New Labour) 218, 220–1; post-war period 2; SET (Selective Employment Tax) 57
SET *see* Selective Employment Tax
Shackleton, Lord 117
Shanks, Michael 24
shareholder power 169–70

Sheffield City Council 159
Sheffield Forgemasters 243
Shenfield, Arthur 67
Sheppard, Right Reverend David 161
Shield 120–1
shipbuilding industry 78, 82, 148, 164
shop stewards 131
Shore, Peter 127
short-term money market 53, 54
Shotton steel works 144
'sick man of Europe' 97
Sikorski 175
Simon, William 126
single currency, European *see* euro; European Monetary Union
Single European Act 1986 187
SIS (Secret Intelligence Service; MI6): and plots against the Labour government 1974–1979 116–17, 118, 120–121
Six Day War, 1967 60
Skybolt missile 14
SMEs (small and medium sized enterprises) 193; post-war period 2
Smith, John 201, 202
Smith, Tim 196
SNP (Scottish National Party) 216, 217, 247; 2015 General Election 244–5
Soames, Christopher 22
Social Chapter (EC) 187, 195, 196, 206, 209, 223
Social Contract 81–2, 102, 110, 122, 125, 127
social democracy 2; Conservative government 1959–1964 13–39; Conservative government 1970–1974 75, 78, 79, 80, 83, 89–90; Labour government 1974–1979 97, 98, 100, 104, 106, 115, 122, 130, 131; Labour government 1997–2010 (New Labour) 203, 208, 209, 212
Social Democratic Party (SDP) 146, 162, 198
Social Science Research Council 160
Solemn and Binding Agreement 68
Sony 195
Soros, George 190
South Africa 3
south-east England: Coalition government 2010–2015 246; Conservative government 1979–1990 (Thatcher) 173; early twentieth century 6; Labour government 1997–2010 (New Labour) 221
Spain 119
'special development areas' 59

Special Drawing Rights (SDR) 99
special relationship with USA 7, 19, 23, 170
sport industries 218
SPVs (Special Purpose Vehicles) 219, 226
stagflation 100
stakeholder democracy 207–8
Standard and Poor's (S and P) 233
State Holding Company 106, 109, 110, 114; *see also* NEB (National Enterprise Board)
State of Emergency, 1966 58
'Statism' 75
steel industry: Conservative government 1979–1990 (Thatcher) 143–4, 146, 164; Conservative government 1990–1997 (Major) 195
sterling: 1925 return to gold standard 62; 1957 crisis 16–18; 1959 crisis 18; 1961 crisis 26; and the Bretton Woods system 51; Conservative government 1970–1974 80; Conservative government 1979–1990 (Thatcher) 152–3, 163, 175–6; Conservative government 1990–1997 (Major) 187–91; floating of, 1971 80; Labour government 1964–1970 49–59, **52, 56, 60**, 63–4; Labour government 1974–1979 101–2, 112, 123–30; Labour government 1997–2010 (New Labour) 210–11; as trading and reserve currency 51–2
sterling M3 152–3, 163
Stewart, Michael 55, 58, 70n24
Stiglitz, Joseph 243
Stirling, David 117, 118, 120
Stock Market crash, October 1987 163
'Stop-Go' economic policies 18, 22, 27, 31, 38, 44, 48, 99
strikes *see* industrial relations; miner's strike 1984–1986; public sector strikes, 1979; seamen's strike, 1966
Sturgeon, Nicola 244–5
sub-prime mortgages 226–7
Suez Crisis, 1956 13–14, 15, 38
Summers, Larry 205
Sure Start programme 212, 215
'sustainable investment rule' 210
Sweden 20, 119
'Switch of Resources Strategy' 63, 64, 65

Task Ahead, The 69, 79
tax credits 211–12, 215
tax evasion 219–20, 242
Taylor Woodrow 121
Tebbit, Norman 154, 155, 156

Teeside: docks modernisation 36
Templer, Sir Gerald 118, 121
Tenzing Norgay 7
TGWU (Transport and General Workers Union) 34, 132; and the EEC 22; and the Labour Government 1974–1979 112; and the sterling crisis 1966 58
Thames Barrier 83
That Was The Week That Was 19
Thatcher, Margaret 97, 119–20, 126, 132; and the 'enemy within' 150, 155, 159; Conservative Party leadership 120; downfall 175–8; Education Secretary 78; and the EEC 171, 175–6; and the Eurosceptics 190–1, 196–7; and monetarism 104; political background 120–1; and President Reagan 170–1; *see also* Conservative government 1979–1990 (Thatcher)
Thatcherism 146–50, 204
Third Way 204–9
Thomas, Hugh 24
Thompson, Sir Robert 121
Thomson, David 25, 174, 208
Thorneycroft, Peter 16, 17, 18
'three circles' doctrine 13
Three Day Week 90–2, 100, 118
Tiarks, F. C. 173
Tomlinson, Jim 2
Townsend, Peter 25
Toyota 159
trade: 1950s 24; 1952–1962 20–1, *21*; 1960–1966 **60,** 60–1; 1964 36, 38; Conservative government 1979–1990 (Thatcher) 146, 153; early 1960s 30; Labour government 1997–2010 (New Labour) 221; mid-twentieth century 6; nineteenth century 4
Trade Associations 193
Trade Union Act 1984 155
trade unions: and the 1944 settlement 2; reform, Conservative government 1979–1990 (Thatcher) 148, 155–9; *see also* industrial relations; TUC (Trades Union Congress)
Trades Union Congress (TUC) *see* TUC (Trades Union Congress)
Transport and General Workers Union (TGWU) *see* TGWU (Transport and General Workers Union)
Treasury: and the 1944 settlement 2; 1957 sterling crisis 17; and CCC (Competition and Credit Control) 85; and the Labour government of 1966–1970 61; sterling M3 152

Treaty of Rome 108; *see also* EEC (European Economic Community, 'Common Market')
Trident missiles 217
Triumph Standard plant, Speke 35
TSR-2 fighter-bomber 46, 54
TUC (Trades Union Congress): and the Conservative government 1970–1974 81–2, 90–1, 92; Conservative government 1979–1990 (Thatcher) 155; and the EEC 22; and the Labour government 1964–1970 46–7, 48; and the Labour government 1974–1979 112, 123, 129, 131, 132, 133; and the NEDC (National Economic Development Council) 31, 32, 33; and the NIC 33; Solemn and Binding Agreement 68; and the sterling crisis 1966 58

UCS *see* Upper Clyde Shipbuilders
UK: breakup of 248; as a nuclear power 8, 14–15
UK Coal 195
UKIP (UK Independence Party) 199n49, 217
unemployment: 1950s 7; 1964 36; Coalition government 2010–2015 243, 244, 246; Conservative government 1970–1974 79–80, 84, 88; Conservative government 1979–1990 (Thatcher) 144–5, 153, 155, 158, 162, 167; Conservative government 1990–1997 192; Labour government 1974–1979 97, 115; Labour government 1997–2010 (New Labour) 211, 213, 221–2; and the Phillips curve 88
Unison 117
United Learning Trust 214
universal (male) suffrage 5
universities: 1961 expansion of 23, 24; Conservative government 1979–1990 (Thatcher) 159, 160; Labour government 1964–1970 56–7; Labour government 1997–2010 (New Labour) 212; Robbins Report 27
University College, Cardiff 160
University of Wales Institute of Science and Technology (UWIST) 160
Upper Clyde Shipbuilders (UCS) 78, 82, 105
urban riots: Conservative government 1979–1990 (Thatcher) 146, 154
US Treasury 126; and the Labour government 1974–1979 121–2; and monetarism 103–4

USA: and the Labour government 1974–1979 121–2; and the Labour government 1997–2010 (New Labour) 204–5; nuclear power 8, 14–15; Paris Summit, 1960 15; special relationship with 7, 19, 23, 170; sub-prime mortgages 226–7; and the Suez crisis 13–14
USSR: invasion of Hungary 14; and the Labour government 1964–1979 118, 119; and Macmillan 19; nuclear power 8, 14; Paris Summit, 1960 15; planning 28; and World War II 7
UWIST (University of Wales Institute of Science and Technology) 160

V bombers (Vulcan, Victor and Valiant) 14
Varley, Eric 111, 113
Vauxhall factory, Ellesmere Port 36
Venture capitalists Association 214
Vietnam 56

wage bargaining *see* pay bargaining
wage restraint *see* pay restraint
Wages Act 1986 155
Wales: Conservative government 1979–1990 (Thatcher) 173, 174; Conservative government 1990–1997 (Major) 195, 198; deindustrialization 144, 221–2; devolution 197, 203, 209
Walker, Peter 147, 156
Walker, Sir Walter 117–18, 120
Walters, Sir Alan 176
Ward, George 137n136
welfare spending: Conservative government 1990–1997 (Major) 195–6; Labour government 1964–1970 47
welfare state 3, 6; 1950s neglect of 23–4; Conservative government 1990–1997 (Major) 186; formation of 7
Welsh Assembly *see* National Assembly for Wales
Welsh Development Agency 113
West Africa 4

West Indies 14
West Midlands: Coalition government 2010–2015 246; Conservative government 1979–1990 (Thatcher) 173; deindustrialization 143–144
Westland crisis 175
'wets' 154
WFTC *see* Working Families' Tax Credit
Whitelaw, William 147, 197n25
Wiener, Martin 1, 2
Wilkinson, Ellen 144
Williams, Marcia 135n56
Williams, Raymond 25–6
Wilson, Harold 34, 58, 99, 171, 177; achievements and legacy 115–16; and Britain's second bid to join the EEC 59–60; character and politics 43–4; coup plotting against 68, 69, 116–19; and the EEC referendum, 1975 110–11; MI5 surveillance of 91; minority administration, 1974 92; in opposition, 1970–1974 78; resignation 115; response to the AES 109–10; *see also* Labour government 1964–1970; Labour government 1974–1979
'winter of discontent' 1978–1979 98, 132–3
Witteveen, Johannes 126, 129, 130
Woodcock, George 38
Woolfson, Charles 171–2
Working Families' Tax Credit (WFTC) 211–12, 215
Working Time Directive (EU) 223
World Bank 98
Wright, Peter 116

Yeo, Ed 126
Young, George Kennedy 117–18, 121
Young, John 14
youth unemployment: Conservative government 1979–1990 (Thatcher) 146

zero hours contracts 223, 245